BULGARIAN COMMUNISM

EAST CENTRAL EUROPEAN STUDIES OF COLUMBIA
UNIVERSITY AND RESEARCH INSTITUTE ON
COMMUNIST AFFAIRS, COLUMBIA UNIVERSITY

Bulgarian
Communism

THE ROAD TO POWER

1934-1944

Nissan Oren

COLUMBIA UNIVERSITY PRESS
NEW YORK AND LONDON · 1971

Copyright © 1961, 1971 Columbia University Press
First published in book form in 1971; portions of this book
were previously published in microfilm form in 1961
International Standard Book Number: 9–231–03457–1
Library of Congress Catalog Card Number: 75–147127
Printed in the United States of America

To My Parents

PREFACE

THIS STUDY is devoted to the politics of Bulgarian Communism during the decade preceding the establishment of Communist rule in Bulgaria. As such, the volume completes the history of the Bulgarian Communist Party in its pre-ruling days. The roots of Bulgarian Communism and the evolution of the Party through the mid-thirties have been described and analyzed in Joseph Rothschild's masterful *The Communist Party of Bulgaria: Origins and Development, 1883–1936*, published by Columbia University Press in 1959. That work has proved indispensable in carrying on the present research.

The peculiarities of Bulgarian politics and the specific conditions of the Communist Party during a period of illegal existence required that special attention be given to the numerous factions and groupings making up the Bulgarian body politic. Chapter 1, therefore, is devoted to the non-Communist formations, their origins, and their place on the political spectrum. The treatment here is essentially functional. The following two chapters deal with the physical and ideological schisms within the Communist Party, involving, in the first instance, the cadres at home and those in Soviet exile, and in the second, the rivalries between the old leadership and the left oppositionists. Organizational problems, the popular front effort, participation in the Spanish Civil War, and relations with the Rumanian Communists over the issue of Dobruja make up the bulk of chapter 4. Chapters 5 and 6 are devoted to Communist involvements in the Soviet-German diplomatic rivalries over Bulgaria in the fall of 1940, the beginnings of wartime resistance, and the conflict with the Yugoslav Communists over Macedonia. Armed resistance and Communist inter-Party maneuvers aimed at the creation of a united opposition front vis-à-vis Bulgaria's wartime regime are given parallel treatment in the concluding two chapters.

Research for this study was carried out in various places in the course of the last few years. The richest sources of materials have been found in the following libraries: the Library of Congress in Washington, the New York Public Library, the Butler Library at Columbia University, the Bulgarian National Library and the Library of the Bulgarian Academy of Sciences in Sofia, the Johns Hopkins University in Baltimore, and its School of Advanced International Studies in Washington, the University of Skoplje, the Hebrew University of Jerusalem, and the Yad Vashem Institute in Jerusalem. I owe a debt of gratitude to the staff of all of the above institutions for their resourceful help.

I wish to acknowledge the assistance given to me by a large number of persons in and out of Bulgaria whom I have interviewed in the course of my work. The evidence of some is documented in the references. My thanks go to the Institute on East Central Europe and the Research Institute on Communist Affairs at Columbia University for their grants to Columbia University Press, without which the publication of this volume would have proved impossible.

I should like to thank Henry H. Wiggins of Columbia University Press for his unfailing aid and advice. The assistance of William Bernhardt, my editor, has been invaluable in the preparation of the final version of this manuscript. I am grateful to Elaine Clark, Marilyn Perkins, and Diane Nielsen of the Washington Center for Foreign Policy Research for having devotedly typed the final draft. Finally, as ever, my thanks to Hannah, my wife, for her wisdom and patience.

NISSAN OREN

New York City
September, 1970

CONTENTS

ABBREVIATIONS

BCP Bulgarian Communist Party

BKP Bulgarska komunisticheska partiia (Bulgarian Communist Party)

BRS Bulgarski rabotnicheski suiuz (Bulgarian Workers' Union)

BZNS Bulgarski zemedelski naroden suiuz (Bulgarian Agrarian National Union)

CC Central Committee

CP Communist Party

CPSU Communist Party of the Soviet Union

CPY Communist Party of Yugoslavia

DGFP *Documents on German Foreign Policy*

DRO Dobrudzhanska revoliutsionna organizatsiia (Dobruja Revolutionary Organization)

ECCI Executive Committee of the Communist International

IIIBKP *Izvestiia na Instituta po Istoriia na BKP* (Announcements of the Institute for the History of the Bulgarian Communist Party)

IMRO Internal Macedonian Revolutionary Organization

Inprecorr *International Press Correspondence*

KUNMZ Communist University for the National Minorities of the West

NOVA Narodnoosvoboditelna vustanicheska armiia (People's Revolutionary Army of Liberation)

NRPS   Nezavisim rabotnicheski profesionalen suiuz (Independent Labor Trade Union)

RMS   Rabotnicheski mladezhki suiuz (Union of Working Youth)

SOE   Special Operations Executive

WEB   West European Buro

BULGARIAN COMMUNISM

INTRODUCTION

ON SEPTEMBER 9, 1944, Bulgaria's old order was overthrown. A government of the Fatherland Front, a wartime coalition under Communist sponsorship, assumed control of the country. Emerging from the underground after years of illegal existence, the Communist Party of Bulgaria, aided by the presence of the Red Army in the country, became the dominant force in Bulgarian affairs. The present study deals with the development of the Bulgarian Communist Party during the decade immediately preceding the 1944 seizure of power.

Two events shaped Bulgaria's politics in the years between the wars, the anti-Stamboliiski coup of 1923 and the Zveno *putsch* of a decade later. The first was an assault on the Agrarian Union. The second, the military *putsch* of May 19, 1934, struck at Bulgaria's political institutions. In both cases, the effect on the political life of the country was profound.

The contrast between the two coups, both in terms of their immediate impact and in terms of their long-range effects, was marked. The blow delivered in June, 1923, by a coalition headed by Professor Aleksandur Tsankov was the end result of a well-prepared political conspiracy. The *putsch* of 1934, on the other hand, had little or no political preparation. The first aimed at a specific objective: the destruction of the rule of peasant populism. The second sought to "regenerate" Bulgaria's political life by means of abolishing the political parties. In both cases, the long-range consequences went far beyond the limits originally envisaged.

In January, 1926, less than three years after his coming to power, Tsankov gave way to the more moderate Andrei Liapchev, who undertook to bring an end to the turmoil and place the country on the road to normalcy. His rule opened the way for free elections in 1931 and the assumption of power of the People's Bloc coalition, giving Bulgaria the semblance of political freedom for the first time in many years.

The instigators of the May 19 coup avoided bloodshed. At the same time, the blow they delivered to the Bulgarian body politic proved deadly, for political parties never recovered. After 1934, Bulgaria was denied the free, if undisciplined, press of the days of the People's Bloc. A newly instituted state-controlled syndicate assumed the place of the free trade unions. Local self-government, which had survived many a past regime, was brought to an end. The centrally appointed bureaucrat took the place of the locally elected politician. The Turnovo Constitution was suspended. The Subranie, Bulgaria's legislature, was dissolved. Organized political meetings were banned. State administration became further centralized. The May conspirators proposed to place a small military clique as the sole counterweight to the growing influence of the monarchy. However, the new regime fell to pieces soon after it took power. Since all political parties were denied organized legal existence, the ambitions of King Boris could not be seriously challenged. Combining a keen sense of intrigue with well-developed political skills, Boris was able to emerge victorious simply by playing off his enemies one against the other. Until his death in 1943, it was in his hands that real political power resided.

Under Boris, Bulgaria did not become a full-fledged totalitarian state. Although crypto-Nazi elements grew in strength and in influence, there remained enough leniency in the Bulgarian political system to allow for a certain political intercourse below the official level. Denied legal existence, most political groupings continued as ghost parties. Some were able to reach the public at large by means of independent newspapers. Nevertheless, throughout the decade following the 1934 coup, Bulgarian political life continued progressively to atrophy. This factor, among others, contributed to Bulgaria's new disaster in World War II. At the time, when open discussion could have stirred Bulgaria to leave the losing Axis camp, the Bulgarian masses remained too disorganized and politically too powerless to bring their weight to bear. This course of events led to still another coup which, executed as it was at a time when the Red Army was already on Bulgarian soil, propelled the Bulgarian Communist Party to power.

The Bulgarian Communist Party sprang from the doctrinaire Bulgarian Social Democratic Party founded in the early 1890s. The division between reformism and Marxist orthodoxy dominated Bulgarian socialist thinking from the beginning. By 1903 a decade of intense ideological rivalry resulted in the formation of two independent factions, the "narrow" Socialists led by Dimitur Blagoev, a Russian-educated Bulgarian intellectual, and a "broad" faction which followed the usual Second International model.

Politically intransigent, Blagoev's "narrows" had at first a smaller popular following than the "broad" Socialists. This power relationship was reversed at the end of World War I when, having renamed themselves the Bulgarian Communist Party, the "narrows" became the second strongest political force in the country after the Agrarian Union.

At the time of the anti-Stamboliiski coup of June, 1923, the Communists stood aloof on the ground that the conflict between the "rural and urban bourgeoisie" did not concern them. In September, 1923, after the establishment of the Tsankov regime, the Communists belatedly joined the radical Agrarians and staged an insurrection which was soon bloodily suppressed. Their leaders, including Georgi Dimitrov and Vasil Kolarov, fled the country and established a Buro-in-Exile, through which they endeavored to maintain control over the Communist Party at home. In 1924 the Communist Party was officially banned. In the following year Communist-instigated terroristic outbursts gave rise to widespread anti-Communist retaliations by the government.

With the coming of Andrei Liapchev to the premiership the Bulgarian Communists resumed their organized activities. In 1926 Communist-backed trade unions began to reappear. In the following year the government agreed to the establishment of the Bulgarian Workers' Party, a front organization directed by the illegal Communist Party. The Young Workers' Union, a front for the illegal Komsomol, was also created.

The early days of the People's Bloc regime saw Bulgarian Communists attain a new height in popular support and organizational strength. Working through the Bulgarian Workers' Party, the Communists elected thirty-one deputies in the general elections of 1931. In the Sofia municipal elections held the following year, the Party received the largest number of votes and the majority of mandates. Provoked by the semi-insurrectionary Communist tactics of the period, the government of the People's Bloc ousted the Communist-elected deputies from the Subranie (April 12, 1933), following which the government initiated a series of legal and extralegal anti-Communist repressive measures. Internal Party strife, conflicts generated within the cadres at home and in exile, and the hardships of underground existence could not but leave their mark. The decade ahead, therefore, found the Communists ill-prepared and ill-equipped, both organizationally and psychologically, in the pursuit of their designs.

CHAPTER ONE

BACKGROUND: THE NON-COMMUNIST SCENE

THE RESULTS OF THE Bulgarian general elections of June, 1931, came as a surprise. In Bulgaria, as in most of the Balkan countries, it was a rarity for a governing party or coalition to be defeated in an election. After eight long and stormy years in power, however, the Democratic Alliance gave way to a newly formed political constellation generally known as the People's Bloc. The changeover was of significance, not only because it was peaceful, but also because it signaled the re-emergence of the Agrarian Union as a governing party. As the outcome of the election became known, a wave of rejoicing swept the nation, particularly the countryside. The peasants, having been the ones most responsible for the victory, hoped for a better deal for themselves and their families. There was an air of expectation forecasting a new era and a better future. However, the new era lasted less than three years. Possibly the change had come too late, or else the times were against an evolution toward liberal democracy. Before long, elements from among the very alliance which had helped engineer the 1923 anti-Stamboliiski coup struck again, thus making almost a profession out of what had eight years earlier appeared to be a mere adventure (nor was their second strike the last one). Therefore, for an understanding of things to come, it is necessary to examine the events leading to the crises of the mid-1930s and to describe the political factions at work at the time.

RISE AND DECLINE OF THE DEMOCRATIC ALLIANCE

The Democratic Alliance dated back to the immediate post-Stamboliiski era and represented in effect an enlargement of a smaller coalition—the People's Alliance—which had carried out the coup against the Agrarian Union regime of Aleksandur Stamboliiski. The core of the People's Alliance consisted of the Military League, headed by General Ivan Rusev and including General Ivan Vulkov and Lieutenant-Colonels Damian Velchev, Kimon Georgiev, and Nikola Rachev. On the civilian side, the coalition was headed by Aleksandur Tsankov, who had succeeded in attracting to himself people like Boian Smilov from the National Liberal Party, Tsvetko Boboshevski from the People's Progressive Party, Yanko Stoianchev from the Democratic Party, Petur Todorov from the Radicals, and Dimo Kazasov from the Social Democrats. Tsankov assumed the premiership in June, 1923, and promptly began to transform a small clique of the People's Alliance into a large political party to include all middle-class political groups in the country. To this end negotiations were started as early as August, 1923, and it was from these exchanges that the Democratic Alliance evolved. The final result was not all that Tsankov had desired. A section of the Democrats under the leadership of Aleksandur Malinov and a section of the Radicals under Stoian Kosturkov refused to enter the new formation. Nevertheless, the coalition as finally constituted was a substantial cluster, quite impressive in its size if not in its cohesion. Only a small minority of Democrats followed Malinov, while most accompanied Andrei Liapchev into the Democratic Alliance; furthermore, Atanas Burov had brought in his conservative Narodniatsi Party (Populists) and they, together with some other minor splinters, helped to strengthen the governing coalition. Thus the Democratic Alliance as it existed around 1925 rested on a tripod of which Tsankov, Liapchev, and Burov constituted the legs. Although Tsankov's wing was considered at the time as the more radical, while the Liapchev-Burov group was thought of as the right wing of the coalition, except for individual inclinations and impulses the Democratic Alliance was devoid of all ideological content. Outside of a fear of Bolshevism, there was little that united the various groupings within the coalition. In a way, the heterogeneity of the Alliance was also its strength, since it was at all times possible to reshuffle the composition of the government without changing the coalition on which it was based.

Tsankov surrendered the premiership in January, 1926. The cabinet was now reorganized under his successor, Andrei Liapchev. Liapchev's emergence at the top was largely due to the support of the Military League under General Vulkov. (The League had its own inner factions. The stronger one, which enjoyed the confidence of King Boris, was led by Vulkov, the minister of war, and supported Liapchev. The other had as its leader Kimon Georgiev, a Tsankovite.) Tsankov did not enter the cabinet but was instead relegated to the presidency of the Subranie (legislature). Thus opened the second stage of the Democratic Alliance regime with Liapchev at its head and with Professor Tsankov heading the internal opposition. Nominally within the coalition, Tsankov proceeded to organize a substantial group of politicians around himself who were antagonistic both to Liapchev's economic policies and to his close association with the pro-Italian General Vulkov.

The history of Liapchev's premiership, which was the longest in Bulgaria's interwar period, was marked by a gradual recovery of Bulgarian party politics. Factionalism from within the government and the growing powers of the opposition forces from without, however, posed an ever growing challenge which not even the durable Liapchev could withstand. Ultimately he fell prey to his own limitless optimism. When after more than five years in office the constituent parts of his coalition proved too unruly, Liapchev strove to bring about general elections which he believed would strengthen him and solidify his grip on his followers. He submitted his resignation on April 20, 1931. After a number of unsuccessful attempts by the King to find a replacement who would command a majority in the Subranie, Liapchev was recalled on May 3, and soon after it was announced that the government would hold general elections on June 21, 1931.

THE ELECTIONS OF JUNE, 1931

In the pre-electoral campaign, Aleksandur Malinov, a Democrat, emerged as the strongest figure of the antigovernment configuration. In the 1927 general elections Malinov had tried his hand at forming a coalition with the extreme right wing of the Agrarian Union led by Kosta Tomov. The results, however, had convinced Malinov that conservative Tomov commanded little support among the peasants. In 1931 he was determined not to repeat his earlier mistake. Furthermore, the Agrarian Union had undergone great changes since 1927. The group led by Dimitur Gichev now commanded the loyalty of the majority of the local organizations as well as the heart of the central leadership. After prolonged negotiations, Malinov's efforts brought success. When later in May the composition of the People's Bloc was announced, its base proved wider than expected. Included were the Malinov Democrats, the Kosturkov wing of the Radical Party, the wing of the Liberal Party led by G. Petrov, and the Agrarian Union under Gichev (known as Vrabcha I). The Social Democrats and the Bulgarian Workers' Party (Communists) remained unaffiliated with either of the two coalitions— the Democratic Alliance or the People's Bloc. The Workers' Party came out with an alliance of its own which it called the Labor Bloc (*Trudov blok*) and which included some Agrarian Union elements from the extreme left. The complexion of the Workers' Party was not changed by these additions. Finally, the group of Kosta Tomov's Agrarians remained isolated.

That the June, 1931, elections were on the whole free was attested to by the results. The government in power interfered, but on a minor scale. When all the results were in, the People's Bloc had won a great victory. It elected 152 deputies as compared to 78 for the Democratic Alliance. The Workers' Party elected 31; the Macedonians (the Mikhailov wing of IMRO), 8; and the Social Democrats, 5. The distribution of deputies among the parties entering the People's Bloc was as follows: Agrarians, 72; Democrats, 43; Liberals, 30; Radicals, 7. Of the seventy-eight deputies elected on the government list, eleven were Liberals.[1]

Malinov proceeded to organize his cabinet. Despite the much greater contribution made by the Agrarians in terms of popular support, the Democrats took the principal portfolios. The distribution of cabinet posts was as follows: the Democrats held, in addition to the premiership and the Ministry of Foreign Affairs (Malinov), the ministries of the Interior (Nikola Mushanov) and Finance (Aleksandur Girginov), leaving to the Agrarians the less important ministries of Agriculture (Dimitur Gichev), Education (Konstantin Muraviev), and Public Works (Georgi Yordanov). The Liberals were given two posts (Trade and Justice), while Kosturkov for the Radicals took over the Ministry of Railroads. The

[1] *Istoriia na Bulgariia*, p. 611; Kazasov, *Burni godini*, p. 423; Swire, p. 242.

Agrarians were dissatisfied and remained so until the very end. Although the Agrarian ministries lacked the glamour of the Ministry of Foreign Affairs or the authority of the Interior, from the point of view of patronage they were far from unimportant, and this, for a time at least, took away some of the bitterness. However, the struggle over ministerial posts dominated the entire period of the People's Bloc and contributed to its downfall. Yet the Malinov and, later, the Mushanov governments had their own logic. In terms of votes, there was no denying that the Agrarians had provided "the muscle" without which the People's Bloc could not have won. At the same time, on their own the Agrarians would not have been permitted to become a governing party so short a time after their 1923 debacle and while prominent Agrarian leaders were still exiles. What the Agrarians needed most in 1931 was a measure of respectability and acceptance which the Democrats had and which they were ready to share. The fact that the Democrats claimed and got the key posts was only proof that a good name was worth as much as power.

The immediate effect the People's Bloc regime had on Bulgarian politics was to intensify the already acute partisan political struggles. Long out of power, the parties of the Bloc undertook to capitalize on their success. Once a ministry changed hands, the entire establishment from the secretary-general down to the last clerk did so too. Abuses were often carried to the very limit of absurdity, with simple policemen, forest guards, teachers, and even unskilled workmen employed by the government awaiting the return to power of the "right minister" who might reemploy them. The government domain was subdivided into party "spheres of influence" which were allocated among the governing groups for patronage exploitation. In a poor economy such as the Bulgarian, already beginning to feel the effects of the worldwide depression of the 1930s, this acute politicization generated resentment. As for the Democratic Alliance, the ordeals were even greater. A heterogeneous grouping of this type could not stay out of power for long and survive. The process of disintegration started immediately after the electoral defeat, and continued until the Alliance all but disappeared from the scene. The first split came right after the elections. The splinter groups were composed of elements that were still in a position to make peace with the victors and thus escape the consequences of defeat. This was particularly true of a great many Liapchev Democrats, who hastened to rejoin Malinov and his party. Then came the splitting off of the Tsankov group. The remaining elements stayed together for a time. They tried the best they could to play the role of an orderly opposition and to gain public support by calling for such measures as a moratorium on debts and a trade monopoly on foodstuffs. Their rank-and-file support continued to shrink.

THE TSANKOV MOVEMENT

Professor Tsankov broke away from the Democratic Alliance in 1932 and launched his own National Social movement. Impressed by the Italian Fascists and the German National Socialists, but insisting on the originality of his social and political ideas, Tsankov began efforts that constituted in effect an endeavor at transplanting Fascism onto Bulgarian soil. The influence which Tsankov exerted on many prominent Bulgarians, not excepting his fellow professors, was substantial during the early and middle 1930s. His was a group which changed with the times and meant different things to different people. When first launched, Tsankov's movement was aided by the spirit of the times. With anti-Bolshevik slogans high on the lists of almost all political parties, and with mounting Fascist successes in Europe, Tsankov was quick to capitalize on the disillusionment which had overcome many elements in the country. There were, however, two fundamental factors which worked against him. First, his appeal was almost entirely restricted to the urban population. In overwhelmingly agrarian Bulgaria this posed an obstacle of the first magnitude. To the majority of peasants he remained "bloody Tsankov" who had murdered Stamboliiski. For this reason, his inroads in the villages remained weak and his few successes localized. Second, Tsankov lacked the ability and the skills of the successful mass demagogue. He was never able to rid himself of the "professor image." While mounting a political platform and facing the crowds he remained the urban intellectual.

His ideas were complex and his formulations vague. He was against political parties because they were based on a class maxim. Tsankov maintained that capitalism, Socialism, Hitlerism, and Bolshevism would in the end converge into what he called "social nationalism." He was opposed to the corporate state even though he favored "the bringing of the factors of production into government." He was for "economic democracy." Tsankov was preoccupied with the drift of youth toward the left, a process he feared. This process, he maintained, could only be arrested by the force of new ideals, which, however, he failed to provide.[2]

At first as he spoke of the "new order" he pointed out that the orders established in Italy and Germany were unsuitable to the Slav temperament. The foreign experience could be dangerous if applied mechanically, since the Bulgarian nation was too young and as yet untrained to respect authority. It did not take long, however, for Tsankov to follow in the direction in which much of Europe was moving. At the height of Nazi military successes, he was to turn to his fellow deputies in the Subranie with the revealing questions: "Are you with the capitalists? No, you are not because they are withering away. Are you with the Bolsheviks? Even less so. With whom are you? I am with the national socialists." [3] This position, however, belonged to a later period. During the early thirties there was a certain freshness in Tsankov's neo-Fascist demagoguery. Much energy was expended by him and by his followers to attract the laboring masses. He spoke of the concessions the employers must make to the workers in order that the era of "peace among the classes" be brought about. To this end he established the National Workers' Syndicate, the main function of which was to divert the workers from the socialist trade unions. He even tried his hand at operating free kitchens for the unemployed. Above all, there were the endless noisy campaigns which Tsankov and his followers kept up and which moved many to believe that a Tsankov regime was around the corner. Part of the Liberals went over to Tsankov, as did the right-wing Agrarian group of Kosta Tomov, together with many other individuals from various groups.

ZVENO

Closely related to Tsankov at first, and in a way constituting an integral part of the Tsankov movement, an influential group of people emerged whose role during the years of the People's Bloc became par-

[2] Tsankov, *Trite stopanski sistemi.* This collection of his lectures on political economy is the single most important source on Tsankov's ideology. His politics, however, had to be judged by his actions. On Tsankov's ideas, see also Kazasov, *Burni godini*, pp. 619–20.

[3] From Tsankov's speech delivered in the Subranie on November 18, 1941; Narodno subranie, *Stenografski dnevnitsi*, pp. 179–86.

ticularly important. This was the Zveno group, which admirers called by its longer and more respectable name of "The Political Circle Zveno" and which detractors simply called the Zveno clique. Having borrowed its name from a publication by the same name, Zveno had one distinction: its size bore no relation to its importance. In fact, in the light of events to come, one could say that Zveno was most influential in the periods when it was smallest in size. Zveno was sometimes jokingly referred to as the *kamion partiia* (truck party) since, so the joke went, its entire membership could be loaded on a single military truck. Another distinction of Zveno was its close association with the army.

The early days of *Zveno* the publication, and thus, also, of the group itself, were associated with a journalist by the name of Dimo Kazasov. A teacher, a trade unionist, and an active member of the Social Democratic Party, Kazasov had made a name for himself in the years immediately following World War I with his journalistic writings. He became a national figure on the day after the 1923 coup when, to the surprise of most, Kazasov was named the minister of communications in the Tsankov cabinet. He was in fact one of the first to be approached by Tsankov while the conspiracy was being hatched. In the coup he participated as an individual without asking or receiving the authorization of the Social Democratic Party. As communications minister, he made his greatest contribution during the September Communist uprising, which he helped to put down with great efficiency. Kazasov continued his association with the Social Democrats and was in fact elected a member of the Party's Central Committee (February, 1924). On February 15, 1924, he left the cabinet in compliance with the decision of the leadership of the Party. By that time he had antagonized many among his fellow Socialists. In 1925 Kazasov published a detailed account of his participation in the 1923 conspiracy as well as of the coup itself.[4] In 1926 he was finally expelled from the Social Democratic Party. This clinched Kazasov's drift to the right. In the middle of 1927, on his initiative, a small group of influential people came together and formed an "ideological circle." A number of meetings were held out of

---

[4] Kazasov, *V tumninite na zagovora* (Sofia, 1925); when first published, this account of the 1923 conspiracy created a sensation, making Kazasov one of the most controversial political figures of the time. His activities up to that time are related in his memoirs, *Burni godini*, pp. 186–89, 227–29, 293–96.

which emerged the decision to launch a weekly publication to be edited by Kazasov. This marked the beginning of *Zveno*, the first issue of which appeared on January 1, 1928. At the time of the paper's appearance, the "circle" around *Zveno* consisted of some eighty individuals belonging to different parties. The overwhelming majority were associated with the 1923 coup and were followers of Tsankov.[5]

What made the Zveno group important in the long run was the fact that not long after its emergence a number of Tsankovites, who had close connections with the army, joined in. Thus, in a small way, Zveno became the vehicle for the political aspirations of certain elements from the Military League, which was then being reorganized. The case in point involved Kimon Georgiev. When in the middle of 1930 Tsankov reentered the government of the Democratic Alliance, Georgiev formally joined the Zveno group, with which he had maintained close connections from the beginning. This association marked the "marriage" between the intellectuals and the military within the Zveno group, a combination which lasted until the eve of the May, 1934, coup. The presence of Georgiev in the leadership of Zveno was particularly significant because of his friendship with Damian Velchev, who was helping to revive the Military League. Velchev had been instrumental in carrying out the 1923 coup. It was he who took control of the army in Sofia in June of that year. During the next five years (1923–28) Velchev served as the commandant of the Military College, a position he used in building a personal following from among the young officer cadres. In 1928 he was again a civilian, having broken with the minister of war (General Vulkov). This development did not prevent Velchev from maintaining his connections in the army and from exercising a great personal influence on many a young officer.[6]

In the meantime, Zveno made progress. From the first, its spokesmen insisted on the non-party, or rather the extra-party, nature of the group. This stand was in part dictated by considerations of logical consistency, since Zveno attacked all parties as decadent and harmful to the Bulgarian body politic. Here is how Kazasov characterized the nature of Zveno in a speech delivered on May 5, 1932:

[5] Kazasov, *Burni godini*, pp. 322–24.

[6] Swire, pp. 159–67, contains a detailed (and on the whole favorable) description of Velchev's activities during this period.

The political circle Zveno is not a political party. Zveno is an organization which stands above all parties, an organization free from dogmatism and narrow-mindedness. Zveno strives to solve Bulgaria's problems on a level higher than the party level, where ideological differences and class antagonisms have conformed to the national interest.[7]

The similarity between this statement and Tsankov's pronouncements was unmistakable. It was therefore natural that most Zveno people continued to belong to the Tsankov movement even after their formal affiliation with Zveno. Differences between the two remained methodological rather than ideological. Zveno was never interested in creating a mass movement. Its leaders relied on what they called the "competent minority" made up of select individuals.[8]

In matters of economic policy, Zveno was in favor of government intervention and, above all, of rapid economic growth. "Our problem is not one of distribution of wealth but one of elevation of the national well-being," wrote Kazasov not long after the launching of Zveno.[9] Economic activism was intended to arrest rather than foster a revolutionary development. Ivan Kharizanov, one of the ideologists of Zveno, insisted that "by means of a radical intervention in the economic sphere on behalf of the middle and lower classes the revolutionary solution could be prevented." [10]

Bold stands were also taken in matters of foreign policy, particularly those affecting Macedonia. At a time when rival factions from among the various wings of IMRO were carrying on their fights in the streets of Sofia, Zveno made history by coming out openly against terrorism, and by calling for the reestablishment of Bulgarian governmental authority in the Petrich Department, where the Macedonians had created a state within a state. This action placed the Zveno group on the side of those who were in favor of a rapprochement with Yugoslavia as the only way out of the intolerable situation created by the Macedonian elements

[7] Kazasov, *Zveno bez grim*, pp. 161–82; this is a collection of his pronouncements, in most cases reproductions of his articles in *Zveno*, published in the aftermath of the 1934 coup.

[8] *Istoriia na Bulgariia*, p. 647.

[9] Kazasov, *Zveno*, December 2, 1928, reproduced in *Zveno bez grim*, pp. 67–69.

[10] *Zveno*, October 9, 1932. Ivan Kharizanov remained one of the principal figures in Zveno until his death on July 7, 1947.

in Bulgaria. In the public mind, therefore, from the very beginning the Zveno people were identified as "pro-Yugoslav." To their enemies, and particularly to the Mikhailov wing of IMRO, they were nothing more than "foreign agents in the pay of Alexander, king of the Serbs." [11] As far as Bulgarian relations with the Soviet Union were concerned, there was nothing "soft" in Zveno's attitude. Partly because the Zveno government was to reestablish diplomatic relations with the Soviet Union (after its coming to power), and partly because of vague prorepublican pronouncements of some of its leaders, there were those who thought Zveno unduly leftist. If Zveno spokesmen did advocate a normalization of relations with the Soviets, it was on grounds of what they considered the national interest. At no time during the early 1930s was pro-Communism an issue within Zveno circles. In 1932, writing in *Izgrev* (a daily newspaper which Zveno had started publishing in addition to its weekly), Kimon Georgiev openly denounced the Bulgarian Communist Party, which, "under the ideological leadership and material support of Moscow, is organizing revolution and spreading anarchy in our country." [12] Nor was Kazasov's stand any different when he stated that "Bulgarian Communism is an instrument of a mighty *gospodar* [master] used against a defenseless beggar." [13] As to the prorepublican sentiments prevalent among some of the leaders (mainly among the military), they were based mostly on grounds of opposition to the dynasty that had brought two defeats to the nation, rather than on ideology.

During the first years of its existence, Zveno restricted its activities to the publication of its weekly and daily organs, remaining organizationally inactive. The first step in the direction of establishing organizations on the local level was made on the eve of the 1931 elections, and was signaled by the publication of a manifesto (June 14, 1931) in which it was said that in the future Zveno would undertake to create local cells of supporters, the function of which would be to popularize its ideas. Similar declarations were made on a number of occasions in the following years. Local units were in fact set up but they remained few and were restricted to the larger towns. Those who affiliated themselves with Zveno were in the main lawyers and other professionals.

[11] Kazasov, *Burni godini*, pp. 490–96.

[12] *Izgrev*, No. 93–94, 1932, cited in Kazasov, *Burni godini*, p. 459.

[13] Kazasov, *Zveno*, November 22, 1931, reproduced in *Zveno bez grim*, p. 72.

DEMOCRATS

The center of the political spectrum was occupied by the Democratic Party of Malinov. Not very powerful in terms of popular support, the Democrats received their strength from the middle and lower-middle classes, which in themselves were comparatively weak. The Democrats derived their influence from their central position as the only group capable of combining with either the left or the right. In addition, they enjoyed the confidence of the court, having always been close to the monarchy.[14] They formed the so-called *tsarska partiia* (king's party). In the person of Malinov the Democratic Party had a leader of great distinction. Malinov's premiership was of short duration. Claiming poor health, he resigned on October 13, 1931, and became the president of the Subranie. His place was taken by Nikola Mushanov, who vacated the Ministry of the Interior. Malinov continued to play an active role in both the Subranie and the Democratic Party, attempting to remain above the day-by-day political struggles.

AGRARIANS OF THE TWENTIES

Because of its size, its structure, and its many inner factions, the Agrarian Union occupied a place on the political spectrum of Bulgaria that cannot be defined with any precision. Nominally the party of the small peasant, the Agrarian Union with its numerous "wings, winglets, and feathers" (as the saying went) spread from the extreme left to far into the right, with its center located somewhere to the left of the Democratic Party.

Factionalism among the Agrarians was the rule rather than the exception, owing to the desire of the Union to represent the entire peasant population. The Agrarians saw themselves as a *suslovna organizatsiya* ("estatist" organization) rather than as a conventional political party. In practice, despite the largely egalitarian character of Bulgarian rural society, there remained sufficient differences between the poor peasant, who throughout his life remained a buyer of agricultural goods,

[14] The Democrats were accused of having been instrumental in passing the constitutional amendment (July–August, 1911) that gave the King the right to conclude treaties without informing the Subranie, as the constitution had originally provided. Alhough the Democrats approved of the amendment, the actual passage of it was done after Malinov had resigned from the premiership (March 16, 1911) and had been succeeded by a government composed of Narodniatsi and Progressive Liberals.

and the richer peasant who produced for the market. There was, of course, more to the factions than mere divergences in economic interest. In the Agrarian Union personalities were very important. As Malinov wrote in his memoirs, "One is compelled to observe, even if with sorrow, that with them passions and appetites were of greater importance than competition between different ideas and platforms." [15]

The Agrarian Union had its left and right wings even at the height of its power. Around 1922 there were two *petorki* (groups of five) within the Stamboliiski regime, the left led by Daskalov and Obbov, and the right by Turlakov, Tomov, and Omarchevski. In the spring of 1923, on the very eve of his regime's collapse, Stamboliiski broke with both Daskalov (who was his first lieutenant) and the Turlakov-Tomov group and reorganized his cabinet to include more easily dominated people. Then came the June coup, which removed the kingpin of the Bulgarian Agrarian Union; with the disappearance of Stamboliiski and under the impact of the White Terror, the Union was split two ways. First, there were those who fled the country. Second, there were the various groups which emerged from among the Agrarians at home.

Daskalov had been abroad at the time of the coup and it was he who became the first exile leader. However, he was soon assassinated in Prague by a Macedonian terrorist. The leadership of the exile Agrarians then passed into the hands of Obbov, who had been Stamboliiski's minister of agriculture. He had been one of the few Agrarian leaders actively to resist the Tsankov forces in June, 1923, by leading an abortive march of several thousand armed peasants into the town of Pleven. In the summer of 1924 the exiled leaders were joined by two more of Stamboliiski's ministers, Atanasov and Stoianov, who succeeded in crossing the Yugoslav frontier. A few months earlier, in January, 1924, Kosta Todorov had been invited to Moscow to negotiate with Georgi Dimitrov and Vasil Kolarov, acting in behalf of the Bulgarian Communist Party and the Comintern, on the terms of a united front to be established between the Communists and the Agrarians with the purpose of overthrowing the Tsankov government.

Dimitrov's proposals [made in Vienna shortly before Todorov left for Moscow] were interesting. He wanted us [the Agrarians] to acknowledge that the goal of our struggle against Tsankov was the establishment of a "workers'

[15] Malinov, *Pod znaka na ostrasteni i opasni politicheski borbi*, p. 185.

and peasants' " government, with the Communist Party dominating. The government would consist of ten members: six Peasants and four Communists. We would hold the premiership, but the key ministries of war, interior and communications would be in Communist hands. The fourth post for his party was immaterial, Dimitrov said.[16]

Nothing came of Todorov's visit to Moscow; nor did later talks (August, 1924) between Dimitrov and the Agrarian leaders conducted in Vienna produce any tangible results.

At home, right and left tendencies in the Agrarian movement became more clearly defined. The right wing was led by Kosta Tomov and Georgi Markov, in whose eyes Stamboliiski had always been too radical. In April, 1927, they split again, with Tomov leading the right wing into an electoral coalition with the Democrats and with Markov assuming a centrist position. The left wing consisted of those Agrarians who, having survived the June coup, were determined to oppose the Tsankov regime by all means possible. Since most Agrarian militants were either in exile or in prison, the leadership of the left-wingers was assumed by relatively unknown people. Some had collaborated with the Communists during their September uprising; others, outraged by the crimes of the usurpers, had decided to join the Agrarian Union. The latter course was followed by Petko D. Petkov, who was elected to the Subranie in the November 18, 1923, elections, thus becoming the leader of the left-wing parliamentary groups. Petkov had earlier made a name for himself as a diplomat, having played an important role in the postwar diplomatic relations of Bulgaria and having become one of the principal advisers to the Stamboliiski government on matters of foreign affairs. His election to the Subranie propelled Petkov to a position of national prominence. Secretly, Petkov joined the Revolutionary Committee which the Agrarian exiles had established abroad.[17] At home, Petkov led the opposition composed of the handful of Agrarians, ruthlessly and brilliantly attacking the government. On June 14, 1924, before the opposition could achieve results, Petkov was murdered. In the years that followed, the name of Petko Petkov became a symbol to all Agrarians who cherished the memory of their comrades, victims of Tsankov's terror. The Communists

[16] Todorov, *Balkan Firebrand*, p. 200; on the early activities of the Agrarian leaders in exile see also pp. 193–98, 200–10, 215–18.

[17] *Ibid.*, p. 200.

remembered Petkov for his support of the united front idea and made use of his memory whenever the question of collaboration with the Agrarians became important. Not least important was the impact which the example of Petko Petkov's career must have made on his younger brother Nikola, who, twenty years later, was to become the champion of an Agrarian-Communist front.[18]

GICHEV'S RISE

Many of the left-wing Agrarian leaders who continued the struggle after the death of Petkov did not survive the terror following the 1925 bombing of the Sofia Cathedral. People like Nikolai Petrini, Kiril Pavlov (whose brother was to become an Agrarian minister after 1944), Dimitur Gruncharov, and others were either shot or otherwise disposed of in the Obshtestvena bezopasnost (Public Safety Police Headquarters). With the coming of the Liapchev government (January, 1926) and the following normalization, the more radical Agrarians were again able to take part in the political life of the country. They formed the left-wing (anti-Tomov) faction within the Agrarian Union and were led by people like Dimitur Gichev, Georgi Yordanov, Konstantin Muraviev, and Vergil Dimov. In the 1927 general elections, while Malinov preferred the more conservative Kosta Tomov, the Gichev wing combined with the Social Democrats and the small Artisans' Party to form the so-called Iron Bloc, from which the Communists' newly formed Workers' Party was excluded. In July, 1928, Gichev and Muraviev further solidified their position. In time, they emerged as the dominant leaders of what had already become the principal body of the Agrarian movement, known under the name of Agrarian Union—Vrabcha I (after the address of the Union's headquarters).

Dimitur Gichev was thirty years old at the time of the 1923 coup. He possessed the personal qualities which went into the making of a substantial political career. Moderate by temperament, he was a man of wisdom and of great persuasiveness who commanded the respect of his followers as well as of his enemies. During the last stages of the Stamboliiski regime he served as the prefect of the district of Plovdiv. He was elected to the Subranie in the last of Stamboliiski's elections (1923).[19]

18 For a short biography of Petko D. Petkov see Dumanov, pp. 53–96.
19 Danchov and Danchov, *Bulgarska entsiklopediia* (Sofia, 1936), pp. 280–81.

At the time of the coup, however, Gichev was not a national figure. In part, at least, this deficiency was made right by the fact that his fellow collaborator, Konstantin Muraviev, enjoyed the distinction of being Stamboliiski's nephew, an advantage which had helped him become his uncle's minister of war a few months before the fateful coup.[20] Otherwise, Muraviev did not distinguish himself as a political figure, overshadowed as he was by the more imposing personality of Gichev. The *troika* of the Agrarian Union—Vrabcha I was completed by Vergil Dimov, who was also Gichev's brother-in-law. Dimov was the youngest of the three (too young, in fact, to be elected deputy in the 1931 elections). These three men kept the Agrarian Union—Vrabcha I together, during the years in power as well as during the years of semilegality; they stuck together until all three found themselves in prison (1944) for having become ministers in the wrong government and at the wrong time.

THE EXILES

The exiled Agrarian leaders abroad tried to maintain contact with political developments at home. Their fate was not enviable, dependent as they were on support from foreign sources, and detached from the day-to-day Bulgarian situation. They received substantial help from the Czech Peasant Party, which also assisted them in publishing the Agrarian Union's organ in exile. As time passed, however, they found themselves gravitating more and more toward Belgrade and Yugoslavia, where most of the rank-and-file exiles had settled from the very beginning. Nor did they stay united. Of the principal four among them, Kosta Todorov and Obbov found themselves at odds with Atanasov and Stoianov. There were mutual recriminations concerning the disposal of funds received from foreign sources and quarrels over tactical and organizational matters. These inner frictions were never fully resolved. Organizational matters remained largely in the hands of Obbov, who was the president of the Agrarian Union's Buro-in-Exile. Todorov, on the other hand, having become the confidant of King Alexander of Yugoslavia (to whose

---

[20] An advantage not without its dangers, however; in later years Muraviev was often accused of having neglected his work in the army and of thus having precipitated the *putsch*. These accusations were unfair and in the main politically inspired. The blame, if any, had to be placed on Kosta Tomov, whom Muraviev succeeded in the Ministry of War only a short time before Tsankov struck; Muraviev thus had little time in which to purge the officers' corps.

court he had earlier been accredited by Stamboliiski), was the man in charge of exile diplomacy. Much of his time in his ten years of exile was spent in constant travels from Belgrade to Prague to Vienna to Paris and back again.[21] Todorov possessed great abilities and great personal charm; journalist, cartoonist, writer of *feuilletons*, organizer, orator, and even historian, Kosta Todorov remained, until the end of his life, one of the most unorthodox and in some ways the most brilliant of Bulgarian political figures.

The exiled leaders knew of Gichev's alliance with the Democrats and, in fact, during the electoral campaign supported him both morally and financially. Thus, when the new People's Bloc government was formed, the Agrarian exiles rejoiced along with the thousands of their supporters at home. "We exiles naturally expected the new parliament to vote an immediate amnesty. But the Government [according to Todorov] was in no hurry to act. Curiously enough, our own party comrades, fearing we might demand the cream of the political posts, were not at all eager to see us in Sofia." [22] It was indeed the government's refusal to grant an immediate and general amnesty which more than any other issue caused the split within the Agrarian Union—Vrabcha I and the emergence of the so-called Pladne group. On the other hand, Todorov's explanation is an oversimplification. Before the elections the People's Bloc coalition had promised an amnesty. Once in power, the new government prepared and passed an amnesty bill on January 5,

[21] Kosta Todorov was born in Moscow to an exiled Bulgarian officer who had fled Bulgaria after taking part in an abortive coup against the anti-Russian regime of Stambolov. Born in exile, he lived much of his life thereafter abroad. A man of free spirit, he seems to have made the most out of his quarrels with successive Bulgarian regimes. As a youth he fought the Turks in a Macedonian revolutionary band. Back in Russia, he spent some time in prison in Odessa for suspected revolutionary activities. The outbreak of World War I found him in France. Todorov fought in the French army and was eventually landed on Bulgarian soil as an emissary of the French commander in chief with orders to establish contact with the Bulgarian military and urge them to capitulate. The last stages of the war he spent in a Bulgarian prison after the Bulgarians refused to listen. It was in prison that Todorov came to know Stamboliiski, who was eventually to make him undersecretary of foreign affairs and later ambassador to Belgrade. Having promised Stamboliiski not to join his Agrarian Union while in power, Todorov formally became a member of the Union only after the June coup; based on Todorov, *Balkan Firebrand, passim.*

[22] *Ibid.*, p. 240.

1932, which, contrary to expectations, did not include the leading
Agrarian exiles and Communists sentenced after April, 1925. Gichev
explained that the amnesty had to be limited on the grounds that the
lives of the former Stamboliiski ministers would be endangered by
Macedonian terrorists who, considering the exiles as "Serbian spies,"
were determined to shoot them down, as they did daily people of
less importance.[23] This explanation, of course, was unacceptable to
many Agrarians. An anti-Gichev assault from within was now organized.
He was attacked for having compromised all principles in order to come
to power and for having given in to pressures from the Democrats as
well as from IMRO.[24] Above all—and this was a powerful argument
among Agrarian intellectuals particularly—Gichev's critics maintained
that, by his failure to bring back the "true disciples" of Stamboliiski, he
had in effect admitted what the enemies of the Agrarian Union had
always maintained, namely, that the exiles were a "gang of Serbian
stooges" and untrustworthy conspirators.

There was little that Gichev could say to his critics. He had always
been a practical politician and had done what he thought was necessary
in order to bring the Union back to normal. In the foreign field, he continued to support Bulgaria's revisionist claims, while at home he went
along with the more conservative economic policies of the Democrats.
His compromise might well have included a promise to try and keep the
former ministers away for as long a period as possible, since their return
would of necessity have further stirred the Macedonians, with whom the
government was not ready to settle accounts.

PLADNE AGRARIANS

One newspaper in particular played an important role in the anti-
Gichev assault. This was the daily *Pladne*, published by one of the most

[23] Swire, p. 258.

[24] *Ibid.*, pp. 242–43; Swire goes into some detail to describe a meeting held between Gichev and Ivan Mikhailov (the IMRO leader) on the eve of the 1931
elections, as well as a meeting between Mikhailov and Vergil Dimov held sometime during 1932. These meetings, according to Swire, produced a deal which
made the participation of the Agrarians in the government acceptable to IMRO,
and which, on the other hand, secured IMRO a degree of freedom of action. The
principal condition on which the Agrarians had to agree was a promise to support
a revisionist foreign policy and thus prevent a rapprochement with Yugoslavia.

capable Bulgarian journalists, Georgi Vulkov. He was an extremely talented writer. In 1922, at the age of twenty-five, Vulkov became the editor of an Agrarian publication by the name of *Zemedelska zashtita*. After the June, 1923, coup and a short time in prison, he resumed his journalistic career. Shortly afterwards he went abroad, established contact with Obbov, and helped put out *Zemedelsko zname* (the organ of the Agrarians in exile) while taking part in a number of international peasant meetings as the representative of the Bulgarian Agrarian Union. Vulkov's true success, however, was achieved during the latter part of the Liapchev regime when, after having returned to Bulgaria, he became the publisher of *Pladne*. "Always just—never neutral" was *Pladne*'s motto, and it was to the latter half of the "maxim" that Vulkov adhered with the greater consistency. Sharply critical of the Democratic Alliance regime, liberal in outlook and pro-Yugoslav in its policy, *Pladne* achieved great popularity and was the first daily to challenge with some measure of success the reactionary and pro-Italian *Zora* of Danail Krapchev, who was Bulgaria's newspaper magnate. *Pladne* was often sued by Krapchev, and the Vulkov-Krapchev literary duels of the 1930s caused a great deal of excitement in Bulgarian political circles.[25]

Pladne helped elect the People's Bloc government but turned against it soon after the election. It was around this hard-hitting and "never neutral" newspaper that the anti-Gichev Agrarians united. "When the attitude of the Peasant spokesmen in the government became clear, [Aleksandur] Obbov, myself [Kosta Todorov], and other leaders organized an independent party which we called the Alexander Stamboliiski Peasant Union to emphasize our continued faith in Stamboliiski's principles—political and economic peasant democracy, and an alliance

[25] The description of Vulkov's early career is based on an article by Mikhail Genovski first published in *Zemedelsko zname*, November 15, 1944, and later reproduced in Genovski's *I v smurta sa zhivi*, pp. 110–16, a useful collection of biographical outlines of some of the more important Agrarian leaders. After the May, 1934, coup, the newspaper *Pladne* was discontinued and Vulkov became a foreign correspondent, traveled to the Soviet Union, and wrote a number of popular books. His writings included biographies of Masaryk and Beneš, a book on the Soviet Union, and an account of peasant wars throughout history (*Selski voini*), a second edition of which was published in 1945. At one time or another Vulkov edited a number of other publications, including the humorous *Sturshel* and *Zvunar*. His reappearance during the first stages of World War II, and his tragic end in 1942 will be dealt with later.

with Yugoslavia as the keystone of a united Balkans." [26] Still in exile, Todorov and Obbov could not at that stage take personal charge of the new group. The actual organizational work in Bulgaria was carried out by Dr. G. M. Dimitrov, a young politician who, together with several fellow deputies from the Agrarian Union, called the first congress of the new "Agrarian Union—Al. Stamboliiski," held in the town of Stara Zagora during November, 1932. Closely associated in the public mind with the newspaper *Pladne*, the new union came to be known simply as the Pladne group, a name which remained attached to it long after the newspaper was discontinued.[27]

In due course, pressure on the government to grant an amnesty to the exiled Agrarian leaders was intensified. In July, 1932, while attending a conference on reparations in Lausanne, Premier Mushanov met with Kosta Todorov, to whom he expressed concern over the violent antigovernment attacks carried out by *Pladne*. At this meeting the Premier promised Todorov that he and his friends would soon be allowed to return to Bulgaria. Mushanov's intervention, which some interpreted as a clever maneuver aimed at weakening the position of the Gichev Agrarians, who were in turn pressing for more ministerial seats, proved decisive.[28] Late in the fall the 1932 amnesty law was amended to include the Agrarian leaders. On January 12, 1933, the amendment

[26] Todorov, *Balkan Firebrand*, p. 240.

[27] Two recent volumes are devoted to the politics of the Agrarian Union in the thirties and the wartime period. Although pro-Communist in their interpretations, the volumes are reliable on the factual side of intra-Union politics: Petrova, *BZNS i narodniiat front, 1934–1939*, and by the same author, *BZNS v kraia na burzhoaznoto gospodstvo v Bulgariia, 1939–1944*. On the ideology of the Agrarian Union in general and the Pladne Agrarians in particular, see the programmatic speech by Dr. G. M. Dimitrov delivered in October, 1944, before the first postwar Agrarian conference and reproduced in *Zemedelsko zname*, October 18, 1944. See also Boris Pashev, *Ideologiiata na zemedelskoto dvizhenie* (Sofia, 1945). Important documentary materials relating to the structure and policies of the Pladne Agrarians and their relations with Gichev and others are contained in the parliamentary minutes of December, 1938, at which time a number of Pladne deputies were expelled from the Subranie: *Narodno subranie, Stenografski dnevnitsi*, debates for December 7–9, 1938, pp. 289–366. On the establishment of the Pladne group, see the account by Dr. Dimitrov in *Svobodna i nezavisima Bulgariia*, October 9, 1952.

[28] This at least is the interpretation given by Swire, p. 258, who had little sympathy for Mushanov.

was passed, thus opening the way for the return of Stamboliiski's former ministers and bringing to an end their ten-year-old exile.

Todorov and Obbov returned to Bulgaria on March 5, 1933. Politically, those were stormy days. IMRO was as active as ever. Parliament was debating the expulsion of the thirty-one Communist deputies elected in 1931. Unemployment was on the increase, while the peasants were sinking into ever deepening poverty. The Agrarians in the government were uneasy, trying to shift the mounting pressures from below onto Mushanov. In January, 1933, they had forced the reorganization of the government and had at last gained the Ministry of Trade, which Gichev took over, surrendering the Ministry of Agriculture to Muraviev. At that time, Vergil Dimov (who had in the meantime been elected deputy) joined the government, replacing old Georgi Yordanov, who in turn assumed the leadership of the "internal opposition" to Gichev. Had the various anti-Gichev Agrarian factions been able to unite, they would have challenged the position of the governing Agrarians. Talks to this end were started even before the return of the exiled leaders. Progress was made at first and by July, 1933, it appeared as if unification was about to be achieved. That was not to be, however. By the time of the May, 1934, coup, Agrarians were split into at least five distinguishable groups: (1) the governing Agrarians of Gichev, (2) the group of Nikola Zakhariev formed in October, 1933, (3) the Pladne group, (4) the union of Georgi Markov (Serdika), and (5) the small group of old Dimitur Dragiev (Stara Zagora), who was one of the founders of the Agrarian movement. In addition, there was a small but vocal group of crypto-Communist Agrarians led by Lazar Stanev who for a time published their own organ under the name of *Zemedelsko vuzrazhdane* (Agrarian Revival). In the 1931 elections they participated in the Communist-sponsored *Trudov blok* (Labor Bloc) and elected a number of deputies who, for all practical purposes, were indistinguishable from the other deputies of the Workers' (Communist) Party. Attacking both Gichev and Pladne, the Stanev group eventually merged with the Communist Party.

In terms of national politics, the various Agrarian factions played minor roles, with the exception of the Gichev and Pladne groups. The return of the exiled leaders proved that Gichev's earlier fears were not without foundation. "My friends [wrote Todorov] organized a bodyguard of three men, each armed with two revolvers, who protected me constantly. Unknown persons were searched before being admitted to see me. I lived as if in a beleaguered fortress and moved about the city only in an automobile, with my bodyguards." [29] Together with Dr. G. M. Dimitrov and his fellow deputies, the newly returned Agrarians plunged into intensive organizational activity. What they needed most was to penetrate the reserved and conservative peasants, who instinctively resented political splits of all kinds. Strong on oratory, promises, and nostalgic reminiscences of the "good-old-Stamboliiski days," Pladne leaders succeeded within a relatively short time in gaining a substantial following. When on November 21, 1933, the Pladne group held its second congress in Sofia, it claimed to have increased its membership from 17,000, as of March of the same year, to 128,000. "The sessions [of the congress] lasted three days, climaxed by the election of a seven-man Central Committee and a governing Party Council of thirty-two members. I [Kosta Todorov] received the largest number of votes; of the sixteen administrative areas, twelve demanded that I represent them in the Central Committee." [30] When on February 18, 1934, elections were held for local rural and communal councils (the first and only election in which Pladne took part as an independent entity), closely trailing the government coalition was Tsankov with 115,193 votes, Pladne with 59,160 votes, followed by the 55,476 votes for the Communists.[31] Although the elections were not national and therefore not indicative of the relative nation-wide strength of the various groups, they did show Pladne in a respectable third position. Despite the progress of Pladne, Gichev's Union remained by far the stronger of the two groups.

RADICALS

Occupying a tiny space to the left of the Democratic Party stood the Radicals. In relation to the Agrarians, their precise position on the spectrum was unclear, owing to the numerous and diversified Agrarian

[29] Todorov, *Balkan Firebrand*, p. 243.

[30] *Ibid.*, p. 248. Exaggerated claims on membership figures were made by all Agrarian groups. There was, however, more to this tendency than the obvious considerations of self-interest. Agrarians would assume *a priori* that they alone had a monopoly of the support of the peasant population. It was this notion that made them take the peasantry for granted.

[31] Kazasov, *Burni godini*, p. 505.

groupings. In February, 1924, under the leadership of Kosturkov, the bulk of the Radicals followed the example of Malinov's Democrats (from whom they had split in 1903) and went over to the opposition. In 1931 they again joined with Malinov in the People's Bloc and were given the Ministry of Railroads (Kosturkov) despite the modest total of seven votes which they commanded in the Subraine. Because of their small numbers, their seat in the cabinet was vulnerable. It was in fact during a government crisis involving the Ministry of Railroads that the May, 1934, coup was executed. The Radicals were of little importance, in terms of both numerical strength and influence. The none-too-glorious reemergence of Kosturkov in the fall of 1945, as an ally of the Communists, belongs to the Sovietization period.

SOCIAL DEMOCRATS

From being the third largest party (after the Agrarians and the Communists) at the end of World War I, the Social Democrats lost most of their strength during the 1920s. In the 1931–34 Subranie they had fewer deputies than the Radicals. The influence of the Social Democratic Party, however, was greater than its size would indicate. In large measure this was due to the prestige which its leaders Sakuzov, Pastukhov, Cheshmedzhiev, and others commanded among working-class circles, as well as among middle-class democratic elements at large. Their association with the Second International and the personal contacts which they were able to establish with Western European socialist leaders enhanced their prestige at home and also tended to make them potential allies of value to governments to whom international good will was important. In terms of influence, not least important were the small but well-organized trade-union movement and the cooperative credit establishments maintained by the Socialists.

Following a short-lived participation in two coalition governments right after the end of World War I, the Social Democrats remained in opposition. Like most other parties, they were happy when Stamboliiski's rule was brought to an end. Although the Party as such did not authorize Dimo Kazasov's participation in the June, 1923, coup, once in, Kazasov was supported by the Party and was elected to its Central Committee. In the November, 1923, elections, the Social Democrats were able to elect the unprecedented total of twenty-nine deputies. As early as December of that year, opposition to Kazasov's participation in the

Tsankov government arose from within the Party ranks. Urgent inquiries were made by the Secretariat of the Second International: How was it that the Bulgarian comrades had given their support to the Tsankov regime? Eventually the Social Democrats withdrew Kazasov's mandate and thus dissociated themselves from the government of the Democratic Alliance. When on March 11, 1924, the Balkan Conference of the Social Democratic parties opened in Bucharest, the Bulgarian delegates sought to explain their past association with Tsankov on the grounds that they had helped mitigate much of the effect of Tsankov's terror. In Prague a year later, the Bulgarian delegation obtained the International's full confidence. By that time, Kazasov had drifted to the right. Expelled from the Party early in 1926, Kazasov, together with several Social Democratic deputies, organized the so-called *Sotsialisticheska federatsiia*. This formation, after some initial successes, soon disappeared from the scene. Most of its members were readmitted to the Social Democratic Party, while Kazasov went over to Tsankov and ultimately into the Zveno group. Thus the crisis within the Party was brought to an end.

Having withdrawn to a position of uncompromising opposition and thus regained the full respect of the Second International, the Bulgarian Social Democrats were never again able even to approximate the parliamentary strength they had achieved in the 1923 elections. "With respectability came poverty" was the saying of their enemies, and the Bulgarian Social Democrats could not help but feel bitter as their strength melted away. As Gichev's partners in the so-called Iron Bloc of 1927, the Social Democrats emerged with eleven deputies. Four years later, they avoided all coalitions and received a mere 25,626 votes, which gave them only five deputies in the Subranie. Still, thanks largely to the caliber of its leaders, the Party continued to be a factor in national politics. In terms of rank-and-file support, the Social Democrats were strongest among the teachers, skilled laborers, and artisans of lower middle-class standing. Their small but well-run trade unions, popular banks, and consumer cooperatives gave them added strength and supplied their organization with a solid, if narrow, economic base. Their greatest asset remained their "good political name" and an accepted international as well as domestic respectability which, so far as the left was concerned, placed the Social Democrats in a position not unlike the one held by Malinov's Democrats among the groups of the right.

THE 1934 PUTSCH

In the early thirties, with authoritarianism on the rise, the prospects of the Bulgarian non-Communist left, as well as of the democratic center, worsened. Committed as they were to the principles of democratic government, both groups faced the assault from authoritarian elements who preferred efficiency to democracy.

The military coup carried out on May 19, 1934, by the Military League placed Bulgaria under a dictatorial regime. The new government of Kimon Georgiev suspended the Turnovo Constitution, dissolved the Subranie, abolished all political parties and organizations (June 14), barred the publication of the various party organs, and confiscated the property of all political parties. Political meetings were prohibited and a severe censorship was imposed. State administration was streamlined and centralized, with the Ministry of the Interior taking over most of the functions of local administration. Local self-government, which had survived through the years, was now all but abolished.

The efficiency with which the *putsch* was executed contrasted sharply with the political character of the new regime. It was only a matter of months before it became obvious that the Military League's shiny armor enclosed a political vacuum; once pierced, it collapsed. This was what Boris proceeded to do and with great success. It took eighteen months and four cabinets for the King to emerge supreme. The Georgiev government fell on January 22, 1935, and was succeeded by the transitional cabinet of General Pencho Zlatev, which in April gave way to yet a new government headed by Andrei Toshev. Following the abortive counter-*putsch* of Velchev (October, 1935), Boris called on Georgi Kioseivanov (November 23, 1935), a career diplomat and a director of the palace office. Real power remained in the hands of Boris, however.

The ease with which Boris capitalized on a deteriorating political situation was not due only to the personal political skill that he undoubtedly possessed. What helped the King greatly was the general trend of the times toward authoritarianism, a phenomenon by no means restricted to Bulgaria. Moreover, a number of factors peculiar to the Bulgarian political situation combined to give him the instrumentality he needed.

The May coup had little political preparation. Between November,

1933, and May, 1934, the period during which the coup was being hatched, the Military League was preoccupied not with mastering support outside its narrow limits but with creating an internal majority. In view of the numerous factions operating within the League, with each following its own chieftain, this was no simple task. Velchev's people, for example, distrusted General Vatev, the president of the League, who was suspected of having been recruited by the King.

The same rivalry was true of the Zveno group, the political front of the Military League. Here, Kazasov, the editor of *Zveno* and founder of the group itself, was kept outside the conspiracy, again for fear that he might have become too closely affiliated with court circles. Only within a very narrow circle of people around Velchev and Kimon Georgiev, such as Ivan Kharizanov (Zveno's ideologist), Petur Todorov, Vasil Karakulakov, and Menakhem Faionov, were the details of the plot known. Throughout the fall of 1933 inner tension mounted. In January, 1934, the Zveno group split wide open; led by Kazasov, ten of the fifteen members of Zveno's governing body broke away and went over to Tsankov. Of the total of one hundred active members of Zveno, according to Kazasov, seventy-six joined Tsankov, eight stayed with Velchev and Georgiev, while the remainder continued unaffiliated.[32]

The main reason for the split was the distrust with which the majority of Zveno members were being treated by the few who were directly associated with the military. Simple opportunism was another factor. In the spring of 1934, the group under Tsankov, thanks largely to the noisy propaganda which it was able to generate, appeared to many to have reached the threshold of power. This feeling was strengthened by the deterioration of the governing coalition's position. The growing influence of the Pladne group, and the mounting economic

[32] Only those aspects of the May coup directly involving the Zveno, Pladne, and Gichev groups—all of importance for their future relations with the Communist Party—are dealt with here. The information concerning the struggles within Zveno and the Military League is based on Kazasov's own *Burni godini*, pp. 490–96, 506–13. Despite his desertion of the Zveno group, Kazasov did not altogether dissociate himself from the Velchev-Georgiev clique. After the coup, he was appointed Bulgaria's ambassador to Belgrade, where he succeeded Kioseivanov. In April, 1935, following the resignation of the Zlatev government, the League proposed Kazasov for the premiership (this was presumably done without Kazasov's agreement), but the proposal was rejected by Boris, who was already strong enough to make his own selections (*ibid.*, pp. 559–60).

difficulties of the Bulgarian peasants, tended to increase the pressures on Gichev, who in turn increased his own demands on Mushanov by requesting a larger share of power in the government. Faced with endless inner bickering, Mushanov was already considering the possible alternatives to the existing coalition with Gichev. In the spring of 1934 he began secret negotiations with the leaders of Pladne for the purpose of opening the way for their entry into the government in the place of Gichev and his colleagues. The negotiations centered on the following main demands made by the representatives of Pladne: (*a*) a new and more progressive approach to the economic problems of the peasants; (*b*) the suppression of the Tsankov movement; (*c*) the ousting of the pro-Italian General Vulkov from his post at Rome; (*d*) close collaboration with Yugoslavia. Mushanov, according to Kosta Todorov, agreed to all the demands except the last, which presumably included an alliance with Yugoslavia. This, Mushanov was reported to have said, was up to the King.[33]

While Mushanov was trying to get Pladne into the government on the very eve of the coup, the conspirators under Kimon Georgiev made a last-minute attempt to secure for themselves some popular support by getting Gichev out of the government and into the conspiracy. Gichev, however, refused to have anything to do with the plot, despite the great pressures and the tempting offers made by the Military League.[34]

In the meantime, Boris did not remain idle. In order to undermine the Military League, he decided to bribe its leader away from the organization. On May 9 the minister of war of the People's Bloc government resigned. Boris pressed for General Vatev, the president of the Military League, to become the new minister of war. Vatev accepted the post and by so doing proved that the suspicions Velchev had of his being the King's man were not without foundation. The general confusion which prevailed was exploited from still another source. Tsankov, always fond of noisy demonstrations, organized a great action for May 20, at which he intended to parade 50,000 of his followers.

[33] Todorov, *Balkan Firebrand*, p. 255.

[34] Swire (*Bulgarian Conspiracy*) goes into some detail to describe the negotiations between Georgiev and Gichev. Among other things, the latter was asked to dissociate himself from Vergil Dimov, who was believed to be too deeply involved in compromising deals with Ivan Mikhailov's IMRO.

On the morning of May 19, with General Vatev isolated in his own Ministry by his subordinates and followers, Velchev and his people executed what appeared to be an ideal coup. In order to undercut any possible resistance, Dimitur Gichev was interned in the Klisurski monastery.[35] General Vatev was banished to Vienna. Kosta Todorov, the leader of Pladne, was expelled from the country, whereupon he found himself back in Belgrade, whence he had come a little more than a year earlier.[36] The King was presented with the list containing the names of the new government, which he hastened to approve. Velchev, whom the League wanted as premier early in May, refused to take any official post, thus opening the way for the assumption of the premiership by his friend Kimon Georgiev. Of the eight members of the new government, only two were known members of the Zveno group, the Premier and Petur Todorov.[37] The others were either technicians or politicians who represented nobody but themselves. Real power resided with a triumvirate of which Velchev and Georgiev were the two permanent members, while the third was anyone from among the members of the government most directly concerned with the issue at hand. This was the "three-man rule" under which Bulgaria was governed for eight months.

The coup of May 19, therefore, was in effect a double coup: a coup against the legally instituted government—which was entirely successful; and a coup of Velchev's people against their opponents within the Military League—which was only temporarily successful. Throughout, the military elements were disposed in one of at least four ways: (1) those who stood outside the League, (2) those inside the League but in favor of the King, (3) those within the League and against the King, and (4) those within the League but otherwise neutral. As events were

[35] Kazasov, *Burni godini*, p. 552. Having failed to attract Gichev, the conspirators turned to N. Zakhariev, an old Agrarian who agreed to join the new government.

[36] Todorov, *Balkan Firebrand*, p. 255.

[37] In 1936 Kazasov made use of this fact in order to clear Zveno by dissociating the group from the coup of May 19, which, in his words, "was exclusively the army's doing." "Zveno," he added, "did not fight parliamentarism but only its defects; it did not oppose democracy but only the falsifications hidden behind the democratic labels." Kazasov, *Zveno bez grim*, from the introduction, pp. 3–5. Had Kazasov been allowed to play a major role in the coup (which he would have greatly liked) and had the coup proved more durable, he would have undoubtedly spoken differently.

soon to show, Velchev's refusal to assume the premiership proved his undoing, for he was unable to maintain his majority within the League. In September, 1934, steps were taken to secure the Ministry of War for Velchev. This proved impossible in view of the League's opposition. With Boris's initiative, one by one Velchev's supporters deserted him. This was the case, for example, with General Zlatev, the minister of war in the Georgiev cabinet, who in January, 1935, after Velchev and Georgiev had all but lost their majority in the League, was selected by the King to head the new government.

Under Zlatev, in order to prevent the opposition from mustering its forces, Georgiev and Aleksandur Tsankov were interned, and Velchev was placed under close supervision. After the Toshev government came to power, Velchev was expelled to Yugoslavia (July 26, 1935), from where, in October of the same year, he sought to organize his abortive counterblow, thus playing directly into the hands of the King. Kosta Todorov (who was in Yugoslavia at that time) and the Pladne leaders at home were accused of having come to an agreement with Velchev and his fellow conspirators. About one hundred of them were arrested. Velchev, Major Kiril Stanchev (who as the secretary of the League was Velchev's contact at home), and General Vladimir Zaimov, among many others, were brought to trial. On February 22, 1936, Velchev and Stanchev were sentenced to death. On March 3 (Bulgaria's independence day), General Khristo Lukov, the new minister of war and Velchev's chief enemy, issued an order for the abolition of the Military League. On March 28, under pressure from abroad, Boris commuted the sentences of Velchev and Stanchev to life imprisonment. With this, the adventure of May 19, 1934, came to a close.[38]

During the early stages of the subsequent Kioseivanov government, the King continued to consolidate his power. The purge of officers from the Military League continued; some were dismissed from the army altogether, while others were assigned to less sensitive posts. All were

---

[38] General Zaimov was shot by the Bulgarian pro-German regime in 1942 for espionage in behalf of the Soviet Union. Velchev stayed in prison until 1940, when he was granted amnesty. Throughout the war, however, he remained under close police supervision and it was only through his personal contacts that he was able to play a role in the army as well as in the Fatherland Front. Kimon Georgiev was not involved in the October, 1935, plot, and therefore retained his freedom.

barred from taking part in any organized activity outside the army. Boris strengthened his influence among the reserve officers' corps as well as among the powerful organization of the reserve noncommissioned officers.

CHAPTER TWO

DIMITROV AND HIS DETRACTORS

DURING 1923–25, as a result of the unsuccessful insurrection of September, 1923, and the violence which followed it, the Bulgarian Communist movement split apart. While the majority of the rank and file remained in the country, a great many emigrated to the Soviet Union. Most of the more prominent Communist leaders found themselves in exile in the Soviet Union as well. This physical schism persisted until the entry of the Red Army into Bulgaria in September, 1944, when the majority of the exiles returned to their homeland. The duality within the Party was characteristic of Bulgarian Communism during most of the interwar and wartime periods. The Party at home and the Party in exile formed the two central columns around which the tangled history of Bulgarian Communism evolved. The emergence of the emigration created a vertical cut, as it were. Yet most of the inner Party conflicts followed complex patterns which more often than not cut across the cadres abroad and at home. The following pages endeavor to describe and clarify these juxtapositions.

BULGARIAN MEN IN SOVIET POLITICS

The politics of the Communist exiles depended equally on their ideology and on their particular political culture, which set them aside and made them unique among the many other foreigners on the Soviet scene. While the particular ideological commitments can and will be traced in some detail, the remarkable adaptability of the Bulgarians to life in Russia can only be illustrated by examples. In general it may be stated that, with the Bulgarians, political radicalism converged with a sentiment for things Russian to produce a relatively rapid acculturation to the new Soviet style of conduct. When Victor Serge, an important raconteur of Comintern affairs, observed that "outside Russia and perhaps Bulgaria, there were no real Communists anywhere in the world," he was referring to the émigrés, who were the only Bulgarians he knew. From the perspective of their tiny and beleaguered land, Russia loomed as the large new world. In contrast to other foreign lands, only in Russia did Bulgarians make first-rate careers for themselves.[1]

The career of Boris Stomaniakov represents an interesting case of a Bulgarian who, having discovered Russia and the Bolsheviks early in life, attained the highest ranks in the Soviet state hierarchy. Born in Ruse (1882), he was sent for his education to Voronezh and later to the Tsarist capital, where he befriended Yelena Stassova. Eventually he turned up as the chief Bolshevik arms-purchasing agent in Western Europe and became the protégé of Lenin and Litvinov. Having spent the war years back in Bulgaria, he was recalled to the Soviet Union and appointed by Lenin the Soviet trade representative to Germany (1921–25) during the early Rapallo years. He was promoted to the post of a deputy commissar for foreign trade, and in 1926 joined the Soviet Foreign Service. From February, 1934, until his purge in 1938, Stomaniakov filled the position of deputy commissar for foreign affairs in charge of the Far Eastern department.[2]

Stomaniakov's was only one in a string of similar "transformations."

---

[1] Evidence on the subject remains sporadic, and the life histories of those who left the fold of their countrymen for careers in the Soviet state bureaucracy are too sparsely documented to allow for systematic generalizations. Still, the phenomenon is too striking to be left unexplored, even if the approach is of necessity typological with only a few selective examples for purposes of illustration.

[2] Only years later did the Bulgarians decide to reclaim him for their dwindling pantheon of revolutionary martyrs. A detailed account of Stomaniakov's life was published in 1963 in a collection of studies devoted to Bulgarian revolutionaries in foreign lands; see Doinov and Draev, eds., *Bulgari bortsi*, pp. 45–56. In 1905 the Bolsheviks appointed Stomaniakov their chief armaments-purchasing agent in Belgium. In the following year, together with Litvinov and Stalin's friend the *boyevik* Kamo (Ter-Petrossian), he organized the dispatch of arms to the Bolsheviks in Russia via the Varna-Odessa shipping route, which had long been used for the clandestine shipment of Lenin's *Iskra*; on these and other details see *ibid*,

In 1919 Kiril Telalov (of Yambol) abandoned his position in the Bulgarian consulate in Odessa to join the Soviet bureaucracy and make a diplomatic career as adviser to the Soviet minister in China.[3] Peitchev and Petrunov served as secretaries of the Soviet legations in Paris and London, respectively.[4] During his brief ambassadorship to Vienna, Joffe had as his Embassy secretary Solomon Goldstein, an old Bulgarian Socialist (since 1908) who had helped found the Bulgarian Metal Workers' Union. Goldstein joined the Bolsheviks in Zurich in 1915, participated in the Zimmerwald left, and was one of the principal founders of the Swiss CP. In 1919–20 he was Lenin's personal representative in Bulgaria, having been sent by him as special emissary to old Blagoev.[5]

At the end of 1917, two high-ranking officials of the Bulgarian delegation in Russia to the Brest-Litovsk talks reestablished old connections with Lenin and the Bolsheviks, now freshly in power. One, Ivan Nedialkov (Shablin), eventually became the official representative of the Bulgarian CP to the Third International in Moscow.[6] The other, Roman P. Avramov, who had worked for Lenin in the early 1900s on a

---

pp. 34–44; Georgi Bakalov, "Staraya 'Iskra' sredi Bolgar," *Proletarskaya revolyutsia*, No. 91–92 (1929), pp. 67–95; Rothschild, pp. 1, 250; *Istoriia na BKP*, p. 109. Antonov, the Bulgarian minister to Moscow in the mid-thirties, knew Stomaniakov personally. His endeavors to arouse the sentiments of the then high Soviet official for the country of his origin and for her interests were of no avail. The man had become thoroughly Russified.

[3] Doinov and Draev, eds., *Bulgari bortsi*, p. 63, has a brief mention of Telalov as well as excerpts of a letter by the person in charge of the Bulgarian consulate in Odessa to his government, complaining of pro-Communist activities by Bulgarians in the Odessa region. On Telalov see also Logio, p. 363n.

[4] Logio, p. 363n.

[5] V. I. Lenin, *Vospominaniia, 1900–1922* (Moscow, 1963), pp. 192–99, 626; see also Serge, pp. 182–83, and Doinov and Draev, eds., *Bulgari bortsi*, p. 74. Serge refers to him as Dr. Goldstein and as the Balkan expert in the Soviet legation in Austria "who carried out the worst possible directives in such a way as to do the least possible damage." Goldstein's relations with Lenin were intimate, dating back to wartime Zurich. His own account published in 1963 conveys a sense of Lenin's great affection for the Bulgarian radicals, referring to Iako Shamli and Roman Avramov (of whom more shortly). Reference is also made of Liiu Kasher. After the death of Lenin, Goldstein appears to have been one of the few Bulgarian exiles who sided with the left opposition in the CPSU (see Atanasov, *Pod znameto na partiiata*, p. 103), which may be attributed to his connections with Joffe. He survived, however, and remained in Russia, retiring in 1956.

[6] He perished in 1925 during the White Terror in Bulgaria.

variety of errands for the Bolsheviks in Germany, Switzerland, and the Balkans, ultimately joined the Bolshevik regime and attained high rank in the state bureaucracy. He headed the Soviet trade mission in Berlin (1921–29), later took charge of Soviet grain exports, and until his purge in 1937 served in various Soviet trade missions in Germany, France, and England.[7]

Whereas the above cases pertain to Bulgarians who made their way directly into the world of Soviet politics (and the list can be further extended), the Bulgarians' aptitude for international revolutionism and their versatility in the wider world of the Comintern would require an extensive cataloguing. None achieved so brilliant (and so tragic) a career as Christian Rakovski, whose name remains intimately associated with the top men of the Soviet state and of Soviet politics during the first two decades of the Bolshevik Revolution. Though born in Bulgaria (he was the nephew of the Bulgarian revolutionary patriot Georgi Rakovski), and actively engaged in Bulgaria's intra-Socialist struggles in the prewar years, he made a greater impact as the organizer of the early Socialists in Rumania. The high points of Rakovski's political career, however, were attained in the Soviet Ukraine, in the politics of the left opposition, and in the realm of diplomacy in postrevolutionary Russia. During this last stage in his life, his involvements in the problems of Bulgarian Communism were incidental, though not unimportant.[8] Boris Stefanov, a Dobruja Bulgarian like Rakovski, was, before his return to

[7] On the life of Roman Avramov and his purge, see *Istoricheski pregled*, No. 4–5 (1967), pp. 177–82. When in 1905 Lenin established his committee of the Bolshevik organizations abroad (KZO), the main function of which was to combat the Mensheviks, he made Roman Avramov its secretary. Avramov was at the same time in charge of money matters for the Bolshevik CC. Together with Stassova, he took charge of the Bolshevik archives when Lenin departed for Russia in October, 1905. Avramov was equally well acquainted with Rosa Luxemburg and the leaders of the German left. Despite his affinity for the Bolsheviks, he did not accept Lenin's principles of super-organizational centralism, and on his return to Bulgaria sided with the Bulgarian "broad" Socialists against Blagoev's "narrows." He was one of the prominent leaders of the Bulgarian Social Democrats, whom he represented in the prewar Subranie. His swing back to the Bolsheviks came after their capture of power, and following his several meetings with Lenin at Smolny at the end of 1917.

[8] On Rakovski's involvements in early Bulgarian Socialism, see Rothschild, pp. 16, 19, 32–36, and *passim*; *Istoriia na BKP*, pp. 124–26. His contributions to Socialism in Rumania are summarized in Ionescu, pp. 2–10; details on his role in

his homeland after World War II, one of the top leaders of the Rumanian CP, and in the thirties its Comintern representative in Moscow.

A whole constellation of lesser luminaries figured prominently in Comintern intrigues in the thirties. There was Stoian Minev, who went under the name of Boris Stepanov. Enlisted by Lenin during the war for work within the various West European leftist factions, Stepanov represented the Italian Communists at the Second Congress of the Comintern under the name of Lorenco Vanini, figured in the left opposition (which he betrayed to the Stalin forces) in the twenties under the name of Lebedev, and was the Comintern chief agent to the Latin American Communist parties and to the Spanish Communists during the Spanish Civil War. Ruben Levi, who under the name Ruben Avramov served as Bulgaria's minister of culture in the mid-fifties, functioned as a Soviet political commissar during the Spanish Civil War in Madrid under the name of Miguel, and later directed the Comintern wartime secret school in Kushnarenkovo (near Ufa) under the name of Mikhailov. Marshal Tito's confidant and one of his principal advisers on Stalin's and Mao's brands of Communism before and after the 1948 Yugoslav break with the Soviet Union was Ivan Karaivanov, a Bulgarian Communist conspirator of remarkable talents, who in the 1920s served as Dimitrov's secretary, and in the 1930s worked in the Cadres Department of the Comintern. A Bulgarian by the name of Georgi Andreichin played a central role in the politics of the old American IWW, helped found the American CP, and in 1921 was elected a member of the Executive Committee of the Profintern in Moscow as an American representative. These names are but a sample.[9] "Among the

---

the left opposition of the CPSU are to be found in Louis Fischer's *Men and Politics*.

A substantial number of Russophile officers of the Bulgarian army were purged in the 1880s; many joined the Tsarist army and some attained the ranks of general officers. The majority returned to their homeland after the Revolution. A number remained and were retained in various capacities by the new regime. Two such generals, S. N. Vankov and P. S. Staev, stayed on and attained important positions, the first as professor of metallurgy and the second as lecturer at the Academy of the Red Army's General Staff. Their careers are traced in *Istoricheski pregled*, No. 4–5 (1967), pp. 105–7.

[9] The careers of Stefanov, Minev, Levi-Avramov, Karaivanov, and Andreichin will be duly traced and documented in the following chapters.

most backward of European countries, Bulgaria produced international
Communism's best bolsheviks." [10]

THE POLITICAL EMIGRATION IN RUSSIA

The bulk of the emigration in Russia was made up of people neither
remarkable for their politics nor particularly noticeable for their personal qualities. They were overwhelmingly of peasant stock—like the
Party at home—with a thin layer of the quasi-intelligentsia radicalized
by the disasters of war and the wretchedness of Bulgarian society. Led
by Kolarov, Dimitrov, and Gavril Genov, the survivors of the 1923 uprising crossed the frontier into Yugoslavia, where they were installed
in refugee camps together with hundreds of Stamboliiski's Agrarian
followers. Selected by the Party leadership which had set up headquarters in Vienna, part of them traveled to Austria and, with the assistance of the International Workers' Red Aid, were dispatched to the
Soviet Union. "During a period of six months, until the end of 1925,
several hundred Bulgarian émigrés went to Moscow via Vienna." [11]
Not all the Communist refugees were withdrawn from Yugoslavia, however. Many crossed back into embattled Bulgaria to feed the fires of the
lingering insurrection and to man the guerrilla bands which had sprung
up all over the countryside. Their survivors joined with the young
militants to make up the second large wave of refugees following the
bombing of the Sofia Cathedral in 1925. There were also Communists
who made their way directly to the Soviet Union on boats across the
Black Sea. Others crossed into Greece and Turkey and eventually, with
Comintern assistance, made their way to Soviet soil. As late as 1927,
small groups of stragglers from the second wave continued to arrive in
Odessa, averaging 10–20 per month.[12] Unspecified numbers of Communists reached Russia in the late twenties and early thirties, many of
them legally. These were the so-called *Apriltsi*, Communists who had

---

[10] The quote is from Rothschild, p. 302.

[11] Vinarov, p. 235. For a time, Vinarov was in charge of the exile transit center
set up in Vienna. His memoirs, together with those of Gilin (*Komunisti*) and
Sh. Atanasov (*Pod znameto na partiiata*, later expanded in a new edition entitled
Zapiski na revoliutsionera), represent major firsthand accounts of the emigration
in Russia.

[12] *Istoricheski pregled*, No. 4–5 (1967), p. 121.

served their prison terms, having been sentenced in the mass trials following the April, 1925, terroristic outrages.

The precise size of the emigration remains uncertain.[13] In the early twenties, before Tsankov's *putsch* of June, 1923, and before the start of the Communist exodus, there were some fifty Bulgarian Communists in Moscow, composed of "the Party's representatives in the Comintern, political émigrés, men sent to the Soviet Union to study in various Party schools and military academies, and clandestine party couriers." [14] During 1924–25, Bulgarian political exiles in the Soviet Union amounted to 17 percent of all political exiles in the country, constituting in absolute terms the second largest contingent of political exiles after the Poles.[15] Some 1,000 Bulgarian exiles were processed in Odessa alone during a three-and-a-half-year period beginning early in 1924.[16] A sum total of 2,000, and possibly as many as 3,000, Bulgarian exiles may reasonably be assumed to have found their way to the Soviet Union at one time or another during the interwar period. Although the vast majority remained in Russia throughout that period, the numbers fluctuated, particularly in the early and mid-thirties when younger functionaries were brought in from Bulgaria for short study periods in the various Party schools.[17]

---

[13] Two whole generations after the emigration arose, and a quarter of a century after its dissolution, Bulgarian historians have yet to make public the vital statistics of the life, size, and history of this most important contingent of Bulgarian Communism. The reason for this silence is as plain as it is cynical: unwillingness to give a full account of those amongst the émigrés who eventually perished in Soviet prisons and Siberian camps during the Great Purge under Stalin, at the very time when Dimitrov, the Party's most illustrious hero, was filling the chair of the Comintern's general secretariatship. First among the adulators of Soviet Russia, the Bulgarians are the last to acknowledge the horrors of this dark chapter in their political history.

[14] Vinarov, p. 172.

[15] *Istoricheski pregled*, No. 4–5 (1967), p. 119. Since the second wave of exiles began reaching the Soviet Union only in the latter part of 1925, and did not reach its peak until the following year, the relative weight of the Bulgarians within the total body of the political emigration in the USSR must have increased.

[16] *Ibid.*, p. 121.

[17] As stated, the Bulgarians have not provided firm figures on the size of their emigration. The above estimates are the author's. They are based on conjecture rather than on hard evidence. Blagoi Popov, the veteran Communist functionary who was a member of the Party's CC in the late twenties, appeared as one of Dimitrov's co-defendants at the Leipzig trial in 1933 and was later purged, spend-

At the outset, at least, the newly arrived were given a hero's welcome. Kolarov made sure that the revolutionary experience of his compatriots, though a failure in its ultimate political objectives, did not become lost on his hosts. The Soviet leaders were all too willing to see, listen, and applaud. An excerpt from Kolarov's *Memoirs* speaks for itself:

Soon after my arrival in Moscow [early 1924] we learned of a large group of Bulgarian insurrectionists from the southern districts [of Bulgaria] who had crossed the Turkish frontier and had arrived at Istambul. I asked the Soviet government to give them visas to enter the Soviet Union and assist them to make their way to Odessa.

When I learned of the group's arrival at Odessa, I asked Stalin that arrangements be made for their reception and dispatch to Moscow by the Odessa Party organization.

In my presence, Stalin dictated the text of a telegram to the Odessa district organization of the Party, along the lines of my request.

In Moscow, a festive reception, with a guard of honor, was organized by the International Workers' Red Aid.[18]

Kolarov was elected an honorary member of a Red Army guard regiment, and a village in the Tomski district in Siberia was renamed after him. A cavalry division in the Ukraine adopted the name of the Bulgarian CP. As Kolarov put it, "The moral blow which the Party had delivered upon itself by its 'neutrality' during the June 9 *putsch* of 1923 had all but withered away, and its prestige as one of the best revolutionary parties was restored."

Elaborate schemes were set in motion in order to maintain an organization of the émigrés, who were now spread all over the Soviet Union. A Central Political Émigré Commission was established at the official representation of the BCP to the ECCI with branches in Moscow

---

ing many years in the Siberian camps, accepted the 2,000–3,000 estimate as reasonable (Popov to author, interview, Sofia, September 6, 1966). The estimates were considered too high by Ruben Levi-Avramov, the person best qualified by virtue of personal experience and official position to be in possession of all the facts (Levi-Avramov to author, interview, Sofia, September, 1966). No counter-estimates were volunteered, however. At the time of the inquiry, Levi-Avramov was a member of the Party's CC and the head of the Institute on the History of the BCP, and therefore under the obvious constraints imposed by the official Party line on the matter.

[18] This and the quotation immediately following are from Kolarov, *Spomeni*, pp. 597–98.

and Leningrad and subdivisions in Kharkov and Odessa.[19] A mutual assistance fund was created and a variety of cultural and literary activities organized. The Bulgarian exiles, who in overwhelming numbers had been members of the Bulgarian CP or had become so on arrival, joined the CPSU and were given Soviet citizenship.

The rank and file were divided into two main clusters: one concentrated in the southern Ukraine, with Odessa as its main urban center, and the other in the large cities of Great Russia, mainly Moscow and Leningrad.

A very large number were sent to the southern Ukraine, or remained there upon arrival. The objective was to reinforce and revitalize the rural and semirural communities of the so-called Bessarabian Bulgarians, who had posed a problem for the Soviet regime from the beginning. These old settlements had been established by Bulgarian migrants a century or more earlier. The history of this remarkable mass migration, which dates back to the early beginnings of the modern Bulgarian national revival, can only be outlined here. Under Turkish rule, Bulgarians in substantial numbers pushed beyond their ethnic boundaries in search of greater opportunities. The rise of Russia as the principal countervailing force to Ottoman power in the Balkans and as chief spokesman for the southern Slavs generated a movement on the part of large numbers of Bulgarian villagers to move beyond the Danube and into the Russian-Ottoman borderlands along the Black Sea. In the latter part of the eighteenth century, and particularly during the first three decades of the nineteenth century, compact Bulgarian communities sprang up in Bessarabia. The migrants came from eastern Bulgaria, mainly from the region of Sliven. Entire villages with their mayors and livestock (and retaining their original names) were transplanted, as it were, into the region lying along the Prut and Dnester rivers, and were reestablished on land grants set aside by the Russian government. Scores of villages clustered around two main towns, Bolgrad and Komrat, and preserved the physical and cultural characteristics of the old country as they evolved. After the Paris Peace Conference (1856), which established Rumanian sovereignty, numerous Bulgarians left Bessarabia, moved eastward across the Dnester, and settled in the south-

[19] *Istoricheski pregled*, No. 4–5 (1967), p. 121.

ernmost regions of the Ukraine and Russia. They continued to be referred to as Bessarabian Bulgarians.

The relative compactness of this migratory people, settled in some
64 villages and the towns of Bolgrad and Komrat, and numbering about
400,000, ensured the preservation of their native tongue and original
ethnic customs. Some fought the Turks in the ranks of the Russian
armies during the Russo-Turkish war of 1877 that led to the San Stefano
treaty and the establishment of an independent Bulgaria. The best among
them returned to Bulgaria to man the new bureaucracy and to help
evolve the new elite. Stagnation gradually set in among the Bessarabian
Bulgarians. The small intelligentsia that they were able to produce in
the following decades drifted into the larger world of Russia and became
thoroughly Russified. This draining process was never successfully arrested. During the Revolution and the Civil War many joined the White
armies and ultimately sought refuge in the country of their ancestors.[20]

Thus the arrival of the Communist émigrés in the southern Soviet
Union in the early twenties converged with the destinies of the century-
old Bulgarian communities along the coast of the Black Sea. It was the

[20] The literature on the history of the Bessarabian Bulgarians is vast. For a brief
bibliography on the subject, mainly in Russian and Bulgarian, see *Istoricheski
pregled*, No. 1 (1967), pp. 55 ff. The estimate of 400,000 is given in *Kratka
Bulgarska Entsiklopediia*, I (Sofia, 1963), 228. In 1960, Soviet statistical estimates
fixed the total number of such Bulgarians at 324,000 (see *Pravda* [Moscow],
February 4, 1960). There are no authoritative estimates on the number of
Bessarabian Bulgarians who became Russified through the years. A favorite game
of many Bulgarian observers of the Soviet political scene in the interwar years
was to endeavor to "uncover" descendants of assimilated Bessarabian Bulgarians
among the Soviet leadership. Such "claims" were made for Kirov, Antonov
(Stalin's secretary), and others (Nikola Antonov to author; Antonov was Bulgaria's
minister to Moscow in the second part of the thirties). The significance of this
phenomenon is in the preoccupation with the subject, rather than in the facts.
Some interesting observations on the national psychology of the Bessarabian Bulgarians are made in Kosturkov, pp. 117–20. Contemporary Bulgarian historians
have gone to great lengths to prove that the majority of the Bessarabian Bulgarians
supported the Bolsheviks rather than the Whites in the Revolution and the Civil
War. A determined, if unconvincing, effort along these lines is made in P. I.
Panaiotov, *Prinosut na bulgari za pobedata na Oktomvriiskata revoliutsiia*. Many
of the Bessarabian Bulgarians who became prisoners of the Germans during
World War II claimed Bulgarian nationality and were turned over to the Bul-
garians. Entire families made their way to Bulgaria during the war while the
Ukraine was under German occupation. After the occupation of Bulgaria by the
Red Army, all were forcibly repatriated to the Soviet Union.

hope of the Comintern that the energies of the émigrés would now be focused on bringing education and a new vitality in political discipline to these culturally fossilized Bulgarian communities.[21]

A volunteering spirit was not readily forthcoming, however. The émigrés preferred to remain in Odessa and spared no effort in searching for suitable employment and the necessary residence permits. Exiles who found themselves in other parts of the Soviet Union were also attracted to the Black Sea metropolis. "The Bulgarian political émigrés," stated a report by the Odessa émigré section, "wherever they find themselves in the Soviet Union, try to come to Odessa sooner or later." As unemployment mounted and the local Soviet authorities became more and more uneasy with the influx of the foreigners, Odessa was banned as a place of residence and a dispersal of the émigrés into the countryside was begun. "For purely political reasons, as well as because of the mounting unemployment in this major borderland city," stated a decision of the local Soviet authorities in consultation with representatives of the Bulgarian section to the ECCI, "Odessa can no longer serve as a place of residence or a place of part-time employment for the legally or illegally arrived foreign political émigrés." The decision did not specify what were the "purely political reasons" for this harsh measure. Conceivably, the Soviet authorities were growing tired of the stream of repeated complaints and demands for better conditions being made by these newly arrived peasant-insurrectionists, unaccustomed to the strict regimentation of Soviet life. "Torn away from their piece of land [in Bulgaria]," Dimitrov was told in no uncertain terms by a spokesman for the émigrés, "our comrades are now forced to work under conditions to which they find it difficult to adjust." The placement of the exiles away from Odessa was obviously the answer to the problem, particularly since it harmonized with the desire of the highest authorities in the Ukrainian SSR to see that the Bessarabian Bulgarians be reinforced from the outside.

By 1926 the number of Bulgarian exiles still in residence in Odessa

[21] The single most important source on the work of the Communist exiles among the Bulgarians in the southern parts of the Soviet Union during the twenties is a study by a Soviet scholar published in *Istoricheski pregled*, No. 4–5 (1967), pp. 118–32. Unless otherwise indicated, the information that follows is derived from this source, as well as from a second article by the same author devoted to the political education of the Bulgarian emigration, *ibid.*, No. 1–2 (1970), pp. 156–78.

proper was reduced to 110. The remainder were distributed among the various Bulgarian villages, where they were assigned minor government and Party positions. A great many became teachers in newly opened elementary schools with Bulgarian as the language of instruction. By 1926, 74 such schools with 109 teachers were in operation. A trade high-school and an agricultural school were also set up. Émigrés helped to establish the first agricultural communes and artels.[22] In 1926 the Lenin district in the Odessa region was renamed for Blagoev, and some 54 émigrés were sent to man the Party and local government positions, with D. A. Mandzhakov, an old member of the BCP and a member of the CPSU since 1924, as the regional secretary. With the launching of forced collectivization in the late twenties, émigré cadres were used to break peasant resistance; even students from the various Party schools in remote parts of the Soviet Union were dispatched to help prevail over the "political neutrality" of the *kolkhozniks*-to-be.[23]

Those who did not settle in the southern parts of the Soviet Union constituted the second and somewhat more diffused contingent of émigrés. The most promising were sent to school; a few were assigned special tasks; bureaucracy and industry absorbed the others. "The question of giving an education to the political emigration was considered most seriously," reported Kolarov years later. "Many of them went to the various institutions of higher learning. For the large mass, which lacked adequate preparation, a special Bulgarian section was set up at the Western university." [24] This was the Communist University for the National Minorities of the West (KUNMZ), whose Bulgarian section, from 1926 to 1932, was headed by Stanke Dimitrov-Marek, who, until his death in August, 1944, was the senior functionary most intimately involved (except for the two-year period 1935–37 when he was back

---

[22] In 1924 an agricultural commune named "D. Blagoev" was established near Poltava by Bulgarian exiles. Ts. Radoinov-Radionov served as its political secretary. The enterprise appears to have been a failure; see Dragoliubov, pp. 56–60.

[23] On the early collectivization of the Bulgarian villages, see *Istoricheski pregled*, No. 4–5 (1967), pp. 108–17. A firsthand account of the participation of Bulgarian émigré-students at KUNMZ in the collectivization campaigns in the late twenties is given in Atanasov, *Pod znameto na partiiata*, pp. 104–5, 107: "Working day and night for two months, we completed the collectivization in the entire region assigned to us."

[24] Kolarov, *Spomeni*, p. 598.

in Bulgaria) with all matters pertaining to the emigration in Russia. At various times, the Bulgarian instructional staff at KUNMZ consisted of such people as Anton Ivanov, Ferdinand Kozovski, Stela Blagoeva, Sava Ganovski, Vasil Karanikolov, Boris Simov, Tsvetan Kristanov, and Koika Tineva, all of whom were to figure in one way or another in future Party affairs. "Hundreds of Bulgarian exiles went through KUNMZ." [25]

The better prepared and more promising were given more specialized training. On his arrival in Russia in October, 1925, Vulko Chervenkov (Vladimirov), who was to become Bulgaria's dictator in later years, was sent to the OGPU Academy in Moscow. He later joined the Lenin International School where he served as a lecturer from 1928 to 1934.[26] The veteran Party leader and ideologue, Khristo Kabakchiev, was a senior member of the faculty of the Lenin International School. He received a doctorate in 1935 and became an associate member of the Soviet Academy of Sciences.[27] Petko Kunin, one of Bulgaria's economic chiefs during the country's Sovietization period, studied at the economic faculty of the "N. Krupskaya" Academy for Communist Education. Ivan Karaivanov attended the University of the Workers of the East in preparation for his later work in China. Ivan Vinarov, a future general in the Bulgarian army, was recruited by J. A. Berzin (on Kolarov's recommendation) for his Fourth Bureau, which was in charge of the Red Army's intelligence section, and was sent to various intelligence schools.[28]

[25] Kasher-Dimitrova, p. 127. This is an interesting biography of Stanke Dimitrov-Marek, written by his widow, Regina Kasher, a Jewish-Polish Communist, and later a member of the German CP in exile. Her account is one of the most vivid portrayals of life in the Bulgarian section at KUNMZ and of the Bulgarian émigrés at the famous Hotel Lux (pp. 123–38).

[26] Chervenkov, *Bio-bibliografiia*, pp. 5ff., has a detailed chronological sketch of his life and functions.

[27] On Kabakchiev's earlier political life, see various entries in Rothschild; see also entries in Kabakchiev, *Bio-bibliografiia*.

[28] Berzin had held a post in the short-lived Soviet Latvian government of 1919. In 1921 he was placed in charge of military intelligence at the General Staff of the Red Army, and was later attached to the Far Eastern command. He played a prominent role in the Spanish Civil War, and was shot on his return to Moscow (Conquest, p. 230). Vinarov became one of Berzin's chief agents (Vinarov, pp. 158–72) and carried out various intelligence missions for the Russians in China during the twenties (*ibid.*, parts III and IV), and in Central Europe in the early

Among the émigrés in the early thirties, none achieved a higher rank or more prominent recognition in the intellectual-scholarly field than Todor Pavlov, the Party's most outstanding Marxist philosopher. He was a professor of dialectical materialism at the Institute of Red Professors, and later the dean of the Faculty of Philosophy at the Moscow Institute.[29]

The emigration was the result of an unsuccessful armed insurrection. It hoped to attain power in the future through military-revolutionary means. The training of military cadres, therefore, received the closest attention. For the rank and file, a special Bulgarian course on military matters was set up at the Section for Special Assignments (ChON). Those with professional military experience in Bulgaria's wars were assigned to the various Soviet military academies. For the Bulgarian Communists, this was an old and well-established practice. Even before the insurrection, at the end of 1921, a number of promising men had been sent to the Soviet military academies.[30] Most prominent among them was Boian Bulgaranov, who later played a central role in Mace-

---

thirties. In addition to Karaivanov and Sh. Atanasov (see various entries in the latter's *Zapiski na revoliutsionera*), many more Bulgarian émigrés were used in intelligence and military capacities in the Far East, China, and Korea. Among them were such people as Khristo Pakov, who trained Kuomintang pilots; Khristo Boev, who was to make a high-ranking military career for himself in later years; Anton Nedialkov; Dr. Yanko Kaneti; Boian Pananchev, who served as Comintern courier; and Vladimir Sedloev (Gorski), who served as colonel in Marshal Blücher's Far Eastern command and was to perish in the Stalin purges; on their respective careers, see Vinarov, pp. 301–2; *Rabotnichesko delo*, September 13, 1963.

[29] He was co-opted as a member of the Party CC in 1924 and was in and out of prison during the second part of the twenties. After his return from the Soviet Union, he played an active role at the time of the Soviet-German Pact and was in a Bulgarian concentration camp during 1941–43. He was the Communist representative at the Regency Council after September, 1944, the president of the Bulgarian Academy of Sciences (1947–62), and a member of the Party's Politburo.

A prolific writer, Pavlov made his main contribution in the field of Leninist aesthetics. He is best known for his *Theory of Reflections*. For some of his writings, see the bibliography at the end of this volume; on his life, see *Rabotnichesko delo*, July 3, 1947, December 15, 1956, and Gana Pavlova, *Ruka za ruka*.

[30] *Istoricheski pregled*, No. 2–3 (1969), p. 174; among them were Vasil Karavasilev, Kuzman Stoikov, Georgi Ivanov (Doktora), Dimitur Georgiev, and Boniu Petrovski.

donian Communist affairs during World War II. Georgi Damianov, a future minister of defense, graduated from the Frunze Military Academy. Peter Panchevski, also a future minister of war, studied at Frunze and the Leningrad Military Academy, and attained the rank of major-general in the Red Army. There were many more, among them Tsviatko Radoinov-Radionov, who served as a colonel in the Red Army, became a senior adviser during the Spanish Civil War, and in 1941 led several parties of émigrés into Bulgaria; also, Ivan Kinov, a future general in the Bulgarian army.[31]

Despite the many ordeals of Soviet life, for the great majority of Bulgarians emigration opened up opportunities for education and professional betterment which Bulgaria could not have provided. The Bulgarians adjusted to Soviet conditions more easily and more harmoniously than any other foreign group. Until the Great Purge struck, the younger Communist cadres in Bulgaria who had come to political maturity after the upheavals of the mid-twenties could expect no greater reward or promise than a period of study in one of the Comintern schools. When the process of Sovietization began after 1944, the Bulgarian Communists had at their disposal more cadres with Soviet exposure than any other East European country. There was no other country where Russianism blended with Communism so perfectly.

THE PURGE OF LUKANOV

Emigration represented a physical schism in the Party. The trauma of 1923 also gave rise to complex psycho-political schisms of no less significance. These became manifested in tortuous doctrinal disputations over the strategies and tactics of the past. Why did the revolutionary attempt fail? This was an inevitable question, the posing of which helped produce the factions. The answers given depended on which faction dominated the organization at any particular time. None of the groups could attain, let alone consolidate, power over the Party organization in exile or at home without the support, or at least the consent, of the Comintern *apparat*. In the final analysis, those whom the Russians endorsed dominated the Bulgarian section in the Comintern, and in turn exercised ultimate authority over the cadres in the emigration and at home.

[31] The careers of most of them will be traced in due course.

A tedious replay of the events of 1923 constituted the central theme in the intra-Party debates: the forums were protracted plenary sessions held in Moscow, Vienna, and Berlin lasting for weeks at a time; the battles were verbal in the main. While the victors tightened their grip over Party affairs, the defeated did not—in the initial stages at least—face the ultimate penalty.

The inevitable right, centrist, and left factions were soon formed. The rightists, or defeatists as they were termed by their rivals, castigated the Party leadership for having ordered the disastrous September insurrection. The centrists, headed by Kolarov and Dimitrov, called the Old Guard by their detractors, defended the Party action of September, 1923. The leftists, who were mainly from among the younger cadres, accused the Old Guard of too much passivity and of lacking a healthy revolutionary sense. Not unlike the internal struggles of the CPSU in the twenties, the factional configurations followed the pattern of temporary alliances established for the sole purpose of dealing with the rivals of the day. Only the sequences varied. In the first engagements, the Old Guard combined with the leftists to defeat the rightists. By 1925–27, this end was all but accomplished. The assault of the left against the Old Guard followed next, and by 1929 the latter were pushed aside and neutralized. The third and last engagement dominated much of the thirties, during which time the Old Guard engaged, defeated, and annihilated their leftist detractors.

Even though opposition to the September insurrection within the Party leadership was formidable, the rightists did not constitute a serious organized challenge to the Kolarov-Dimitrov leadership. The latter had forced the insurrection as the result of Comintern instructions and with Zinoviev's blessings. A repudiation of the September uprising therefore inevitably led to a repudiation of the Comintern itself, with all that this implied. Already in November, 1923, only weeks after the insurrection had been put down, the Tsankov regime felt strong enough to hold general elections. The Communists elected eight deputies. In December they reconstituted themselves into a new Independent Labor Party, and declared severed all connections with the Third International. Their leader, Nikola Sakarov, announced in the newly elected Subranie that the insurrection had been forced on the Communist Party by Moscow, against the best advice of old Blagoev, and contrary to the wishes of the

Central Committee. Henceforth, he pledged, the Independent Labor Party would restrict itself to strictly legal activities and would remain committed to constitutional methods. Kolarov's and Dimitrov's particular roles were repudiated by many.

Exile gave immunity to the main perpetrators of the insurrection, however. The fact that they had not only survived the uprising but were in a position to set themselves up as the Party leadership in exile, claiming sole legitimacy over the Communist movement at home, was of crucial importance. Their exit from the Bulgarian scene meant that the rights and wrongs of the September insurrection were not to be settled on home grounds but in foreign forums, set up, paid for, and mastered by the Comintern. From the safety of Vienna, Kolarov announced that Sakarov and anyone supporting him were henceforth expelled from the Party. "I and Dimitrov found ourselves abroad," Kolarov related later. "However, the role we played in the insurrection, and the positions we held in the Comintern (I as general secretary and Georgi [Dimitrov] as a prominent functionary of the International), gave us the decisive word in selecting the new Central Committee." [32] In an endeavor to check Sakarov's organized opposition, in January, 1924, the Party of Labor was created within Bulgaria as a new Communist front true to the leadership in exile. In May of the same year an improvised Party conference of Kolarov's followers convened secretly near Sofia and selected Stanke Dimitrov-Marek to be the man in charge of Party affairs at home. The conference gave a retroactive approval to the September insurrection. The line was tilted further to the left and preparations were begun for a renewal of armed resistance. These recommendations were indeed the Comintern's. Exasperated by what they perceived as irresponsibility bordering on political madness, Sakarov and those who had joined with him in the Independent Labor Party, as well as other defectors, became further repelled and moved away from Communism altogether. Some drifted into sectarianism and into political insignificance. Others, like Sakarov himself, strove to maintain their personal

---

[32] Kolarov, *Spomeni*, p. 593. There is an unavoidable duplication between the events related in the following pages and the same events traced in detail in the last two chapters of Rothschild's study on the earlier years of Bulgarian Communism. All that is endeavored here is not to retrace the close chronology of developments, but to establish a bridge between the emergence of the emigration in Russia and the purges of the middle thirties.

independence and remained unaffiliated. Still others traveled the entire length of the spectrum and joined the various formations of the middle class all the way to the reactionary right. Having once left the fold of the Party, and thus having renounced moral and material support from the outside, none succeeded in stabilizing a Communist position in mid-course and maintaining a meaningful organizational posture.[33]

Some moderates did not leave the Party. "There remained within the Party the right opportunists who," as Kolarov described them, "tried to blunt the Party's revolutionary spear by working from within. They came forward in opposition to the Party's representation in exile and against the publication of [Kolarov's] *Rabotnicheski vestnik* abroad. Distrusting Vasil Kolarov and Georgi Dimitrov, they dispatched to Vienna Todor Lukanov, who, by becoming a member of the representation in exile, was expected to arrest the intervention of the emigration into the affairs of the Party at home." At this point, Kolarov discovered a hitherto unknown blessing of exile life, namely, the feasibility of creating an exile within an exile. "I arranged that Lukanov be sent to Moscow as a political émigré. By so doing, the attempt on the part of the right opportunists to impede the work of the representation abroad was defeated." [34] It was a discovery which in a few short years his many rivals were to put to good use against him and Dimitrov, his closest and ultimately world-famous collaborator.

Todor Lukanov, the rightist leader from within, was an old friend of Kolarov's. He had been made organizational secretary of the Party in 1922. His opposition to the September insurrection (for the failure of which he was blamed in part) had been consistent and unequivocal and he did not publicly change his stand.

The threat from the right "liquidationists," as Lukanov's forces

---

[33] Sakarov, among other things, was an able economist and made substantial contributions in the economic field. He was one of the very few oppositionists in the wartime Subranie where he performed his last public service in an altogether distinguished career. He died in 1943. The number of people who left the fold of the Party and found their way into the "enemy camp" is much too great to be traced. Yordan Yordanov, a close collaborator of Sakarov's, later joined the right-wing National Liberal Party. Dimitur Vasilev, who in 1922 represented the Party in Moscow, found himself minister of construction during the wartime pro-Fascist regime and was eventually placed on trial for war crimes.

[34] Kolarov, *Spomeni*, p. 591.

were termed, continued to preoccupy the Old Guard throughout much of the middle twenties. The danger from the right dominated the discussions at the first general gathering of the émigré leadership, which convened in Moscow (with Manuilski in attendance as the representative of the ECCI) and which lasted forty days (from July 30 to the beginning of September, 1925). The Moscow consultations were held in the aftermath of the Cathedral bombing in Sofia (April, 1925), which the exile leadership condemned as an aberration of its insurrectionist line. It was now recognized that the revolutionary upsurge had come to an end, that "the temporary stabilization of capitalism" was a fact of life in Bulgaria as well as elsewhere, and that armed resistance had become senseless and was to be suspended. This moderation of the general line, it was thought, necessitated increased watchfulness of the Lukanov forces, whose prognosis had proved correct. To keep the rightists at bay, the Old Guard made increased use of the young militants freshly arrived in the Soviet Union as the vanguard of the second wave of émigrés escaping Bulgaria after the April outrage. A center-left alliance was thus created and solidified by the increasing co-option into the exile leadership of spokesmen for the younger cadres, soon to emerge as the left opposition. Before the second engagement took place, however, the rightists were purged. The final act came at the Second Party Conference, held in Berlin (December 8, 1927–January 15, 1928), at which time Todor Lukanov and his collaborator Georgi Popov were expelled from the Party. By that time, the equilibrium of forces within the émigré leadership had shifted in favor of the leftist young militants. From the viewpoint of the Old Guard, the expulsion of Lukanov, when it came, did not signify the elimination of a real threat, but was more an act of appeasement toward the leftist allies, whose thrust for power was already being felt. Kolarov and Dimitrov were committing one more tactical mistake which they were soon to regret.[35]

---

[35] On the expulsion of Lukanov, see *Istoriia na BKP*, p. 350. Lukanov remained in the Soviet Union but his political fate, particularly during the Great Purge, is unknown. He was "preparing his return to Bulgaria" when he died in Moscow on February 17, 1946, according to the official report (*Rabotnichesko delo*, May 17, 1947), which added that he had "gradually overcome his errors of September, 1923." His son, Karlo Lukanov, played an important role in the emigration, in the Spanish Civil War, and in Communist Bulgaria, where for a time he served as foreign minister.

ISKROV AND THE LEFT OPPOSITION

Unlike the opposition from the right, which, because of its inherent anti-Comintern posture, failed to attain a durable organizational base, the challenge from the left was soon translated into an overwhelming victory over the Kolarov-Dimitrov forces. The left opposition was not Trotskyite, nor was it influenced or infiltrated by Trotskyite elements. With very few exceptions, the Bulgarian emigration in Russia sided with the Stalin forces from the first. The few exceptions centered on a number of émigrés who found themselves in Leningrad and came under the influence of the Zinoviev opposition.[36] A few more came under the personal influence of Christian Rakovski. In both cases, the numbers involved were small and their affiliations temporary. A small Trotskyite group emerged within Bulgaria (to be dealt with later), but its impact remained insignificant. None of the above affected the left opposition, which emerged, developed, and perished within the strict confines of Stalin's Comintern. To the end, the left opposition was as fanatically devoted to the Soviet Union as was the Old Guard.

From the late twenties until well into the thirties, the leftists formed a solid majority. This was true in the emigration as well as in the Party at home. In this sense, the term "left sectarians" affixed to them by the official Communist historiographers is a misnomer. (The term "left opposition" is used in these pages only for the purposes of convenience.)

The ideological roots of the left opposition are traceable to the so-called Iskristi (named after *Iskra*, a short-lived newspaper published in

[36] Trotsky had criticized the Bulgarian Party both for its neutrality during the June, 1923, *putsch* and for its insurrectionary tactics during the September uprising. On his arrival in Moscow, Kolarov undertook to answer these charges in an article published in the Soviet *Izvestiia* (September 23, 1924) and in *Pravda* on the following day. According to Kolarov, the Party's actions constituted a clear-cut anti-Trotsky stand taken in the early stages of the Stalin-Trotsky conflict (Kolarov, *Spomeni*, p. 596). "Our political emigration had to take a stand in the conflict," reported a prominent exile later. "It must be noted that the orientation was the correct one. Only separate individuals supported the platform of the opposition. These were Goldstein [of whom reference has already been made], the son of Sider Todorov [who was a prominent leader of the small Trotskyite group in Bulgaria in the thirties], the Iskristi [of whom more shortly], as well as some ultra-leftists such as Krum Buchvarov, who served as professor at the Tolmachov Military Academy in Leningrad, and Mitko Zlatarov. Soon, however, they corrected their stand." (Atanasov, *Pod znameto na partiiata*, p. 103.) Buchvarov perished in the Great Purge; his story will be related later.

Bulgaria in 1919), who had emerged as an ultra-left group in the aftermath of Bulgaria's defeat in the war. They resented the ineptness of Blagoev's "narrows," whom they criticized for having failed to capitalize on the revolutionary fervor of 1918. The Iskristi had favored direct action and had been opposed on principle to participation in elections and to parliamentarism as political methods. They resembled and were inspired by the "ultra-left" in Germany. Soon, however, they were beaten back by the Blagoev forces and gradually sank into political insignificance.[37] The crushing disappointments of 1923, and above all the insurrectionary fervor generated by violence and terrorism in the following years, helped to resurrect some of the ideas of the old ultra-leftists, which ideas became the core of the left opposition's ideology.

The principal features of this ideology were arrived at deductively. There was an underlying determinism in the repeated failures of Bulgarian Communism. How else could the blunders be explained but by the incapacity of the Party leadership to become properly infused with the maxims of Leninism? It was no accident, according to the ideologues of the left opposition, that old Blagoev had sided with Plekhanov and against Lenin before World War I. The "narrow" tradition was nothing but social democracy raised on Bulgarian soil. Blagoev and his followers were irreparable social democrats. As a saying of the left opposition put it: "It is easier for a camel to pass through the eye of a needle than for an old 'narrow' to become a true Bolshevik." The left opposition perceived the greatest tragedy in the development of Communism in Bulgaria to lie in the fact that the "narrows" had joined the Third International en bloc, without having undergone a split. Thus the Party had become the carrier of the old baggage of ideas and habits that made its Bolshevization impossible. The Old Guard could not discard this baggage, to which it had become sentimentally attached. The prehistory of the September insurrection properly belonged to the heritage of the "narrows," who were Bulgaria's Mensheviks. Year One of Bulgarian Communism, according to the left opposition, began with the uprising of 1923.

Above and beyond the critique of the Party's past, the left opposition undertook new and extreme formulations on the national problem

---

[37] On the Iskristi, see *Istoriia na BKP*, pp. 222–23, and Kolarov, *Spomeni*, p. 591.

and on Bulgaria's class structure. In the main, these were adaptations of the Comintern's post-1928 leftist orientations applied to Bulgaria, rather than doctrines exclusive to the Bulgarian experience. In political terms, Bulgaria was seen as being under a semicolonial regime. The country was, as it were, under class occupation. Liberation was attainable only under the principle of "class versus class." Chauvinism was converted into what amounted to national nihilism. Self-determination was to be applied not only to those regions such as Dobruja and Thrace which lay outside the Bulgarian sovereign domain, and over which Bulgaria had had a historic claim, but also to the region of Pirin Macedonia (or the Petrich region, as it was called at the time), which was an integral part of Bulgaria. Political alliances were to be tolerated only with the destitute peasantry, while the middle peasants were to be fought *in toto*.

Finally, there were two allied quasi-theories which gave the left opposition much of its particular distinctiveness. The one had to do with the generation gap within the Party; the other, not unrelated to the first, dealt with the problem of revolutionary courage as contrasted with revolutionary cowardice. Inevitably, age came to be identified with meekness and lack of resolution, while youth was identified with revolutionary valor. Simplistic as these dichotomies were, their application to the intra-Party warfare which the left opposition launched had resounding consequences.[38]

These were the particularistic Bulgarian features of the left opposition's outlook. The resentment against the Old Guard was deeply rooted and would have persisted independent of the general orientations of world Communism. Yet only when Moscow moved to the left, and the specific Bulgarian critique could be merged with the mainstream of the new thrust, did the left oppositionists carry out a successful assault.

The general shift to the left was made sometime late in 1927 and early 1928, and was directly connected with the Comintern's failures abroad (mainly in China), as well as with the inner struggles of the CPSU manifested by Stalin's attacks on Bukharin. The "temporary and

[38] The ideological profie of the left opposition is a composite based on a number of sources, the most important of which are the following: Kolarov, *Protiv liiavoto sektantstvo i trotskizma v Bulgariia*; *IIIBKP*, XI (1964), 124–57; Barov, *BKP v noviia podem na antifashistkoto dvizhenie, 1929–1935*; *Istoriia na BKP*, pp. 362–87.

partial stabilization of capitalism" dominant during the mid-twenties came to an end; the future was to witness a new revolutionary era.

The change of tactics was mild at the beginning. But the new trend had its own momentum which drove it to ever more furious exaggerations. The outbreak of the world depression and the launching of the industrialization effort in Russia helped push the new policy to new and greater extremes.

Under Communist guidance, the proletariat was called upon to prepare for the "inevitable revolutionary outbursts." This necessitated the sharpening of the class struggle and an intensified struggle against the Socialists, who were now termed "social fascists." There were, according to the new Comintern thesis, no differences between the Fascists and the Socialists, since they were both equally bourgeois. Thus, cooperation with Socialists meant alliance with bourgeois elements and therefore betrayal of the cause of Communism. Also, democracy and fascism were equated. Ordinary parliamentary activities and normal trade-union work in the labor movement were condemned as traitorous. All through the period, the war cry of "social fascism" was raised and was followed up by demonstrative political strikes and physical clashes.

The Bulgarian left opposition sprang from within the leadership of the Bulgarian Komsomol, into whose hands the conduct of insurrectionary and terroristic activities had passed after the September uprising. The left oppositionists acquired their political experience in the streets of Sofia, in the hills of the Bulgarian countryside, and in Tsankov's jails, rather than in conference rooms, Party meetings, and interparty polemics, as had been the case with the Old Guard. The first formulations of their ideas into a more or less cohesive body of doctrine were undertaken in Soviet exile. Younger émigrés formed their first audiences and provided the first recruits for the new doctrines in the various political schools organized for them in Russia. The majority of the left opposition leadership that ultimately took control of the Party within Bulgaria consisted of returnees from the Soviet Union, graduates of the political schools in the late twenties. The very fact that the emigration became a bastion of left-opposition ideas infuriated Kolarov no end.[39]

[39] The facts of the leftists' influence on the emigration are incontestable. For a firsthand report by a Party functionary, himself a Dimitrov follower, see Gilin, pp. 63–70. Attacking the Old Guard (or more plainly "the beards," as they were

Theoretical preeminence went to Petur Iskrov, who emerged as the chief ideologue of the opposition. A stern doctrinaire and a dialectician of some brilliance, Iskrov, unlike his younger collaborators, had served his political apprenticeship during the "narrow" period. In October, 1923, right after the collapse of the uprising, he was brought into the Party leadership that had remained in Bulgaria. As secretary of the Komsomol, he experienced a rise in his political fortunes at the same time that increased responsibility was placed on the younger cadres who were to prepare the new armed uprising. The secret Party conference held near Sofia in May, 1924, co-opted him to membership in the Party's Central Committee. The exact date of Iskrov's arrival in the Soviet Union is unclear, but he was present at the exile gathering in Moscow (summer of 1925) that gave the leftists a first opportunity to air their views. Iskrov was then formally elected to the Central Committee. The left opposition, still in a minority, maintained its own at the Enlarged Plenum assembled in Vienna in September, 1926, at which Iskrov was reelected to the CC. At the same time, Nikola Kofardzhiev, a young functionary of the illegal Komsomol and a rising force within the left opposition, was elected a member of the Executive Buro within Bulgaria.[40]

The conflict between the Old Guard and the left opposition surfaced at the Second Party Conference in Berlin, held in the winter of 1927–28. In this meeting, attended by Julian (Leszczynski) Lenski as the representative of the Comintern and Manuilski as the official delegate of the CPSU, Kolarov and Dimitrov were openly assaulted. The scapegoat of the Berlin conference was Lukanov, who was dropped from the Party in the vain hope of maintaining the semblance of a center-left unity. This conference was the last Party forum (until 1936) in which

---

called) became fashionable and virtually all joined in. Even Vulko Chervenkov-Vladimirov, the husband of Dimitrov's sister and his protégé in later years, did not shy away. In this campaign encouragement was given not only by the leaders of the left opposition within the Party but also by such Comintern notables as Piatnitski, Kun, and Valetski; on these and many more details, see the two articles by Karaivanov in *Glas na bulgarite v Yugoslaviia*, October 14, October 21, 1952.

[40] On the 1925 gathering in Moscow, see the monograph by Stela Dimitrova, *Moskovskoto suveshtanie na BKP, 1925*. Iskrov's career within the Party hierarchy is pieced together from *Istoriia na BKP*, pp. 307, 318, 336, 342.

the Kolarov forces succeeded in mastering a majority. Soon the distribution of power within the leadership shifted unmistakably in the
direction of the leftist forces. Stalin had already begun to veer to the
left. The switch was not yet openly visible, but the Comintern and the
Bulgarians within that body were taking notice. The Berlin conference
settled the formal structure of the Party's leading organs, which had
been ambiguous ever since 1923. There was to be a small Buro-in-
Exile, formally in charge of the emigration, but in effect in an overlord-
ship position concerning the affairs of Bulgarian Communism as a whole.
The Buro-in-Exile was to have its formal representative to the ECCI.
A Central Committee was placed in charge of the Party within Bulgaria. Kolarov, Dimitrov, and Iskrov were elected as the sole members
of the Buro-in-Exile, with Kolarov as the formal representative to the
Comintern.[41]

Soon the Bulgarian quarrels spilled over into the larger forums of
the Comintern. At the Sixth Congress of the Comintern held in Moscow
in the summer of 1928, Richard Schüller, a leading functionary of the
Youth International, referred to the strife within the Bulgarian Party and
castigated Kolarov for not allowing sufficient scope to the rising younger
cadres. The Sixth Congress confirmed Kolarov's and Dimitrov's positions
on the ECCI, the first as full member and the second as a candidate
member, but it also elected Iskrov to the International Control Commission. At the Fifth Congress of the Youth International (August–
September, 1928), Ilia Vasilev-Boiko and Georgi Lambrev-Rosen, both
leading members of the Bulgarian Komsomol, bitterly attacked the Old
Guard of their own Party. Earlier, Kolarov had warned them of their
outspoken left-oppositionist utterances. But the unmistakable leftward
winds prevailing in Moscow were reassuring. Vasilev-Boiko became a
member of the Executive Committee of the Youth International.

The final blow to the Old Guard was delivered at the Second
Plenum of the Party, again held in Berlin (August–September, 1929).
This was the last formal Party gathering to be held abroad. By that time,
Vasilev-Boiko, who had been sent to Bulgaria to reinforce the illegal

---

[41] *Istoriia na BKP*, pp. 349–51. As an institution the Buro-in-Exile continued to
exist until the dissolution of the emigration after September, 1944. In future years,
the Central Committee was to contain members working and residing within
Bulgaria as well as in exile.

Komsomol, had imposed himself on the leadership of the Party and had in effect captured control over the Party at home. Thus the left opposition was able to appear in Berlin with a strong slate of delegates who were in a majority at the Plenum. Left oppositionists were in a clear majority within the newly elected thirteen-member Central Committee. Most important of all, the leftists captured control of the editorial board of the Party organ *Komunistichesko zname*, making Iskrov its chief editor in place of Kolarov. The three-member Buro-in-Exile remained unchanged, with Kolarov, Dimitrov, and Iskrov as its members. This situation was not to last long, however. In August, 1930, the Buro-in-Exile was permanently moved to Moscow. Bela Kun became its third member in place of Dimitrov, who was demoted to candidate membership.[42]

DIMITROV'S "EXILE" IN BERLIN

With their majority now firmly secured, the leaders of the left opposition began the consolidation of their power. The appeals of their rhetoric had a powerful effect on the Bulgarian emigration, which in overwhelming numbers joined the Iskrov forces as the spearhead of the new trend. The few who resisted were pushed aside. More and more, the struggle with the Old Guard shifted into the unchartered world of Comintern intrigue. There were also the inevitable "affairs." "A group of Bulgarians were arrested when attempting to return to their country without permission. They belonged to a group of left nationalists [?] within the Bulgarian Party. Dissatisfied with the official policy of Kolarov and Dimitrov, they had tried secretly to leave Odessa in a small craft. They were arrested as they were setting foot on board. One of the comrades had betrayed them to the Kolarov-Dimitrov group. They were arrested by the GPU and sent to the mines of the Ural." [43] The incident, probably insignificant in itself, was symptomatic of the ways and means by which the quarrels began to be settled.

---

[42] Except for excerpts, neither the full texts of the resolutions nor the stenographic records of the Second Plenum have been made public. The materials were turned over to the ECCI for adjudication. Good summaries are to be found in *Istoriia na BKP*, pp. 62–65; Barov, pp. 47–53. On the co-option of Bela Kun and the demotion of Dimitrov, see *IIIBKP*, XVI (1967), 215

[43] Ciliga, p. 63.

Symbolically, however, the Odessa incident went to the root of the problem facing the left opposition. The fact was that not only had Kolarov and Dimitrov established for themselves solid reputations within the Comintern *apparat*, but they were also well connected with the larger world of Soviet politics. They had also become, like Kuusinen, Stalin's favorites. Throughout the twenties, Moscow had come to depend on "the Bulgarians" whenever it needed to "discipline" veering European parties. Kolarov was an old and reliable hand in the techniques of split-and-purge. He was dispatched to Oslo in 1923 to help cleanse the Norwegian CP, as well as to various Communist conferences in Rome, Paris, Frankfurt, Leipzig, and Prague as the Comintern roving emissary.[44] When in May, 1927, the Italians Togliatti and Silone (in the presence of Stalin) naïvely refused to condemn a Trotsky statement on the Chinese question which they had not seen, the session was adjourned "so that the old Bulgarian Communist Kolarov could go over the question with the recalcitrant Italians in private. He told them quite frankly that it was not a question of getting to the truth, but of the struggle of power. The Comintern must go along with the Soviet Politburo majority, and that was all there was to it." [45]

All this was not lost on the left opposition. Even though he was a doctrinaire-dogmatist and an ideologue rather than an organizer, Iskrov must have realized that the Old Guard would not be easily dislodged, his majority within the Party leadership notwithstanding. The path he followed was, under the circumstances, a strategy of the second best. As much as possible, Kolarov and Dimitrov were to be kept away from purely Bulgarian affairs and were to be removed from the Comintern headquarters, even if this meant their being promoted in the formal Comintern hierarchy. Above all, the two were to be kept separated. Kolarov they despised and hated, but Dimitrov was feared for his energy and hard work. As Ruth Fischer observed, Dimitrov was "regarded as an excellent organizer but a zero in matters of political theory." [46] On the theory that as long as the two were not permitted to work together they would not constitute an immediate threat to the dominance of the

[44] On Kolarov's ventures, see Rothschild, p. 300, and the various entries in Kolarov's *Spomeni.*

[45] Conquest, pp. 427–28.

[46] Fischer, p. 308.

left opposition, Iskrov and his immediate followers pressed their demand for the removal of both. A search was started for an appropriate place of "exile." Several posts were suggested to Dimitrov, including missions to France, England, and the United States. Dimitrov objected on the ground that these assignments were hardly suitable to his particular talents. "I will be better off in Turkistan," he countered. A compromise settled on Berlin. As far as Dimitrov's leftist rivals were concerned, the German capital was as good a place as any so long as he was not permanently present in Moscow.

From January, 1929, until his arrest in March, 1933, and subsequent trial in Leipzig, Dimitrov (alias Dr. Hediger) was stationed in Berlin. The Ninth Plenum of the ECCI (1928) had decided to establish a West European Buro (WEB) in Berlin which was assigned to maintain operational coordination between Moscow and the various Comintern sections in Europe. First co-opted as a member, Dimitrov became the head of the WEB in April, 1929, a position he held for the following four years. In this capacity he was in contact with numerous European CPs as well as in over-all command of a number of international Communist-front organizations, particularly the Communist-sponsored Anti-Imperialist League. After the resurrection of the old Balkan Communist Federation at the end of January, 1929, Dimitrov served also as secretary of its Executive Committee. Under his capable hands and boundless energy, the WEB became the largest of all the Comintern's branch agencies and its most important communications center outside Moscow. Except for the Bulgarians in Moscow, only very few among the best-informed people in the Comintern understood that Berlin was in effect a place of banishment for the Bulgarian functionary. From the WEB headquarters in the Wilhelmstrasse, disguised as the *Führer-Verlag*, Dimitrov's jurisdiction ran "from Iceland to Capetown," but he could not command the band of young militants who had taken over his own Party. He had, as it were, by losing a kingdom gained an empire; yet his most pronounced ambition during his entire Berlin days was to regain control over his native organization. With persistency bordering on the pathetic, he continued to correspond with Kolarov in Moscow, bombarded the ECCI with written suggestions on the various problems of Bulgarian Communism, and kept up his intrigues with Bulgarian Communists passing through Berlin. When in the summer of 1930 the

Bulgarian intra-Party disputes were examined in the ECCI, Dimitrov asked permission to attend, but was turned down by Manuilski and Kuusinen. In August of the same year he was refused attendance at the Fifth Congress of the Profintern as a delegate of the Bulgarian Party by the Political Secretariat of the ECCI, which asked him to remain in Berlin. In March, 1931, he wrote Piatnitski of the ECCI (with a copy to Bela Kun) asking that he be relieved from the WEB "in order to be able to participate more actively in the affairs of the Bulgarian CP." This was not to be. The Comintern had decided to back Iskrov on all matters pertaining to Bulgarian Communism. At the same time, it maintained Dimitrov as its viceroy in Western Europe. The arrangement had its contradictions. Dimitrov's personal enemies in the Comintern (as Bulgarian sources were later to suggest repeatedly) may well have played a hand in the matter. They were, for the time being, powerful enough to sustain his rivals and maintain him in his splendid isolation. His friends, on the other hand, both in the ECCI and more importantly in the Soviet hierarchy itself, made sure that his misfortunes with his countrymen did not affect his career as a most capable functionary-conspirator.[47]

The remaining prominent leaders of the Old Guard were handled with greater ease. Kolarov stayed in the Soviet capital and was made a director of the Soviet Agrarian Institute and the editor of *Agrarnie Voprosy*. Kabakchiev, who had been removed from the Party Central Committee in 1928, became a contributor to *Istorik Marksist*. Gavril Genov, who had been in charge of the military side of the September insurrection, was given a post in the International Peasant Council.[48]

---

[47] On Dimitrov and the WEB, see Nollau, pp. 142–46. On Dimitrov's various functions in Berlin and his petitions to the ECCI, see *IIIBKP*, XVI (1967), 213–29. The author is indebted to Joseph Berger-Barzilai for information, insight, and firsthand accounts relative to Dimitrov's years in Berlin and his relations with Iskrov, then in the Comintern headquarters in Moscow. One of the founders of the Palestinian CP, Berger-Barzilai was in charge of the Anti-Imperialist League in the early thirties in Berlin, during which time he maintained intimate personal contacts with Dimitrov. He also knew Iskrov and was in a position to observe the reactions of the Bulgarians in Moscow before and after the arrest of Dimitrov in connection with the Reichstag affair. Berger-Barzilai was himself arrested in 1934 and spent the following two decades in various Siberian camps, part of the time with Blagoi Popov, Dimitrov's co-defendant in the Leipzig trial, who was eventually to be purged as a member of the left opposition.

[48] Rothschild, p. 290.

In 1930 Anton Ivanov, another important functionary from the old cadres who was in later years to reemerge in wartime Bulgaria, was removed from his post as Party delegate-resident in Vienna and replaced by Lambrev-Rosen from the left opposition.[49] The latter was soon moved to Berlin in order to undercut Dimitrov's intrigues with the Bulgarian Communists who continued to frequent the German capital. When in 1932 Lambrev-Rosen became entangled with the German police and was arrested, his place as the Party's resident in Berlin was filled by Blagoi Popov, yet another left oppositionist who in the following year turned up as Dimitrov's co-defendant at the Leipzig trial.[50]

With these reshufflings, the left opposition gained a clean slate for itself. Not before the radical turn to the right by the Comintern in the mid-thirties could the leftist dominance be challenged. Even then, the Old Guard's return to power was to prove a major and painful undertaking.

[49] Vinarov, pp. 403–4.

[50] *ИИBKP*, XVI (1967), 227–28.

CHAPTER THREE

THE PURGE OF THE LEFT OPPOSITION

THERE WAS LITTLE DOUBT in the minds of all concerned that the Old Guard would muster its energies in an endeavor to execute a comeback. Such, after all, was the unwritten rule of factionalism and secretarian warfare among political organizations in general, and of Communist parties in particular. Intra-Party upheavals were, of course, not unique to the Bulgarians. Most of the European parties underwent purges and counterpurges in the twenties and early thirties. The specifics differed, as did the political colorings of the factions. Yet the patterns had their uniformity. At various times and in different fashions, the Communist parties of the Germans, the Italians, the Czechs, the Rumanians, the French, and the Spaniards, to mention but a few, went through "sectarian" dominations and "sectarian" disestablishments. In 1925 the Fischer-Maslow group in Germany was overthrown in favor of Thalmann. In the following year in Italy, Bordiga was replaced by Togliatti and Longo. Gottwald, in 1929, successfully rid himself of the Czech "sectarians" who had captured control two years earlier. His fight with the Slovak Eugen Fried still lay ahead of him. The Rumanians went through their own internal upheavals in 1929, until the Party leadership was replaced in 1931. Henri Barbé, who rose rapidly in the French Party hierarchy and reached the top as its representative in the Comintern, was purged in 1931 and sent back to France. In 1932 the Spanish

Party dropped its "sectarians" who had been in a position of dominance a considerable period of time. Whether or not the ideological roots of the Bulgarian left opposition were basically similar to those of the purgees from the other parties, as was later claimed, is not easy to prove. What is indisputable, however, is the fact that "in none of the other parties did the sectarians hold power as long and as solidly as did the left opposition" in the Bulgarian Communist Party.[1]

To regain its supremacy, the Old Guard required almost a full decade. Its comeback was made possible by the convergence of a number of independent developments which tipped the scales in its favor. Uppermost among them was the sudden rise of Dimitrov to world prominence. The military *putsch* of May, 1934, in Bulgaria and the turn to the right by the Comintern followed in quick succession. Finally, the Great Purge in Russia made possible the physical elimination of the left opposition in exile. Except for the military takeover in Sofia, all were extra-Bulgarian events.

COMMUNISM ON THE HOME FRONT

Within Bulgaria, the leaders of the left proved immensely successful. Led by young militants such as Vasilev-Boiko, Kofardzhiev-Sasho (later shot by the police in the streets of Sofia, October 31, 1931), Andrei Georgiev (alias Dancho-Boian), Ivan Pavlov-Encho, and others, Communism in Bulgaria attained new levels of activity. With a view toward exploiting opportunities made possible by increased political freedoms in the late twenties, the Bulgarian Workers' Party was set up in 1927 as a legal front for the illegal Communist Party. The creation of the Workers' Party as the official face of Communism in the country represented an interesting novelty for the times. Both organizations grew rapidly. From a membership of about 1,000 in 1929, the illegal Communist Party increased to 3,732 by 1933. The Workers' Party did even better. It rose from 6,180 members as of January, 1931, to a sum total of 27,078 as of April, 1932. None of the figures included the Party emigration in Russia, which was never officially accounted for. Similar policies with equal success were pursued in the field of organized youth. In 1926 the illegal Komsomol created the RMS (Rabotnicheski mladezhki suiuz) [Union of Working Youth] as a legal front. Komsomol

[1] *IIIBKP*, XI (1964), 149.

membership rose from 500 in 1928 to 2,254 by the end of 1932. The
RMS numbered 1,100 at the end of 1930, and 20,000 two years later.[2]
A legal front organization for Communist university students (including
those studying in foreign universities) was set up in March, 1930. This
was the General Bulgarian National Union of Students, which continued
to be active throughout the thirties.[3]

These were but a few of the indications of the remarkable recovery
which organized Communism made during the period. A Communist-
inspired organization under the name of Workers-Peasants Solidarity
was set up for the purpose of aiding villagers in natural calamities
through volunteer work. Schemes were worked out for free legal aid to
sympathizers and fellow travelers. Accusations leveled by the Old Guard
against the left opposition leaders to the effect that Communism was
bound to lose popular support because of their "dogmatism" and "sectarian tactics" broke down in the face of concrete achievements. In local
rural elections, the popular vote of the Workers' Party rose from 2,282
in 1928 to 10,912 in 1930 and all the way to 122,113 in 1932. In the
1932 municipal elections in Sofia, the Workers' Party received a majority, polling 16,405 votes, which gave it 19 out of 35 seats in the
municipal council. Eventually most of the Workers' Party candidates
were invalidated by the courts, thus sparing the Bulgarian capital the
disgrace of a Red mayor. Finally, in the two general elections in which
the Workers' Party participated, its popular vote increased five-and-a-
half-fold, from 30,329 (four deputies) in 1927, to 165,606 (thirty-one
deputies) in 1931.[4] "Is it not true," asked the conservative paper *Mir*

[2] Throughout the text references are made to the "Party" without distinguishing
between the Communist Party and the Workers' Party. A distinction is made only
when specifically relevant. Membership figures for the Communist Party are taken
from Nedev, p. 60; for the Workers' Party, from *Rabotnicheskata partiia v
Bulgariia*, pp. 231, 325; for the youth organization, from Rothschild, p. 287.

[3] On the creation and work of the Union, see Michev and Kolev, pp. 16 ff. To
counter the Communists, the Bulgarian Anarchists established their own university
student organization in the same year (*ibid.*, pp. 22–23). One of the founders of
the Communist Union, and for a time its president, was Asen Georgiev, who was
to carve a prominent career for himself after 1944. He was tried and executed in
1963 for spying activities (to which he confessed) on behalf of the United States
(*ibid.*, pp. 15–23).

[4] All figures are from *Rabotnicheskata partiia v Bulgariia*, p. 348.

in August, 1933, "that 30% of our people is clearly bolshevized and that a large part of the remainder has no faith and no guiding principles?"[5]

While successes mounted, the commitment to "direct revolutionary action" became further exacerbated. The revolution was judged to be around the corner, and no political "constructivism" was to be tolerated. "A general and open offensive" against the regime became the order of the day. The cadres were urged to "dominate the streets" and "occupy the land." In the Subranie, the thirty-one deputies of the Workers' Party used their parliamentary immunity to turn the house into a street-corner platform for their revolutionary oratory. In April, 1933, the government of Mushanov decided to rid the Subranie of their presence. On the grounds that they were members of the illegal Communist Party rather than bona fide delegates of the Workers' Party, the expulsion measure was rushed through the house and was approved on April 12.[6]

In December, 1930, the left opposition had secretly held the Third Party Plenum in Bulgaria,[7] at which the defiance of the Old Guard by the home Party was confirmed. In August, 1933, the Fourth Party Plenum, again held in Bulgaria, gave an overwhelming approval to the policies and leadership of the left opposition. Coming four months after the expulsions from the Subranie, the Fourth Plenum was held at the very time when Dimitrov, already in the hands of the Gestapo, was working on the defense which was to make him world-famous. It was in fact in the fall of 1933 that the dominance of the left opposition reached its high mark. Although the left opposition was to maintain itself for a long while yet, the Comintern's shift to the right was about to begin. Dimitrov's heroic emergence from the Leipzig trial, the military coup in Sofia in May, 1934, and the arrival in Bulgaria of the vanguard of the executors of "Dimitrov's new course" followed in quick succession.

[5] Quoted in Logio, p. 468.

[6] On the expulsion debates, see Narodno subranie, *Stenografski dnevnitsi*, debates for April 11–12, 1933, pp. 1689–1752. Only twenty-nine deputies were expelled, since at the last moment two (D. Ikonomov and N. Doichinov) disavowed any Communist affiliations. Cheshmedzhiev of the Social Democrats and young Dr. G. M. Dimitrov of the Pladne Agrarians opposed the expulsion measure on legal grounds. The complete list of the expellees appears on p. 1752.

[7] On the Third Plenum, see *BKP v rezoliutsii i resheniia*, p. 312.

DIMITROV'S RISE TO WORLD FAME

At no time during its political disgrace at the hands of its young militant detractors did the fortunes of the Old Guard in exile reach as low an ebb as during the first weeks following Dimitrov's arrest by the Nazis. As the news of the arrest reached Moscow, the consensus at Comintern headquarters was that the Bulgarian functionary had committed an unforgivable blunder, that he had endangered the entire *apparat* in Europe, and that his repudiation by the Soviet hierarchy was inevitable. In the Hotel Lux, in the Comintern building, and within the colony of foreign Communists in Moscow, anybody known to be a friend of Dimitrov's was ostracized for fear of the retributions that were believed forthcoming. Only gradually did this silent indignation turn to unreserved enthusiasm. The first signs of approval came from leftist circles in Europe. Then came the first bold public utterances from the accused himself. Ultimately, Moscow adopted the Bulgarian as its hero. The official acclaim signified the beginning of the new Soviet orientation.

Dimitrov was arrested on March 9, 1933.[8] A few days earlier, on February 26, he had attended a conference of the Yugoslav Communist

[8] Dimitrov, *Suchineniia*, IX, 554–67, contains a detailed chronology of Dimitrov's activities from the time of his arrest to his return to Moscow at the end of February, 1934. The volume as a whole is almost entirely devoted to the Leipzig trial itself, and includes Dimitrov's speeches as well as his correspondence from prison. On the same subject, see also the volume published by the Bulgarian Communist Party shortly after the September coup of 1944: *Georgi Dimitrov pred fashistkiia sud*.

While the ultimate political consequences of the Reichstag affair are clear to all, the technical side of the problem, namely, who started the fire, etc., remains unresolved to this day. A succession of revisions and counterrevisions has marked the historiography on the subject. The 1963 study by Fritz Tobias (*The Reichstag Fire: Legend and Truth*) contends that the Nazis merely exploited rather than engineered the fire. Tobias has been refuted by a special committee of historians and political figures set up in January, 1968, to investigate the case. Including figures such as Willy Brandt and André Malraux, the committee reestablished Nazi guilt. In these pages the affair is dealt with only in the narrow context of Bulgarian Communism.

There is no reason to question Dimitrov's courage and boldness of conduct during the trial, as does Ruth Fischer (*Stalin and German Communism*, p. 308), who suggests that the Gestapo had made a deal with the Soviet GPU for Dimitrov's release and that Dimitrov knew of the deal in advance. Rothschild (pp. 292–93) has successfully refuted this contention.

The best account of Dimitrov's arrest and trial in relation to the impact on the Bulgarian Communist Party and Bulgarian politics in general is given in Nedev,

Party in Munich. On September 11, 1933, six whole months after the arrest, he was finally presented with the indictment. The trial opened in Leipzig on September 21 and lasted through more than fifty stormy court-sessions until December 23, 1933, at which time he was pronounced innocent for lack of evidence. By then, Dimitrov had gained the sympathy and acclaim of progressive world public opinion, thus giving the international Communist movement a much-needed lift. This was particularly significant in view of the low mark which Communist prestige had struck, chiefly because of the ultra-left "social fascism" line pursued by the Comintern during the preceding years.

The general excitement surrounding the Leipzig trial did not fail to affect Bulgarian public opinion. Here, however, reactions were more complex. Unlike the situation in other countries, in Bulgarian political circles Dimitrov was well known. There was hardly a politician of importance with whom Dimitrov had not, at one time or another, exchanged heated words in parliamentary debates. Memories of the abortive Communist uprising of 1923, in which Dimitrov had played a leading role, were still sharp; so was the hatred of his enemies. Many Bulgarians nevertheless felt a sense of pride regardless of their attitude toward the cause Dimitrov was defending. It was not often that a Bulgarian could claim to have captured the attention of the world press; Dimitrov not only made the front pages of the world's newspapers, but he did so while fighting the regime of mighty Germany. The reaction of some groups was altogether positive. The Central Committee of the Pladne Agrarians dispatched a telegram to the court in Leipzig affirming the Agrarian Union's conviction of Dimitrov's innocence; its leader, Kosta Todorov, went so far as to help finance the trip abroad of Dimitrov's mother.[9] The intervention of Todorov, an outsider in the matter, was not accidental. Old Parashkeva Dimitrova, having lost three of her revolutionary sons, had asked the Central Committee of the Bulgarian Communist Party for help, but was turned down.[10] The fact of

---

Otrazhenie na laiptsigskiia protses v Bulgariia (Sofia, 1962). The present author has had the opportunity of exploring some of the aspects with Blagoi Popov (during a 1966 interview), a co-defendant and at that time the only living survivor.

[9] See Todorov, *Balkan Firebrand*, pp. 245–46.

[10] *Istoricheski pregled*, No. 2 (1953), pp. 156–79. Eventually, Dimitrova succeeded in going abroad, where she made several appearances in mass meetings organized in behalf of her son.

the matter was that "the man upon whom the whole world looked as a model of heroism was regarded as half a traitor by the Communist Party of his own country." [11] At first, the left opposition leadership in Bulgaria could not see why the man it had termed "renegade" should be honored as a hero. In a special issue commemorating the tenth anniversary of the September uprising which the Party made public in the fall of 1933, the names of both Kolarov and Dimitrov appeared alongside the names of other Communist leaders who in the opinion of the leftists had "failed the Party." Only at the last moment were the names of these two scratched out and replaced by a dotted line. "This," according to Kolarov, "did little to change the situation, since all who read the issue knew perfectly well what the dotted line stood for." [12] In fact, in the course of 1933, the leadership at home had gone even further; at one point it proposed the liquidation of the Party's Buro-in-Exile and suggested that Iskrov return to Bulgaria. According to the proposed plan, the leadership in Bulgaria was then expected to oppose the re-election of Kolarov to the Executive Committee of the Comintern and eventually replace him with one of its own partisans to be dispatched for that purpose from Bulgaria.[13] The suggested maneuver came to nothing because, in the words of a recent article on the subject, "the victory of Dimitrov in Leipzig made the eventual defeat of the 'left sectarians' a matter of certainty." [14]

Already at the Thirteenth Comintern Plenum (December, 1933), the Bulgarian delegate had to take note of "comrade Dimitrov's Bolshevik tenacity," which was to serve as "a brilliant example of how communists should fight." [15] Iskrov, the leader of the Party at the Comintern, while maintaining his attack against the "right-wingers"

---

[11] Borkenau, p. 384. The reaction of the "left sectarians" to the Leipzig trial as seen by present-day Communist historians is described in Nedev, pp. 90–92, 139–49, 194–95.

[12] *Rabotnicheski vestnik*, No. 4, 1933. On the reaction of the leftists in Bulgaria to the Leipzig trial see also the speech of the Bulgarian delegate delivered before the Seventh Congress of the Comintern and reproduced in *Inprecorr*, October 10, 1935, pp. 1300–1.

[13] Kolarov, *Protiv liiavoto sektantstvo i trotskizma v Bulgariia*, p. 127.

[14] *Novo vreme*, November, 1959, p. 109.

[15] "The XIII Plenum of the Executive Committee of the Communist International —Comrade Planinski (Bulgaria)," *Inprecorr*, March 5, 1934, pp. 396–97.

among the Communists in Bulgaria, went even further. After giving an outline, a most complimentary one, of Dimitrov's revolutionary life, Iskrov urged that the "international mass campaign [in connection with the Leipzig trial] be raised to a higher level." [16]

Then came the release of Dimitrov by the Nazis (February 27, 1934). On May 17, 1934, Dimitrov attended a gathering of Bulgarian Communists in Moscow. The occasion was the commemoration of the tenth anniversary of the death of Blagoev, the late leader of the Bulgarian "narrows." Dimitrov's speech to the exiles was significant. He admitted having made mistakes in his long revolutionary career. The neutral position assumed by the Party during the June, 1923, coup and the failure to realize the great importance of the immediate "bolshevization of the 'narrow' Party" he saw as his two most important errors, errors which, in his words, "can neither be forgotten nor forgiven." [17] Yet, according to Dimitrov, in terms of the Party the "narrow" past should not be looked at altogether negatively, assuming, of course, that "the traditions and the old Marxist experience are dissolved in the large Bolshevik kettle."

THE MOSCOW EMISSARIES

While Dimitrov was reestablishing his lost authority over the Bulgarian exiles in the Soviet Union, the military elements around Velchev in Bulgaria were preparing to strike. The irony of the situation was that while the Velchev-Georgiev coup was aimed at the Mushanov-Gichev government, and while the Communist Party under the leadership of the left opposition militants played no role in the May, 1934, events, the coup, when it came, helped the veterans under Dimitrov and Kolarov to regain control over the Party at home as well as in exile. At that time, of course, Velchev could not have been aware of the influence which his *putsch* would have on the struggles within the Communist Party. Least of all would he have liked to see the two insurrectionists he helped to expel from Bulgaria in 1923 being assisted by his political exploits.

The fact remained, nevertheless, that the success of the military

---

[16] "The XIII Plenum of the Executive Committee of the Communist International —Comrade Iskrov (Bulgaria)," *Inprecorr*, May 7, 1934, pp. 738–40.

[17] Dimitrov, *Suchineniia*, IX, 455–59.

helped the Old Guard. Party leaders at home, after issuing a number of high-sounding appeals, sank into inactivity. They continued to theorize and rationalize the May events. To them the coup was nothing more than a change of government. The new regime was merely "an overt organ" of the "middle-class Fascist dictatorship," no different from all the governments since June, 1923.[18] The *putsch*, their analysis continued, was a further indication of the "inner contradictions" of a political system under a death sentence.

The Comintern did not agree with that analysis. Kolarov's lobbying for his cause, which had never stopped, now combined with Dimitrov's new fame to produce the first fruits of a long-anticipated victory. Pavlov-Encho, the political secretary of the Central Committee of the home Party, was called to Moscow to give an accounting. In August, 1934, the Political Secretariat of the ECCI considered the Bulgarian events. It criticized the Party behavior during and after the coup and called for a change of tactics. Pavlov-Encho was handed the text of a resolution ("The Bulgarian Communist Party and the Events of May 19, 1934") with which he was to familiarize his colleagues at home. He was further instructed to commence preparations for a Fifth Party Plenum, to convene not in Bulgaria but in Moscow. These instructions Pavlov-Encho found difficult to carry out after his return home. The Central Committee in Sofia could not defy the Comintern. At the same time it could not accept the stipulation that the Plenum be attended by Kolarov and his fellow companions. The quarrel with the Old Guard had already gone too far and the hatred had become too deep to be effectively bridged. The leaders of the left opposition were now fighting for their political life.

A series of complicated maneuvers were put in motion, involving the illegal Central Committee in Bulgaria and their friends in the Buro-in-Exile on the one hand, and Kolarov and Dimitrov on the other, all endeavoring to swing the ECCI their way. On December 11, 1934, Dimitrov, still recuperating from the ordeals of his imprisonment and trial, wrote Kolarov of his apprehensions over the attitude of their opponents at home: "We are obviously faced with a conscious sabotage" by the Central Committee, a situation which, he added, must be over-

---

[18] The quotations are from a public pronouncement made by the Party's Sofia district organization of May 26, 1934, and reproduced in *Rabotnicheskata partiia v Bulgariia*, pp. 409–10.

come "in one way or another." What had angered the Old Guard most was a decision by the Central Committee to convene the Fifth Party Plenum within Bulgaria, or, as an alternative, outside Bulgaria but at a place where neither Dimitrov nor Kolarov could be present. Obviously the alternative was to include neither Moscow nor any other place in the Soviet Union, where the gathering could be packed by émigrés who were gradually but inevitably moving in the direction of Dimitrov's rapidly rising star. The next move was up to the ECCI. Impressed by the solid control of the left opposition over the Party organization in Bulgaria, and fearful of a possible break and all that this might involve, the ECCI decided to compromise. It informed the Central Committee that Pavlov-Encho must be removed from his position as political secretary. At the same time, it agreed that the planned plenum be held in Bulgaria, but let it be known that an emissary would be sent as the representative of the Buro-in-Exile. The man chosen to serve as emissary was Traicho Kostov.

The left opposition in Bulgaria countered the ECCI's compromise directives with a compromise of its own. Pavlov-Encho was indeed dropped. At the end of January, 1935, the underground Fifth Party Plenum assembled in Sofia. Kostov, who in the meantime had arrived from Moscow, was not invited to attend. The Party at home was not yet ready to accept dictation from the Buro-in-Exile, where the Kolarov-Dimitrov forces were gaining the upper hand. Consisting of some twenty functionaries, with the left opposition in a position of dominance, the Fifth Plenum endeavored to comply with the new policy directives of the Comintern and strike a note of accommodation vis-à-vis the Buro-in-Exile, without surrendering to the wishes of the Old Guard.[19]

The Fifth Plenum approved the resolution entitled "The Bulgarian Communist Party and the Events of May 19, 1934" which the ECCI had worked out in August. The tactics of passivity during and after the military *putsch* were condemned. The Party leadership was criticized for having gone too far in its attacks against the Agrarians while overlooking the perils presented by the Military League, Zveno, and the Tsankov forces. "Under the present conditions, the Agrarian Union cannot be classified as a fascist organization." The formation of a "united anti-

[19] The intricate diplomacy between Moscow and the Sofia leaders is pieced together from a number of recent studies, the most important being the account given in Barov, pp. 208–11.

fascist people's front" was now deemed to be the Party's most urgent task. Dimitrov could no longer be disregarded. "In conclusion the Plenum addressed a letter of greeting to Comrade Georgi Dimitrov, expressing the great satisfaction felt by the whole Party in possessing in him a universally beloved and authoritative leader, who combines the best traditions of the 'narrow' socialists . . . with the Bolshevist-Leninist spirit." In the future, Dimitrov was to be the Party representative to the ECCI. The Buro-in-Exile elected by the Fifth Plenum included, in addition to Iskrov, Kolarov, and Dimitrov, also Georgi Damianov and Anton Ivanov, both identified with the Old Guard. A number of older cadres were co-opted into the new Central Committee. Significantly, however, the left opposition retained control over the Politburo, thus for the time being securing for itself a commanding position over the Party at home.[20]

In Moscow, Dimitrov was outraged. He was already being groomed for an illustrious role to be played at the forthcoming Seventh Congress of the Comintern, now in preparation. Yet, despite the concessions made at the Fifth Plenum, as far as he was concerned the rebellion at home had not been put down. Kostov, the purger-to-be, had been outmaneuvered and pushed aside. On March 10, 1935, in a letter to Moscow, Kostov confessed that "a turnabout" in the Party "will not be easily forthcoming." [21] Pressure was now applied at the ECCI to come to the assistance of the Dimitrov forces in order to force the issue over the unruly militants in faraway Bulgaria. On March 7, Dimitrov addressed a special session of the Balkan Secretariat at which he insisted that all steps be taken in order "to fortify the Bulgarian Party." A commission made up of Gottwald, Valetski, Kolarov, and Dimitrov, among others, was set up at the Secretariat for the purpose of working out the specific measures to be undertaken "in order to overcome the weakness" in the Party.[22]

One measure resorted to was the Comintern's well-tested technique of summons to Moscow "for report." Petko Kunin, an old Party functionary who had been co-opted as a member of the Central Committee

[20] On the decisions of the Fifth Plenum, see "Enlarged Plenum of the C.C. of the C.P. of Bulgaria," *Inprecorr*, March 23, 1935, pp. 367–68; *BKP v rezoliutsii i resheniia*, III, 315–23; Barov, p. 220, has the names of the persons elected.

[21] Barov, p. 221.

[22] *Ibid.*, p. 222.

in 1929 following his return from a study period in the Soviet Union, was recalled and placed before an improvised Party court of trial. He was able to prove his "innocence" by pointing out that he had not always sided with the leaders of the left opposition.[23] Also brought to Moscow— never again to return—was Vasilev-Boiko, one of the most prominent leaders of the left opposition.[24] Another way of dealing with the problem was, of course, dismissal by direct command of the ECCI. In the first half of 1935, "with the assistance of the ECCI the left sectarians were expelled from the Politburo" of the home Party. By no means was this the end of the fight. The left opposition, which had to its credit impressive achievements, was yet to show great resiliency.[25]

Until the summer of 1935, at which time senior Party emissaries were dispatched from Moscow for the purpose of putting down the opposition, Traicho Kostov formed the Old Guard's bridgehead within Bulgaria. An intense and studious Marxist, Kostov epitomized the typical intellectual turned professional revolutionary. A law student and a stenographer in the Subranie in his younger years, Kostov came to prominence in the mid-twenties, at the height of the White Terror. During police interrogations, he attempted suicide by throwing himself from the fourth floor of the Sofia Police Headquarters. His life was saved, even though he was left with a permanently crippled back. While serving his sentence, he was in charge of the Communist Party organi-

---

[23] See the articles on Kunin by Karaivanov in *Glas na bulgarite v Yugoslaviia*, February 5, 1952. In the late forties, Kunin was implicated in the Kostov affair and jailed. One of the charges against him was his alleged "left sectarian" past. After years in prison, Kunin reemerged, a broken man, and was restored as a member of the Central Committee.

[24] See the article by Dr. G. M. Dimitrov in his anti-Communist émigré paper published in Washington, D.C., and entitled *Svobodna i nezavisima Bulgariia*, July 7, 1949. Vasilev-Boiko's hatred for Dimitrov was not a secret. During the Leipzig trial he is quoted as having said that "Dimitrov had been sent to Germany to prepare a revolution, but he had spoiled everything; if you want to spoil things, send Dimitrov."

[25] Barov, p. 221. Even at this late stage, the leaders of the left opposition remained confident of their influence on the rank and file. To beat the Old Guard on its own grounds, as it were, they proposed that a regular Party Congress convene in Moscow. So confident were they that they could master a majority that for the purpose a technical commission was set up for the election of the Congress candidates. The exact date of this extraordinary proposal remains obscure. The plan was blocked by the Dimitrov-Kolarov forces and came to nothing. Only in 1948 did the Party convene a Congress. On the proposal, see *IIIBKP*, XI (1964), 155.

zation in the Sofia Central Prison. After a period in Moscow, he returned to Bulgaria in June, 1931, and became a member of the Central Committee early in 1932. During the same period, Kostov edited the legally published (Communist) *Rabotnichesko selsko zname* and was responsible for the legal activities of the Party, including the work of its parliamentary group. Again in Moscow, he was in charge of the Cadres Department in the Balkan Secretariat of the Comintern from 1933 until his return to Bulgaria. Kostov's alignments in the intra-Party disputes were never very clear. Like the great majority of functionaries, he pursued the leftist orientations so long as they were the official line. He was in Moscow during Dimitrov's triumphant return from Germany and no doubt enjoyed the trust of the Old Guard, without which his mission to Bulgaria would have been inconceivable. When the leading left oppositionists were forced out following the Fifth Plenum, Kostov was made a member of the Politburo, a position he was to hold until his tragic end.[26]

The period between the conclusion of the Fifth Plenum and the opening of the Seventh Congress of the Comintern (July, 1935) saw an intensification in intra-Party activity. The center of attention shifted from Bulgaria to the Soviet Union. In the spring of 1935, the Bulgarian émigrés held a general meeting in Moscow which lasted from March 28 to April 3. The spotlight was on Kolarov, who, in his opening speech, demanded that the Party rid itself of oppositionist elements and clean up its entire apparatus.[27] After extended debates during which several leading members of the opposition from among the exiles appear to have

[26] Kostov's life and earlier career are based on two detailed sketches in *Rabotnichesko delo*, June 17, 1947, and December 27, 1962; his prison days are related in Terpeshev, p. 100; many interesting details are found in the court minutes of his 1949 trial (*The Trial of Traicho Kostov and His Group*), although facts and fiction are difficult to separate. At the time of that trial he was accused of having been a leading member of the left opposition, charges he denied but was not allowed to explain (*ibid.*, pp. 66–75, 98, etc.; see also Kolarov, *Izbrani proizvedeniia*, III, 504–6). Whatever his leanings and earlier preferences, there is little doubt that after 1934 he was firmly committed to the Dimitrov forces. The fact that he was back in Moscow (1936–38) during the climax of the émigré purges, and returned safely to Bulgaria, is not without significance. In 1964 a collection of his writings and speeches was published (Kostov, *Izbrani statii, dokladi, rechi*), substantiating his contribution to the purge of the left opposition.

[27] Kolarov's report is reprinted in Kolarov, *Protiv liiavoto sektantstvo i trotskizma v Bulgariia*, pp. 35–68.

made statements of self-criticism, the meeting resolved to punish two leading exiled "leftists" by demoting them to "lower Party work," and called on all to examine their stands and unite around the leadership of Dimitrov. Blagoi Popov and Vasil Tanev, Dimitrov's co-defendants at the Leipzig trial, were condemned for their failure to follow his example of "selfless Bolshevik behavior"; their "sin" was that during the trial they concentrated on personal self-defense rather than having stood up for Communism as a whole and pointed at the rising Fascist danger.[28] Dimitrov (who seems not to have been present at the meeting) made an appearance before the Bulgarian Communist exiles in Moscow on May 11, 1935, on the occasion of the eleventh anniversary of Dimitur Blagoev's death. On the whole, his speech did not differ much from the one delivered the previous year during the commemoration of the tenth anniversary. This time, however, he was in a position to report that the Communist Party in Bulgaria, "with the help of the Comintern, is in the process of overcoming its deviations," and was making "a decisive turnabout in the direction of Bolshevik mass activity." He warned against overoptimism and stated that the correction of past mistakes and "perversions allowed during the course of the Party's Bolshevization" should not be interpreted as a return to the "narrow" past. The Party's present task, according to Dimitrov, was the creation of a "broad united

---

[28] *Ibid.*, pp. 69–75, contains the text of the adopted resolution. A month earlier (February 25, 1935) Popov and Tanev had already criticized themselves (see B. Popov and V. Tanev, "Our Behavior at the Leipzig Trial," *Communist International*, January, 1936, pp. 88–90), although they continued to be attacked by Kolarov (V. Kolarov, "The Behavior of Comrades Tanev and Popov at the Leipzig Trial," *Communist International*, January, 1936, pp. 86-87) and by the Central Committee of the Party ("Decision of the C.C. of the C.P. of Bulgaria on the Declaration of Comrades Popov and Tanev," *Communist International*, January, 1936, pp. 90–92).

In July, 1936, the two expressed further self-criticism ("B. Popov and V. Tanev to Dimitrov and the Central Committee of the Communist Party of Bulgaria," *Communist International*, July, 1936, pp. 902–7), since the Central Committee appears not to have been satisfied with their original statement.

After the German attack on the Soviet Union, Tanev was sent back to Bulgaria (he parachuted from a Soviet plane), but was immediately apprehended by the Bulgarian authorities and shot in October, 1941; *Rabotnichesko delo*, October 16, 1956.

Blagoi Popov was a leading member of the left opposition. His fate will be traced along with those of the purged émigrés.

front against the fascist dictatorship." [29] This, of course, was the central theme of the Seventh Congress of the Comintern (July 25–August 20), at which the Bulgarian Communist Party was represented by Kolarov, Petur Iskrov, and Krumov.[30] Dimitrov was already an international rather than a strictly Bulgarian figure; except for occasional references to Bulgarian problems, his report added nothing to the Bulgarian Party's situation as such. The same was largely true of Iskrov's report dealing with the fascist danger in general. Kolarov, an expert on agrarian problems, had some harsh words to say against the Bulgarian "left sectarians" and their failure to collaborate with the Agrarian Union. The Bulgarian Party, he said, "demonstrated how a united front ought not to be established and how a struggle against fascism ought not to be conducted." It was Krumov, however, who concentrated entirely on an attack against the "left sectarians." In his words, "the evil consequences of the sectarianism and factionalism of the Party leadership made themselves felt in the intensified offensive of reaction and fascism (dissolution of the workers' fraction in parliament [1933], dispersal of the workers' fraction in the Sofia municipality [1932], the assassination of a number of popular proletarian leaders . . .)." This was the strongest public assault made against the "leftists" to that time. Like Dimitrov in his speech of May before the émigrés, Krumov could not say more about the immediate present except to assert that the "leftists" were in the process of being purged.

With the closing of the Seventh Congress, the focus shifted back to Bulgaria. The Buro-in-Exile, determined to put an end to the running fight within the Party ranks at home, decided to strengthen the nucleus around Kostov by dispatching two of its senior functionaries. These were Stanke Dimitrov-Marek and Georgi Damianov, both of whom returned to Bulgaria after the closing of the Seventh Congress in Moscow in the face of death sentences imposed on them in the mid-twenties by the Tsankov regime.

Of the two, Dimitrov-Marek was to play the major part. His role as head of the Bulgarian section at KUNMZ has already been related.

[29] Dimitrov, *Suchineniia*, X, 6–10.

[30] For the texts of the reports of Kolarov, Iskrov, and Krumov, see the following articles in *Inprecorr*: November 21, 1935, pp. 1537–40; January 11, 1936, pp. 80–81; October 10, 1935, pp. 1300–1.

This was not the first time (nor was it the last) that he was called upon to steer the Party on its "correct" course. After the debacle of 1923, Dimitrov-Marek led the "healthy elements" within the underground Party. He fled to the Soviet Union in 1925 and joined the CPSU.[31] In 1932 he was appointed to a position in the Balkan Section of the Comintern.[32]

Georgi Damianov, who in 1950 became the Bulgarian head of state, was more a practical rather than an intellectual revolutionary. A member of the Party since the age of twenty (1912), he participated in the soldiers' rebellion that broke out at the end of World War I, and in the Communist rising of 1923.[33] In 1926 he emigrated to the Soviet Union where he studied at the Frunze Military Academy, after which he became a commander in the Red Army and an instructor in the same academy.[34]

The reappearance of the two emissaries in Bulgaria coincided with the return from Moscow of two Party delegates to the Seventh Congress, namely, Encho Staikov and Georgi Chankov. The former was sent to the Congress to represent the home Party, while Chankov, a young functionary of the Party's youth organization, had been in Moscow since 1934.[35] These four, together with Kostov and his partisans, now

---

[31] *BKP v rezoliutsii i resheniia*, III, 31.

[32] *Yarki imena v nashata istoriia*, pp. 171–76. He was born in 1889 in the town of Dupnitsa (renamed after him following the Communist takeover) to a father who was a shoemaker. As a youth he became involved in socialist propaganda activity, which he never abandoned. He was first arrested in 1906. A teacher, a student abroad (Switzerland, 1912–13), and a law graduate from Sofia University (1914–19), he was first elected a Communist deputy in 1919. He was arrested on the eve of the 1923 uprising, became implicated in the 1925 bombing, and was sentenced to death after his escape.

[33] During the uprising, Damianov was a member of the Party district committee of Vratsa, which served as the center of the rebellion. On this and other details, see *Rabotnichesko delo*, November 28, 1958.

[34] On the years at the Frunze Academy, see the article by General Ivan Kinov in *Rabotnichesko delo*, November 29, 1958.

[35] Chankov was a representative of the young generation of Communists who had reached maturity in the years following the 1923 uprising. He was only twenty-three in 1932 when the Party sent him to study at the Lenin International School in Moscow. Back in Bulgaria, Chankov became a member of the Central Committee of the Party's youth organization, returning to the Soviet Union in 1934

undertook to complete what the Fifth Plenum of January, 1935, had left undone.

Ever since the spring of 1935, the surviving oppositionists had been fighting a losing battle. For a time, some tried to hang on "by endeavoring," as they were later accused, "to interpret the [Fifth Plenum] resolution . . . according to their own ideas." [36] The trends within the Communist world, however, were working against them. Their sectarian militancy was becoming anachronistic in a movement in which the slogans of the united front were the order of the day. Nor could they fight against Dimitrov's prestige, which the Seventh Congress had done much to enhance. Those who returned from Moscow made sure that Dimitrov's message would not be lost. The Party in Bulgaria printed and distributed illegally 5,000 copies of Dimitrov's report to the Congress. In September, the Party's Central Committee made public a resolution condemning the "left sectarian" leadership for its failure to "raise" Dimitrov's role at Leipzig "to its proper heights" during and after the trial.[37] On October 1, the Central Committee came out with an "open letter" which for the first time brought the internal Party rifts to the attention of the rank and file:

The Left opportunist, sectarian course taken by the Party was due to the fact that a number of petty-bourgeois elements, sectarians and doctrinaires, had gained the upper hand in the C.C. of the party. . . . These elements rejected the whole of the revolutionary experience of the Bulgarian proletariat and of the Party and waged fractional war against the best bearers of this experience, comrades Georgi Dimitrov and Vasil Kolarov; they trained the young Party cadres in this spirit.

Then followed the operative part of the Central Committee's declaration:

With the aid of the Communist International, and with the closest collaboration of comrade Dimitrov, the Left opportunist and sectarian course of

---

on Party instructions; *Rabotnichesko delo*, December 12, 1947. His return to Bulgaria in 1935 marked the beginning of a brilliant career in the Party which was to take him to the highest and most responsible posts, positions he continued to hold until his sudden purge in 1957.

[36] "A Historical Letter from the C.P. of Bulgaria," *Inprecorr*, November 16, 1935, pp. 1516–17.

[37] *Rabotnicheski vestnik*, No. 8, September, 1935, quoted in "Decision of the C.C. of the C.P. of Bulgaria on the Declaration of Comrades Popov and Tanev," *Communist International*, January, 1936, pp. 90–92.

the Party was subjected to an annihilating criticism, its advocates removed from responsible Party positions, and the political line of the Party corrected.[38]

In a matter of months, Dimitrov-Marek accomplished what Kostov had failed to do earlier, in large measure owing to the greater conspiratorial talents of the former. More importantly, however, with Dimitrov-Marek's arrival in Bulgaria, the ECCI placed in his hands financial resources never before brought to bear on the Bulgarian Communist scene. Since all legal Communist organizations were banned after the 1934 coup, the left opposition had little or no funds on hand. No such limitations operated on the purgers. A clandestine two-way radio transmitter was set up by Dimitrov-Marek to provide instant liaison with Moscow. A number of illegal Communist presses were established. Eight secret flats were placed at the disposal of the Moscow emissaries in the capital alone. There was money available for the building of a new permanent *apparat*. At no time before 1935 was organized Communism in Bulgaria so overwhelmingly dependent on Moscow money. This dependence was to grow rather than lessen in the following years.[39]

The *coup de grâce* was delivered to the opposition leaders in February, 1936, at the Sixth Party Plenum held in Sofia under the chairmanship of Damianov and with the active participation of Dimitrov-Marek and Kostov. Retrospective approval was given to all that the Moscow emissaries had accomplished, including the ousting of the leftists from the Politburo on ECCI orders. Dimitrov-Marek was formally elected political secretary. Kostov's co-option into the Politburo of the spring before was affirmed. With these steps, the purge of the left oppo-

[38] A photostatic reproduction of the "open letter" appears in *Nelegalni pozivi na BKP*, pp. 126–30; this is a collection of Party leaflets published illegally throughout the years. For the English text of the same "open letter," published by the Comintern, see "A Historical Letter from the C.C. of the C.P. of Bulgaria," *Inprecorr*, November 16, 1935, pp. 1516–17.

[39] Kasher-Dimitrova, pp. 138–80, gives a detailed account of the activities in Bulgaria of Dimitrov-Marek and Damianov (whose cover name while in Bulgaria was Rusiia). The former returned to Moscow in the summer of 1937 and the latter somewhat earlier. The statement on the Party's dependence on Comintern money is conjectural since there are no firm figures given anywhere. Firsthand accounts on their work in Bulgaria are also given in Dimitrov-Marek, pp. 321–33.

Insights into the conduct of the purge at home are to be found in a revealing letter by Kostov to the Buro-in-Exile of July 10, 1936, reproduced in Kostov, *Izbrani statii, dokladi, rechi*, pp. 292–99.

sition leadership at home came to an end. For the future, there remained the problem of restoring "order" within the provincial Party organizations as well as among the rank and file.[40]

THE PURGE OF THE EMIGRATION

The fateful quarrel between the Old Guard and the left opposition, which overshadowed all other intra-Party struggles for an entire decade, was destined to be resolved not in the conference room but in the prison cellars and concentration camps of the NKVD. In the course of Stalin's Great Purge, the leaders of the left—those who were in Russia as well as those who were recalled to Moscow—and most of the rank-and-file émigrés who had supported the leftist cause, perished, and were condemned to oblivion. The victims of Stalin's homicidal fury in the Comintern involved more than the left opposition. With only minor exceptions, the wholesale massacre which befell the Bulgarian Communist emigration in Russia remained hidden behind an iron blanket of silence which has never been officially lifted.

On September 23, 1936, barely four weeks after the sixteen ex-oppositionists headed by Zinoviev were arraigned for public trial on capital charges, Kolarov issued a brochure devoted to Trotskyism in the Bulgarian revolutionary movement. The Bulgarian Trotskyites, Kolarov said, had at one time called for the establishment of a "proletarian court" to try "the Stalinist faction of Kolarov and Dimitrov" for their treason of 1923. Why were the Trotskyites left unmasked? Obviously, Kolarov answered, because of the domination of the Party by the "left sectarians," who covered up for the treasonous agents of Trotsky. At this point, the insinuations were only oblique. Given the frenzy into which the Soviet public was being whipped over the Zinoviev affair, however, the hidden meaning of Kolarov's message was not lost. The final act of pinning the Trotskyite label on the people of the Bulgarian left opposition was now only a matter of time.[41]

---

[40] On the conduct of the Sixth Plenum, see Kostov's account given in 1945 at the first postwar Plenum, Kostov, *Politicheskoto polozhenie*, p. 59; see also Kostov, *Izbrani statii, dokladi, rechi*, pp. 298–99. For the names of the Politburo and Central Committee members elected, see *BKP v rezoliutsii i resheniia*, p. 327, and *Istoriia na BKP*, p. 415.

[41] Kolarov, *Protiv liiavoto sektantstvo i trotskizma v Bulgariia*, pp. 99–153, reproduces the text of the brochure.

In June, 1937, Kolarov called yet another Bulgarian émigré meeting in Moscow. The main report dealt with the Trotskyite dangers in the past and in the future. Here, the unmistakable link between Trotskyism and the Bulgarian left opposition was firmly established. This gathering was to prove fateful, for the mass arrests of the émigrés began soon thereafter.[42]

When the blow fell, it was massive. Stalin's police hit hard and without much discrimination. Two main conspiracies were concocted, implicating hundreds of exiles. The one was the "Ukrainian conspiracy," involving Bulgarian exiles from among those settled in the southern parts of the Soviet Union. The other involved the emigration at large, and had as its core the leaders of the left opposition. It included persons employed in the Comintern *apparat*, the state bureaucracy, and the Red Army.

More than two hundred exiles were arrested in connection with the "Ukrainian conspiracy." They were accused of belonging to a spy organization working for the annexation of the Ukraine to Bulgaria! How this feat was to be achieved when Bulgaria had no common frontier with the Ukraine, the NKVD did not bother to explain. The main body of this group was made up of Bulgarian Communist émigrés working among the Bessarabian Bulgarians in the southern Ukraine and the Odessa region. The great majority perished. Those who were not dealt

---

[42] *Ibid.*, pp. 157–85, reproduces Kolarov's report. In the Russia of mid-1937, the timing rather than the content of the accusations was significant. Charges of Trotskyism against the opposition had been made before. Accused of Menshevism by the left opposition, the Old Guard naturally replied with a countercharge. Dimitrov appears to have taken a slightly qualified position from that of Kolarov. Addressing the Balkan Secretariat earlier, Dimitrov was reported to have said that "Kolarov's contention that the attitude of the left opposition toward the Comintern is Trotskyite is incorrect. From these roots, however, both Trotskyism and Zinovievism can spring. When they decided to convene a Party Plenum [Fifth Plenum of January, 1935] without awaiting the instructions of the Comintern, then this was a hidden attack against the Comintern. One more step in the same direction, and we will have Trotskyism-Zinovievism." *IIIBKP*, XI (1964), 140. The publication in 1964 of this subtle differentiation was no doubt aimed at lightening the implicit blame on Dimitrov. Only after 1956 was the charge of Trotskyism dropped from the official Bulgarian literature, and only in the early sixties did the official sources (*ibid.*, p. 140) acknowledge the truth, namely, that not only were the left oppositionists not Trotskyite, but they consistently fought the Trotsky people tooth and nail.

with immediately in the Odessa prison were dispatched to the concentration camps, never to return.[43]

A number of well-known Communists among the victims of the "Ukrainian conspiracy" perished. The most prominent was Dr. Nikola Maksimov, who, as a member of the Central Committee, had represented the Bulgarian Party at the Second Congress of the Comintern. Maksimov had sided with Lukanov and the right opposition after 1923. His stand had placed him at odds with the Kolarov-Dimitrov faction in the Vienna exile, which may or may not have been the reason for his purge. Genko Krustev was another well-known figure who lost his life. In Bulgaria he had been the head of the Bulgarian Teachers Union, and after his emigration to the Ukraine had become the editor of a Bulgarian-language newspaper. Some of the others who perished from the "Ukrainian group" were the engineer Tseniu Ninchev (a brother of Tsola Dragoicheva, herself a Politburo member during World War II and later the general secretary of the Communist Fatherland Front); Vasil Manafov, a lawyer; and his wife, Nevena Gencheva, who was a veteran Party member and became a teacher in the Ukraine (she died in the Odessa prison two months after her arrest). Raina Kandeva, alone among the

[43] Ivan Karaivanov, in *Glas na bulgarite v Yugoslaviia*, January 15, 1952. Unless otherwise indicated, the information given above and in the following pages, pertaining to the purge, is based on this major source. Much the same grounds are covered, also by Karaivanov, in his "Stvarnost Staljinovog carstva," *Trideset dana*, September-October, 1951, pp. 33–44, though in much more general terms. Karaivanov has already been mentioned briefly as a Bulgarian Communist who was Tito's confidant before and after Yugoslavia's break with Moscow. Since he emerges as the main *rapporteur* on the purge of the Bulgarians in Russia, a brief outline of his career is called for.

Karaivanov was born in 1889 in Pirdop, Bulgaria. He was not a Macedonian. He was old Blagoev's protégé and received his socialist schooling as a Bulgarian "narrow" socialist. From December, 1923, until his arrival in Russia in 1926, Karaivanov remained in Austria helping Dimitrov with his propaganda work. He graduated from the University of the Workers of the East and later worked in China (1929–34) as a Comintern agent. Back in Moscow, he was employed in the Comintern's Cadres Department (1934–37), in propaganda work, and in 1943 was sent as an agent to the Arab east. Karaivanov returned to Bulgaria in November, 1944, together with the surviving exiles. However, he went over to the Yugoslavs (before the 1948 break) for reasons which remain obscure, and was a member of the Central Committee of the Yugoslav CP until his death. (For his autobiography, see Karaivanov, *Narodna republika Makedonija*, introduction.) In January, 1949, the People's Front of Yugoslavia began the publication of a

better-known Bulgarians in the "Ukrainian conspiracy," survived and returned to Bulgaria after 1944.[44]

More than four hundred Bulgarian émigrés were arrested in connection with the second "conspiracy." They were accused of being "the agents of Fascism, working on Hitler's behalf." Those who were not shot in the prisons were sent to the Siberian Kolyma concentration camps where they perished. Only a few survived to return to their homeland after the war.[45] The entire leadership of the left opposition, consisting of Petur Iskrov and a score of his closest collaborators, was disposed of. The great majority of those arrested in the second "conspiracy" were made to sign the inevitable written confessions as spies of Nazi Germany. Of the more prominent left opposition leaders, only

---

Bulgarian-language weekly under the name of *Glas na bulgarite v Yugoslaviia* for the purpose of mastering the 50,000-strong Bulgarian (not Macedonian) national minority in the Yugoslav regions of Tsaribrod and Bosilgrad. It was in the pages of this periodical, published at the height of Belgrade's conflicts with Moscow and Sofia, that many of Karaivanov's revelations were made. In Soviet exile, Karaivanov belonged to the Old Guard of the Party and had no sympathy for the left opposition. If anything, his biases were pro-Dimitrov and anti-Iskrov. A surviving member of the left opposition expressed a belief commonly held by Bulgarian exiles in Moscow when he said that Karaivanov had given a hand in purging the left by siding with Kolarov (Blagoi Popov to author, interview, Sofia, September 6, 1966). This claim cannot be substantiated, particularly since Karaivanov lost a sister in the purge. Yet, given the hell into which Stalin turned his country in the thirties, nothing can be strictly excluded. Karaivanov was clearly not a scholar but a politician. The particular circumstances of his defection to Yugoslavia, and Tito's break with Moscow, created the political conditions which made his revelations possible. Without them, the fate of the Bulgarians in the Comintern would have remained buried in the archives of the Bulgarian Central Committee. Once revealed, his evidence could be corroborated. This the author did to the best of his ability. Karaivanov's information appears trustworthy. And yet, only the pinnacle of the iceberg has so far become visible. On revelations concerning the purge of some Rumanian Communists in the Comintern, see Karaivanov, *Ljudi i pigmeji*, p. 112.

[44] On the earlier careers of Maksimov and Krustev, see Rothschild, pp. 40, 101*n*, 154.

[45] Some of the survivors who showed up in Bulgaria after the war were Mladen Stoianov, who was a Central Committee member in the twenties; Raicho Karakolov, who later became a professor of Marxism; and Anton Nedialkov, who joined the Foreign Ministry. As of January, 1952, Karaivanov was aware of no more than twenty survivors who had returned. Blagoi Popov returned in 1954. There were a few more who followed him, but their numbers were very small.

Blagoi Popov, one of Dimitrov's co-defendants in the Leipzig trial, survived. He was arrested in 1937 and tried in 1939, whereupon he was sent to the Siberian camps. He was freed in 1952, but remained in Siberian internment until 1954, at which time he was permitted to return to Bulgaria.[46]

The massacre claimed the lives of the most prominent leaders of the Bulgarian Komsomol. A few sprang from the emigration, returned to Bulgaria as Party functionaries, and were eventually recalled to the Soviet Union where they paid the ultimate penalty. V. Ganchev-Koprinkov emigrated in 1925 and studied in the Rostov Party school. In 1927, at the age of twenty-four, he returned to Bulgaria in the double capacity of a member of the Party's Central Committee and secretary of the Komsomol. He was arrested in 1929 and kept in prison until 1934, at which time he resumed his functions as Central Committee member in charge of the legal activities of the Workers' Party. In the fall of 1934 Ganchev-Koprinkov was recalled to Moscow, and in the following year was appointed head of the Bulgarian section at the Lenin School (under the name of Ivan Nikolaevich Aleksandrov), which was the last position he held before his arrest and death "during the period of the cult of personality." [47] Another casualty of the purge was Zh. Zhelezov-Kiranov, who went to Moscow in 1935 and became the Bulgarian representative to the Youth International and a member of its

[46] Blagoi Popov believed that Iskrov and his friends were shot in 1938. A firsthand account of Popov's initial two years in the Norilsk camp is to be found in Berger-Barzilai's memoirs (see Barzilai, pp. 116–20). Popov was in a state of depression largely because of the lack of solidarity he had witnessed among the Bulgarian exiles in Moscow during the purge. As indicated earlier, Popov and Tanev were criticized for their "non-Bolshevik" behavior at the Leipzig trial. In 1939 Popov was sentenced to fifteen years at hard labor. The accusation against him was that he had planned to murder Dimitrov. Despite numerous written appeals to Dimitrov during and after the war, he served his sentence to the very end. Twelve years after his return to Bulgaria, Popov did not know whether or not his Communist comrades had tried to intervene on his behalf after they had assumed power in Bulgaria. Popov had married Otto Kuusinen's daughter, who abandoned him after his arrest. Following his return to Bulgaria, he was used in various public appearances as a living memorial to Dimitrov's heroism at the Leipzig trial (see *Rabotnichesko delo*, February 28, 1963, for Popov's speech in East Berlin on the thirtieth anniversary of the Reichstag fire).

[47] On his career and posthumous rehabilitation, see *Rabotnichesko delo*, November 10, 1963.

Executive Committee. His arrest followed in time.[48] Vulko Radinski, a graduate of the Lenin School (1932–34), became the secretary of the Komsomol in Bulgaria in the middle of 1935. At the end of 1936 he returned to Moscow to represent the Komsomol at the Youth International. He was arrested in the fall of 1937 and perished "under cruel circumstances." [49] Dimitur Lambrev was yet another former member of the Executive Committee of the Youth International who perished. A lawyer by profession, he was on Party work in Vienna and Berlin from 1923 until 1932, at which time he went to Moscow and worked in the Soviet Law Institute before falling prey to the secret police.[50] Before his arrest and death, Krum Buchvarov served as professor of history at the "Tolmachov" (later "Lenin") Military Academy in Leningrad and as brigade commissar in the Red Army. His purge may have been connected with his past leanings toward the Zinoviev organization in Leningrad in the mid-twenties.[51] The execution of Colonel Vladimir Sedloev-Gorski of the Far East command of the Red Army may or may not have been related to the fact that Sedloev was a Bulgarian émigré. He escaped to Russia in the twenties and was a distinguished graduate of the Frunze Academy.[52]

The murder machine did not discriminate even when its victims had relatives highly placed in the Communist hierarchy. The purge claimed the life of Dobri Terpeshev's émigré son.[53] Terpeshev (the father) was a member of the Politburo from 1937 on, and became the commander in chief of the Communist resistance in wartime Bulgaria. Georgi Atanasov was given a ten-year sentence, never to return from the Siberian camps. At the time of his arrest his brother, Shteriu

[48] *Rabotnichesko delo*, January 31, February 1, 1964, on his rehabilitation, and the special memorial in the village of his birth (attended also by A. Zolotov, the Soviet consul in Varna), respectively.

[49] Radinski's life and posthumous rehabilitation appear in *Rabotnichesko delo*, May 18, 1963.

[50] *Rabotnichesko delo*, June 5, 1963.

[51] For the life and rehabilitation of Buchvarov, see the article by General of the Army Ivan Mikhailov in *Rabotnichesko delo*, September 5, 1962.

[52] *Rabotnichesko delo*, September 13, 1963.

[53] Blagoi Popov to author. Yet another victim from the same family was Zheliazko Terpeshev, according to Atanasov, *Pod znameto na partiiata*, p. 22.

Atanasov, was the liaison man between the Buro-in-Exile and the Comintern, having replaced from the same position Boris Filipov of the left opposition.[54]

The horrors occasionally had a sardonic twist. The irrepressible Georgi Andreichin (already mentioned), having been purged, survived the ordeals in Russia and at the end of the war returned to Bulgaria, where he made a career in the Foreign Ministry, only to perish in the purges of the late forties in Bulgaria.[55]

There were a number of notable Soviet officials of Bulgarian origin whose lives were claimed by the Great Purge. Their careers have been discussed already. They were Bulgarians who for all practical purposes had become Russified. Most probably, their ultimate fate bore no relation to their ethnic origin or previous experiences in Bulgarian Communism. Christian Rakovski was tried, given a sentence of twenty years, and eventually perished (as did his wife and only daughter). Boris Stomaniakov, the deputy commissar for foreign affairs, was arrested in 1937 and died in 1941. Roman Avramov, who, among other things,

---

[54] *Ibid.*, pp. 111, 114.

[55] Andreichin was born in 1894 in Macedonia, which was under Turkish rule until 1912. He was educated in Samakov (Bulgaria). Like Vladimir Poptomov, whose friend he was, he drifted into Socialism via the Macedonian revolutionary movement. He fought the Turks in the Balkan War, and at the end of 1913 immigrated to the United States, working in the mines of Minnesota. He became actively involved in the politics of the IWW and was arrested several times during World War I. Andreichin joined the American CP from its inception. He joined the Executive Committee of the Profintern as an American delegate in 1921, and served as chief of its Anglo-Saxon Section. Boris Souvarine, who knew Andreichin well, described him as "an unsophisticated, generous, spontaneous young fellow, whose eclectic anarch-syndicalist views were in sharp contrast to the dogmatism of the Social Democrats converted to communism." (Drachkovich and Lazitch, eds., p. 182, also pp. 166, 392–93.) In the late twenties, Andreichin appears to have sympathized with the Trotsky opposition. American Ambassador William Bullitt knew Andreichin well while in Moscow, as did a number of foreign correspondents. Before Andreichin's arrest and purge he was employed as censor. On his return to Bulgaria after the war he headed the office of the President of the Republic, later worked in the Foreign Ministry, and was a member of the Bulgarian delegation to the Paris Peace Conference. On his life and posthumous rehabilitation, see *Rabotnichesko delo*, January 19, 1964; no mention is made in this source of Andreichin's purge in Russia. Blagoi Popov believed that, after his arrest in the late forties, Andreichin was taken to the Soviet Union and was liquidated there.

headed the Soviet Grain Export, was arrested in 1937 and died in the Magadan camps.[56]

On a few occasions at the height of the purge, Dimitrov intervened on behalf of his protégés. Sometime during 1937, Dimitrov found out about the forthcoming arrest of his brother-in-law, Chervenkov-Vladimirov, whereupon the latter took refuge in Dimitrov's villa in Kuntsevo. He remained in hiding for a fortnight until the danger expired, presumably as a result of Dimitrov's intervention with the NKVD.[57] Dimitrov helped, but did not quite save, old Khristo Kabakchiev, who was arrested and thrown in the infamous Lubyanka prison in Moscow. The accusa-

---

[56] On Avramov's death, see *Istoricheski pregled*, No. 4–5 (1967), p. 181. The date of his death is not given. He was posthumously rehabilitated by the Russians in 1954. During the 1938 public trials of the major figures of the Soviet opposition, a group of well-known physicians was also tried on charges that they had helped to murder prominent Soviet leaders. One of them, Dr. I. N. Kazakov (the others were Drs. Levin and Pletnev), was tried and executed for having allegedly helped to murder V. R. Menzhinsky (Yagoda's predecessor as head of the OGPU). (Conquest, pp. 400 ff.) Kazakov was a Bulgarian (Nikola Antonov, the Bulgarian minister in Moscow, knew him personally), even though it is not clear whether he was born in Bulgaria or else born to Bulgarian parents from the so-called Bessarabian Bulgarians. In either case, his death was unrelated to the purge of exiles.

There are passing references on the purge of the Bulgarian exiles in several sources. Most important are those in Drachkovich and Lazitch, particularly pp. 168–70; Conquest, p. 433: "There were many other victims [among the Bulgarians]. One Bulgarian is mentioned in a Vologda camp being thrown into a hole in the ground without food for thirteen days, and dying." There are two references made by Dr. G. M. Dimitrov, the Agrarian leader, in his anti-Communist émigré paper, *Svobodna i nezavisima Bulgariia*, August 17, 1949: "The greatest idealists in the Bulgarian Communist Party were called to Moscow and shot"; see also *ibid.*, July 7, 1949.

[57] Karaivanov, "Vulko Chervenkov," *Glas na bulgarite v Yugoslaviia*, October 14, 21, 1952. This is not to imply that Dimitrov's villa in Kuntsevo had any immunity vis-à-vis the NKVD. There is a vague reference in Karaivanov's article to the effect that arrests were carried out on the premises of Dimitrov's residence. A somewhat different version of Chervenkov's escape is supplied by Vlahovic and reported by Djilas (p. 34), according to which Chervenkov's "exposé" of "the political school where he was an instructor had already been published," whereupon "he took refuge with Dimitrov."

Even though Chervenkov appears to have been carried away with the slogans of the left opposition, after Dimitrov's return to Moscow a great intimacy between the two developed. "Chervenkov's son and daughter," reports Karaivanov, "were for all practical purposes raised in Dimitrov's villa."

tions against him were the same as those made against hundreds of Bulgarian émigrés, namely, spying activities on behalf of Hitler's Germany. At the time of his arrest Kabakchiev was an associate in the Soviet Academy of Sciences. The left opposition had purged him from the Central Committee as far back as 1928. His good standing in the Party was restored after the purge of the left. In fact, he was brought forth by Kolarov to speak against the leaders of the left opposition at the Moscow émigré meeting of March, 1935. After a long span in Lubyanka, Kabakchiev was finally freed as a result of Dimitrov's insistent interventions. The secret police, however, had succeeded in breaking the health of the old man, who never recovered, and died soon thereafter.[58] Also freed from arrest through Dimitrov's efforts was Ferdinand Kozovski. At the beginning of the purge, Kozovski was in Spain together with a large group of Bulgarian émigrés who volunteered to fight on the Republican side (developments yet to be related). He was recalled to Moscow and arrested on unknown charges.[59]

There were two Communist "emigrations" which were outside the reach of the NKVD. The one was the Bulgarian Communist colony in Paris; the other was the much larger Communist colony in the Bulgarian jails. The first could be reached through special emissaries from Moscow. The second remained immune, except for the followers of the Old Guard who were themselves prisoners.

The Bulgarian Communist contingent in Paris was made up predominantly of "economic émigrés," or people who went to France in

---

[58] The story of Kabakchiev's arrest is related by Karaivanov in "Stvarnost Staljinovog carstva," *Trideset dana,* September-October, 1951, pp. 33–44. Kabakchiev died in Moscow on October 6, 1940. The death announcement was carried by *Pravda,* October 8, 1940, under the signatures of Dimitrov, Kolarov, Manuilski, Pieck, and Chervenkov-Vladimirov. Kabakchiev's ordeals have never been acknowledged in official sources. In a detailed chronicle of his life published in 1958 (Kabakchiev, *Bio-bibliografiia*) there is a gap in his activities for the years 1936–37; he is reported gravely ill as of April, 1938. The same source omits the name of Trotsky from a joint publication (Trotsky and Kabakchiev, *Ocherki politicheskoi Bolgarii* [Moscow, 1923]). It is just possible that this joint venture crossed the collective minds of the NKVD when the arrest was made.

[59] Karaivanov, *Glas na bulgarite v Yugoslaviia,* January 15, 1952, relates the arrest and release of Kozovski. According to Herbert Wehner, a witness to the purges of the foreigners, Dimitur Vlakhov (or Vlahov), the former Macedonian revolutionary turned Communist, was also arrested and freed as a result of Dimitrov's intervention (see Drachkovich and Lazitch, eds., pp. 168–69).

search of better employment than they could find in Bulgaria. There were also students among them, as well as an uncertain number of political émigrés. Inevitably, the quarrel between the Old Guard and the left opposition reached the Bulgarians in Paris. Followers of the left opposition prevailed, and although they were fewer in number, the leadership of the Bulgarian Communists in Paris fell into their hands. This state of affairs was thought intolerable by the Kolarov-Dimitrov people in Moscow, particularly after the outbreak of the Spanish Civil War when Paris became the focal point for Bulgarian Communists on their way to Spain. Tsola Dragoicheva, the veteran woman-functionary, was dispatched to France to deal with the "left rebellion." When she failed, in October, 1936, Dimitrov sent Shteriu Atanasov, who was the liaison man between the Buro-in-Exile and the Comintern. "After receiving detailed instructions from Dimitrov," Atanasov reported, "I explained to them the need for having a unified Party organization." The emissary further told the Parisian émigrés that in the future, on Comintern instructions, all Bulgarian Communists on French soil must join the French Communist Party. This the left opposition had refused to do, maintaining membership in the Bulgarian Party alone. The "rebellion" was eventually put down. Having been forced into the ranks of the French CP, the opposition dissolved.[60]

The Bulgarian jails represented an entirely different situation. Since left oppositionism meant militancy, and since the young militants were most apt to clash with the police and find themselves in prison, the left opposition reigned supreme in all Bulgarian jails. The older cadres were intimidated, sneered at, and placed in a position of being in "prison within a prison" as it were. The norms of "direct action" were rigorously observed. Those who deviated from the set line were driven to despair. "I was isolated as if I were a leper," wrote Terpeshev years later, "and considered taking my own life." Terpeshev was an old revolutionary in prison since 1925. Jailed Communists were expected to turn down government pardons on grounds that true revolutionaries could not accept favors from the class enemy. In the 1931 general elections, G. Petrov from the Liberal Party ran for election in the district of Kharmanli, where the same Terpeshev was a well-known figure from his pre-prison days. To gain electoral support, Petrov promised to arrange for the re-

[60] Atanasov, *Pod znameto na partiiata*, pp. 114–17.

lease of Terpeshev if successful. He was duly elected and became a minister in the first government of the People's Bloc, whereupon he arranged for clemency with the minister of war. The Party line was not to be crossed, however. From prison Terpeshev telegraphed to the minister of war his refusal to accept the pardon or any other favors from "the Fascist regime." He remained imprisoned six more years and was released only in 1937, again by an act of government pardon. By that time, however, the Party line had changed and such favors were permitted.[61]

The purge of the left opposition within the prisons was slow in coming. Long after the leadership of the Party at home was in the hands of the Old Guard, the spirit of the left opposition lingered on among the hundreds of Communists in prison. The Old Guard never tired in its endeavors to penetrate the prison walls and win over to its side the exponents of the left line. From his Gestapo detention, while awaiting trial, Dimitrov kept writing his friends in Bulgaria (a privilege never taken from him while in Nazi hands) hoping to establish contact with the cadres in jail.[62] Later, he used the platform of the Seventh Congress of the Comintern to send greetings to Yonko Panov, a leading left oppositionist member of the Central Committee who was serving a sentence in Bulgaria.[63] What many left oppositionists did not realize at the time, but what they came to realize later, was that their lives were spared thanks to their Bulgarian jailers. Being in prison meant that they could not be recalled to Moscow to give an account of themselves, and possibly perish in the process.

[61] Terpeshev, pp. 102–3, 123–24. His actions gave Terpeshev the distinction of becoming the "dean" of Communists in prison; during his life he remained in jail the sum total of seventeen years. Avram Stoianov, who in 1932 would have become Sofia's Red mayor had it not been for the court abrogations of the Communist seats, on being pardoned refused to leave his jail cell for fear of being branded a renegade by his comrades. He was finally forced out of prison with the aid of the police!

[62] Nedev, p. 215.

[63] For Dimitrov's reference to Panov, see Dimitrov, *Suchineniia*, X, 38. Years later, during the Party Congress of 1948, Panov apologized for his past "sectarianism"; *Peti kongres na BKP*, I, 356–60. Once out of jail, Panov played an active role in the wartime resistance. This helped restore his good standing. He became a general of the Frontier Guards after 1944, and a deputy minister of interior later, only to be purged for "factionalism" in mid-1957.

DIMITROV, THE COMINTERN, AND THE PURGE

It was probably inevitable that Dimitrov's interventions with the NKVD, rather than the tragic ordeals of his compatriots, would capture the attention of the foreign Communists in Moscow. While Bulgarian Communists perished by the hundreds, those few protected by the General Secretary became the quiet sensations of the purge. Because of their Russian-sounding names and their Russian accents, the Bulgarians died in the camps of Kolyma, often unrecognized as such by fellow prisoners. "The Bulgarian émigrés were lucky that Dimitrov was Secretary of the Comintern," wrote Djilas, recalling his conversations in Moscow in 1944. "He saved many of them." [64] Luck was a relative matter. The blood tribute which the Bulgarians paid during Stalin's Great Purge was possibly not as high as that paid by some of the other foreign parties. Yet the "Bulgarian exception" was a myth, kept alive by the Bulgarian purgers who set out to fortify their own careers in the Comintern.

The extermination of a large part of the Bulgarian emigration posed one of the important landmarks in the stormy development of Bulgarian Communism. As far as the exiles were concerned, the intra-Party debate, which had lasted a full decade, was now settled. Probably the majority of those who perished could not even be accused of consistent and conscious "left sectarianism" as defined by Kolarov. But the Stalin purges had their own logic, which the Old Guard could not alter or modify once it initiated the purge of the Bulgarian exiles. As Dimitrov told Tito years later, when speaking of the purges, "it was cutting into good flesh in order to get rid of the bad." [65] No doubt some lost their lives not as Bulgarians as such but as functionaries in the state and military bureaucracies. Personal vendetta, on political grounds or otherwise, must have claimed the lives of others who were merely turned in to the secret police. There were, no doubt, yet others who were arrested and for whom "he [Dimitrov] would have thrust his hand into the fire." [66] Neither the few survivors, nor the managers of the Party archives, would ever know with any degree of certainty who perished when and where and for what reason.

[64] Djilas, p. 34.

[65] *Ibid.*, p. 58.

[66] Dedijer, p. 391.

All this requires that final judgments be put off for the remote future. However, there is one judgment which can be made on the basis of present knowledge. Kolarov's identification of his rivals with Trotskyism, elaborated in public at the height of the Great Purge, constituted a crucial and irretrievable act. He knew that the accusations were untrue. He must have known into what hands his charges would deliver his opponents. How else could his accusations be judged but as an act of vengeance for insults and degradations sustained during a long decade? Iskrov, Lambrev-Rosen, Vasilev-Boiko, and Pavlov-Encho might well have perished in any case, as did so many others for no "guilt" at all. Kolarov's accusations, when they came, meant an almost certain death. This was not the last time that Kolarov's name became associated with a mass purge of the Party. He presided over the liquidation of the "Kostov conspiracy" in 1949, using much the same methods and making much the same insinuations.[67] This was after the death of Dimitrov and just before his own death. In the minds of the Party, Kolarov remained associated as the purger.

Yet, if Kolarov served as Stalin's stooge, in the mid-thirties he was the spokesman for the Old Guard in general and for Dimitrov in particular. In the last decade, official Communist historians have endeavored to draw a subtle distinction between Kolarov and Dimitrov. Small bits and pieces of Dimitrov's oratory have been produced to show that Dimitrov was opposed to "cutting" the bad elements out of the Party and in favor of co-opting healthy elements. He was said to have tried to draw Iskrov to his side, since Iskrov, so the stories go, unlike his younger colleagues, was never opposed to the Comintern directives. These differentiations have been made without any acknowledgment of Iskrov's and his comrades' ultimate ends. Yet, as late as 1948, Dimitrov made sure that the original charges against the left opposition were sustained. "The Fascist dictatorship," Dimitrov told the Fifth Party Congress, ". . . found its best allies in the leaders of the left sectarian faction. What is more, as was subsequently revealed in the USSR in connection with the foreign enemy agencies within the Bolshevik Party and some other Communist Parties, some of these left sectarian leaders were in the service of these agencies." [68]

[67] Much of what we know of the left opposition was indeed made public by Kolarov at the time of the Kostov affair.

[68] Dimitrov, *Political Report Delivered to the V Congress of the BCP*, p. 26.

There remains the problem of the global numbers of those who perished. Ivan Karaivanov, the chief *rapporteur*, puts the total figure of those arrested from the two main groups at more than 600. Of the more than 200 arrested in the Ukraine, the great majority perished. He is more specific on the second group, where, from the more than 400 arrested, he cites the names of a dozen who returned after the war and adds that "at most there were ten more who survived." He writes as of 1952. Popov, we know, did not return until 1954, and although he was one of the very last to return, there were a few more who followed him. Some allowance, therefore, would have to be made for the late survivors. Still the picture would not be changed radically. During the purges themselves, Karaivanov was best placed to know the details, since he worked in the Cadres Department of the Comintern from 1934, the date of his return from China, until 1937. He returned to Bulgaria in November, 1944, and was in a good position to follow developments from there until the break with Tito, even though his identification with the Yugoslavs came soon after his return. Few things could have escaped his attention in the years after the break, since it was his function to cover Bulgarian affairs closely at the height of the conflict. There remains the problem of his trustworthiness. Karaivanov was a sharp antagonist of the Iskrov faction, a fact clearly indicated in all his writings. He could not therefore be suspected of sympathies toward the leftist opposition. Moreover, after the break of Tito with the Cominform, Karaivanov remained closely attached (he may well have been the architect of this specific approach) to the Yugoslav line of treating Dimitrov as a friend, somewhat pathetic but always consistent in his favorable disposition toward Tito and Yugoslavia. This stand was well reflected in Karaivanov's writings, where he devoted more space to Dimitrov's good deeds in saving some of the purged than to the victims themselves. One could speculate on the motives of the Yugoslavs in maintaining Dimitrov as their friend. Furthermore, there was no accident in the fact that Karaivanov wrote on the purge in some detail only in the Bulgarian exile paper in Yugoslavia, which was clearly directed at the Chervenkov regime, and which had but a small circulation. The stories he told his Yugoslav friends, which eventually found their way to the West, pertained only to the cases in which Dimitrov intervened in order to save his compatriots. These facts would in general confirm Karaivanov's reliability. Blagoi Popov, the only other source of information on the number of

Bulgarian émigrés involved in the purge, estimated those who perished at 400.[69] Having himself been arrested in 1937, Popov had no precise knowledge on the matter. In sum, so long as no further information is supplied, the Bulgarian blood tribute to the Great Purge can be accounted as anywhere between 400 and 600.

At the time of the purge and for many years thereafter, the Communist cadres at home and the families of the victims were kept ignorant of events. Some information did filter in, thanks to the two-way traffic between Moscow and Bulgaria which Party functionaries maintained well into the war. Furthermore, the Bulgarian police, who knew a great deal on developments within the emigration in the Soviet Union thanks to their very efficient inquisition methods put to work on Communist returnees, made sure that their secrets were shared, even if only by spreading rumors. The defection of F. F. Razkolnikov, the Soviet minister to Bulgaria, his subsequent public attacks on Stalin, and his ultimate death were widely publicized in the Bulgarian press, and could not but make an impact on the Communist rank and file, even though the affair was not directly connected with the Bulgarian émigrés in Russia. Razkolnikov was a popular figure in Russophile and left circles in Sofia ever since assuming the post as the first Soviet minister to Bulgaria in November, 1934. He was admired by the Communists, and during the first years of his tenure, at least, assisted the Party with advice and funds. In April, 1938, upon being recalled to Moscow, Razkolnikov chose to go to France. His criticism of the Stalin tyranny was widely publicized in Bulgarian newspapers, as was his mysterious death in September, 1939.[70] How many of these scattered pieces of news and information were in fact believed by the Russian-loving Bulgarian Communists was, of course, another matter altogether.

[69] Popov to author, interview, Sofia, September 6, 1966. When pressed on the matter, Communist officials in a position to know refused to supply their estimates. They claimed that a figure of 400 constitutes an exaggeration. Their interestedness makes them suspect.

[70] On Razkolnikov's success with Bulgarian Russophiles, see Todorov, *Balkan Firebrand*, p. 274. A man of considerable literary talents, Razkolnikov became a legendary figure during the October Revolution with his exploits as a Bolshevik naval commander in the Baltic and Caspian seas. Sofia was his last post in a colorful diplomatic career spreading from Afghanistan to Estonia and Denmark. In his last years in Bulgaria he was already under the surveillance of Yezhov's secret agents. In July and August, 1939, he issued his open attacks on the Soviet

Only after the return of the surviving exiles at the end of the war did the fate of the emigration become an acute issue.[71] Yet the matter was classified as a state secret. In time monetary compensations were made to the victims' families, but except for a few individual posthumous rehabilitations in the sixties, the Party chose not to make public revelations. There was one final gruesome note to the tragedy. Having established itself in power, the Party was asked by its Soviet masters to reimburse the Soviet government for the costs sustained through the years in maintaining the Bulgarian Communist emigration in the Soviet Union.[72]

For the long run, the impact of the massacre on the fortunes of the Bulgarian Communist Party is not easily assessable. In terms of intellectual talents, organizational abilities, and sheer militancy, the loss was enormous. Even at the height of anti-Communist repressions during the wartime resistance, the intellectual elite of the Party in Bulgaria was preserved. The Boris regime persecuted and killed only those Communists who either conspired against it actively or fought with arms in hand. One of the ironies of the purge was that it struck shortly before the Party was to find itself in dire need of cadres with precisely the insurrectionary talents that the left opposition possessed in such abundance. The purge left an unhealed wound on the body of Bulgarian Communism which was to break open again during the Sovietization campaign. The gap left within the Party ranks was only partly filled by the return of the émigré survivors soon after September, 1944.[73]

On the ruins of the emigration, those Bulgarians in Moscow who survived the purge went on to build or restore their own personal

---

leadership. He was rehabilitated at the end of 1963, "the only defector to have received this extraordinary honour." On his rehabilitation and life, see *Voprosy Istorii*, No. 12 (Moscow, 1963), pp. 90–94; *Rabotnichesko delo*, January 30, 1964; Conquest, pp. 456–57; Fischer, *Men and Politics*, pp. 495–96.

[71] Atanasov, *Pokhodut na zapad*, p. 24.

[72] The story is related by Karaivanov in *Glas na bulgarite v Yugoslaviia*, February 12, 1952. The Soviet request was made to Petko Kunin, who was in charge of Party economic affairs. Kunin replied that the matter was one for the Bulgarian government to consider. According to Karaivanov, Kunin's purge a few years later was due to his non-cooperation on this very issue. It is not clear (nor is it materially important) whether payments were eventually made.

[73] In the case of some, alas, only in order to pay the ultimate price in Bulgaria's own purges in the late forties, such as Manol Sakelarov, who returned after

careers. Dimitrov, the general secretary of the Comintern from 1935 until the dissolution of that organization in 1943, held the central position. Outwardly this station was the culmination of his life as a revolutionary. A self-made man, and lacking the advantages of formal education and academic training that Kolarov possessed, Dimitrov was one of the few foreigners to attain prominence of the first rank in the Soviet state. Yet his illustrious position was drained of real content from the first. In Stalin's kingdom no man was sovereign, least of all the man in charge of world Communism. Even though Dimitrov maintained intimate relations with Stalin throughout his career, he did what he was told, at the same time giving a non-Russian label to what was a thoroughly Russian instrument. Above and beyond Manuilski, who was Stalin's known man in the Comintern, Dimitrov was never left without an imposed entourage of "ideological advisers" who reported his words and edited his writings. Although the persons in this personal cabinet changed, the institution remained. The first to fill the post of an "adviser" was the young Marxist philosopher, G. F. Alexandrov, who later went on to become minister of culture under Malenkov.[74] Several more followed. The last to serve as Dimitrov's political watchdog was Mirov (a former secretary of Trotsky and Zinoviev), who stayed with him throughout the war and followed him to Sofia after Dimitrov returned to Bulgaria in 1945. Afflicted with personal misfortunes and bad health, Dimitrov was a declining man long before he reappeared on the Bulgarian scene.[75] His assumption of the premiership in Sofia revived but did not restore his past vigor. Toward the late thirties and during the war, he

---

eighteen years in Soviet exile, or Lulcho Chervenkov (not to be confused with the future dictator), who represented the Party at the Third Congress of the Comintern and headed the Sofia Fatherland Front organization during the war, or Vasil Markov, who in the 1920s was active in Communist affairs in Germany and Austria, to mention only a few.

[74] In 1939 Alexandrov succeeded Zhdanov as head of the Agitprop Department, a position he lost to Suslov in 1947. He became minister of culture in March, 1954, but was attacked and disgraced right after Malenkov's downfall.

[75] Dimitrov's first wife committed suicide soon after his arrest by the Gestapo. Dimitrov married a woman of German-Sudeten origin after his return to Moscow. In 1935 he had a son, an only child, who died in 1943 in Kuibyshev. There are interesting eyewitness reports on Dimitrov and Kolarov in Castro Delgado, pp. 17, 29–30, 212, and for the period 1944–45, pp. 305–8. On Kolarov in Moscow, see Gilin, p. 66; Djilas, pp. 34–35.

retained interest in the Bulgarian Party, even though the day-by-day affairs were left to the heavy-handed and spiteful Kolarov.

Having escaped the purge, Chervenkov-Vladimirov went on to carve a high-ranking career in the Comintern hierarchy. A compulsive imitator of Stalin's manners, he was a man of considerable theoretical-doctrinal abilities. He was first employed in the Agitprop Department of the Comintern under Bedrich Geminder (known in Moscow as Friedrich and later executed in Czechoslovakia together with Rudolf Slansky). Following the purge of Kirsanova (Yaroslavski's wife), Chervenkov became the director of the Lenin School (1937–38). From 1938 until the outbreak of the German-Soviet war he was director of all the Comintern schools, as well as the head of the Department of Education in the Propaganda Section of the ECCI. During the war he was in charge of the clandestine radio broadcasts beamed to Bulgaria.

From 1937 until the dissolution of the Comintern, the Cadres Department was in the hands of Georgi Damianov (alias Belov in the Comintern). This assignment was given to him following his return from Bulgaria, where together with Dimitrov-Marek he carried out the purge of the home Party. After 1935, Vladimir Poptomov, the old Macedonian revolutionary turned Communist, worked with Wilhelm Pieck in the Balkan Section. Stela Blagoeva, the daughter of the late leader of the "narrows," was in charge of the Latin Section in the Cadres Department. Also working with the Latin Communist parties in varying capacities was Stepanov-Minev, freshly arrived from the Spanish Civil War.[76]

[76] On Damianov-Belov's life, see Damianov, pp. 7–27; on Poptomov, see the biography written by Bitsin and Yurukov; on Blagoeva, see *Diplomaticheski slovar*, I, 190, and Castro Delgado, pp. 13–17; Stepanov-Minev will be dealt with in the section dealing with the Spanish Civil War.

CHAPTER FOUR

COMMUNISM AND THE POPULAR FRONT

THE INNER LOGIC of the purge was rooted in the determination of the Old Guard to eject its rivals and restore itself to a position of unchallenged dominance. Outwardly, the purge was justified by the contention that only the old cadres could carry out a successful campaign aimed at creating a popular front movement. This claim was never verified because the leaders of the left opposition were not permitted to demonstrate whether or not they were capable of making an adjustment to the new requirements put forward by the Comintern.

In large measure, the purge overlapped with the popular front effort. The search for allies outside the Communist camp was undertaken while the internal Party struggles went on. This did not enhance the credibility of the Party in the eyes of potential and prospective political partners. Furthermore, a complicated reorganization of the Communist Party structure intervened in the process. Finally, while these contradictory trends developed, the regime increased its anti-Communist repressions.

ANTI-COMMUNIST REPRESSIONS

The May, 1934, coup was aimed at parliamentarism. Bolshevism was also an issue, although a secondary one. Whatever complaints the conspirators had against the regime of the People's Bloc, Mushanov could not be accused of having treated the Communists softly. To the

Communists the immediate effect of the coup was expressed in the abolition of the Workers' Party, the legally operated front of the Communist Party, and in the intensification of the legal and extralegal struggle against individual Communists. In the months immediately following the coup, anti-Communist repressions were greatly increased. At the end of August, official Comintern sources estimated the number of those arrested during the same month at more than 500. Among the more prominent Communists arrested in Sofia were Zhak Natan, a Marxist economic historian, and Boris Bogdanov, a noted Communist functionary; in the town of Plovdiv alone, 130 workers and soldiers were arrested for having undertaken pro-Communist propaganda. Despite this, the Communist *Rabotnicheski vestnik* was reported appearing "more punctually" than ever before.[1] By the end of 1934, the Comintern estimated the total number of those arrested since the coup at 2,000, of whom the majority were Communists.[2] In February, 1935, the figure was revised upwards to 2,200, with twenty-two "revolutionary leaders murdered" and seven anti-Fascist soldiers executed.[3] On the first anniversary of the coup, Kolarov put at forty-four the number of Communists and anti-Fascists murdered during the previous year. According to him, a committee known as the "Friends of the Bulgarian People" had been formed in Paris whose function it was to tell the world of the anti-Communist terror in Bulgaria. The same committee organized legal help for those being tried in Bulgaria.[4] On May 9, 1935, Yordan Liutibrodski, a communist district organizer, was hanged. On June 25, 1935, Aleksandur Voikov, a district secretary of the Communist youth organization in Sofia, was also hanged.[5] Large-scale repressions continued through 1936. At the beginning of that year, Communist circles in Bulgaria estimated the total number of political prisoners in the country at 2,500. The same sources made public a letter signed by

[1] D. Vlachov, "The Situation in Bulgaria," *Inprecorr*, August 31, 1934, p. 1208.

[2] D. Vlachov, "The Situation in Bulgaria," *Inprecorr*, December 15, 1934, pp. 1692–93.

[3] D. Vlachov, "Scene-Shifting in the Military Fascist Dictatorship in Bulgaria," *Inprecorr*, February 2, 1935, pp. 121–22.

[4] V. Kolarov, "Reply to the Base Provocation of the Sofia Hangmen," *Inprecorr*, May 18, 1935, pp. 569–70.

[5] *Istoriia na Bulgariia*, pp. 678–79; see also Dimitrov, *Suchineniia*, X, 167–68.

thirty political prisoners from the prison house in Shumen, which gave some idea of the cruel reality under which Bulgarian prisoners lived:

Our long stay in prison and the deadly regime under which we have been compelled to live have drained our strength and destroyed our health. Many of us suffer from tuberculosis, acute rheumatism, pleurisy, and other diseases . . . it will not be years but months before we are all dead in this damp hole. . . . We do not want to die.[6]

On November 16, 1936, in the town of Stara Zagora a large-scale Communist trial opened. Of the ten death sentences, four were commuted to life imprisonment on the grounds that they had been issued against minors. The International Juridical Association sent a lawyer from England, but he was not allowed to take part in the trial and was eventually evicted from Bulgaria.[7] In January, 1937, a Communist source from Sofia stated that thirty Communist prisoners had been suffering "living death" in Bulgarian jails ever since 1924.[8] In the middle of 1937, the Bulgarian section of the International Red Aid compiled a statistical report on the state of political prisoners in Bulgarian jails. Their number was estimated at 1,500, among whom were fifteen editors, five former deputies, three writers, and many lawyers. The report also contained a vivid description of the prevailing conditions in the prisons. Political prisoners were worse off than the criminals.[9]

ORGANIZATIONAL DUPLICATION AND PARTY MEMBERSHIP

In the midst of repressions, the Party held its Sixth Plenum in February, 1936. While the principal undertaking of the Plenum was to give a retroactive approval to the expulsion of the leftist leaders, the organizational structure of the Party received close attention.[10]

---

[6] *Rabotnichesko delo*, February 15, 1936, cited in *Rabotnichesko delo, izbrani statii i materiali, 1927–1944*, pp. 316–18. The latter is a collection of articles published in the organ of the Workers' Party.

[7] Stepan, "The Death Sentences in Bulgaria," *Inprecorr*, January 2, 1937, p. 19.

[8] Stepan, "The Struggle for the Amnesty in Bulgaria," *Inprecorr*, January 30, 1937, p. 98.

[9] Boris Ivanov, "The Situation of the Political Prisoners in Bulgaria," *Inprecorr*, July 24, 1937, p. 711.

[10] The following discussion on the organizational restructuring of the Party is based on three major studies, all devoted to the subject: *Novo vreme*, November,

In the years 1927–34, there were two Communist organizations in
being, the illegal Communist Party, which had been outlawed since
1924, and the Workers' Party, created in 1927 as a legally constituted
Communist front. Throughout the period, real power remained in the
hands of the leaders of the illegal Communist Party. Some leading
cadres were members of both organizations. The rank and file, however,
split between the two, leading a parallel but separate organizational
life. Within the smaller Communist Party, membership requirements
were stricter and discipline tighter. On the other hand, membership in
the Workers' Party grew rapidly, inevitably including many nominal
Communists. While the dominance of the left opposition lasted, it was
natural that the young militants belonged to the Communist Party, while
the older cadres tended to be relegated to the Workers' Party.

On September 8, 1934, several months after the May *putsch*, the
Politburo, still in the hands of the left opposition, decided to dissolve the
Workers' Party. On the surface, the decision appeared logical enough.
The Workers' Party was of significance only so long as it could operate
in the open. Since the regime established after the May *putsch* banned
all political parties, there seemed little sense in maintaining two parallel
Communist structures, both underground. There was, however, a more
compelling reason for the decision. In the fall of 1934 the left opposition
in Bulgaria was already being challenged by the Old Guard in Moscow.
Since the Workers' Party included many of Dimitrov's protégés, it was
feared that it might be used as an instrument against the left opposition.
That group therefore hastened to enforce the decision of September 8.
The more reliable militants from the Workers' Party were co-opted into
the Communist Party. The majority were told to join various antigovernment organizations. In effect they were suspended. Many traveled their
own ways and gradually left the Communist fold. Only later were great
efforts made to reclaim the former members of the Workers' Party, a
process which lasted a long while and proved only partly successful.

The maneuver was not lost on the people in Moscow. The emissaries who were dispatched to Bulgaria to carry out the purge were instructed in no uncertain terms to restore the Workers' Party as soon as

---

1957, pp. 69–80; *IIIBKP*, VIII (1961), 93–139; *ibid.*, XX (1969), 455–502. The
1969 study reproduces extensive texts from the correspondence carried out between
the Buro-in-Exile and the ECCI on the one hand, and the Party Politburo in
Bulgaria on the other, during the period 1934–40.

possible. Much of Dimitrov-Marek's stay in the country was devoted to this particular task. To re-create the Workers' Party as rapidly as possible, the admission requirements for membership were relaxed. The introduction of the popular front line, it was thought, would also be helped if the Workers' Party were restored, despite the extralegal tactics that would have to be followed in view of the Party's illegal existence. Moreover, there were practical problems of immediate importance to be considered. The 1924 law banning the Communist Party provided extremely heavy penalties, up to fifteen years in prison for its members. On the other hand, the June, 1934, law which outlawed all political parties (including the Workers' Party) carried lighter penalties of up to three years in prison. This meant that if a Communist formally belonging to the Workers' Party were to be caught, his sentence would be much lighter than if he were arrested as a member of the Communist Party.

The switch, when made, caused great confusion. Some had already become full-fledged members of the illegal Communist Party. Most, however, were left "hanging in air," disconnected from both the Workers' Party and the Communist Party. Thus the first task of the new leadership was to repair the damage by reestablishing contact with the "lost" membership. In view of the mounting anti-Communist campaign and the insecurity and dangers involved in underground operations, this task proved most difficult.

Following the Sixth Plenum the dual organizations were restored, with both parties operating illegally. In tactical matters, the Workers' Party continued to be subordinated to the leadership of the Communist Party. Within leading Communist Party circles, however, matters concerning the organizational structure of the Communist movement were debated throughout 1936. No sooner was the Plenum over than opinions favoring the dissolution of the Communist Party and the retention of the Workers' Party as the sole organizational framework of the movement were expressed with ever growing insistence. It was reasoned that, in order to be successful in carrying out the objectives of the popular front, Bulgarian Communism needed an organizational form of mass appeal. The Workers' Party had such an appeal, as the successes of the 1931–32 elections had shown. By submerging the Communist Party, it was hoped to attract progressive elements that would be willing to collaborate with Bulgarian labor but not with Bulgarian Communism.

The chief exponent of a merger of the Communist Party with the

Workers' Party was Dimitrov-Marek. His views were pressed with vigor after his return to Moscow in 1937. In October of the same year, the entire matter was brought to the attention of the Secretariat of the ECCI. The merger proposal found an easy majority. However, the idea was opposed by Dimitrov and his word proved decisive. His contention was that Bulgaria was moving in the direction of a political liberalization that might bring about the restoration of all political parties. If this were to happen, he argued, the Workers' Party would be well suited to assume its role and make a meaningful contribution. If, however, the illegal Communist Party were to be merged with the Workers' Party, the image of the latter might become impaired in the eyes of the non-Communist groupings with which it was hoped a popular front could be established. The proposed merger was thus turned down. At this point the ECCI failed to take a clear stand on how the Bulgarian Communists were to reorganize their affairs.

For the time being, because of developments in Bulgaria, all further considerations toward reorganization were suspended. Sometime after the departure of Dimitrov-Marek to Moscow, the composition of the leadership of the Communist Party elected at the Sixth Plenum became known to the police. This discovery was preceded by the arrest of several leading Communists. Fearful that everybody of importance might be arrested, it was decided to dissolve the Central Committee. The leadership of the Party was now assumed by an emergency Secretariat composed of three persons, of whom Dobri Terpeshev was the senior. On its part, working on the assumption that the functionaries of the intermediary Party apparatus had also become known to the police, the new Secretariat decided to reorganize the district and local Party organizations by cutting off contact with the old functionaries and starting afresh. The effect of this decision, coming as it did at a moment when anti-Communist repressions reached a new peak, could not but lead to most unfortunate results as far as Party organization was concerned. Many local functionaries, including secretaries of intermediary organizations who escaped arrest, suddenly found themselves abandoned and without any contact with the center. The same was true of the rank-and-file membership. For them, with much more limited knowledge of the underground workings of the Party, the reestablishment of contacts proved difficult if not impossible. Many dropped out of active participation altogether and were in many cases not able to restore their Party connections before 1940, at which time, for reasons to be pointed out later, the pressure on the Party was slightly relaxed.

Throughout 1938–39 the debate between Moscow and the home Party over structural matters continued. Gradually all concerned realized that the duplication was inefficient and that some type of merger was inevitable. The prevailing opinion within the Central Committee was that the fusion should take place, although not in the full sense of the term. Maybe deep in their hearts the leaders of the Communist Party could not help but agree with the thesis of their formal enemies from the left opposition to the effect that the functionaries of the Workers' Party could not be fully trusted, in view of their insufficient preparedness in matters involving Marxist-Leninist orthodoxy. In any case, the final decision was based on a compromise. In the future, only the Workers' Party would be entitled to organize members. At the same time, the central and intermediary apparatus of the Communist Party would be preserved in order to serve as a "school for Communism." The newly created situation therefore presented the following picture: both the Workers' Party and the Communist Party would continue to maintain separate Central Committees as well as Party committees on the district and local levels. Primary organizations, on the other hand, would be maintained exclusively by the Workers' Party. In this way, it was thought the Communist Party would be in a position to supervise the activities and control the actions of all the organs under the jurisdiction of the Workers' Party. Control it did. Throughout 1939, the dual organizational principle continued to be maintained much as before. This is the way Terpeshev described the organizational situation in a letter addressed to the Buro-in-Exile from Paris on March 1, 1939:

Both parties taken together constitute the Communist movement in the country. The difference between the two arises from the division of labor which has been imposed on them in view of the particular conditions under which operations must be carried out at this moment. The Communist Party remains the vanguard of the Bulgarian proletariat. The Communist Party is not being dissolved. Its new organizational structure has been tailored to fit the present requirements. The main objective of the Communist Party remains its determination to serve as a "school for cadres."

Frictions between the leaders of the two parallel organizations mounted. At a time when all energies were to be concentrated on the popular front effort, the Bulgarian Communist leadership remained occupied largely with operational matters. Repeatedly, functionaries from the Communist Party attempted to interfere with the activities of the Workers' Party. Disputes of this nature continued unresolved for long periods of time, despite the fact that in several cases leading functionaries were members of the Central Committees of both parties.

Sometime in 1939, the Buro-in-Exile answered Terpeshev's letter of March 1 in the form of a directive that noted the unfortunate features of the dual organizational structure and warned that as long as the two organizations continued to be maintained separately there would continue to be manifestations of "competition" between them. The directive presumably insisted on the complete and immediate fusion of the Communist Party with the Workers' Party. The fusion was finally effected in 1940. After a publishing history of forty years, *Rabotnicheski vestnik*, which in the previous decade had served as the organ of the underground Communist Party, was discontinued. *Rabotnichesko delo*, the Workers' Party organ published since 1927, now became the only official publication of the Party.

The failure to achieve timely reorganization, and the organizational dislocations caused by police interference, combined to produce confusion and weakness at a critical point. As late as February, 1939, Anton Ivanov (writing under the Party name of Bogdanov), in a letter from Paris addressed to the Buro-in-Exile in Moscow, observed that "organizationally, we remain very weak, primarily because we have failed to carry out the reorganization of the Party." When the merger was finally realized, the principal reason behind the determination to reorganize, namely, the desire to appear more acceptable to potential popular front allies, had already lapsed since, with the signing of the Russo-German treaty, the popular front era had come to an end.

Internally, there was more to the procrastination than mere failure of organizational ability. Bulgarian Communists, with their long and hard schooling in Bolshevik orthodoxy, with years spent in Bulgarian prisons, and with long memories of repression and retaliation, were finding it difficult to exhibit the necessary flexibility required in carrying out tactical shifts.

Endless confusion over organizational matters, coupled with the adverse effects of illegality, affected total membership in the most profound manner. Within a decade, membership shrank fivefold. In 1932–

33, there were over thirty thousand organized Communists (27,078 in the Workers' Party as of 1932, and 3,732 in the Communist Party as of 1933). Toward the end of 1934, following the May coup and the dissolution of the Workers' Party, membership dropped to a low of 4,000. The situation improved somewhat after the reestablishment of the Workers' Party. In October, 1936, total membership reached 7,252 (3,857 in the Workers' Party and 3,395 in the Communist Party). In the following few years it again declined. In the middle of 1940, following the merger, there was a sum total of 6,890 organized Communists.[11] The drastic decline in membership did not indicate a decline in the appeals of Communism. Rather, the loss was to be attributed to the hardships of illegality, and in large measure to the failure on the part of the Party's high command to set clear organizational policies. Comparatively, the Communist-sponsored youth organization (RMS) did better. At the end of 1940 it claimed a total membership of 15,000.[12]

Endeavors to increase the number of women in the Party were never very successful. For those in charge of cadre policies, the failure was particularly painful considering the fact that 70–80 percent of the industrial labor force in the main branches of industry (textiles and tobacco) were women. No absolute figures on women's affiliation with the Party are available. Efforts to recruit women were greatly intensified in the late thirties, not without success. By the summer of 1940, women accounted for 20 percent of the Party membership in Sofia, 30 percent in Plovdiv, and 15 percent in Sliven, the three major industrial centers in the country.[13]

Despite these efforts, the Party remained largely nonproletarian in its social composition. Industrial workers accounted for 10.2 percent of the membership in 1919 and 11 percent in 1935. The overwhelming majority of Party members were peasants, followed closely by self-employed town dwellers and intelligentsia. A telling sample of a Communist Party with a large peasant content is provided by the Party organization in the district of Plovdiv. In 1935 there were 92 Party cells

[11] Figures for 1934, 1936, and 1940 are based on *IIIBKP*, VIII (1961), 96, 119, 135, respectively.

[12] *Ibid.*, p. 138.

[13] *Ibid.*

in the district, 37 in the city proper and 55 in the villages of the district; the corresponding membership figures were 169 and 308 respectively. Of a total of 477 Party members in the district as a whole, 81 were industrial workers, or double the national average. Yet Plovdiv was the major center for the tobacco industry in the country.[14] While in narrow Marxist terms the social composition of the Party was looked upon as a major weakness, in nondoctrinal political terms it was precisely the appeal to the peasants which made the Party a formidable force in an overwhelmingly peasant country.

TRADE UNIONISM

One of the first aims of the Georgiev government was to restore "order" within the trade-union movement. Soon after it came to power, the government expressed its determination to take over the existing trade-union organizations, the Communist-sponsored Nezavisimi rabotnicheski profesionalni suiuzi, or NRPS (Independent Labor Trade Unions), as well as the trade unions supported by the Social Democratic Party. These organizations were denied legal existence, along with the dissolved political parties, as early as June, 1934.[15] During the summer of the same year, the first preliminary steps were taken in the direction of converting the trade-union movement into a state-controlled syndicate. In September, a government decree directed the establishment of state trade unions with compulsory affiliation for both workers and professionals. This directive was further elaborated and formalized in a decree-law of January 11, 1935, which established the various trade unions later united within the state-controlled Bulgarski rabotnicheski suiuz, or BRS (Bulgarian Workers' Union). The actual establishment of the unions was undertaken by the short-lived transitional govern-

[14] *Ibid.*, p. 97. The 1919 figures are from Rothschild, p. 95. Even in 1947 the Bulgarian Party figured as the least "industrial" (except for the Albanian) in its social composition as compared to all other East European parties; its "middle-class" contingent was the largest; on this and more comparative statistics, see Burks, pp. 35, 52.

[15] There is a vast literature on the trade-union movement relevant to the interwar period. Here is a sample of the most important works. Kodzheikov *et al.*, *Rovoliutsionnoto profsuiuzno dvizhenie v Bulgariia*, is a major study; also important are his memoirs (*Rozhdenie i suzizhdane*) and his *Materiali* . . .; another important author on the same subject is Asen Boiadzhiev (for his works, see the bibliography at the end of this book). Much of what follows here is based on Kodzheikov *et al.*

ments that followed the downfall of the Kimon Georgiev cabinet. The state readily gave material support to its trade unions. Former syndicalists, trade-union functionaries from Tsankov's movement, and opportunists of all kinds were attracted by the state and were given high positions in the new bureaucracy. The BRS held its first congress in October, 1935, and beginning with 1936 started publishing an official organ under the name of *Trud*.[16]

Following the May coup, the Communist-sponsored NRPS was ordered underground. Deterioration and decline resulted. The influence of the NRPS before the coup was never great. In 1932–33 it numbered some 10,000 members. By 1935 their number had shrunk to the insignificant total of 1,200.[17] The semi-insurrectionary tactics pursued by the leadership of the Communist Party found their reflection in the trade-union movement. The main effort of the NRPS before the coup was directed against its Social Democratic counterpart. Demonstrative actions rather than economic strikes dominated the period before as well as immediately after May, 1934. Toward the end of 1933, Planinski, the representative of the Party at the Thirteenth Plenum of the Comintern, stated with great satisfaction that "the Communist Party and the revolutionary unions [NRPS] have delivered a decisive blow at the social fascists and practically squeezed them out from the privately owned enterprises and the leadership of strikes." [18] Planinski went on to illustrate the type of strikes in which the NRPS found itself involved:

For example, the miners of the Hadjiliper and Chumerskav mines marched to the city where the management is located, and in the course of twenty days took possession of the building and carried on the struggle for payment of back wages to the amount of 1,200,000 leva. They succeeded in getting half of the sum paid up.

If anything, the militancy of the underground NRPS sharpened following the coup. In March, 1935, *Inprecorr*, the organ of the Comintern, stated that "the revolutionary struggle of the masses in Bulgaria is going on from strength to strength." It went on to report on the methods used during strike demonstrations: "On January 26 [1935] a

[16] Kodzheikov *et al.*, pp. 218–20, includes a good description of the organization and workings of the BRS.

[17] *Ibid.*, p. 221.

[18] "The XIII Plenum of the Executive Committee of the Communist International —Comrade Planinski (Bulgaria)," *Inprecorr*, March 5, 1934, pp. 396–97.

number of Communists forced their way into a factory in the neigh-
borhood of Sofia, bound the watchman, cut the telephone wires, addressed the workers and disappeared after they had finished their
meeting." [19]

At the same time, the government was making progress with its
labor policy. Despite opposition, the state-sponsored BRS expanded.

The organizations of the BRS were becoming more numerous as well as
stronger [reports Kodzheikov, whose intention was not to overstate the case
for the government]. Substantial labor masses joined in. Hundreds of paid
agitators and organizers, who received the active assistance of factory owners
and employees, went on organizing meetings and conferences in which they
tried repeatedly to impress on the workers fascist "theories" of "compatibility" between the interests of the workers and the bosses, and of "elimination" of the conflict between labor and capital through mediation by the
state syndicates.[20]

To emphasize the "compatibility" between labor and capital, the
state was ready to go a long way, including the adoption of some newly
introduced Nazi techniques.

On the First of May [1936] the capital and some other cities of Bulgaria
[wrote Kolarov] saw an unforgettable picture: the priests in their elaborate
religious vestments "blessed" the red banners; generals and lieutenants
figured as "god-fathers"; military bands accompanied the "First of May"
demonstrations; royal adjutants, high military officers and the government
ministers in frockcoats and silk hats marched in the demonstrations.[21]

Persuasion, propaganda, and police measures were all used together
in order to achieve the complete domination of organized labor. The
NRPS found itself more and more isolated as a result. During the period
from the middle of 1934 to the fall of 1935, there were, all told, 130
small-scale strikes involving a total of 5,745 workers. Of these strikes,
45 were political and only 85 economic; 42 were organized, while the
remaining were spontaneous.[22]

[19] D. Vlachov, "The Political Situation in Bulgaria," *Inprecorr*, March 2, 1935,
pp. 257–58.

[20] Kodzheikov *et al.*, p. 222.

[21] V. Kolarov, "How the Fascists 'Buried' the Class Struggle in Bulgaria," *Communist International*, August, 1936, pp. 993–1003.

[22] Kodzheikov *et al.*, p. 223.

In the months following the Seventh Congress of the Comintern, the Party line in relation to trade unionism changed slightly. A certain amount of infiltration into the BRS took place, although, as a rule, this was done on individual initiative. Even after the purge of the left opposition leadership was completed, the Party organ continued to urge that Communist workers in factories "seize upon every manifestation of dissatisfaction and use every pretext in order to bring the struggle into the open." [23] In this respect the Sixth Plenum (February–March, 1936) did not introduce any changes. The resolution it adopted on trade unionism continued to maintain that "strikes are of the greatest importance even if the results they bring are minimal." [24] No steps were taken to dissolve the Communist unions. Powerless vis-à-vis the state, the Party was still finding itself hanging on to the old methods instead of relaxing its tactics in an attempt to gain the confidence of those elements it required in order to establish a popular front. The state-sponsored BRS was termed a "serious danger" which Party members were urged to continue to fight "with all their might." The only mention of the popular front remained hidden between the lines of paragraph seven of the resolution, which stated that "in places where the state-sponsored syndicates appear active . . . the Communists should work together with Social Democrats, Agrarians, Anarchists, etc." [25] Such cooperation was in fact achieved on several occasions, although it remained restricted to the local level. Overtures made by the Central Committee of the NRPS to the centers of the trade unions sponsored by the Social Democrats and others, before as well as after the Sixth Plenum, remained unanswered.

The tactical approach started to change in the spring and summer of 1936. Following the Sixth Plenum, the new leadership of the Party decided to reverse the tactics of noncooperation with the state-sponsored BRS and urged Communist trade unionists to enter the BRS and infiltrate its apparatus. Finally, in the summer of that year, the Party decided to dissolve the NRPS altogether. In its place, the Politburo of the Workers' Party created a Central Syndicate Commission composed of leading Communist trade unionists such as Nacho Ivanov (a member of the

[23] *Rabotnichesko delo*, December 10, 1935, cited in *Rabotnichesko delo, izbrani statii i materiali, 1927–1944*, pp. 262–65.

[24] *BKP v rezoliutsii i resheniia*, p. 340.

[25] *Ibid.*, p. 341.

Central Committee), Todor Prakhov (who was to become a Politburo member in the period after 1944), Yordan Milev, Boris Blagoev, Nikola Penev, Dragoi Kodzheikov, and others.

The publication of *Edinstvo*, the organ of the NRPS, was discontinued. Efforts were gradually directed at subverting the state-run bureaucracy. Occasionally such methods proved successful, thanks primarily to the greater experience of Communist functionaries in matters concerning trade unionism than that of officially appointed state functionaries. Communists were called upon to take up popular causes, such as the organization of protest actions against unpopular regulations dictated by the BRS. These were the days of what later became known as the "protest delegation movement," of which the Communists were particularly proud. The "movement" made sure that grievances expressed by workers were heard and that appropriate protests were delivered to the official authorities. Attempts were made to capitalize on the turmoil which the strike movement, on the increase in 1936, generated. The largest strike of the year was that of the tobacco workers which broke out in May and involved anywhere between 18,000 and 25,000 workers. Although Communists undoubtedly played a major role in the initial stages of the strike, they were unable to maintain their leadership because of the intervention of the BRS, which was able to negotiate a compromise settlement involving a wage increase of 12 percent. To a greater or lesser degree, Communists participated in most of the other strikes of the period, despite penalties of up to three years in prison decreed against instigators of strikes.

Local cooperation between Communist and Socialist trade unionists was in fact achieved in various localities. In August, 1936, for example, representatives of both parties participated jointly in a local trade-union conference held in Sofia; a joint committee was selected that was empowered to deal with labor problems involving local disputes. In January, 1937, in Sofia, a joint session attended by Communist, Socialist, Agrarian, and Anarchist trade-union representatives "established permanent contact" among the various elements and called on the workers to establish "unity committees in defense of their rights." [26] Such collaboration remained limited, however, partly because of the hardships

[26] B. Ivanov, "Revival of the Strike Movement in Bulgaria," *Inprecorr*, April 17, 1937, p. 421.

involved in illegal activity and partly because no broad political agreement among the various formations had been reached.

UNITED FRONT APPEALS

The attainment of an agreement for political cooperation among the various groups was, at least after 1936, the major preoccupation of the Party. Having done much to antagonize other political groups during the early thirties, Bulgarian Communists now found themselves handicapped.

The Party's point of departure, going as far back as early 1930, had been that, among all non-Communist political formations in the country, no differences existed so far as fundamentals were concerned.[27] Following the 1931 elections, the Agrarian Union was considered "the social base for the Fascist dictatorship." [28] This pronouncement was made on the morrow of one of the freest elections Bulgaria had ever seen. The Social Democrats, as well as the Agrarian Union "with all its wings," were repeatedly accused during the People's Bloc government (which the Party invariably called "the government of the anti-people's bloc") of having "given their support to the regime along with all other middle-class parties." [29] After the expulsion of the Communist parliamentary group from the Subranie, the Agrarian Union was pointed out as "the main enemy" of the Party and was accused of being the vanguard of the Fascist counterrevolution in Bulgaria. In its peasant policy, the Party continued to use the same old militant slogans it used among the workers.

Of the greatest importance at the present moment [wrote the Party organ in January, 1934] are such forms of peasant mass struggle as the organization of mass peasant resistance, the expulsion of the tax collectors from the village limits, the seizure of church lands as well as large private and state holdings including pastures and forests.[30]

[27] From a Party manifesto of February 17, 1930, cited in *Novo vreme*, November, 1959, p. 105.

[28] *Komunistichesko zname*, July, 1931, cited in *Novo vreme*, November, 1959, pp. 105–6.

[29] From a Party leaflet reproduced in *Nelegalni pozivi na BKP*, pp. 101–3.

[30] *Rabotnicheski vestnik*, January 1, 1934, cited in *Novo vreme*, November, 1959, p. 103.

In many cases, these slogans were not empty words, but expressed factual situations. "There are villages which no creditor, no lawyer and no judge would dare enter for fear of being beaten up or even killed," a non-Communist paper was quoted as having written toward the end of 1933.[31] The Party was therefore determined, according to its spokesman at the Thirteenth Plenum of the Comintern, to exploit this situation by "applying the tactics of the united front from below."

During the "no enemies on the left" period of the united front, the Party switched from its earlier stand, but only slightly. This change was not due to the "left sectarian" course, since even after the May coup the organ of the Comintern continued to maintain that "all the bourgeois parties in Bulgaria, including the social democrats and the peasant leaguers, are fascists." [32] Nominally the Party accepted the call for the establishment of a united front, although it continued to insist that this be a united front from below. "The political line of a united revolutionary front," wrote the Party organ less than a month after the coup, "does not mean the establishment of a coalition from above which would involve the Communists with the Agrarians and the Social Democrats." Why should the Party enter into alliances when, as the same paper wrote at the beginning of July, "the revolution is inevitable," and when "the immediate problem is one of rapid revolutionary mobilization of the masses"? [33] This line continued to be pursued as late as September, 1934, at which time the Agrarians and Social Democrats were still being

---

[31] This and the quotation immediately following are from "The XIII Plenum of the Executive Committee of the Communist International—Comrade Planinski (Bulgaria)," *Inprecorr*, March 5, 1934, pp. 396–97.

[32] "Military Fascist Coup d'Etat in Bulgaria," *Inprecorr*, June 1, 1934, pp. 836–37.

[33] *Rabotnicheski vestnik*, July 5, 1934, cited in *Novo vreme*, November, 1959, pp. 103–4. On the interparty relations through the thirties and on the endeavors aimed at establishing some kind of popular front cooperation, see Kolev, *Borbata na BKP za naroden front*, and Petrova, *BZNS i narodniiat front*. The first centers on the Communist efforts, while the second relates the reactions of the various Agrarian groupings. Although both follow the standard Communist line, Petrova's monograph supplies valuable information on the Agrarians not available otherwise. There are, in addition, three compilations of the writings and speeches of the most important Communist functionaries on the scene, devoted in part to the united and popular front efforts: Dimitrov-Marek, *Izbrani proizvedeniia*, pp. 178–206; Kostov, *Izbrani statii, dokladi, rechi*, pp. 140–299; Damianov, *Izbrani proizvedeniia*, pp. 93–96.

accused of having united "around the counterrevolutionary program of the *putschist* government."

The end of 1934 brought a measure of self-examination. Even dogmatists could no longer fail to see that not only was the revolution not imminent, but that the very existence of the Georgiev government was being threatened by pro-monarchist right-wing elements from within the Military League. At the same time, the Social Democrats and Agrarians who were suspected of supporting the government were in fact breaking up under the hardships of illegality.

In January, 1935, the Party amplified on the conditions which were to form the basis for the united front. "We are prepared to refrain from all mutual attacks during the period of the joint struggle against Fascism and place in the forefront only that which unites us . . . and which renders the united front possible and necessary." Moreover, in order to calm any suspicions which the sought-after allies might have toward the Party and its semi-insurrectionary slogans of the not-too-distant past, the Bulgarian Communists hastened to add that the "united front should not be employed as a means of exposing the unrevolutionary character of the social democracy and of the Peasants' League, but must embody the earnest will to gather all forces for its extension." [34]

Throughout 1935 the Party continued to speak of the united front. Communist pronouncements, however, proved in many cases self-contradictory. In others, they expressed wishful thinking rather than existing situations. The fact was that the Party was caught in a cross fire. With the Comintern insisting on immediate results on the one hand, and with the internal purge on the other, Bulgarian Communists were finding it difficult to make progress.

The message of the Comintern was clear enough. At the Seventh Congress, Kolarov stated clearly that "if we want to wage a successful struggle against fascism, we must take the peasants as they are—with their organizations and with the leaders who still enjoy the confidence of the peasants." [35]

Following the publication of the Party's "open letter" of October

[34] "Enlarged Plenum of the C.C. of the C.P. of Bulgaria," *Inprecorr*, March 23, 1935, p. 367.

[35] Communist International, *Seventh Congress of the Communist International: Abridged Stenographic Report of the Proceedings*, pp. 343–47.

1, 1935, which marked the nominal end of the purge, the newly instituted leadership undertook to broaden the platform of the proposed common action with the other parties. In a Party leaflet published in October, the term "popular front" appeared for the first time. The same publication outlined the general conditions on which a popular front could be established: (1) restoration of the Turnovo Constitution; (2) calling of a Grand Subranie; (3) restoration of political freedoms; (4) electoral rights to women; (5) immediate local elections. In November, the Comintern was still hopeful that such a front could be achieved in Bulgaria, although it attacked the Bulgarian Social Democratic Party for being "one of the most Right wing parties in the Second International," and as such quite unreceptive to progressive efforts.[36] Hopes that a popular front was about to be established continued to be expressed through January, 1936.[37] Then, at the end of February, the Party held its Sixth Enlarged Plenum, which examined the progress, or rather the lack of it, in some detail. Noting the rapprochement between Communist and leftist elements on the local scene, the Plenum admitted the absence of progress among the leaders of the various parties. It renewed its appeals, which were now directed toward the Democratic and Radical parties as well, and insisted that, once established, the popular front would serve to strengthen the determination of the masses vis-à-vis the growing powers of the central government. And yet, even at the Sixth Plenum, at a moment when the problems of the popular front were commanding the attention of the Party, the leadership did not fail to repeat and emphasize that "only a Soviet-type government can really improve Bulgaria's situation." The reassuring statements which followed and which asserted that at the present time under the growing Fascist danger the Party was ready to collaborate with any and all anti-Fascist elements did little to dissolve the suspicions of those who knew at firsthand the meaning of tactical maneuvers.

The reaction of the parties toward which these appeals were directed was not uniform. As a rule, there was interest in the things that the Communists had to say, particularly since it was not often that

[36] Stoico, "The Bulgarian Bourgeoisie Looks for a Way Out," *Inprecorr*, November 2, 1935, pp. 1430–31.

[37] See the article by Stephan, "The Bulgarian Bourgeoisie in a State of Confusion," *Inprecorr*, January 11, 1936, p. 389.

Communists approached anywhere near the cooperative mood they now showed. In relation to the larger problems with which all parties were preoccupied, however, the question of cooperation or noncooperation with the Communists was of secondary importance. Under the stresses of illegality, the Democrats, the Gichev Agrarians, the Radicals, the Pladne Agrarians, and the Social Democrats strove hard to keep their groups organizationally alive. Depending on the momentary disposition of the government, this proved possible to a degree. The Democrats remained weak and disunited, although the presence of Malinov with his towering personal prestige kept the party from disintegration. They maintained their channels of communication with the King and never completely lost hope of being recalled to the government. Boris, on his part, did nothing to discourage them.

Gichev's prestige among the peasants as well as among his fellow politicians remained undamaged. In the period 1936–37 he attempted to keep the local Agrarian associations functioning by the dispatch of periodic circulars. Having lost their command over patronage, however, the Gichev Agrarians could not preserve their organizations intact. By comparison, the Pladne Agrarians did better. With them, patronage was never an important factor since they were never in power. The Pladne people depended much more on powerful oratory and colorful personalities. Of the surviving Stamboliiski ministers, the majority were on their side: Obbov, Stoianov, and Atanasov could be counted on to deliver fiery speeches. None of them displayed the "color" supplied by Todorov, who remained the hero of thousands. His talents for the written and spoken word were hard to match. His popularity in the villages grew despite his prolonged trips abroad. The young Dr. Dimitrov, with his energy and organizational abilities, contributed much to the cause of Pladne during the period of illegality. There were many other city professionals whose political aspirations were fulfilled in the services of Pladne. Among the younger peasants who reached maturity in the decade following the 1934 coup, Pladne rather than Gichev made the greatest inroads.

The Radicals lost most of their significance in the years following the May coup. There were two wings, the one under Kosturkov, who had quarreled with his People's Bloc partners, and the other under Professor Georgi Genov, who kept up his connections with Gichev and Mushanov.

The Social Democrats remained united although organizationally weak. Sakuzov, the grand old man of the Social Democrats, was still active although it was Krustiu Pastukhov who became the guiding spirit behind the political activity of the Party. *Narod* (People), the Party organ, appeared occasionally in stenciled form. The paper of their cooperatives, *Duga* (Rainbow), appeared openly and was used by leading Social Democrats to convey information concerning their limited activity.

The rightist groupings, which were not the object of Communist popular front appeals, found themselves organizationally in still worse shape. The small Liberal Party lost its political significance altogether and was never revived. Liapchev's Democratic Alliance broke up into its component parts. Individual leaders like Atanas Burov, the former foreign minister, Grigor Vasilev, Professor Petko Stainov (who was to become foreign minister after September, 1944), and Stoicho Moshanov gathered small groups around themselves and waited. Some did not wait long. Stoicho Moshanov, who was to become Speaker of the 1938 Subranie, became minister of labor in the 1935 Toshev government. Professor Stainov, on the other hand, having associated himself with Zveno elements, was made Bulgaria's minister to Paris after the May coup. Of the Zveno group, nothing but the name remained. Those from among the Military League who collaborated in Velchev's abortive October coup were in jail. Kimon Georgiev was free but under close police surveillance. Other Zveno members stayed true to Tsankov. Kazasov, after his term as ambassador to Belgrade, devoted himself to journalism. The only one who remained an important factor was Tsankov. Little hampered by the authorities, he continued to organize conferences, print leaflets, and in general prepare himself for the day when his movement would take over.

The political atmosphere in which these groupings and subgroupings survived was one of insecurity. Unlike the leaders and functionaries of the Communists, the leaders of the non-Communist parties were, on the whole, not persecuted. As long as they did not overstep themselves, the regime was ready to tolerate their limited political activities. Moreover, 1936 was a relatively good year for Bulgaria. There were signs of economic revival. Bulgaria's diplomatic position was improving. After the suppression of IMRO by the Georgiev government, the King did much to better relations with Yugoslavia. Sofia saw the arrival of the first Soviet representative following the reestablishment of Russo-Bulgarian diplomatic relations in 1934. Boris, in an attempt to gain popularity, showed the milder side of his complicated personality. On July 4 the Kioseivanov cabinet was reorganized. The new cabinet declared that the regime intended to normalize the political life of the country and that in order to achieve this the government hoped to hold general elections in the "nearest future." A few days later, the Prime Minister announced that such elections would be held "not later than October 25, 1936."

THE PETORKA

The regime's expressed desire to liberalize the political life of the country raised the hopes of the traditional political leaders. If a genuine political revival were possible, collaboration with the Communists could only prove an impediment. Determined to see to it that the government fulfilled its promises, Gichev and Pastukhov proceeded to establish a "popular front" of their own.

This was the so-called *petorka* (quintet) established in 1936 in the form of an informal grouping of five party leaders, namely, Gichev, Pastukhov, Professor Genov for the anti-Kosturkov Radicals, Smilov for the former Liberals, and Grigor Vasilev for the milder elements of the now defunct Democratic Alliance. The Pladne group, Kosturkov's Radicals, and Malinov's Democrats remained aloof, first, because they were not prepared to follow Gichev's initiative, and second, because their rivals under Professor Genov were taking part. With its formation, the *petorka* proceeded to prepare an appeal to the King calling for the restoration of the Constitution and free, general elections.

The prospects for an early popular front were now all but dead. Even the Pladne group, potentially most receptive to the idea, held back. In November, 1935, the Comintern tried to help by attempting to make a deal with the Pladne leaders. In that month Kosta Todorov was in Brussels as the Pladne representative to an interparliamentary conference of Europe's leftist parties. On his return to Paris, he was approached by Communist agents who asked him to go to Moscow and meet Dimitrov concerning the "future of the Balkans." [38] Todorov remained noncommittal. Early in 1936 he met in Belgrade with his Pladne associ-

[38] Todorov, *Balkan Firebrand*, p. 268.

ates from Sofia. He was then told of the insistence of the Communists for an early popular front from which Tsankov would be excluded. "I advised my followers," Todorov wrote later, "to delay their decision until we see how the united front worked in France." With this, for the time being, Pladne withdrew from the bargaining table.[39]

THE PEOPLE'S CONSTITUTIONAL BLOC

In their frustration, the Communist leaders at home concentrated on the establishment of a front "from below" throughout the spring and summer of 1936. Great efforts were made to attract leftist elements into local popular front committees. In a small way, committees of this kind did come into being in a number of larger urban centers such as Sofia, Plovdiv, Ruse, and the like. These examples remained isolated successes. "The wavering and stubborn leaders of the Agrarian Union and of the Social Democratic Party," wrote Kolarov in August, 1936, "will have to take into account the militant sentiments of the workers and peasants, will have to give up their attempts at compromise with reaction, and follow the path of developing the mass struggle on the basis of the People's Front." [40]

In the meantime, however, it was the Party that had to take into account the emergence of the *petorka* and take a stand. This the Party proceeded to do in the late summer of 1936 by deciding to join forces with the *petorka* and back Gichev's and Pastukhov's appeals for the restoration of the Turnovo Constitution. The Pladne group and the Democratic Party did the same. This marked the beginning of the People's Constitutional Bloc, which was not a bloc but a loose confederation between the *petorka* on the one hand, and the forces of the Communists, Pladne, and the Democrats on the other. The initiative remained in the hands of Gichev and Pastukhov, the two principal figures in the *petorka*. They prepared a protest letter to the King which was supported by the Communists.[41]

[39] *Ibid.*, p. 270.

[40] V. Kolarov, "How the Fascists 'Buried' the Class Struggle in Bulgaria," *Communist International*, August, 1936, pp. 993–1003.

[41] *Narod*, No. 8, 1937; this single, crudely produced issue of the organ of the Social Democratic Party contains the text of a letter of protest to the King with the supporting signatures of many prominent democratic figures. It reports on the work of the *petorka* and on the support given to it by the Workers' Party.

The Constitutional Bloc was in no way a full-fledged popular front. A dispatch from Sofia to the Comintern (December, 1936) stated that "this joint struggle will perhaps mean the commencement of the formation of a People's Front in Bulgaria." The same dispatch spoke merely of a "rapprochement" between the Workers' Party and the "democratic parties . . . for the purpose of fighting for the return of the Constitution and democracy." [42] The principal significance of the rapprochement lay in the fact that it opened the way for the establishment of so-called People's Constitutional committees on the local level. Many such committees came to be established in the following months. They provided local Communist activists with the opportunity of carrying out agitation and propaganda.

The general elections promised for October 25 remained only a promise. Instead, the government announced its decision to hold local elections for municipal and communal councils. For the purpose, a special electoral law was prepared and made public in January, 1937. This law proved to be one of the most reactionary electoral laws ever promulgated. Candidates were asked to place their own nominations as private individuals. They were required to submit written declarations that they were not Communists. The minimum age of electors was raised from twenty-five to thirty years. Women were allowed to vote, although this concession was restricted to mothers. The government hoped that Bulgarian women would on the whole vote for the official candidates. Most importantly, the law allowed for elections to be held on different dates for each and every region. In this manner, the regime could concentrate its police forces at a given locality on election day and shift them to the next in accordance with the electoral schedules.

In view of large-scale repressive measures before the elections the groups affiliated with the People's Constitutional Bloc decided to ask their supporters to protest by defacing the ballots with slogans ("restore the Constitution"), thus rendering them invalid. The Communists carried out the most energetic campaign in support of the protest ballot. When in April, 1937, the returns were in, 20.78 percent of the ballots cast were invalid, in most cases because they carried write-in slogans. For both the government and the opposition, the significance of the 1937 local elections was not in their immediate impact but in the fact

[42] Stephan, "The Fight for Democracy in Bulgaria," *Inprecorr*, January 9, 1937, pp. 34–35.

that they served as a full-dress rehearsal for the general elections yet to come.

In the period between the establishment of the People's Constitutional Bloc and the 1938 general elections, the effort of the Party went into infiltration of nonpolitical organizations, mass propaganda on behalf of the Soviet Union, "peace appeals," petitions on behalf of political prisoners at home, and campaigns on behalf of Republican Spain. These efforts did much to change the popular conception of the stereotyped Bolshevik image. The nonmilitant intellectual Communist came to the forefront, and it was he, together with the intellectual Communist sympathizers, who emerged as the symbol of the new Communist.

Demonstrations were either directly organized or indirectly supported by Communists. On June 14, 1936, the anniversaries of the murder of Stamboliiski and Petko D. Petkov were commemorated in public meetings in which Communists participated together with thousands of Agrarians. On November 27 a student demonstration was organized to protest the Neuilly treaty imposed on Bulgaria at the end of World War I. The Party line in relation to Bulgaria's foreign position was modified.

Maintenance of peace and fraternal agreement [according to an appeal of the Central Committee made in 1937] with other nations—this is the certain way to break the murderous and degrading chains of the Treaty of Neuilly, to defend the oppressed Bulgarian minorities and to save them from assimilation by foreign countries. By these peaceful means the question can be faced under favorable conditions, of the unification of the oppressed Bulgarian districts of South Dobrudzha and the Western Provinces with Bulgaria.[43]

This was a far cry from the earlier stands taken on the national problem.

Communists were urged to take up popular causes ranging anywhere from organizing a local citizens' committee for improvement of sanitation services that would eventually take a complaint to the municipal authorities, to the infiltration of a cultural or artistic association. In the fall of 1936 the Central Committee sponsored a meeting of Communist women activists. The Bulgarian Union of Women was infiltrated to a substantial degree. More impressive were Communist successes achieved in such associations as the Union of Bulgarian Esperantists and the Bulgarian Temperance League. In the case of the latter, so absolute

[43] "Appeal of the C.P. of Bulgaria," Inprecorr, October 30, 1937, pp. 1053–54.

and far-reaching was the Communist infiltration that the authorities ordered its dissolution.[44] Modest in scope although significant politically were Communist activities within the Bulgaro-Soviet friendship associations, the creation of which became possible after the establishment of diplomatic relations with the Soviet Union. The first such association was created in Sofia on September 1, 1934, under the presidency of Professor Dolapchiev, a non-Communist Russophile. Several branches were eventually established in the provinces. Under Razkolnikov, the Soviet minister, the Soviet legation in Sofia became a leading cultural and literary center. Razkolnikov himself was a writer and was thoroughly familiar with Bulgarian literature.

Many activities during the period were geared to the so-called international peace movement. The Party established a special commission (attached to the Central Committee) "to direct the peace campaign." The commission was composed of Communist theoreticians and men of letters, such as Todor Pavlov, Georgi Bakalov, a well-known Communist editor and literary figure, and Sava Ganovski, also a Marxist theoretician.

THE 1938 ELECTIONS

As 1937 came to a close, the regime felt secure enough to attempt a cautious step in the direction of "controlled democracy." Accordingly, in October the government announced its intention to hold a general election, the first since 1931. The government also made public some provisions which it hoped to incorporate in the new electoral law. These included a proposal that a certain number of deputies would not be elected but appointed by the government. To this, the various political leaders reacted by preparing a protest memorandum to the King which renewed the demand for the restoration of full political freedom. The Communists found themselves momentarily isolated. They alone refused to sign the memorandum on the ground that they would never place their signatures alongside that of Aleksandur Tsankov, who participated in the protest action. To make up for its refusal to sign, the Party came out with a similar statement of its own.[45] Eventually the government

---

[44] *Istoricheski pregled*, No. 5 (1956), pp. 3–26. See also Kazasov, *Burni godini*, pp. 625–26.

[45] B. Ivanov, "The Peculiarities of the New Franchise Law in Bulgaria," *Inprecorr*, November 13, 1937, pp. 1199–1200.

dropped its appointive proposals, although the electoral law, when finally promulgated, did little to please the various political groups.

Essentially, the main features of the local electoral law were retained, namely, the nonparty character of the election as well as the "geographic provisions" which allowed elections to be held on different dates in different districts. The principle of proportional representation applied in the 1931 elections was abandoned altogether, and a single constituency system was substituted. There were 160 constituencies, each electing one deputy. This opened the way for large-scale gerrymandering. Districts where the opposition was thought to be strong were split up and the various "slices" attached to the "safe" constituencies. Furthermore, since the number of electors in constituencies varied anywhere from 20,000 to 40,000, the government made sure that the "safe" constituencies included 20,000 electors, while the doubtful ones were as large as possible. The electoral law included numerous other provisions, all cleverly tailored to serve the government.

The restrictive clauses in the law notwithstanding, the political leaders of the antigovernment camp saw in the forthcoming elections an opportunity which they decided not to miss. The Buro-in-Exile and the ECCI were dissatisfied with the performance of the Party in the 1937 local elections, and said so. In their estimation, the tactics of invalidating the ballots by write-in slogans were little more than a carry-over from the strategies of the left opposition of the past. Popular frontism meant an endeavor to check the rise of rightist authoritarianism, and that required a positive rather than a negative approach. If the Communists were to make a meaningful contribution in a general assault on the regime, they must cooperate with anybody and everybody ready to lend a hand in the effort. Collaboration with the democratic forces in general, and with the two main wings of the Agrarian Union in particular, had to be effectuated even if this meant reducing the political price to the very minimum. In the face of these dictates, the Communists entered the pre-electoral interparty negotiations with a greatly reduced bargaining posture. It did not take long for Gichev and the remaining democratic leaders to grasp the potential advantages hidden in the new configuration. If they could make use of Communist influences with the voter, without affixing to themselves the label of Communist allies, cooperation with the Party was both possible and desirable. It was in this context that the actual terms were eventually worked out.

A minimum electoral platform acceptable to all the opposition forces was fashioned. This agreement was not to be formal, however. Its terms could be stated orally in the electoral campaign, but the platform was not to be published, not even as an underground document. The democratic leaders did not want to have the stigma of Communism inflicted on them for fear of official retribution. What was even more important, they wanted the anonymous support of Communist and pro-Communist voters, but were not prepared to take the risk of repelling the determined anti-Communist voters.[46]

The Communists had no choice but to accept the terms, by which the opposition parties, including the Communists, agreed not to oppose each other's candidates but to concentrate instead on defeating those of the government. An informal electoral agreement at the top, therefore, was all that the popular front effort achieved. Given the concrete conditions prevalent on the Bulgarian political scene in 1938, this was possibly the most that could be attained.

The electoral campaign of 1938 represented an admixture of official fictions and hard realities. The official fiction to which the government subscribed stated that the elections were apolitical, that political parties were nonexistent, and that candidates represented only themselves rather than any particular political philosophy. The realities were quite different. The voters could and did discriminate among the various candidates. They were aware of their political affiliations and

[46] Several versions of the electoral platform were published abroad; these were picked up by Radio Moscow, which broadcast them in its emissions in the Bulgarian language. Of the lot, the most reliable version appeared in the Bulgarian-language newspaper *Narodna voliia* of March 18, 1938, published in Detroit. This text is reproduced in *IIIBKP*, IX (1962), 379–82. The text itself is not important since it states in general terms the desire of all for the restoration of free political institutions. *Narodna voliia* was launched in February, 1938, as a Communist paper aimed at Bulgarian émigrés in the United States. The moving spirits behind the publication were Sharenkov and Petur Grigorov. The latter was a Communist lawyer who participated in the defense of Dimitrov at Leipzig, and eventually both found themselves in the United States. Persecuted by the American authorities, they returned to Bulgaria after World War II. For a time, Grigorov served as Dimitrov's chief of cabinet during his premiership. *Narodna voliia*'s editor after 1948 was Nikola Kovachev (1899–1964), a Bulgarian Communist who emigrated to America in 1923. Kovachev died in Detroit. Another Communist-sponsored Bulgarian-language newspaper by the name of *Suznanie* appeared in Detroit before *Narodna voliia*. There were at least two more Bulgarian Communist papers in the thirties aimed at émigrés abroad: *Narodna tribuna*, published in Buenos Aires, and *Fraternité* published in Paris; *IIIBKP*, IX (1962), 162.

acted accordingly. Political parties were formally nonexistent. Yet, in some way or another, and with varying degrees of success, most of them preserved their political identity as well as a semblance of organizational structure. Despite the organizational duality between the Workers' and Communist parties, the Communists had a clear advantage over most other opposition formations, in that the central leadership could enforce discipline on the rank and file and control its provincial functionaries. This power was possible because of the doctrinal rigidity which went with Communism, and also because the Communists maintained a full-time Party *apparat* which none could rival. The leaders of the democratic opposition could not exercise the same degree of control over their following. They relied on their personal authority, their influence with provincial followers, and their prestige.

The above differences became manifest in the concrete implementation of the electoral agreement. In practical terms the selection of candidates had to be done on the local level. Once matters were brought down to the constituency, it was natural that variations in the degree of interparty cooperation appeared. In those localities where the respective political representatives agreed on a single common candidate who was also acceptable to the government judges (whose approval was an essential prerequisite), a popular front was indeed established. In some localities, however, no such agreement was reached. The result in those cases was that two or more opposition candidates ran against each other, as well as against the official government candidate. Such breaches in popular front discipline were common. They would have been more frequent if not for the great difficulties which the Communists faced in getting the necessary approval for their candidates. Even persons with the remotest affiliation to Communism found it difficult to establish their eligibility in the eyes of the official government judges. In the end, the Communists and their sympathizers contributed more to the opposition cause than they received.[47]

The elections were held throughout the month of March. The

[47] On the popular front effort in general and on the elections in particular, see the author's "Popular Front in the Balkans: Bulgaria," *Journal of Contemporary History*, V, No. 3 (1970), 69–82. On the electoral interparty talks between the Communists and the two wings of the Agrarian Union, see Petrova, *BZNS i narodniiat front*, pp. 75–81. On the breaches in discipline, see "Letter from Bulgaria," *Inprecorr*, May 21, 1938, p. 640.

police edited election appeals and written statements of the opposition candidates. They superintended the election meetings called by the candidates and dispersed those which they considered undesirable. The police were sent successively to the districts where polling was held, in accordance with a calendar plan drawn up by the government (March 6, 13, 20, 27). On polling day, the police literally besieged the villages hidden from the eyes of foreign observers. The object was to prevent the distribution of opposition ballots and, of course, to arrest opportunists. Local Communists were rounded up in order to prevent them from carrying on agitation. In the larger urban centers, the electoral campaign was relatively freer. Early returns indicated a victory for the opposition.[48] The government, however, improved its position as returns from the rural districts came in. By the end of March, official sources claimed 103 seats for the government-supported candidates and 57 for the opposition.[49] The opposition, on the other hand, insisted that it had elected more than 100 candidates. It was pointed out that, of the seven mandates from Sofia, the government received none, while five were won by the democratic opposition and two by Tsankov.[50] The fact was that, even after all the returns were in, neither side knew its exact relative strength. Once elected, nominal oppositionists saw the advantages presented by crossing over into the government camp, their campaign promises notwithstanding. For two whole months after the elections, government functionaries carried out what amounted to a postelectoral campaign aimed at recruiting supporters from among the doubtful deputies. Threats, promises, flattery, and plain bribery were all put to use, with the result that a considerable number of wavering deputies were drawn to the government side.

The magnitude of the opposition's strength became evident only when the new Subranie convened in May, 1938. In the first crucial vote for the election of the government-supported Speaker of the House, the opposition mustered 67 votes against the government's 93.[51] Considering the constraints placed on opposition candidates during the elections, this

[48] *New York Times*, March 8, 1938.

[49] *Ibid.*, March 28, 1938.

[50] *Christian Science Monitor*, March 27, 1938.

[51] Kazasov, *Burni godini*, p. 615.

was an impressive success. By far the strongest contingent within the opposition consisted of the deputies affiliated with the two wings of the Agrarian Union. As many as 45 Agrarians were claimed by the opposition. In addition, there were eight Social Democrats and an unspecified number of Democrats. A small but vocal group of Tsankov's followers formed the antigovernment opposition of the extreme right. The Communists elected five deputies.[52]

To the government, the electoral results came as an unpleasant surprise. Although its majority in the Subranie was not seriously endangered, the government of Kioseivanov was never quite satisfied with the parliamentary composition. The newly elected Communists became its first target. On June 8, 1938, their expulsion was requested. Police evidence was produced to show their affiliation with Communist causes. The fact that Radio Moscow had supported their election and had mentioned their names was used as proof against them. The expulsion measure was debated at length. It was opposed by Gichev and the Agrarians, as well as by Tsankov, who claimed that common sense dictated that the Communists be left in the Subranie instead of driven underground, prognosticating that "with their expulsion, Bolshevism will not be defeated." [53] On June 15, Todor Samodumov, the leader of the

[52] The lack of precision on the relative strength of the various opposition groups reflected the uncertain character of their respective affiliations. The figure of 45 opposition Agrarians is inflated. Gichev claimed 27, and the Pladne Agrarians 18 (Todorov, *Balkan Firebrand*, p. 287). Both claims were exaggerated. Included in the Gichev claim were a number of deputies who either immediately, or else soon after the opening of the Subranie, crossed over into the government camp and joined the so-called co-opted Agrarians. The Pladne 18, on the other hand, included a number who were closer to Gichev than to Kosta Todorov. In the case of the Democrats, those from the Liapchev wing belonged to the government majority, as did Stoicho Moshanov, who was elected Speaker. Only the Democrats from the Malinov wing of the party were in the antigovernment opposition. Malinov died a few months before the elections. The opposition Democrats in the Subranie were led by Nikola Mushanov, the last premier of the People's Bloc government. The number of Communist deputies was in fact larger than indicated. However, only five were identified as belonging to the Workers' Party, while the remaining were nominal Communist sympathizers. They have been disclaimed in the official Communist literature altogether.

[53] On Tsankov's speech, see Narodno subranie, *Stenografski dnevnitsi*, debates for June 17, 1938, pp. 360–61. Tsankov further stated that the establishment of diplomatic relations with Moscow was a grave mistake he had opposed.

Communist group, spoke in his own defense. He was expelled, nevertheless, as were two of his friends.[54] Having thus rid itself of a few of its enemies, the government majority proceeded to extend its victory.

The sharpest antigovernment opposition in the 1938 Subranie emanated from the Pladne Agrarians, the most outstanding of whom was D. Matsankiev, a lawyer who had been the chief of the police department during the Stamboliiski regime. Another Pladne deputy who distinguished himself in the parliamentary debates of 1938 was Nikola Petkov. The government retaliated in December. Six Pladne deputies were accused of having in effect formed a political group, and of having "sought to reduce royal prerogatives." Following stormy debates, their expulsion was confirmed on December 9, 1938.[55]

The spirit of cooperation between the Communists and the democratic opposition—never very intimate—reached its high mark during the first months of the 1938 Subranie. The Munich agreements and their aftermath cast their shadow soon thereafter, bringing to an end whatever little had remained of the appeals of popular frontism.

There was one more aspect to the Communist popular front effort which remained hidden at the time, but which in the long run proved of particular significance. While courting the democratic opposition leaders, Communist representatives undertook an extensive exploration of a possible alignment with nondemocratic elements from within the antigovernment opposition. As early as 1936, and through 1937, secret talks were held with the leaders of Zveno and representatives of the

[54] Samodumov's speech is reproduced *ibid.*, debates for June 15, 1938, pp. 342–47. The other two expellees were Ivan Georgiev and Bocho Bachev. The government had requested the expulsion of all five. The cases of Ivan Boiadzhiev and Matiu Matev, however, were returned back to committee for reconsideration. It is not clear whether they too were eventually expelled. Samodumov was a well-known writer in the pedagogical field. The year before, he had been expelled from the Party, presumably for not showing sufficient devotion for the cause. He appealed the case to the Buro-in-Exile, whereupon he was restored to membership; the incident is related in Vranchev, p. 388.

[55] The six were D. Matsankiev, N. Petkov, D. Angelov, T. Lazarov, N. Nikolov, and K. Slavov. On the expulsion debates, see Narodno subranie, *Stenografski dnevnitsi*, debates for December 8–9, 1938, pp. 295–366. Significant for the future were Nikola Petkov's parting words to the deputies. "I am confident," he said, "that at the first free elections, this House would have a majority made up of the elite of the Bulgarian peasantry and the elite of the Bulgarian working class."

Military League. Significantly, the initiative came from Zveno. Negotiations were opened between former Premier Kimon Georgiev and a Communist functionary serving as spokesman for Dimitrov-Marek, the Comintern's delegate in Bulgaria. A number of retired young army majors from the Military League (now formally dissolved) were brought in. Georgiev's view was that an alliance between the Communist Party and the democratic formations, even if successful, could bring no tangible results. Instead, he suggested the formation of a narrower Communist-Zveno alliance which, backed by the more radical anti-royalist elements from the Military League, could take power by means of a military *putsch*. In due course, the proposals and counterproposals were put in writing. The Communists showed interest, and reported to the Buro-in-Exile. After a careful and sympathetic consideration, Moscow issued its verdict. The newly established liaison with Zveno and the Military League was to be continued and strengthened. At the same time, the Zveno people were to be told that for the time being a military *putsch* was inopportune and could not be supported by the Communists. The newly found friendship was to be cultivated for its possible future value. The initiators were disappointed but not discouraged. For Zveno and its military friends, this alliance was the beginning of a course which was to lead them into an unholy marriage with their historic enemies.[56]

[56] There are a number of authoritative accounts on the Zveno-Communist rapprochement in the thirties. Of the lot, the most detailed is related by the man who represented the Communist side in the talks, namely, Vranchev, pp. 326–35, 360–69; the chief representative for Zveno was Ivan Kharizanov, one of the original founders of the group and its ideologue. Kharizanov was of Macedonian origin and participated in the Macedonian revolutionary movement. His original anti-Communism and that of his friends in Zveno were well known. In the late twenties, Kharizanov served as president of the Bulgarian Anti-Comintern League. The latter had as its vice-president Geshev, who as head of the political police in later years figured as the most ruthless persecutor of Communists. The most important members of the Military League who took part in the discussions were the retired majors K. Lekarski, T. Toshev, and S. Trendafilov, who participated in the Communist resistance movement during the war and were made generals of the Bulgarian army after the entry of the Red Army in September, 1944. On the same subject see also Terpeshev, p. 133; *Otechestven front*, July 27, 1947. It would be wrong to conclude from the above evidence that Zveno's liaison with the Communists had become irrevocable as early as 1937. Zveno was always a small opportunist political group with no popular following. Had Bulgaria's wartime political fortunes not brought the Russians, Zveno could have, and probably would have, acted differently. Discussions on a possible military *putsch* were re-

THE SPANISH CIVIL WAR

The impact of the Spanish Civil War on the development of the popular front effort in Bulgaria was slight. Those of the democratic camp sympathized with the Republican side, but agreed with the government's policy of neutrality in the conflict. The Pladne Agrarians were the one notable exception. Their leader, Kosta Todorov, visited Spain on the invitation of the Republican government, whose cause he tried to help the best he could.[57] The conflict in Spain, however, had a significant effect on intra-Communist relations, since it brought together Communist cadres from Bulgaria with a large number of Bulgarian exiles in the Soviet Union.

As early as August, 1936, the Bulgarian government associated itself with the policy of keeping military supplies out of the hands of either side. On April 9, 1937, the government issued a decree prohibiting Bulgarian nationals from participation in the conflict. Normal diplomatic relations with the Republican government continued to be maintained, even though an unofficial representative of General Franco was permitted to open an office in Sofia. On September 8, 1938, a Bulgarian trade delegate was assigned to the Franco government. Yet, only on March 4, 1939, following the lead of the great Western powers, did the Bulgarians extend recognition to the Franco regime.

Despite limitations, as many as 460 Bulgarians participated in the Spanish Civil War. The majority came from Bulgaria proper, about one hundred from Soviet exile, and an unspecified number from the Bulgarian emigrations in Western Europe and the United States. A special committee under the veteran Bulgarian-Macedonian Communist functionary Metodi Shatarov (alias Atanasov) was established in Paris. Its function was to receive arriving volunteers traveling with regular Bulgarian passports and arrange for their dispatch into Spain.[58] Some

---

opened before as well as after Munich. Consideration was given to the possible participation of the Pladne Agrarians in addition to the Communists, Zveno, and the more moderate (Protogerov) wing of the Macedonians; again, the talks proved abortive, as indicated in Petrova, *BZNS i narodniiat front*, pp. 116–17.

[57] Todorov, *Balkan Firebrand*, pp. 282–83.

[58] One monograph, a number of major articles, and several autobiographies constitute the major sources on the Bulgarian participation in the conflict. Most important is the work of D. Sirkov, *V zashtita na ispanskata republika*, and his two

reached Spain on their own, traveling illegally all the way from Bulgaria by boat, or following an intricate clandestine route worked out by functionaries in Sofia. Participants from the Bulgarian emigration in Russia came as Soviet personnel, on board Soviet ships.

The Bulgarians were distributed among the various units of the International Brigades. Plans made to create a single fighting unit composed solely of Bulgarians never materialized. Most of the Soviet émigrés figured as Russians and were only occasionally identified as ethnic Bulgarians. The dichotomy between the two groups was maintained throughout. In May, 1937, the Buro-in-Exile appointed Subi Dimitrov (alias Vladimir Mikhailov) as the official representative of the Bulgarian Communist Party in Spain. He was made a political commissar and was provided with a small staff in charge of the education and training programs for the Bulgarian volunteers. Subi Dimitrov had been the leader of the Communist parliamentary group in the Subranie (1931–33). He went to the Soviet Union as a delegate to the Seventh Congress of the Comintern, and arrived in Spain directly from Moscow. Even though he was formally in charge of all Bulgarians in Spain, his primary responsibility was for those who had come directly from Bulgaria. He edited a Bulgarian-language newsletter called *Bulgarski interbrigadist* and supervised the Bulgarian-language broadcasts originating from Barcelona.[59]

In the military and political spheres, by far the leading roles were played by the émigrés. The more important among them went to great lengths not to be identified as Bulgarians. The principal representative of the Comintern in Spain was Boris Stepanov-Minev (known in Spain as Moreno).[60] Dimo Dichev (Yanov) headed the section of the volunteers

---

articles in *IIIBKP*, IX (1962), 143–93, and X (1963), 163–210. See also two articles by a Russian participant published in *Novyi mir* (Moscow), July, 1960, pp. 142–80, and August, 1960, pp. 141–77. The autobiographies of Telge, Velichkov, and Stoev-Shvarts are both interesting and important.

[59] Milev, *Subi Dimitrov*, provides details on the work of the Bulgarian political commissar in Spain; see also Sirkov, pp. 100–3. Broadcasting was done first by Zhak Asher and later by Raiko Damianov, who became a major Party and government figure after 1944.

[60] Stepanov-Minev has already been mentioned in different contexts. He was Comintern representative to the Spanish CP from 1928 to 1939 and was the real power behind the Argentinian of Italian origin by the name of Vittorio Codovilla

from the Slavic countries at the Central Committee of the Spanish CP.[61]
For a time, Captain T. Ivanov Nenov represented the International
Brigades at the War Ministry of the Spanish Republic.[62] Ruben Avramov-Levi, in Soviet exile since 1925, became first a divisional political
commissar in the Spanish Republican army under the alias of Miguel.
At the end of 1936 he was appointed general inspector of all political
commissars in the Republican army on the Madrid front. Later he became the director of the School for Political Commissars in Madrid, and
also the editor in chief of *El Comisario*, the organ of the General Military Commissariat.[63] From 1937 until the end of 1938 the director of
all medical services for the International Brigades was Dr. Ts. Kristanov
(known in Spain as Oscar Telge); his deputy was Dr. Petur V. Kolarov
(Vasil Kolarov's son, known in Spain as Dr. Franek).[64] The organizer
and head of supply and logistics for all the International Brigades was
L. Todorov-Karbov.[65]

A number of Bulgarian émigrés who had become career officers in
the Red Army figured prominently on the various fronts. P. Panchevski
was the senior adviser to the corps of engineers in the Republican army.[66]
Ts. Radoinov-Radionov, an instructor of tactics at the Frunze Academy,
served as senior adviser to the Republican general staff.[67] Ferdinand

---

known in Spain under the name of Comrade Medina. A brief biographical outline
of Stepanov-Minev's life is given in *V pomosht na izuchavashtite*, p. 179. Also on
Stepanov, see Thomas, pp. 72, 622; Salvador De Madariaga, *Latin America
Between the Eagle and the Bear* (New York, 1962), p. 139; Castro Delgado, pp.
6, 17.

[61] *IIIBKP*, X (1963), 179. Dichev spent ten years in prison. In 1936 he went to
Russia and from there to Spain. He was later active in the wartime resistance in
Bulgaria and after 1944 rose to the top ranks in the Party and the government.

[62] *Ibid.*, p. 179.

[63] *Ibid.*, pp. 181, 184; also, Avramov-Levi to author, interview, Sofia, September,
1966. His name has appeared earlier. His Spanish experience was to be put to
good use during World War II when he headed the Comintern School in Ufa.

[64] Sirkov, p. 117. Telge *et al.* relates in great detail what is probably the most
authoritative account of the military medical services for the International
Brigades.

[65] *IIIBKP*, X (1963), 180.

[66] Sirkov, p. 115. Panchevski served as major general in the Red Army during
World War II and was Bulgaria's minister of defense in the fifties.

[67] On the life of Radoinov-Radionov, see the biography by Dragoliubov.

Kozovski (known in Spain as Colonel Petrov) commanded the Dombrowski battalion of the Eleventh International Brigade in the early stages of the battle for Madrid. He later became deputy commander of the Twelfth Brigade, a position held until his recall to Moscow and eventual arrest.[68] The chief of staff of the Twelfth Brigade was Karlo Lukanov (known in Spain as Major Belov), the son of the veteran Todor Lukanov who in the twenties headed the right opposition to Kolarov and Dimitrov. In July, 1937, Lukanov-Belov was made commander of the base at Albasete, which was the administrative and training center for the International Brigades.[69]

Anton Ivanov (Spiridon), a member of the Buro-in-Exile, served as the Comintern troubleshooter in Spain. His special mission was with the Italians and Poles in the International Brigades, whom he helped organize (and purge).[70] Vlado Georgiev was commander of a tank battalion.[71] Vlado Trichkov (known in Spain as Captain Pavlov) commanded all machine-gun units in the Ebro offensive.[72] The latter three perished in the Bulgarian wartime resistance. I. Grebenarov commanded the "G. Dimitrov" battalion and perished in Spain. These are but a few of the more outstanding participants.

About 70 percent of the Bulgarian volunteers in Spain were Communist Party members (or became so while in Spain). A quarter were members of the "intelligentsia" (including students), while less than

---

[68] Sirkov, pp. 132, 135. Kozovski's arrest in Moscow during the purge and his release through the intervention of Dimitrov have already been related in connection with the purge of the émigrés.

[69] *Ibid.*, pp. 107, 135. Karlo Lukanov was born in Geneva in 1897. He studied law and followed in the footsteps of his father into the Bulgarian Socialist and, later, Communist movements. He went to Russia in 1926 where he worked in state planning. It is not clear whether or not he was penalized because of his father's rightist tendencies. In 1945–46 he served as director of the Bulgarian State Radio, became deputy premier in 1951, and was minister to Moscow in 1954–56. Lukanov was appointed foreign minister in 1956, a position he held until 1962.

[70] Mikhailov, p. 113.

[71] Bogdanov, *Vlado Georgiev*; this is a brief biography with many interesting details on Spain as well as on Georgiev's activities in the Bulgarian wartime resistance.

[72] Nestorov, *Vlado Trichkov*; this is the life story of a professional revolutionary. Trichkov spent eleven years in prison. In 1936 he went to the Soviet Union and later to Spain; he perished in the Bulgarian wartime resistance.

8 percent were workers. About one-half were of peasant origin.[73]

The only other organized group among the Bulgarians in Spain were the Bulgarian Anarchists. Although few in number, they engaged in lively propaganda warfare with the Communists in Spain, and by way of pamphlets and leaflets printed in Barcelona carried their verbal battles into Bulgaria as well. The Federation of Anarcho-Communists had been founded in Bulgaria in 1919. The Anarchists took an active part in the 1923 uprising and, despite persecution, managed to survive throughout the interwar period. In the early thirties they claimed that 130 peasant groups were affiliated with the Anarchists' Union of Vlassovden in addition to 40 syndicalist groups in the cities.[74] The outbreak of the Spanish Civil War revived their spirits, and some managed to reach Spain. They published a Bulgarian-language newsletter in Barcelona with which they tried to contact the Bulgarians in Spain. The Bulgarian Anarchist group in Paris published a periodical entitled *Nash Put* (Our Way).[75] Given the heavy involvement of numerous Bulgarians in the Comintern and Soviet military *apparat* in Spain, the Anarchists could not make important inroads.

The over-all military contribution of the Bulgarian forces in Spain is difficult to assess. They were good warriors and many came with substantial military and insurrectionary experience from the Bulgarian wars, the 1923 uprising, and the Soviet military academies. A sum total of 68 were killed in Spain; 27 of the participants perished later in the Bulgarian wartime resistance, and 4 died in the resistance of other European countries.[76] When the Russians pulled out of Spain, the majority of

[73] Sirkov, pp. 98–99; the figures are based only on 334 volunteers for whom exact records are available.

[74] On the Anarchist movement in Bulgaria, see *Bulgaria, a New Spain: The Communist Terror in Bulgaria*. The Anarchists condemned Blagoev and the leaders of the Communist Party for their "three-fourths from abroad" thesis, which meant that the Communists expected three-fourths of the force behind a triumphant revolution in Bulgaria to come from the outside. On Anarchist participation in the 1923 uprising, see P. Svobodin, "El Movimiento anarquista en Bulgaria," *Timon*, November, 1938, cited in Rothschild, p. 143*n*.

[75] Sirkov, p. 99; *IIIBKP*, IX (1962), 157–59. The illegal organ of the Anarchists in Bulgaria was *Khliab i svoboda* (Bread and Freedom). In addition, they published the legal *Kompas* (Compass) and *Nov sviat* (New World); Anarchist views and news also found their way into the daily *Nova Kambana* (New Bell).

[76] *Rabotnichesko delo*, January 19, 1958. An up-to-date list of names of Bulgarian participants is printed in Sirkov, pp. 235–50.

Bulgarian exiles returned to the Soviet Union.[77] The remaining were interned in French camps and returned to Bulgaria only in 1940 when an amnesty was granted.[78] The American émigrés returned to the United States.[79] In January, 1958, the veterans from Spain were honored by the Party. In May, 1963, a Committee for Solidarity with the Spanish People consisting of the more prominent survivors was set up in Sofia.

RUMANIAN COMMUNISM AND DOBRUJA

With the introduction of the popular front line, the Party adjusted its orientation toward the Dobruja question, which for Bulgaria remained a major national issue throughout the interwar period. In 1878 the Congress of Berlin had split the territory of Dobruja. Northern Dobruja was awarded to Rumania in compensation for southern Bessarabia, which went to Russia. Southern Dobruja, on the other hand, was assigned to the new Bulgarian state. However, the Bulgarians lost the region to the Rumanians at the end of the Second Balkan War, a loss confirmed in 1919.

As in all other matters, the Communist line closely followed Comintern dictates. In 1919 the Bulgarian Communists called for the establishment of "Soviet Dobruja." Such narrow sectarianism did little to enhance the Communists in the eyes of the thousands of Bulgarian refugees from Dobruja, whose only desire was to see the region revert to Bulgarian rule. Despite great efforts, the Dobruja refugee organiza-

---

[77] Except for meager indications, there is no evidence on the fate of those who returned to Russia. Kozovski-Petrov's arrest and release have been mentioned. Colonel Radoinov-Radionov "was treated badly by the people of the cult of personality, but did not despair"; Telge *et al.*, p. 222. Whatever the ordeals of Radoinov-Radionov, he survived to lead a number of parties of émigrés into Bulgaria after the outbreak of the Soviet-German war. The Bulgarians, like all other returnees from Spain, could hardly have escaped the political quarantine imposed by the Soviet authorities.

[78] Sirkov, p. 197. There were 160 interned in the French camps as of August, 1939; their number was reduced to 40 in March, 1941. Repatriations continued after that date as well.

[79] On this, and on efforts undertaken by Bulgarians in the United States to force an amnesty on the Bulgarian government, see *Narodna voliia* (Detroit), March 11, 1938, and August 18, 1939. As far as the global figures of Bulgarian participants are concerned, there is undoubtedly a degree of double-counting on the part of Bulgarian and Yugoslav sources, involving Macedonians both in the United States and in Macedonia proper.

tions in Bulgaria remained under the influence of supernationalist elements rather than the Communists. The latter did better in southern Dobruja proper, where oppressive measures by the Rumanians inevitably resulted in the radicalization of the younger Bulgarian elements.

With Comintern inspiration, the Dobruja Revolutionary Organization (Dobrudzhanska revoliutsionna organizatsiia, or DRO) was created in September, 1925, in Vienna. The leadership of DRO went to Dr. Petur Vichev, who, although not a Communist, followed closely the Comintern line until his death in 1933.[80]

The real importance of the Communist-sponsored DRO was in the underground revolutionary cells established and operated by Bulgarians in southern Dobruja itself. While serving the cause of Dobruja, many DRO functionaries were at the same time members of the Rumanian Communist Party. Inevitably, the problem of double allegiance arose. A hidden antagonism between the Rumanian and Bulgarian Communist parties over the Dobruja question persisted throughout most of the interwar years, mitigated somewhat by the presence of prominent Bulgarians in positions of central importance in the hierarchy of the Rumanian Party.

The problem of national minorities dominated Rumanian Communism from its inception. Not until after World War II was the Rumanian Party truly "nationalized." In the interwar years it resembled more a confederacy of radical national minorities than a Rumanian revolutionary movement. Probably more than any other single national group, the Bulgarians figured prominently in the affairs of Rumanian Communism. The role of Christian Rakovski (himself of Bulgarian Dobruja origin) as one of the founding fathers of Rumanian Socialism has already been mentioned. In later years, Kolarov could proudly claim that "the 'directives' of the Bulgarian Communists played a key role in the formation of the Rumanian sister party." [81] When the first unified Central Committee of the Rumanian Party was elected in October, 1922, there were at least three Bulgarians among its members, namely, Boris Stefanov (not to be confused with Stepanov-Minev, the Comintern delegate to the Spanish Communist Party) as delegate of the Rumanian

[80] On the establishment of DRO, see Rothschild, pp. 198–203. Vichev was shot dead in Sofia on June 16, 1933, by a Macedonian gunman.

[81] *Ibid.*, p. 199.

Party from the Old Kingdom, Dimitur Donchev, and Colev, the latter two from the Dobruja Party organization. Stefanov (who was related to Rakovski) was elected to the Rumanian parliament in June, 1920, from the district of Dobrich in southern Dobruja.[82] He played a central role in the formative years of the Rumanian Party. Persecuted by the Rumanian police, he went underground in 1924, but was captured in 1926 and remained in Rumanian prisons until 1933. When in 1925 the decision to establish DRO was taken, Boris Stefanov was secretary of the underground Central Committee of the Rumanian Party. The moving spirit behind DRO, of which Dr. Vichev was the formal head, was a Communist from southern Dobruja by the name of Georgi Krosnev with whom Stefanov maintained intimate relations.[83] All through their active political lives, these Bulgarians remained associated with the Dobruja cause in one way or another, even though their main contributions were made to Rumanian Communism. In the mid-thirties, Stefanov appeared in Moscow and functioned as Rumanian representative at the Comintern. In the fall of 1939 an article which appeared under his name caused a sensation for its insistence that Rumania seek direct alliance with the Soviet Union, implying that the principle of self-determination be applied to Bessarabia. After World War II, Stefanov was repudiated by his Rumanian comrades and found refuge in Sofia.[84]

[82] Ionescu, p. 20. For obvious reasons, official Rumanian historians have tended to minimize and sometimes completely omit the roles of Bulgarians in the ranks of the Rumanian Party. Furthermore, Bulgarian names appear Rumanianized and are difficult to trace. On the Bulgarian side, the single most important source on the politics of Bulgarian Communists in the affairs of Rumania is the book by Ivan Georgiev, *Dobrudzha v borbata za svoboda, 1913–1940*, on which much of the information in the following pages is based. Another Bulgarian Communist elected to the Rumanian parliament in June, 1920, was Kosta Stoev from the town of Silistra in southern Dobruja; on the elections, see Georgiev, p. 41.

[83] Georgiev, p. 105.

[84] Stefanov's early career is pieced together from Georgiev, pp. 41, 80, 105. On his 1939 article, see Henry L. Roberts, *Rumania: Political Problems of an Agrarian State* (New Haven, 1951), and Ionescu, p. 59. For Stefanov's repudiation as an "opportunist" in 1961 by a Rumanian Communist leader, see Ionescu, pp. 356–57. The Bulgarian *Rabotnichesko delo* of June 11, 1963, carried Stefanov's speech on the occasion of Georgi Dimitrov's birthday. He was described as an old friend of the late Dimitrov, and as having been "the Secretary of the CC of the Rumanian CP." As late as September, 1966, Stefanov was alive in Sofia, working in the publishing field.

Dimitur Donchev (alias Doktora), while a member of the Central Committee of the Rumanian Communist Party, preoccupied himself with the affairs of the Bulgarian Communists in southern Dobruja until the end of his life. He went to Soviet Russia for military training (1927–28), returned to Bucharest, and in 1931 was placed in charge of a special *apparat* in the Central Committee of the Rumanian Party whose function it was to coordinate the revolutionary activities of the Communists from Transylvania, Bessarabia, Bukovina, and southern Dobruja. Before long, however, Donchev was shot dead (September 12, 1931) by the Rumanian police.[85]

Much of Georgi Krosnev's work on behalf of the Dobruja revolutionary movement was done in exile, into which he was forced by the Rumanian authorities. In the late twenties he was in Berlin. Under Dimitrov's supervision (at the time when he was in charge of WEB), functionaries of DRO convened in Berlin (June–July, 1929) to consider the Dobruja issue, at which time Krosnev served as a member of the Central Committee of the organization. He was later sent to Moscow, became a "red professor," and worked in the Comintern *apparat*. In the latter part of 1935 he was sent to Bucharest where, together with Ana Pauker, he helped reorganize the central leadership of the Rumanian Party. As a member of the Central Committee of that Party, Krosnev headed the Agitprop section and served as the editor of the illegal *Scanteia*. He was arrested on October 16, 1936, and died in a Rumanian prison on February 7, 1937.[86]

As long as the Comintern persisted with its line of "A Free and Independent Dobruja," the differences between the Bulgarian and Rumanian parties remained largely invisible. Led by the left opposition, the Bulgarian Communists in southern Dobruja, like their comrades at home, were expected to pursue the revolution for revolution's sake. A rift occurred only when the Bulgarian Communists began insisting that southern Dobruja revert to the Bulgarian state. The change of signals came from Moscow in April, 1933. At that point, the Comintern dis-

[85] On Donchev's life and death, see Georgiev, pp. 209, 213, 272–76, 302–7. The Moscow *Pravda* published an article on his revolutionary activities on October 4, 1931.

[86] Krosnev's story is pieced together from Georgiev, pp. 80, 105, 207–13, 421–22; see also Ionescu, pp. 25, 50, where he appears under the name of Dmitri Kroshneff.

patched Kuzman Stoikov (alias Vangel) to southern Dobruja to serve as its delegate to DRO.[87] Stoikov's message, delivered at a secret plenum, was plain and simple. DRO was no longer a revolutionary organization for all the national elements in southern Dobruja but only an organization for the ethnic Bulgarians, who were numerically in a position of clear plurality (the others being Turks, Gypsies, Rumanians, and Tartars). The slogan "A Free and Independent Dobruja" was to be dropped. In the future, the principle of "Self-determination with the Right of Secession" was to become the guiding line of Communist endeavors. The central point was not lost on the participants of the plenum. Southern Dobruja was to achieve freedom not through independence, but through secession, which meant reversion to Bulgaria. This the Rumanian comrades were to be told in no uncertain terms.[88]

To supervise the execution of the new line, the Bulgarian Party in Sofia selected Dimitur Ganev, who was sent to southern Dobruja in mid-July, 1933, as the new head of DRO. Ganev was also co-opted as a member of the Central Committee of the Rumanian Party. His work, however, was short-lived. In July, 1935, the Rumanian police uncovered and arrested many of the members of the Central Committee of the Rumanian Party, including Ganev. He was tried in July, 1936, and sentenced to ten years in prison.[89]

[87] Stoikov was not from southern Dobruja but from Nova Zagora in Bulgaria proper. He had been in Soviet exile since 1925.

[88] On the plenum presided over by Stoikov and held in the town of Dobrich, see Georgiev, pp. 370–78. According to Bulgarian official estimates, at the end of World War I there were 282,131 people altogether in southern Dobruja. Of them, 48 percent were Bulgarians, 38 percent Turks, and the rest Gypsies, Tartars, and Jews. Ethnic Rumanians were estimated at 2 percent. After 1924, Bucharest undertook to create a Rumanian majority by the settlement in southern Dobruja of Kutso-Vlakhs from Macedonia on land expropriated from the non-Rumanian elements. As a result, 40,000 Bulgarians and 20,000 Turks were displaced and became refugees; see Rothschild, p. 198.

[89] Dimitur Ganev (1898–1964) was not a native of southern Dobruja. He became a member of the CC of the Bulgarian CP in 1929, and a member of the CC of the Rumanian CP in 1934. Some of his time in Rumanian prisons he spent together with Gheorghiu-Dej, the future Rumanian Communist dictator. When Dobruja reverted to Bulgaria in 1940, Ganev was granted amnesty. He was co-opted into the Bulgarian Politburo in 1942 and was in charge of the resistance in the northeastern parts of Bulgaria. In the postwar years he held top Party and government positions. He served as minister to Bucharest and as minister of

With the arrest of Ganev, relations between the Sofia and Bucharest Communists deteriorated. The latter claimed, not without good reason, that the pursuance of the secessionist line, at a time when Rumania faced the danger of being dismembered, placed Rumania's very existence as a sovereign state in peril. In the nature of things, the Dobruja question could not be squared with the interests of the two parties. While for the Bulgarians the popular front effort required that the Communists support Bulgaria's national demands, the same effort in Rumania necessitated that the Rumanian Communists support their country's political integrity.[90] In August, 1938, in his capacity as secretary of the Party, Traicho Kostov dispatched to southern Dobruja a special emissary for the purpose of discussing the problem directly with the Rumanian comrades. The latter, however, refused to meet with the Bulgarian delegate. Only at the beginning of 1940, when the future of Rumania's frontiers had become a pending international issue, and when the much more important regions of Transylvania and Bessarabia were about to be surrendered, did the Rumanian Communists modify their stand on southern Dobruja. Ironically, when Bulgaria did fulfill her revisionist aspirations vis-à-vis Rumania, the credit went neither to the Soviet Union, nor to the Bulgarian Communists, but to Nazi Germany.[91]

---

foreign trade. His fortunes fell in the early 1950s (possibly not unrelated to the purge of Ana Pauker in Rumania), but in 1958 he was made head of state, a position he held until his death on April 21, 1964. On Ganev's work in Dobruja and his trial before a Rumanian court, see Georgiev, pp. 380, 406–10.

[90] Georgiev, pp. 426–29.

[91] *Ibid.*, pp. 429–30. The person who appears to have helped swing the Rumanian Communist leadership was a functionary of DRO by the name of Petur Georgiev, who at about the same time became a member of the Central Committee of the Rumanian Party. Georgiev later became secretary of the Rumanian Party organization in Bucharest. In 1943 he fell into the hands of the Rumanian police, stood trial, and was shot later in the year (*ibid.*, p. 430). From the Bulgarian Communist cadres associated with DRO in the thirties, at least one person lived to become a top functionary of postwar Communist Rumania. This was Dimitur Kolev, or Dumitru Coliu in the Rumanian version. He served as regional secretary of Dobruja just before the war, spent the war years in Russia, and returned to Rumania with the Tudor Vladimirescu division. He became a member of the CC of the Rumanian CP in 1948, a candidate member of the Politburo in 1952, and secretary-general of the Bucharest Party organization in 1953. In 1955 he was made chairman of the State Control Commission; on his career, see Georgiev, p. 331, and Ionescu, p. 351.

CHAPTER FIVE

SOVIET DIPLOMACY AND BULGARIAN COMMUNISM

BETWEEN THE MUNICH PACT and the German attack on the Soviet Union, the Bulgarian Communist Party went through three distinct stages. The first began with Munich and ended with the signing of the Russo-German Pact. Of the three, this was the least eventful. It saw the virtual end of the rapprochement with the democratic groups, thus bringing the Party back to its customary state of political isolation. In the second stage, between the outbreak of World War II and the opening of the Soviet diplomatic effort for the conclusion of a treaty of non-aggression with Bulgaria (fall of 1940), in matters of fundamental policy the Communists found themselves in general agreement with the Bulgarian government, for despite the government's leaning toward Nazi Germany, it maintained Bulgaria's neutrality and by so doing fulfilled the minimum requirement of Soviet diplomatic interests in the Balkans. As if overnight, the Communists realized that they no longer needed the good will of allies. Thus the middle of 1940 saw Sofia politics in a state of paradox. While Mushanov, Gichev, and Pastukhov had still not recovered from the crushing blow which German arms had delivered to the Allies (and to their illusions), Communists could walk the streets of Sofia, openly buy a copy of the Moscow-printed *Izvestiia*, and listen to news of the presence of Communist parliamentary leaders at official court receptions.

The third stage began with the refusal of the Bulgarian government to respond to Soviet diplomatic overtures for an alliance. Momentarily, Bulgaria became the focal point of Russo-German diplomatic rivalry, with the Communist Party as the sole backer of the Soviet line. Allies were now again of importance, although they were hard to come by. Almost singlehandedly, the Communists, acting as an extension of Soviet foreign policy, carried out an impressive mass mobilization.

FROM MUNICH TO THE RUSSO-GERMAN PACT

Bulgaria's foreign relations and local elections dominated the attention of the Party during the first stage. On July 31, 1938, Bulgaria signed the Salonika Agreement, which formally nullified the military clauses of the Treaty of Neuilly. This action was a victory for the regime. With the agreement at Munich, the hopes of the government rose. If Germany could shatter the fetters of 1919, why not Bulgaria? Extremist right-wing organizations such as the Ratnitsi and the Legion intensified their agitation. So did Tsankov and his followers. With Nazi assistance, the IMRO, dormant for the past several years, came to life.[1]

The reaction of the Communists was predictable. The Munich Pact was, of course, condemned. Yet Bulgarian revisionism was not attacked, although stress was placed on the concept of mutual security. In July, 1939, the Party organ appealed to the government to sign the Balkan Pact. The organ saw the only solution for Bulgaria's international problems in the establishment of a Balkan defense bloc, with Bulgaria at its core. The Communists went on to propose a detailed plan for comprehensive Balkan cooperation.[2]

Cooperation with the antigovernment opposition was all but gone. Despite the spirit of independence which the opposition continued to exhibit in parliamentary debates, the Western compromise at Munich could not but make its leaders hesitate about the wisdom of their anti-German orientation. Nor could they fight against the rising wave of Bulgarian irredentism. They themselves believed in the justice of Bulgaria's national aspirations. The government, on its part, strove to tighten national discipline. In the fall of 1938 a number of new laws were promulgated that were aimed at regulating the press. The effects of

[1] Stoyan Christowe, "IMRO Resurrected," *Living Age*, July, 1939, pp. 408–12.

[2] *Rabotnichesko delo*, July, 1939, cited in *Rabotnichesko delo, izbrani statii i materiali, 1927–1944*, pp. 330–33.

these laws were best described by a foreign observer: "Every journalist will now have to carry a little rule book, to see the worth—in jail sentences—of every news item. Most punishments seem to be three years in the penitentiary."[3]

The fiction of representative government continued to be maintained. In the spring of 1939, the mandate of the municipal and rural councilmen elected in 1937 expired. The government announced its intention to hold new local elections, which were fixed for May. The restrictive electoral provisions, as well as the old police techniques, again came into play. At the end of April, police repressions were intensified. From Sofia alone, twenty-five Communist functionaries were interned to the provinces. In many localities, the only electoral lists to be posted were the official slates of candidates. This meant that government-supported candidates got "elected" automatically. Isolated attempts at cooperation between Communist and non-Communist oppositionists came to nothing. The government emerged overwhelmingly victorious, with the Communists almost completely isolated from their allies of the day before.[4]

The news of the German-Soviet Pact surprised the Communists, as it did everybody else. Momentarily, their attention was directed away from the political and organizational problems with which they had been preoccupied.

Outwardly the pact was accepted without question. In September, the Party organ stated flatly that "the signing of the pact shows the complete and total capitulation of Hitler to Soviet might." Immediately afterwards came a counteraccusation. "The Soviet Union," stated the newspaper, "is not responsible for the outbreak of war. Had France and England not protracted their negotiations for four long months, and had they come to an agreement, Hitler would not have dared make a move." Finally, hope was expressed that "the German people, come what may, would find strength to topple Hitler and restore peace."[5]

---

[3] *Christian Science Monitor*, September 6, 1938. See also *Times* (London), October 17, 1938, on the internment of many Pladne Agrarians accused of spreading alarming rumors.

[4] *Istoriia na Bulgariia*, pp. 740–41.

[5] *Rabotnichesko delo*, September, 1939, reproduced in *Rabotnichesko delo, izbrani statii i materiali, 1927–1944*, pp. 334–38.

On September 17, with fighting in Poland still going on, Todor Pavlov, the Party theoretician, published a fifteen-page pamphlet entitled "Against Confusion of the Terms." The purpose of the pamphlet was to answer doubts from within and to explain the Soviet intervention in Poland. This Pavlov attempted primarily by quoting from Molotov's speech and by reassuring the orthodox militants that "the pact does not represent a programmatic retreat but a step toward peace." He praised Kioseivanov's declaration of Bulgaria's determination to remain neutral "as the only correct stand for the moment," and concluded by giving the full text of the published portion of the pact, which the Bulgarian press had somewhat distorted.[6]

GENERAL ELECTIONS

Communist spokesmen concentrated on three major objectives. First, Bulgaria's neutrality was to be maintained at any price. Second, the only way neutrality could be secured was for Bulgaria to seek the friendship of the Soviet Union. Third, the pro-French and pro-British democratic leaders were to be discredited as warmongers. It was along those lines that the Communist electoral campaign for a new Subranie was carried out during the fall of 1939. The decision to have new general elections was reached by Boris soon after the outbreak of the war. The reason why new elections were necessary so short a time after the general elections of 1938 was not explained by the government. Yet it was well known that Boris was dissatisfied with the composition of the 1938 Subranie. Despite its government majority, the Subranie had retained a degree of independence. In matters of foreign policy in particular, independent thinking went far beyond what the King deemed tolerable. In July, 1939, Stoicho Moshanov, the Speaker of the Subranie, elected to the post with the support of the government majority, undertook a private tour of Western European capitals that included, among others, London and an official reception by George VI.[7] Although

---

[6] Todor Pavlov, *Protiv oburkvaneto na poniatiata.*

[7] Moshanov, p. 51; on the same subject, see also Kazasov, *Burni godini*, pp. 637–39. Stoicho Moshanov was a nephew of Nikola Mushanov. He had adopted an alternative spelling of his last name in order to distinguish himself from his uncle, with whom he did not agree. Moshanov's "English connections" were remembered in the summer of 1944 when the government of Ivan Bagrianov decided to send him to Cairo in order to negotiate Bulgaria's withdrawal from the war.

Moshanov had no authority to negotiate, a fact repeatedly stressed by official sources, his visit to England invited attacks from Germanophiles. Such independent behavior Boris found not only irritating but also dangerous in view of his determination to keep foreign policy exclusively in his own hands. It was in order to stifle independence that the 1938 Subranie was dissolved and new elections fixed for the period December 24, 1939, to January 28, 1940.

In the fall of 1939, the revival of the People's Constitutional Bloc was out of the question. In a pre-electoral circular prepared by the Party, it was made clear that the main theme of the Communist campaign would be the "struggle against the imperialist war" and the "war instigators." [8] The Party did not hesitate to identify the Bulgarian representatives of the "war instigators." A Communist leaflet issued in November, 1939, delivered a concentrated attack on Nikola Mushanov, Gichev, Pastukhov, Kosta Todorov, and other leaders of pro-French and pro-British orientation.[9] The government's nominally neutral foreign policy, on the other hand, was spared criticism. The Party continued to press for closer ties with the Soviet Union although, in view of improved Russo-Bulgarian relations, the subject was not stressed. On November 26, one whole month before the start of the elections, 100 Communists and Pladne Agrarians were interned to rural places. Similar internments continued throughout December. A number of provincial constituencies ran single candidates who were proclaimed as elected before election day. Thanks to the procedure followed by the government in past elections, the police were able to concentrate their entire force in a given locality and move it according to the electoral schedules.

The electoral results surpassed Boris's expectations. Of the 160 deputies elected, the regime could count on the support of 140, as opposed to twenty for the opposition. Of those twenty, ten were Communists or nominal Communists, and five were identified as Pladne Agrarians, the most prominent of whom was Angel Derzhanski. The remaining were single individuals, the most notable among them being Nikola Mushanov, the leader of the Democrats, Professor Petko Stainov, nominally affiliated with Zveno, and Dr. Nikola Sakarov, the inde-

[8] *Rabotnichesko delo*, No. 1, 1939, cited in *Istoriia na Bulgariia*, p. 749.

[9] *Nelegalni pozivi na BKP*, pp. 229–31.

pendent leftist economist who had broken away from the Communist
Party after the 1923 uprising. Kimon Georgiev of Zveno, as well as
Stoicho Moshanov, the Speaker of the previous Subranie, failed to get
elected. The Gichev Agrarians were all but obliterated. They were
represented by a single deputy in the person of D. Iliev. Gichev himself
was defeated by a government-backed Agrarian, as was Vergil Dimov.
The new Subranie included fourteen deputies who had dropped out of
the Agrarian Union before the outbreak of the war, as well as ten Gichev
Agrarians who had crossed over into the government majority either
before or during the elections. None of them counted as oppositionists.[10]
Professor Tsankov was reelected, figuring as an oppositionist to the
right of the government majority.

As in the 1938 elections, the relative strength of the oppositionists
in the new Subranie bore no relation to the true influence of their respective groups in the country at large. Police measures and administrative constraints accounted primarily for the electoral outcome. At the
same time, the timing of the elections had proved masterful from the
regime's viewpoint. Europe was at war, while Bulgaria had remained
peaceful and neutral. The country enjoyed mild economic prosperity.
The Western Allies, in whom the democratic leaders believed, had
proved indecisive and weak. If Bulgaria hoped to bring about a revision
of her frontiers, Boris with his pro-German neutrality could be trusted
to be more successful than the Francophiles from the opposition.

On the face of it, the Communists doubled their representation,
from the five deputies elected in 1938 to the ten elected to the new
Subranie. The increase in strength was due not to increased influence
with the public at large but to the virtual absence of any electoral agreements with the forces of the democratic groups. While in the 1938
elections pro-Communist voters contributed more to the election of
opposition candidates than to their own candidates, in the 1939–40
elections Communists and their sympathizers could vote only for candidates identified as Communist nominees. The elections were held in the
aftermath of the Soviet-German Pact and in the midst of the Russian

[10] Details on the composition of the opposition are derived from Petrova, *BZNS
v kraia* . . . , pp. 8–19. Gichev ran in the Third Sofia rural district and received
4,172 votes against the 9,089 votes given to a government-backed Agrarian
candidate.

war on the Finns. Whatever adverse effects these developments might have had, they were balanced by improved Soviet-Bulgarian relations, the first signs of which were clearly visible.

The Communist deputies were faceless persons little known to the public at large. The two exceptions were Dr. Liuben Diukmedzhiev and Todor Poliakov. Diukmedzhiev, who became the spokesman for the Communists in the Subranie, was a well-known lawyer, long associated with Communist causes. He was a friend of Georgi Dimitrov. He was, furthermore, a good orator and a capable debater.[11]

For the Communists, the months following the elections brought a measure of official acceptability to which they were long unaccustomed. Seeing their uncompromising attacks on the leaders of the pro-Western democratic groups, and with an eye on the Soviet Union, the government willingly decided on a policy of restrained toleration. This policy did not change with the premiership of Professor Bogdan Filov (February 15, 1940), whom Boris substituted for Kioseivanov.[12] At the opening of the new Subranie (February 25, 1940), the Communist deputies nominated Diukmedzhiev, their parliamentary leader, for the post of Speaker; he was given thirteen votes.[13] The government, of course, elected its own man, who received 121 votes.[14] Also at the opening of the new session the Communist deputies attended the official

[11] On Diukmedzhiev, see Dimitrov, *Suchineniia*, VIII, 62, 70, 438. During the Leipzig trial he was asked by Dimitrov to maintain connections with Dimitrov's German lawyers and to take care of his legal problems in Bulgaria. This was not the last time that Diukmedzhiev became involved in defending leading Bulgarian Communists. In 1949 he served as the chief legal counsel for Traicho Kostov, not an enviable task by any means. Neither Diukmedzhiev nor Poliakov was in any way to be considered a Party functionary.

[12] At the time, several reasons were given as the possible causes for the decision to drop Kioseivanov. First, he was believed to be closely associated with the policy of Bulgarian-Yugoslav friendship unsuitable to Boris at a time when he was about to open a revisionist campaign. Secondly, Kioseivanov was at odds with his minister of agriculture, Ivan Bagrianov, who, as the second most important person in the cabinet, was believed to be more suitable for the premiership. Thus the choice of Filov, an apolitical professor of archaeology and the minister of education, was interpreted as a compromise decision; see *New York Times*, February 16, 17, 1940.

[13] Kazasov, *Burni godini*, pp. 652–53.

[14] *Times* (London), February 27, 1940.

reception given by the King.[15] In matters of foreign policy, Diukmedzhiev continued to support the government's neutrality.[16] In fact, throughout the spring of 1940, in both foreign and domestic policies, the Communists did what the government dared not do, namely, attack openly the Western countries and discredit their protagonists at home. Here is what a Party leaflet of April 20, 1940, wrote about the Norwegian campaign:

Having failed to create a new front thanks to the peaceful policies of the Soviet Union and its heroic Red Army, the Anglo-French imperialists established a new theater of war in Scandinavia. Norway is in the flames of a new imperialist war. However, out of this new adventure the Anglo-French imperialists are emerging badly crippled.[17]

In May, the Party organ turned its attack against the democratic leaders:

For us, the danger is not only from abroad. The agents of Anglo-French imperialism in our own country are not idle. The followers of Mushanov, Pastukhov, Moshanov, Dimov, and similar political careerists have placed themselves at the disposal of Anglo-French imperialism. Rejected by the Bulgarian people, they see their only hope in the support they might receive from the British and the French. . . . In the meantime, they are being supported by the political adventurers and open agents of the Intelligence Service around Kosta Todorov and Grigor Vasilev [leader of the former Liberal Party]. And what is the government of Professor Filov doing about all that? While making declarations to the effect that Bulgaria's neutrality would be defended, it allows these Anglo-French agents to carry out their designs freely.[18]

The article closed with an appeal for mass demonstrations and for telegrams to be sent to the government asking that (1) internationalist "agents" be immediately arrested, (2) Bulgaria secure for herself the support of those nations interested in her neutrality, namely, the Soviet Union, and (3) freedom of expression be restored to the working people.

Fundamentally, Communist writings and deeds during the period

[15] Kazasov, *Burni godini*, p. 653.

[16] "The Bulgarian People Against the Imperialist War," *World News and Views*, April 13, 1940, pp. 229–30.

[17] *Nelegalni pozivi na BKP*, pp. 234–37.

[18] *Rabotnichesko delo*, May, 1940, quoted in *Rabotnichesko delo, izbrani statii i materiali, 1927–1944*, pp. 344–47.

were dictated by the immediate requirements of Soviet foreign policy. Similarly, the government's attitude toward the Party was in large measure determined by the state of Soviet-Bulgarian relations. These, compared with 1938, had improved immeasurably.

A certain warming up of Soviet-Bulgarian relations was evident even before the conclusion of the Russo-German Pact. In April, 1939, on his way to Turkey, Deputy Foreign Commissar V. Potemkin stopped over in Sofia where he met with Kioseivanov.[19] He returned to Sofia on his way back and was this time received by Boris. On both occasions he warned the Bulgarians against drastic shifts in their foreign orientation and explored the possibilities of a Soviet-Bulgarian rapprochement. Early in August, 1939, prompted by the worsening of relations with Turkey, a delegation of twenty-one deputies went to the Soviet Union, where they visited the Agricultural Exposition in Moscow and were received by Molotov in person.

With the signing of the Russo-German Pact, the Bulgarian government felt encouraged. Not only was the Soviet Union on the same side as Germany, but the Russians, having abandoned Litvinov's line, could be expected to support Bulgaria's revisionist claims. In the middle of September, 1939, the Soviet Commissariat for Foreign Affairs presented Bulgaria's minister to Moscow with a proposal for an agreement of mutual assistance. This was rejected by Kioseivanov.[20] The Bulgarians were ready to go but a certain distance. Instead of reaching a comprehensive understanding, the government decided on a number of limited commercial and cultural agreements. The first in the series was an agreement (December 11, 1939) for the establishment of direct air communications between Moscow and Sofia, followed by a trade agreement (January 5, 1940) in which the Soviet representatives met Bulgarian demands more than halfway.[21] In the spring of 1940 the Soviet Union participated for the first time in the international exposition at

---

[19] Lukacs, p. 216.

[20] On these proposals and the Bulgarian refusal, see *DGFP*, VIII, 277, 484–85. No attempt will be made in the following pages to trace in detail the diplomatic developments. Only occasionally were Communist functionaries given details by the Soviet legation in Sofia. Otherwise, they acted along the general lines of Soviet diplomatic initiatives.

[21] A comprehensive survey of the spectrum of Russo-Bulgarian trade relations is given in V. Khadzhinikolov, *Stopanski otnosheniia*, pp. 185–235.

Plovdiv; the Soviet pavilion was an immediate success and visitors by the tens of thousands showed their enthusiasm. By that time, Soviet movies and books were being widely distributed. The Bulgarian government permitted *Izvestiia* to be sold openly on the newsstands of Sofia. What Bulgarian Communists had striven to achieve for years, namely, the wide distribution of Soviet literature, Professor Filov made a reality. Nothing was more successful in terms of popular enthusiasm than the August, 1940, visit to Sofia of a Soviet football club.

The Soviet planes arrived at five [according to the colorful, if somewhat exaggerated report of a well-known Bulgarian correspondent]—two twin-engined silver-coated machines gleaming bright in the rain. The peasants [who had come to Sofia airport for the occasion] yelled "Ura"—the Russo-Bulgarian war cry. They surged forward, heedless of a barrier of bayonets, and forced their way through the cordons. In a few minutes they had overcome all resistance and entered the airport triumphantly. Cheering wildly, they surrounded the two planes. Their intention was as fantastic as it was pathetic: in their enthusiasm they wanted to lift the planes onto their shoulders! [22]

The reception given the Soviet athletes by the people of Sofia proved again that two decades of continuous anti-Bolshevik propaganda by successive regimes had not succeeded in stamping out the Bulgarians' widespread feeling of friendship toward the Russian people.

THE SOBOLEV MISSION

The visit of the Russians to Sofia marked the opening stage of a political battle of the first magnitude. It was on Bulgarian soil that Soviet and Nazi diplomacy soon clashed for the first time since the pact of August, 1939. In this collision, the Bulgarian Communist Party, acting as the chief sponsor for the Soviet cause, played a significant role. Moreover, since throughout most of the confrontation it was mainly through the actions and writings of the Party that Soviet designs became manifest, Communists received the close attention of Western observers.

The spring of 1940 saw the first signs that the era of good feeling between the Communists and the regime was coming to a close.

In June Germany stepped up its pro-Bulgarian campaign. A joint German-Bulgarian cultural agreement was signed in Berlin by Filov, whom Hitler in turn rewarded with the Grand Cross of the Order of the

[22] Quoted from Padev, p. 233.

German Eagle. With Filov's return to Bulgaria, the press began a campaign for "territorial adjustments." Impressed by the relative ease with which the Rumanians agreed to return Bessarabia to the Soviet Union, the Bulgarian government reopened its demand for the return of southern Dobruja.

In the following months, Bulgaria's demand received the attention of all the Great Powers, each of whom tried to improve its position in Bulgaria or at least prevent the others from doing so. While the Axis preferred the method of direct Bulgarian-Rumanian negotiations, the Soviet Union openly supported Bulgaria's demands. At the same time, in order to weaken the Axis position in the Balkans, Britain indirectly associated herself with the Soviet stand by terming the Bulgarian demands reasonable.[23] The Bulgarian government placed its trust in Germany alone, trying its best to keep the Soviet Union out of the negotiations. Rumors circulated by pro-Nazi elements to the effect that Germany was ready to lend her hand in order to "liberate" the Macedonian people did not strengthen the position of the Soviets, who at this stage, much as they wanted to improve relations with Bulgaria, were not ready to antagonize Yugoslavia in the process.

In early August, 1940, on the eve of the Craiova conference at which the Dobruja issue was settled, the Soviet Union expressed anger for its exclusion from the actual negotiations. It was at this point that the Bulgarian Communist Party entered the scene. Sometime before August 12, it issued a lengthy manifesto which was equally hostile toward the Bulgarian government, which it termed a "Fascist dictatorship," toward the Rome-Berlin Axis, and toward "British imperialism." The manifesto accused the government of having refused a Russian offer for the conclusion of a pact of friendship and mutual assistance. Since no official communication to this effect had been made public, it now became clear to the country at large for the first time that the Bulgarian government had indeed been approached, but that it had turned down the offer.[24]

Most of the manifesto was devoted to a violent attack on alleged German attempts at inducing Bulgaria to intervene on the side of the Axis by holding out prospects of the realization of a Greater Bulgaria

[23] Lukacs, p. 314.

[24] *Times* (London), August 12, 1940.

at the expense of Yugoslavia. If realized, the manifesto added, such a plan would in effect prepare a "new slavery for Macedonia: its conversion into a new Albania." The "just struggles" of the Macedonians should be carried on in conformity with the fundamental duty of all the Balkan nations, which was to avoid anything that could assist the great imperialists in extending the war to the Balkans. To maintain that the rapprochement between the Soviet Union and Yugoslavia "sanctioned the *status quo* and perpetuated Macedonian slavery," the manifesto said, was a "misrepresentation." The document closed with an attack on middle-class opposition groups—the Agrarians and the Social Democrats—who were accused of wanting "to harness Bulgaria to English imperialism." The Party proclaimed its determination to follow an independent line and form "a large People's Front of workers which will lead Bulgaria to security along the path of rapprochement and cooperation with the Soviet." [25]

The significance of the manifesto lay in that it constituted the first open Communist attack on Axis foreign policy in the Balkans. To the hard-pressed British watching for the slightest indication of a German-Soviet rift, this was good news. As it was, the manifesto was only the first of a number of similar pronouncements, each going a step further in the anti-German campaign. Later in August, in a leaflet entitled "An Appeal for Struggle Against Reaction and the Opportunistic Foreign Policy," the Communists openly called for the expulsion of the German "tourists" from Bulgaria. The same leaflet warned against an orientation toward the Axis which would threaten Bulgaria's political and economic independence, and repeated the demand for the conclusion of an agreement for mutual assistance with the Soviet Union.[26] This line continued to be pursued with ever growing vigor during the first half of September. Toward the middle of the month, the Party issued a new manifesto (the third in ten days) in which it openly charged that "Germany wants to organize anti-Soviet bases in the Balkans." The government was urged to cut off its exports to Germany in order to contain the inflationary trend within the country.[27]

By that time, however, the Filov government had scored a victory

[25] *Ibid.*, August 13, 14, 1940.

[26] *Poziv na borba protiv reaktsiiata i avantiuristicheskata vunshna politika* (August, 1940).

[27] *New York Times*, September 15, 1940.

which neutralized the Communist campaign. The Craiova agreement for the return of southern Dobruja was signed on September 7, 1940. Although two days later the Bulgarian minister to Moscow officially thanked the Soviet government for its assistance, the government at home did everything in its power to overlook the role of the Soviet Union and attribute the diplomatic success exclusively to Germany and Italy. The Soviet government was unhappy and said so in the Moscow publication *Trud*, although it continued to be careful not to offend the Germans by putting the blame on "those [Balkan] statesmen who allowed the Western European powers to mislead them." [28] In Bulgaria mass celebrations were organized.[29] The Communists tried to hold the attention of the public in other ways. In the Subranie, on the eve of the official reoccupation of Dobruja, the Communist parliamentary leader asked that the government grant an immediate general amnesty to all political prisoners. His proposal was defeated.[30] Later, in mid-November, the Communists joined with Nikola Mushanov to protest against the first anti-Semitic laws proposed by the Filov government. The protests went unheard and the Subranie proceeded to approve the measures on November 20, 1940.

All through the fall of 1940 the Soviet government remained officially silent on the question of Bulgaria's pro-German orientation. On November 18, Molotov summoned the head of the Bulgarian legation and told him orally of a Soviet proposal for a guarantee to Bulgaria. He stated that the Soviet Union supported Bulgaria's territorial aspirations, and that his government was determined to leave the Bulgarian monarchy and government intact, if and when such a guarantee came into effect. The official written version of the Soviet proposals was delivered on November 25, 1940, by Arkadi Sobolev, the secretary-general of the Soviet Commissariat for Foreign Affairs, who came to Sofia for the purpose.

The Soviet proposal opened with a statement of good will. It reminded the Bulgarians of the "friendly relations" between the two coun-

---

[28] Quoted *ibid*.

[29] *Ibid*., September 9, 1940.

[30] *Ibid*., September 21, 1940. A little later, an amnesty was in fact granted (*ibid*., October 3, 1940) which freed some 3,000 political prisoners, more than half of whom were said to be Communists.

trics, relations that "have frequently been put to the test," and gave the settlement of the southern Dobruja question as an example. "The Soviet Union has full understanding for the interests of Bulgaria in western Thrace and is prepared to cooperate in their realization." Western Thrace was the region which Bulgaria had won from the Turks in the Balkan Wars, giving her access to the Aegean Sea. Following Bulgaria's defeat in World War I, the region went to Greece. Yet, in the Soviet text, Greece was not once mentioned by name. "There are authentic reports that Turkey will oppose by military means the advance of Bulgaria toward the south and that she will prevent the realization of Bulgaria's plans with all available means," the statement went on. At the same time, the Russians made clear that they were vitally interested in the security of their Black Sea border with Turkey "and cannot permit a repetition of the threat constantly directed against southern Russia through the Straits." The final link was now set between the USSR and Bulgaria on the one hand, and Greece and Turkey on the other. "If Bulgaria should be threatened by an attack, or be attacked by Turkey," under the proposed agreement "the Soviet Union will assist Bulgaria with all available means and support her in the realization of Bulgaria's well-known claims in the European part of Turkey." The last point was of particular importance, since the Russian offer on Turkey's account could not be matched by the Germans. In view of the fact that the Soviet Union was "opposed on principle" to unilateral guarantees, "which stress the inequality between the two partners," the offer was for mutual assistance. The only obligation of the Bulgarians was to render assistance to the Soviet Union "in case of a real threat to the interests of the Soviet Union in the Black Sea or in the Straits." Bulgaria's internal regime was not to be affected by the terms of the proposed agreement. Furthermore, the Russians were prepared to give "suitable assistance in the form of a loan of money, food, arms, and material, if Bulgaria should need them." The USSR was prepared to drop its objections to Bulgaria's entry into the Tripartite Pact, assuming the proposed mutual assistance agreement was accepted.[31]

The Bulgarian government, after making known the text of the proposals to the German ambassador in Sofia, rejected the offer. On

---

[31] The full text of the Soviet draft agreement is reproduced in *DGFP*, XI, 772–73.

November 30, Soviet Minister to Sofia A. Lavrishchev was called in by
Bulgaria's Foreign Minister Popov, who presented his government's oral
reply. Bulgaria was interested in the revisions of her frontiers, but such
revisions were to be accomplished peacefully. In view of her past misfortunes, Bulgaria had no desire for grand ventures. Bulgaria was interested in the Straits only indirectly. Finally, Popov told the Russian,
his government had already decided in principle to join the Tripartite
Pact, a decision which precluded other engagements.[32]

Except for Sobolev's visit to Sofia, the Bulgarian public did not
learn of the Soviet proposals, which the government had no inclination
of publishing. It was at this point that the Bulgarian Communist Party
took over. In a matter of days it printed thousands of leaflets containing
a popularized version of the more attractive aspects of the Soviet offers.
These leaflets, distributed throughout the country, produced what
amounted to an explosion of popular excitement, with heavy pro-
Russian overtones.

> Bulgaria has been profoundly shaken [reported a foreign correspondent on
> December 10] by what may be considered as the greatest subversive activity
> organized from abroad in the country's recent history. During the last ten
> days thousands of Communist leaflets have been circulated throughout the
> country declaring that Soviet Russia is proposing a "pact of mutual assist-
> ance," and that Bulgaria will receive the Adrianople district west of the
> Enos-Media Line from Turkey and the whole of the Aegean coast from
> Greece.

"Thousands of telegrams have been received in Sofia from the
whole country," continued the same source, "and most of the deputies
have requested an audience with the king. About 100,000 signatures
have already been collected in the provinces urging the government to
accept the Russian proposals." The government counterattacked by
organizing a press and radio campaign "for the defense of Bulgaria's

---

[32] On the Bulgarian reply, see *ibid.*, pp. 756–57. The Popov-Lavrishchev interview
ended with mutual recriminations on account of the many thousands of leaflets
which had already appeared all over Sofia, containing details of the Soviet proposals. Popov assured the Soviet Minister that the matter had been kept secret by
the government. Lavrishchev stated that in no way had there been any indiscretion
on the part of his legation, to which Popov replied that "undoubtedly the publication originated with the local Communists and asked for an investigation as to
where they received their information."

independence." This failed to stifle the pro-Russian campaign. Leaflets continued to be pushed "under the doors of every house in Sofia" throughout much of December.[33] By that time, the "battle of the leaflets" was joined by an unexpected participant, a development which, if nothing else, helped complicate matters further. The Germans, seeing that the leaflets had an anti-Turkish flavor, decided to produce and distribute some themselves.[34] It was not long before several versions of the affair were in circulation. The government encouraged rumors to the effect that the Soviets were only looking to establish naval and air bases in the port towns of Varna and Burgas. The Communists made efforts to explain the differences among the many versions.

At the height of the pro-Russian effort, the Party's Buro-in-Exile decided to send assistance to the leadership at home, headed by Kostov as secretary of the Central Committee. In December, 1940, he was joined by Anton Ivanov, a member of the Buro-in-Exile, who arrived clandestinely on board a Soviet freighter. With his arrival in Bulgaria the campaign for a pact with the Soviet Union reached the peak of its intensity. As the new year arrived, Communist propaganda was given a new twist. The danger from the Turks, reported massing troops on the Bulgarian frontier, was emphasized. In an article, Anton Ivanov compared the attitude of the Bulgarian government to that of Colonel Beck, the Polish foreign minister. "It seems that we Bulgarians have become envious of Colonel Beck's great foresight and caution and have turned down a brotherly offer for fear that it might endanger our independence." The Soviet offer, he went on to stress, did not constitute interference in Bulgaria's internal affairs. "The Soviet proposals do not prevent Bulgaria from joining the Tripartite Pact," concluded his article, "if such a step were found to be in the interest of Bulgaria." [35]

---

[33] *New York Times*, December 27, 1940.

[34] *Times* (London), December 11, 1940. The full range of Bulgaria's relations with Germany in the period before and after the Soviet initiative is dealt with in detail by Marin V. Pundeff in his "Bulgaria's Place in Axis Policy" (an unpublished doctoral dissertation, University of Southern California, 1958). For the principal documentation on Bulgarian-German relations on the one hand, and German-Soviet relations as pertaining to Bulgaria on the other, see, *DGFP*, XI, 364–66, 560–61, 651–54, 672–78, 691, 713, 726, 1022, 1202–3.

[35] *Rabotnichesko delo*, January, 1941, reproduced in *Rabotnichesko delo, izbrani statii i materiali, 1927–1944*, pp. 556–60.

This last sentence showed that the Party was growing wary, if not desperate, for in January, 1941, the government evinced no signs of softening.

A LAST EFFORT

The bonds with Germany grew stronger daily. The first day of 1941 found Filov conferring with German government officials in Salzburg. In January, the police almost succeeded in capturing the entire Central Committee, the Politburo, and all the regional Party secretaries assembled in the Macedonian quarters of Sofia in order to attend the Seventh Party Plenum.[36] The decision to hold a plenum at this time indicated the Party's concern over the prevailing situation. The Party leadership now realized that the campaign for a pact with the Soviet Union could not succeed. Therefore, prime emphasis was once more placed on complete neutrality.[37]

The Seventh Plenum attacked the Social Democrats and the Gichev Agrarians for their failure to support the Communist campaign.[38] At the height of the pro-Soviet effort Gichev, Pastukhov, Grigor Vasilev (Liberal), Kosturkov (Radical), and Professor Petko Stoianov were alleged to have assembled to draft a pamphlet with which to counter growing pro-Soviet sentiments.[39] Significantly, Nikola Mushanov and the leaders of Pladne were not attacked, the former because of his energetic condemnation of Filov's foreign policy in the Subranie debates, and the latter because of a certain inclination to collaborate with the Communist Party despite their pro-Western orientation.[40]

The Plenum was hardly over when its resolutions on Bulgaria's international position became obsolete. The end of January saw an intensi-

---

[36] For unexplained reasons, the meeting place of the Plenum was changed at the last minute. Had this not been done, all would have fallen into the hands of the police, who occupied the place originally designated for the purpose. These facts were made public by Kostov at the Eighth Plenum held in the spring of 1945; Kostov, *Politicheskoto polozhenie i zadachite na partiiata*, p. 59.

[37] The text of the resolution dealing with the effort of the Party for the conclusion of a pact with the Soviet Union is reproduced in *BKP v rezoliutsii i resheniia*, pp. 379–86.

[38] *Ibid.*, p. 382.

[39] Gornenski, p. 31.

[40] *Ibid.*, pp. 25–27.

fication in both domestic and international activities. With German backing, a Bulgarian-Turkish rapprochement was effected, culminating in the signing of a joint declaration (February 17, 1941) that restated the determination of both governments to maintain good neighborly relations. The infiltration of German "visitors," which had been in progress for several months, was stepped up. On February 1, 1941, the Bulgarians concluded an agreement with the German authorities regulating the ways and means in which the German army was to be supplied while in Bulgaria. Throughout February, more and more German officers dressed as civilians entered the country from Rumania.[41] On January 29 the Bulgarian cabinet adopted a plan prepared and presented by Petur Gabrovski, the minister of the interior, laying out the details of an anti-Communist scheme to be put into action at any given moment in order to immobilize the Party.[42]

On January 29 the fifteen Communist and Pladne Agrarian opposition deputies presented a petition asking the government to explain how it proposed to safeguard Bulgaria's neutrality. The government was also requested to state its position in relation to the pact proposed by the Soviet Union. At this late hour, the feeling that only the immediate acceptance of a Soviet guarantee could save the country from German occupation grew among some non-Communist opposition elements.[43] Open support for a pact with the Soviet Union was expressed by moderate democratic elements early in February.[44] These reports came amid a wave of rumor and speculation of a second visit to Sofia by Sobolev, who had delivered the original proposals late in November.[45]

After prolonged insistence by the opposition, on February 10 Filov

[41] M.B., "German Threat to Bulgaria," *Bulletin of International News*, February 22, 1941, pp. 191–97.

[42] Based on Filov's diaries as printed in *Otechestven front*, December 6, 1944.

[43] *Times* (London), January 31, 1941.

[44] *Ibid.*, February 5, 1941.

[45] *Ibid.*, February 10, 1941. Added to this was the small-scale sensation caused by the sudden resignation of Ivan Bagrianov, the minister of agriculture. Bagrianov was a pro-German and a believer in the "new order," and therefore his exit from the cabinet (February 5, 1941) had no immediate political significance. Probably the single most important reason for his resignation was his ambition and desire to become prime minister. Nevertheless, the resignation on the eve of the German entry into Bulgaria and his formal dissociation from the signing of the Tripartite

agreed to meet with a delegation of the parliamentary opposition leaders. They came armed with the full text of a recent speech by Churchill in which Bulgaria was warned against allowing the entry of the German army on Bulgarian soil. The references concerning Bulgaria had been suppressed by censorship and Filov was now asked to explain the course of his foreign policy. Furthermore, the leader of the Communist parliamentary group pressed the Prime Minister for a definitive answer concerning the Soviet proposals. Filov did all he could to calm down his unwelcome visitors, but evaded all direct questions.[46] Three days later, Pastukhov, who, not being a deputy, was not present at the meeting of February 10, sent Filov a personal telegram in which he warned of the disastrous results which any shift from the policy of strict neutrality would have on Bulgaria. He also protested the presence of German military personnel on Bulgarian territory.[47]

All this time Boris remained behind the scenes. Repeated requests for an audience with him were invariably turned down. Knowing full well that the final word had been given on matters concerning foreign policy, ten opposition leaders forwarded a protest memorandum to the palace on February 21, 1941.[48]

A day before the presentation of the protest memorandum, the Germans had already thrown a number of pontoon bridges across the Danube that allowed them to enter in force. On February 21, Field-

---

Pact made Bagrianov a suitable candidate for the premiership when Bulgaria contemplated a switch from her pro-German course in the summer of 1944. On the resignation and the immediate reaction, see *New York Times*, February 5, 6, 1941, and *Times* (London), February 8, 1941.

[46] *Times* (London), February 11, 1941.

[47] *Ibid.*, February 15, 1941.

[48] The memorandum was initiated by Dr. G. M. Dimitrov of Pladne. It carried ten signatures, namely, two for Pladne, one for the Communists, as well as those of Gichev, Pastukhov, S. Kosturkov for the Radicals, K. Georgiev for Zveno, N. Mushanov, A. Burov, and G. Vasilev. The document represented the minimum on which all signers could agree. It demanded the preservation of Bulgaria's neutrality but made no mention of the Soviet initiative. On the memorandum, see Dr. Dimitrov's article in the *Saturday Evening Post*, December 6, 1947, pp. 28–29; see also Petrova, *BZNS v kraia . . .* , p. 38. The latter is an important source on the attitude of the non-Communist oppositionists throughout the campaign over the Sobolev mission, and particularly that of Gichev, whose slogan was "peace and true neutrality without pacts and military alliances" (*ibid.*, p. 36).

Marshal List, the commander of the German forces, established his headquarters in Sofia. On the following day the government, undertaking a preventive action, struck a swift blow at all potential opposition, concentrating in particular on the more outspoken pro-British elements. Prominent Agrarian leaders (especially from the Pladne group), journalists and correspondents for Western newspapers, "cosmopolitans," Communists, and other persons "with foreign connections" were arrested and herded into Gonda voda, a detention camp prepared earlier by the government for precisely this purpose. A few succeeded in evading the police and escaped across the border.

The formal adherence of Bulgaria to the Tripartite Pact (March 1, 1941) and the official government announcement about the entry of German troops came as an anticlimax. On March 3, Vyshinsky, Soviet deputy commissar of foreign affairs, presented the Bulgarian minister to Moscow with a mildly worded protest and expressed the fear that the decision would serve to broaden the war.[49] At home, a number of opposition deputies tried to protest in the Subranie, but were prevented from speaking. The people of the Legion and other crypto-Nazi elements were enthusiastic. The public at large remained uncertain and confused, although in all cases impressed with the mechanized German columns that were visible everywhere.

The Communists were disappointed. The intensity of their pro-Soviet campaign had given rise to great expectations which were now shattered. Their effort was not completely wasted, however. It brought to the surface pro-Russian sentiments and thus reminded Bulgaria's rulers that the Bulgarian people would not tolerate open hostility with the Soviet Union.

The coming of the German armies into Bulgaria resulted in the first armed resistance effort. It sprang not from within the Communist Party, for which the dictates of the Soviet-German Pact still applied, but from among the Pladne Agrarians. The effort was backed by the British and the Yugoslavs. In military terms the endeavor proved of no importance. Yet for the long run its political significance was considerable.

Anticipating the German occupation of the Balkans, in the winter of 1940–41 the British undertook to organize resistance centers in the

[49] For the texts of the Soviet reactions over the German entry into Bulgaria, see Degras, III, 482–84.

various Balkan countries, which they hoped would carry on the struggle against the Germans after their own departure from the region. In all cases, the clandestine resistance organizations rested on pro-Western democratic political formations. Advice, material, and money came from the secret British organization for sabotage and subversion known as the SOE and supervised by the Foreign Office.[50]

The resident agent of the SOE in Sofia was Norman Davies. Under his inspiration, collaboration was established with Dr. G. M. Dimitrov of the Pladne Agrarians, who in turn organized a number of clandestine groups among his followers. On the day following the submission of the opposition protest memorandum of February 21, Dr. Dimitrov was placed under arrest. He succeeded in evading the police and was eventually smuggled to Istanbul in a vehicle of the British legation in Sofia.[51] From Turkey, Dr. Dimitrov traveled to Yugoslavia where he organized a contingent of young Agrarian followers from among the Bulgarian students there. They received military training and were on their way to cross into Bulgarian territory as partisans when the Germans invaded Yugoslavia on April 6, 1941.[52] With the fall of Yugoslavia, Dr. Dimitrov was flown to the Middle East where he remained throughout the war.

[50] Details on the SOE and its operations became known only in the mid-sixties with the publication of B. Sweet-Escott's *Baker Street Irregular*. By October, 1943, the SOE had something like 80 separate missions in the Balkans (*ibid.*, p. 170). Unlike the American OSS under William Donovan, which it resembled, the British SOE did not produce a single authoritative head. Coordination between the two organizations was almost nonexistent. Early in 1944 Donovan and the SOE clashed over "jurisdictional rights" in their Bulgarian undertakings (*ibid.*, p. 194). In the early years of the SOE's operations, much of its work in the Balkans was amateurish and produced little result. From the first it maintained close contact with the Rumanian peasant leader Maniu.

[51] Details of Dr. Dimitrov's escape to Turkey are given in the memoirs of George Rendel, the British minister to Bulgaria (*The Sword and the Olive*, pp. 174–78). In January, 1941, D. Matsankiev, the leader of the Pladne parliamentary group in the 1938 Subranie, escaped over the Rumanian frontier, went to the Middle East, and later to London (see his account in the *Central European Observer*, December 22, 1944, pp. 398–99). Another Pladne Agrarian who escaped to the Middle East was Ivan Kostov.

[52] On this there are the accounts by Dr. Dimitrov in *Svoboda*, October 7, 1944, and *Svobodna i nezavisima Bulgariia*, September 14, 1949. In a manifesto to his followers, printed in Yugoslavia and distributed in Bulgaria by the Yugoslav legation in Sofia, Dr. Dimitrov called for resistance to the Germans; on this, see Petrova, *BZNS v kraia . . .* , p. 44.

In April, 1941, the secret resistance organizations set up by Dr. Dimitrov in Bulgaria were uncovered by the police. Thirty persons were arrested in Sofia and the provinces. Sabotage and propaganda materials, as well as a radio transmitter, were found. In May, the authorities made public the names of the arrested in connection with the conspiracy. A mass trial was held near the end of the year, and sentences were pronounced at the end of December. Eleven death sentences were issued, seven *in absentia*. Of the four condemned people in custody, none was executed. They remained in prison until 1944, at which time they were freed together with the remaining persons sentenced to various prison terms.[53] In later years, Dimitrov and his Pladne collaborators could claim, not without good reason, that it was they rather than the Communists who first fostered armed resistance. In February, 1942, the authorities executed Georgi Vulkov, the former editor of the newspaper *Pladne*, on charges of espionage on behalf of Great Britain.[54]

[53] On the first public announcements concerning the conspiracy, and on the persons sentenced, see, respectively, *Dnes*, May 9, 1941, and *Zora*, December 26, 1941. Among those sentenced to death *in absentia* were Dr. Dimitrov, Ivan Kostov, Norman Davies of the SOE, and a number of Yugoslavs. Four received life terms, two were given terms of fifteen years each, ten received twelve and a half years each, and the remaining six received lighter sentences. Many of those involved in the conspiracy were indeed Pladne members, or persons close to them. Yet the antigovernment conspiracy was organized by Dr. Dimitrov personally, without the knowledge of other Pladne leaders.

[54] *Zemedelsko zname*, October 2, 14, November 25, 1944; *New York Times*, February 12, 1942. Vulkov's execution was unrelated to the activities of Dr. Dimitrov. He was found guilty of having given information of military value to agents of the British intelligence.

CHAPTER SIX

THE PARTY DURING THE INITIAL STAGES OF THE WAR

BULGARIA DID NOT BECOME an occupied country with the entry of the German troops. Throughout the war years the government retained control over the administration and was responsible for its actions. The Bulgarian government played the role of a willing ally of the Axis against her Balkan neighbors and the Western Allies, and a nonbelligerent helper against Russia.

Bulgaria's reward for her assistance to the Germans was the annexation of extensive territories from her two neighbors. Yugoslav Macedonia and Greek Thrace were incorporated into the Bulgarian state, although the Germans made clear that this change would have to be confirmed by the peace treaties after the final victory. Within Bulgaria, the annexation was universally popular. What the Bulgarians called "our historic national unification" remained the single most important political factor throughout the war years. For its part, the government did everything to capitalize on its accomplishment, claiming that it had given the people what two wars had failed to achieve.

Added to the feeling of national fulfillment was the sense of well-being which the majority of the people continued to have throughout much of 1941 and 1942. With most of Europe in flames, Bulgaria remained relatively peaceful. The economy appeared to be booming. Bulgaria's export trade rose steadily, the bulk going to Germany. Much of the prosperity was of course due to inflation. The fact that Germany became increasingly unable to deliver real goods was not felt until later.

Bulgaria's formal declaration of war on the Western Allies in December, 1941, left most Bulgarians apathetic. Their indifference was due to the realization that, for the time being at least, this was to be a "paper war" and that as long as the Germans retained their grip on the Balkans, Bulgaria was not to be faced with the danger of an active front. The British had always been disliked by the masses. The United States was too remote to cause any concern.

The Soviet Union presented a special case. Most Bulgarians felt emotionally involved with Russia. After June, 1941, they were bewildered. Their surprise was not so much over the German attack on the USSR as over the Russian failure to withstand the Nazi assault. On the morrow of June 22, the Party decided to prepare for armed resistance. This decision proved difficult to implement because the Party itself was divided on the issue of armed struggle. It was only in 1943, after the Soviet success in Stalingrad, that Communists, aided by Tito's Yugoslavs, made some progress in that direction.

THE SPRING INTERLUDE

The Party position did not undergo radical change with the entry of the German army. As long as the Russo-German Pact remained intact, the Communist attitude toward the Germans in Bulgaria remained one of restrained hostility. Following the Soviet protest to the Bulgarian government of March 3, the Party organ came out with a statement of its own (March 6) which repeated the Soviet fears that by its policies the Filov government had helped to expand the war.[1] Throughout the spring of 1941, the line remained unchanged: oppose the Germans by propaganda, but not by force.[2]

The extended debates over the dual organizational structure which dominated much of the Communist leaders' thinking after 1934 had come to an end with the final fusion of the illegal Communist Party with the Workers' Party. In mid-1941 the number of organized members was estimated at 10,600; that of the RMS, the Party youth organization, at 19,000.[3] Compared with the 30,000 to 35,000 organized Communists before the 1934 May coup, the figure was not impressive, although con-

---

[1] *Rabotnichesko delo*, March, 1941, reproduced in *Rabotnichesko delo, izbrani statii i materiali, 1927–1944.*

[2] *New York Times*, February 23, 1941.

[3] Vasilev, p. 210.

sidering the semilegal conditions of the past seven years, it represented achievement. Thousands of ex-Communists remained unaffiliated, some because of their past "left sectarian" associations, and others because of lost contact with local Party organizations. The Seventh Plenum gave much of its attention to the problem of organization. It urged Communist functionaries and activists to initiate a search in order to bring former members back into the Party.[4] Lack of discipline and a growing number of *agents provocateurs* within Party ranks remained the cardinal organizational problem. With the efficiency of the police growing daily (soon to be further increased thanks to collaboration with the Gestapo), the Party found the maintenance of conspiratorial standards increasingly difficult. In January, 1941, it introduced a plan which stipulated a thorough check of all the cadres.[5]

In the spring of 1941 the Politburo consisted of the following five members: Kostov, Anton Ivanov, Dragoicheva, Radenko Vidinski, and Anton Yugov.[6] Of the five, Kostov was the only holdover from the Politburo elected at the Sixth Enlarged Plenum in 1936. Ivanov was also a member of the Buro-in-Exile. The new additions—Vidinski (also known as Rangelov), Dragoicheva, and Yugov (whose real name was Anton Tanev)—were significant, first because all three had spent the middle thirties in the Soviet Union, and secondly because within a year, with the arrest of both Kostov and Anton Ivanov, the entire Party apparatus would fall into their hands.

Vidinski, a contemporary of Kostov, was a Communist deputy in the 1931–34 Subranie and a member of the Agrarian Commission of the Party Central Committee. After the dissolution of the Subranie he emigrated to the Soviet Union, remaining there until his return to Bulgaria in 1935.

Tsola Dragoicheva, the only Bulgarian Communist woman ever to reach the higher echelons of the Party, was largely a product of the

---

[4] *BKP v rezoliutsii i resheniia*, p. 361.

[5] *Ibid.*, p. 362.

[6] *The Struggle of the Bulgarian People Against Fascism*, p. 32; see also Vasilev, p. 119. The latter source omits the name of Radenko Vidinski, although he was reported elected a Politburo member in January, 1941. At the same time, Vlado Georgiev, reported elected to the Politburo together with Vidinski, is unaccounted for. He was killed as a resistance fighter sometime after 1941.

Bulgarian prisons, in which she spent eight years of her youth (1923–24, 1925–32). After being sentenced to death during the Tsankov terror of the mid-twenties, she avoided execution by becoming pregnant and giving birth to a child in prison. Granted amnesty in 1932, she went to the Soviet Union to undergo theoretical training. Dragoicheva returned to Bulgaria in 1936 to take part in the purge, and entered the Central Committee in the following year. In the middle of 1940, after a second trip to Russia, she became a Politburo member, taking over also the editorship of *Rabotnichesko delo*, the Party organ.[7]

Short, quick-witted, tough, and able, Anton Yugov, the youngest of the five (born in 1904), distinguished himself as trade-union organizer among his fellow tobacco workers. Born and raised in Greek Macedonia, Yugov, with his family, was repatriated to Bulgaria after World War I. He became active in the Communist youth movement, joined the Party in 1928, and was eventually sent to the Comintern School (1934–36). After his return to Bulgaria, he concentrated on trade-union work and was instrumental in the general strike of tobacco workers that broke out in the middle of 1940.[8]

The only other significant addition to the top Party leadership made in 1941 was the inclusion of Vulko Chervenkov in the Buro-in-Exile.[9]

REACTIONS TO THE GERMAN ATTACK ON THE USSR

On the day following the German attack on the USSR, the Central Committee issued a manifesto condemning both the attack and the pro-German policies of the Filov government. "Beware and resist all measures which the government will undertake in order to bring us into the war or place our country in the services of the fascist criminals." The manifesto went on:

Never before in history has there been a more brigandlike, more counter-revolutionary and imperialist war than this one Fascism is now waging on the USSR. . . . So just a war cannot but enjoy the sympathy and support of

[7] Her biographical sketch is based largely on the following sources: *Rabotnichesko delo*, December 12, 1947; *ibid.*, November 29, 1958.

[8] On Yugov's life, see *Rabotnichesko delo*, August 7, 1945; *Free Bulgaria*, August 1, 1949.

[9] *BKP v rezoliutsii i resheniia*, p. 359.

every honest and progressive person in the world. . . . The Bulgarian people, who in their overwhelming majority harbor a deep love for the fraternal Soviet peoples and pin on them their greatest hopes for a better future, are faced with the colossal task of preventing their country and army from being used for the criminal purposes of German Fascism. . . . Not one grain of Bulgarian wheat, not one piece of Bulgarian bread for the German Fascists and plunderers. Not a single Bulgarian in their service.[10]

On June 24 the Politburo decided to start preparing for armed resistance. A Central Military Commission was created and empowered with the preparation and conduct of the "armed struggle against the Nazi occupationists and their local Quislings." [11] As first constituted, the Commission was composed of five members: Khristo Mikhailov, Dimo Dichev, Gocho Grozev, Ivan Maslarov, and Georgi Minchev, with Anton Yugov as Politburo representative.[12]

The Central Military Commission met for the first time at the end of June and considered organizational problems. A full-fledged plenary session was held a month later (July 21, 1941) in the Vitosha mountains, where further details regarding the establishment of parallel military committees on the local district level were considered.[13] Khristo Mikhailov, a veteran Communist with military experience, was given over-all command.[14]

For the Party, these measures were in the nature of reflex actions: the "Socialist fatherland" was in danger and the Bulgarian Party was

[10] *Ibid.*, pp. 447–50.

[11] Dimitrov, *Political Report Delivered to the V Congress of the Bulgarian Communist Party*, p. 34.

[12] In one form or another, the Central Military Commission (later renamed the general staff of the resistance) existed throughout the war years, although its composition underwent constant changes owing to arrests and executions. On the Commission's initial composition, see Vasilev, p. 126.

[13] Gornenski, p. 58.

[14] Mikhailov had served as an officer in the Bulgarian army during World War I and had been a central figure in the 1923 Communist insurrection. With that, his military experience had come to an end. Following the 1925 terroristic outbursts, he had been imprisoned for years (1925–37) and interned four times between 1938 and 1940; *Rabotnichesko delo*, February 9, 1947. Mikhailov continued to operate from the underground until February, 1944, at which time he was shot to death by the police. Later, he was posthumously made a colonel general of the Bulgarian army (*Rabotnichesko delo*, June 16, 1945) and has since been honored as the first commander in chief of the Bulgarian wartime resistance.

going to its assistance. Two decades of indoctrination could not have failed to teach Bulgarian Communists the first maxim of Soviet Bolshevism, which stated that the safety of the Soviet Union was the prerequisite for the survival of the international Communist movement. Only when the maxim came to be put into practice, did the discrepancies become obvious. The strategic mistakes of the past were all too fresh in the minds of many Communists. They had revolted in 1923 after the opportunity had passed. They took no action in 1934 when the opportunity was there. Were they to act in error once again? The fact was that opposition to armed struggle developed from the outset. It affected the top leadership no less than the rank and file. At an early stage, the Central Military Commission, which was responsible for resistance, opposed the armed effort on the ground that acts of violence would bring police retributions that the Party could not withstand.[15]

Within the Party [according to Kostov], the course of armed resistance was opposed by many. According to some comrades, if we were to resort to armed struggle, the Party would have to face the danger of becoming isolated from the masses and of having to carry the burdens of the fight all alone. Their advice was that we wait with decisive actions until the course of the war had changed. Thus it was necessary first that we carry out within the Party a great struggle in order to uproot the prevailing inclination toward passivity. Furthermore, it soon became clear that the organization of armed resistance was by no means an easy undertaking. We needed war materials as well as the skills required in order to put them to use. At that time we did not have such skills. Nor had we prepared ourselves for this kind of work.[16]

Interested in maximizing the extent of the wartime Communist resistance effort, Party historians after 1944 did all they could to conceal the true magnitude of intra-Party opposition. There was little doubt that throughout the war, and particularly during its initial stages, such opposition was both powerful and widespread. Only occasionally did Party spokesmen give any indication of the seriousness of the inner crisis. "The policy of armed resistance," according to Anton Yugov,

[15] The revelation was made in 1945 by Kostov himself, then first secretary of the Party. His report, printed right after it was made, has never been republished since. It was not included in his collected works published after his posthumous rehabilitation; see Kostov, *Politicheskoto polozhenie i zadachite na partiiata*, pp. 88–89.

[16] *Ibid.*, pp. 5–8.

particularly during the temporary successes of Hitler's hordes on the eastern front, gave rise to certain doubts among Party circles, including Party cadres in a position of leadership. Some of them, frightened by the difficulties of the moment, became the authors of all kinds of opportunistic theories. Openly or secretly, they expressed disagreement with the political line of the Party. They justified their position of virtual capitulation by saying that under the prevailing Bulgarian conditions the policy of armed resistance was nothing more than an "adventure" and that the main effort should be made in the direction of political agitation and propaganda.[17]

The decision having once been made not to support the line of armed resistance, the inevitable followed. Again according to Yugov:

Not only individual rank-and-file Party members, but also some leading comrades, at the most decisive moment for our people, disobeyed the Central Committee directive [of June, 1941] which had instructed all Communist functionaries to go underground, and surrendered into the hands of the enemy.

Immediately after the outbreak of the Nazi-Soviet war, the Party sustained its first major blow. In June, the police presented the government with a list of 291 prominent Communist functionaries and recommended that they be arrested; the report also urged the government to step up the establishment of internment camps.

On July 3 the police struck all over the country and arrested a total of 244 people, many of whom were sent to the Gonda voda concentration camp, where they joined other Communists and Agrarians arrested during the winter and spring of 1941.[18]

It was not long before Radenko Vidinski, a member of the Politburo, also found himself in Gonda voda. In September, 1941, he was joined by Yugov and Dimo Dichev, a member of the Central Military Commission. At the same time, Tsola Dragoicheva was also arrested and placed in the Sveti Nikola camp for women. Thus, in September, three out of the five Politburo members were in the hands of the police. In October, however, Yugov, together with four other Communists— Radenko Vidinski, Nikola Pavlov (a technical associate of the Central Committee), Emil Markov, and Boris Kopchev—succeeded in escaping

---

[17] *Novo vreme*, September, 1953, pp. 59–75.

[18] *Istoricheski pregled*, No. 4 (1959), pp. 172–79.

from Gorda voda. Vidinski and Pavlov were recaptured immediately.[19] Anton Yugov reached Sofia on October 17, 1941, and assumed his position in the Central Military Commission; he was soon rejoined by Tsola Dragoicheva, who had also escaped.[20]

Police repressions continued throughout the fall and winter of 1941. On July 10, 1941, the parliamentary immunity of the Communist deputies was lifted and they were arrested.[21] At the same time the government rushed through the Subranie amendments to the penal code which raised the penalties for subversive and antigovernment activities. In November, four Communists were executed under the new provisions.[22] Up until the end of 1941 the government succeeded in uncovering and breaking up seventeen Party and seventeen youth organizations involving 769 Communists altogether, of whom 474 were brought to trial. In Greek and Yugoslav Macedonia under Bulgarian occupation, the respective figures were six local organizations involving 272 Communists, of whom 115 were brought to trial.[23]

Demoralized by Soviet failures on the eastern front, even militant Communists retained little fighting spirit. Here and there tiny combat groups sprang up. In all cases they were formations of from three to six persons who occasionally undertook a small-scale operation against the local police.[24] They were not partisan units. Their participants continued

[19] This information has been pieced together from the following sources: Vasilev, p. 217; Dinev, pp. 316–17; and Belev, *Katorgata na fashizma*, pp. 37, 41, 62, 141, 173–78. Belev, a well-known Communist novelist, knew the concentration camps at firsthand. His *Katorgata na fashizma* gives a good description of the prevailing conditions and the mood of the inmates.

[20] *Rabotnichesko delo*, August 7, 1945.

[21] In all, nine deputies identified as Communists were expelled. They were Dr. L. Diukmedzhiev, T. Poliakov, D. Zakhariev, P. Mitev, A. Gachev, A. Kudrev, K. Svetlov, B. Belev, and N. Dzhankov. On their expulsion, see *Utro*, July 10, 1941; see also Narodno subranie, *Stenografski dnevnitsi*, debates for July 9–10, pp. 4, 11–12. Mushanov and Professor Stainov protested the measure, to no avail. Mushanov spoke again on the subject during debates held on November 14, 1941 (*ibid.*, pp. 162–71), on which occasion he expressed regret for the expulsion of what he considered to be honest people. He stated his lifelong opposition to Communism but attacked "the brutal anti-Communist" measures taken by the government.

[22] *New York Times*, November 18, 1941.

[23] The above figures are taken from Gornenski, p. 121.

[24] *Istoricheski pregled*, No. 4 (1959), pp. 132–56.

to live a legal existence, joining in occasional night ventures. Fighting groups also undertook small-scale activities of economic sabotage with which they hoped to cripple Bulgaria's ability to supply the Germans. Since no one knew what was going to be exported, the net result of such sabotage was to antagonize local merchants or manufacturers whose merchandise was damaged. There were exceptions, although few. On October 19, 1941, a Communist by the name of Leon Tadzher ignited gasoline dumps servicing the Germans. He was caught, sentenced to death, and eventually hanged.[25]

The only centrally organized undertaking during this early period was an abortive attack on the Gonda voda concentration camp carried out on August 15, 1941. On orders from the center, a group of Communists from southern Bulgaria assembled. They were instructed to attack the camp and free the Communists there, many of them important functionaries. Poorly armed and badly organized, the attackers failed. A new attempt was made a fortnight later (August 31) without result. Before reaching the camp, the attacking force was intercepted, dispersed, and pursued. Several of the participants were caught and eventually executed.[26] This was the only case throughout the war years in which an attack on a concentration camp was ever attempted. Toward the end of 1941, the Gonda voda camp was closed and the prisoners shipped to the occupied territories, where they were placed in a former military camp of the Greek army.[27]

SOVIET CONTRIBUTIONS: THE ARRIVAL OF THE PARACHUTISTS

On July 23, 1941, one month after the German attack on the Soviet Union, the Party Buro-in-Exile launched its first broadcast in the Bulgarian language. This marked the beginning of the broadcasting station "Khristo Botev" (named after a Bulgarian poet and a nationalist hero),

---

[25] On this, see Tadzher's biography by Samuilov. Tadzher acted on his own. He had emigrated to Palestine and had been active as a member of the Palestinian CP until deported back to the country of his birth by the British colonial authorities.

[26] Gornenski, p. 67; see also *Times* (London), December 5, 1941, for a description of the attack and other Communist armed undertakings. Michael Padev (*Escape from the Balkans,* pp. 243–49), a Bulgarian journalist who in the spring of 1941 spent some time in Gonda voda, participated in one of the attacks.

[27] Dinev, pp. 316–17.

which throughout the war years beamed its message to Bulgaria.[28] Some of the more important exiles in the Soviet Union, such as Vulko Chervenkov, Karlo Lukanov, and Ferdinand Kozovski, were associated with "Khristo Botev" and continued to work in it throughout the war. In the fall of 1941, a second broadcasting station, "Naroden glas" (People's Voice), operating on the same wave length as Radio Sofia, began operations. The moving spirit behind "Naroden glas" was Stanke Dimitrov-Marek. The technique used was to interfere with the regular newscasts of the official Bulgarian radio by answering, correcting, or contradicting the announcer on the spot. From September 1, 1941, until September, 1944, the Moscow radio maintained a regular Bulgarian broadcast with which Vasil Kolarov was closely associated.[29] To the Bulgarian Communists the broadcasts were mainly of morale-boosting importance.

In the summer of 1941, Moscow came to the assistance of the Communist resistance in Bulgaria. Groups of Bulgarian Communist émigrés were dispatched, some of whom were landed on Bulgarian territory by Soviet submarines, while others were parachuted from Soviet aircraft.[30] There were several such groups involving a total of 58 people. On July 14 the Bulgarian authorities uncovered a group of parachutists in southern Dobruja. Their objective, never carried out, was to act in the rear of the Rumanian army. This discovery placed the Bulgarian military on notice. Special measures were undertaken to safeguard against similar incursions on Bulgarian territory.

On August 11 a party of fourteen was landed on Bulgaria's Black Sea coast by a Soviet submarine. The group was led by Radoinov (alias Radionov), whose career as a colonel in the Red Army and senior adviser in Spain has already been related. After being landed at the mouth of the Kamchiia River, Radoinov split his people into groups

---

[28] Later, the "Khristo Botev" broadcasts were published in seven volumes under the name of *Govori radiostantsiia Khristo Botev*.

[29] Kolarov, *Protiv khitlerizma i negovite bulgarski slugi*. This volume contains the texts of many of the scripts written by Kolarov and broadcast over the Moscow radio.

[30] There are a number of authoritative accounts of this expeditionary force manned by Communist exiles. The single most important monograph is Vidinski's *Podvodnicharite*; see also *IIIBKP*, X (1963), 325–54; Vinarov, pp. 557–72; Gilin, pp. 100–6; Atanasov, *Pod znameto na partiiata*, pp. 126–28. The account in the following pages is based on the above sources, unless otherwise indicated.

which he dispersed. One, headed by his second-in-command, the ex-Communist deputy Subi Dimitrov, succeeded in reaching the town of Sliven and established contact with the local Communists. Dimitrov, however, was soon discovered by the police and committed suicide to avoid capture.[31] The other groups were sent to the towns of Shumen and Burgas respectively. Radoinov himself, together with a number of his men, remained on the spot of the landing awaiting the arrival of a new group from the Soviet Union. He was discovered, and after an exchange of fire in which most of his people were shot, succeeded in reaching Sliven and later Sofia where he took command of the Central Military Commission, becoming also a member of the Party Central Committee.[32]

The second group landed by submarine arrived a fortnight later. Other groups were parachuted during September and early October: two of them over Dobruja, one near the town of Khaskovo, one near Triavna, and the last in the Bulgarian-occupied territories in Greece. The last group included Vasil Tanev, one of Dimitrov's co-defendants at the Leipzig trial. Before reaching Bulgarian territory, he and his fellow parachutists were apprehended and shot.[33]

The participants in all the groups were Bulgarian Communist émigrés who had undergone special training for sabotage and underground subversive activities in the Soviet Union. Most were people of high training, including officers and engineers. Many had had military experience in the Spanish Civil War. Their main objectives were to inter-

---

[31] Milev, pp. 29–42. Subi Dimitrov (alias Mikhailov) was in charge of the Bulgarian Communist volunteers in Spain. Earlier, he had led the Communist parliamentary group in the Subranie (1931–33). Sliven was his home town, from which he had been elected deputy in 1931. Despite his popularity and his extensive connections with the Sliven Communists, he was forced to remain in hiding in a cave in the Sliven hills. As related in his biography, his ordeals reflect the intolerable hardships under which Communist conspirators were forced to live in the fall and winter of 1941. Before he was driven to despair and suicide, Dimitrov discovered what the Buro-in-Exile failed to realize, namely, that conditions in Bulgaria were radically changed from what they had been in the early and mid-twenties. Far from being on the brink of revolution, Bulgaria's Communists lived under a prevailing mood of resignation.

[32] Details on Radoinov's arrival and his activities until his arrest are supplied in Dragoliubov, *Ts. Radoinov.*

[33] *Rabotnichesko delo,* October 16, 1956.

fere with the German lines of communication within Bulgaria and, above all, to help organize an efficient armed resistance network using local Communists.[34] The results were nil.

Of the 58 persons involved, twenty were shot on arrival. The remaining were caught soon after landing on Bulgarian soil; they were tried and the majority were executed. Only a few succeeded in avoiding immediate arrest and were able to operate for short periods of time.

On November 19, 1941, Premier Filov told the Subranie that the entire affair, which he described as a Communist outrage, had come to an end. He claimed, not without reason, that "the people had helped the authorities in apprehending the invaders." [35] In later years the Communists maintained that the expedition failed because of organizational and technical mismanagement. There were elements of truth in both claims. There was, however, another reason for the failure which was revealed later. In addition to the Bulgarian émigrés landed on Bulgarian soil, also attached were a number of Russians serving as radio operators for liaison with Moscow. At least one of them became a police collaborator and gave direct aid to the authorities in rounding up the newly arrived.[36] In faraway Russia, Dimitrov and the Buro-in-Exile, who had

[34] In human terms, the venture involved great personal dramas. The group landed by the second submarine included Avram Stoianov, an old functionary of the Party who has already appeared in these pages in connection with the Sofia municipal elections of 1932. Stoianov evaded arrest until the summer of 1942, at which time he was discovered and, like Subi Dimitrov, took his own life rather than fall into the hands of the police. Stoianov's son, Luchezar Avramov, also an émigré, arrived in Bulgaria with one of the parachutist groups. He was apprehended, but being a minor was not executed. He spent the war years in jail and survived to become a top Party functionary after 1944. Stoianov's story is related in Angel Georgiev, *Avram Stoianov* (Sofia, 1954).

The Bulgarians were the first among all the peoples in Eastern Europe to have cadres sent from the USSR into their respective countries. On the Soviet side, the Bulgarian operation involved considerable investment in terms of military effort. Soviet submarines participated in early reconnaissance along the Bulgarian coast and in escort missions, as well as being used for transportation (Vidinski, p. 63).

[35] Filov, *Putut na Bulgariia*, pp. 20–24. Much of Filov's speech dealt with the Communist threat. He warned against underestimating the Communist influence in the country, but expressed complete confidence in the government's ability to cope with the subversion.

[36] It is not clear whether the Russian radio operators were expected to watch over the Bulgarians, or whether they were co-opted into the landing parties because

engineered the expedition, were distressed. Plans for the dispatch of fifty additional émigrés were suspended. The failure had to be explained to the Soviet authorities who had provided the means. Added to the military failure, the venture proved a political blunder as well. Bulgaria had remained neutral and her diplomatic relations with the Soviet Union were intact. The apprehension of the émigrés created an uproar in Bulgarian public opinion. Voices from the extreme right insisted that Bulgaria declare war on the Soviet Union.[37] The crisis blew over eventually, thanks to Boris's fear of military involvements with the Russians. Why the Soviet Union became entangled in this marginal operation with all the political risks it involved at a time when the Red Army was in full-scale retreat was never explained. Were the Russians taken in by Dimitrov's enthusiasm to show his and his countrymen's devotion to the cause? In any case, the endeavor proved the last such undertaking for the remainder of the war. The Russians soon discovered that Bulgarian neutrality was of greater value than anything Bulgarian Communists could show for themselves. Not until the Red Army reached the Bulgarian frontiers in early September, 1944, did they change their minds. Then it was they rather than the Bulgarians who declared war.

After the fall of 1941, the energies of the Bulgarian exiles in the Soviet Union were employed in three main spheres. Led by Chervenkov, and supervised by Kolarov, the intellectual elite occupied itself with the radio broadcasts beamed to Bulgaria. The younger cadres with military training behind them were enlisted in the International Regiment of the Brigade for Special Assignments which was assembled in Moscow. A third group was sent to the Comintern School at Kushnarenkovo near Ufa.

The creation of a fighting unit composed of foreign political émigrés

---

of their technical skills. The *provocateur* appears to have sought to surrender from the first. For a time he continued the radio link with the Soviet Union under police supervision; on this, see the account in Atanasov, *Pod znameto na partiiata*, pp. 127–28. Atanasov, who remained in the Soviet Union, was in charge of the organizational aspects of the entire venture.

[37] On the diplomatic charges and countercharges over the landings of the Bulgarian émigrés, involving, on the one hand, Vyshinsky in Moscow and Lavrishchev in Sofia, and, on the other, Bulgaria's minister to Moscow, M. Stamenov, and the secretary-general of the Bulgarian Foreign Office in Sofia, M. Shishmanov, see *Soviet Foreign Policy During the Patriotic War*, I, 79–80, 88–89, 93–96.

in the Soviet Union was suggested by the ECCI immediately after the German attack. The result was the formation of the International Regiment, which, together with a second regiment of Russian cadres from Moscow, constituted the Brigade for Special Assignments. At its inception, the International Regiment numbered less than a thousand people, of whom the Spaniards made up one-third, followed closely by the Austrian political exiles. The remainder were émigrés of various nationalities (at the end of 1941 the Poles were withdrawn to form their own independent brigade). The Brigade for Special Assignments fell under the triple auspices of the NKVD, the Red Army's military intelligence, and the Comintern. Its commander was Colonel M. F. Orlov and its political commissar Colonel A. A. Maksimov (later replaced by Studnikov). V. V. Gridnev became the commander of the International Regiment, and the Bulgarian Ivan Vinarov its political commissar. In the winter of 1941–42, the Brigade participated in the battle of Moscow.

Later, the Brigade's chief military assignments were behind the German lines in the occupied parts of Soviet Russia. In 1942 the command of the International Regiment was assumed by Ivan Vinarov, a veteran Bulgarian Communist. For years, Vinarov had worked as an agent for the military intelligence of the Red Army. Before joining the Brigade he was an instructor at Frunze with the rank of colonel. There were about one hundred Bulgarian émigrés in the International Regiment. Several groups of Poles from the Regiment were parachuted near Warsaw in December, 1941. In later years, as the Red Army moved westward, small groups of Czechs, Yugoslavs, Austrians, and Hungarians were dispatched to their home countries. Eventually, Vinarov himself was parachuted over partisan-held territory in Yugoslavia where small detachments of Bulgarian partisans operated.[38]

From fifteen to twenty Bulgarian exiles received training in the secret Comintern School at Kushnarenkovo near Ufa. The school's main function was to give selected cadres from among the foreign political émigrés in the Soviet Union theoretical background on Communism and the world revolutionary movements. Mikhailov, the school's director, was the veteran Bulgarian exile Ruben Avramov-Levi, who under the

[38] Vinarov, pp. 557–72, 576–97. The story of the International Regiment is based entirely on Vinarov's own accounts. The sons and daughters of many of the Comintern's luminaries served in the International Regiment.

name of Miguel had directed the School for Commissars in Madrid. In late June, 1943, a few weeks after the announcement of the dissolution of the Comintern, the Kushnarenkovo school was closed. The director, Avramov-Levi (alias Mikhailov), joined the Chervenkov staff of the "Khristo Botev" radio station, where he remained until his return to Bulgaria in 1944. The Bulgarian group from Kushnarenkovo was returned to Moscow. They were soon sent to a special training camp near the Soviet capital where they joined other Bulgarians undergoing military training in preparation for dispatch to the free partisan territory in Yugoslavia.[39]

THE GREAT COLLAPSE OF 1942

The virtual obliteration of the parachutists and those landed by submarine in the fall of 1941 was soon followed by the collapse of the entire political and military hierarchy of the Party. For a few short

[39] On the Comintern School and on Mikhailov's work, see the detailed accounts in W. Leonhard, *Child of the Revolution*. Mikhailov's true identity became known only in 1960 with the publication of Gilin's memoirs (*Komunisti*, pp. 116–17). This identity was confirmed by Avramov-Levi in an interview with the author in September, 1966. Gilin was sent to Kushnarenkovo by Damianov-Belov, the head of the Cadres Department of the Comintern, in August, 1942. He was later parachuted onto Yugoslav soil, returned to Bulgaria after the entry of the Red Army, and was made a general in the Bulgarian army.

Avramov-Levi has already appeared in these pages a number of times. In Soviet exile he was known as Ruben Levi. He changed his name to Avramov several years after his return to Bulgaria. He was born in the town of Samakov in 1900, joined the Party in 1921, and served as secretary of the Sofia district organization of the Komsomol from 1921 to 1923. Under a sentence of death, he fled to the USSR in 1925. (A brief official biography appears in *Kratka bulgarska entsiklopediia*, I, 9.) Throughout much of his career, Avramov-Levi followed in the footsteps of Chervenkov, who was in charge of all Comintern schools at the outbreak of the Russo-German war. On his return from Spain in 1939, Avramov-Levi participated in the debates among the Spanish émigrés over the causes for the failure in Spain (see Castro Delgado, p. 23). On his return to Bulgaria, Avramov-Levi rose steadily in the Party hierarchy. He was elected a member of the Central Committee in 1945 and became Chervenkov's deputy in the Agitprop Department, which he headed after 1949. He took over the Committee for Science, Art, and Culture in 1952. In February, 1954, that body was transformed into the Ministry of Culture with Avramov-Levi as minister. He survived Chervenkov's downfall and retained his place in the Central Committee, becoming the director of the Institute for Party History. He edited Kolarov's and Dimitrov-Marek's selected works, among others.

months, Radoinov, the senior commander of all the groups dispatched from the Soviet Union, evaded arrest. Upon reaching Sofia, he was co-opted as a member of the Central Committee. He was also placed in charge of the Central Military Commission. A military expert by profession, Radoinov endeavored to introduce a measure of vitality into the work of the Commission. Yet his work had hardly started when the entire organization caved in.

On February 4, 1942, the police arrested one of the technical associates of the Central Committee. His arrest was followed by others. As the number of those apprehended increased, the information in the hands of the police widened. It was only a matter of days before it became clear that the police had achieved what amounted to a major breakthrough. Throughout March and April the authorities pressed their advantage with vigor and determination. On March 4 the police arrested forty-six leading functionaries, including several members of the Central Committee and the Central Military Commission. Radoinov was apprehended on April 25.[40] Kostov was also arrested in April and was identified to the police by four of his co-defendants.[41] On the basis of extensive disclosures, the police were in a position to identify Communists they had interned without knowing or being able to prove their leading Party positions. Soon the purge spread to the provinces, where one after another Party organization was broken up.

In the spring of 1942 the regime concentrated on the preparation of a mass trial of Communists in which about one hundred leading functionaries were involved. Initially the government was inclined to combine the trial of the parachutists with that of the members of the Central Committee and its technical apparatus, on the grounds that Radoinov had participated in both groups. Eventually it was decided to separate them.[42] The trial of the émigrés, popularly known as "the trial of the parachutists," opened on June 22. There were 27 defendants in all. They were defended by a panel of well-known Sofia lawyers, most prominent among whom was Stefan Manov, who for more than a decade was the leader of Bulgaria's Trotskyites. That group, never very numerous, had

[40] Gornenski, pp. 122–24.

[41] *Ibid.*, p. 78.

[42] *Ibid.*, pp. 199–222.

sunk into political insignificance by the late thirties. For Manov personally the trial represented an opportunity to absolve himself of his "sins"
against the Soviet Union.[43] Also participating in the legal defense were
Grigor Cheshmedzhiev, a leader of the Social Democratic Party, and
Mikhail Genovski of the Pladne Agrarians.[44] The counsels for the defense realized full well that the only way they could save the émigrés
from execution was for them to prove that the defendants were members
of the armed forces of the Red Army, and request that they be treated
as prisoners of war under the Geneva Convention. To this end, confi-
dential approaches were made by the defense to the Soviet government
through the Soviet legation in Sofia. These proved futile. Moscow remained silent. The Russians were not going to risk a break in relations
with neutral Bulgaria and endanger their legation in Sofia—the only
one in German-occupied Europe—for the sake of a few Bulgarian
Communists. The trial ended on June 26. Of the twenty-seven, nine
were given prison sentences for being minors. Eighteen were sentenced
to death. They were executed on the same day in the tunnels of the
School for Noncommissioned Officers in Sofia.[45]

The "trial of the 62," involving the Central Committee, members

[43] The Bulgarian Trotskyites were few and never formed a full-fledged political
party. The more prominent among them were Manov, Sider Todorov (whose son
in Soviet exile was inclined toward the Zinoviev opposition in Leningrad), and
Spas Zadgorski. Manov and Todorov had started as Social Democrats and had
later joined the Communist Party, from which they were expelled because of their
opposition to the 1923 uprising. In the early thirties they formed the Left Marxist
Opposition with *Osvobozhdenie* as their journal. Lack of resources coupled with
inner dissensions brought the almost complete withering away of Trotskyism as
an organized force (see Rothschild, pp. 294–97; also, *Rabotnicheski vestnik*, III,
406–10). Soon after the trial Stefan Manov was sent to a detention camp where
he is said to have joined the Communist Party (Natan, *Biakhme v "Enikioi,"*
pp. 141–42). After the Communists came to power, he took a leading part in the
People's Courts set up to try Bulgaria's wartime leaders. His good deeds for the
Communist cause did not save him. He was arrested in the late forties as an
ex-Trotskyite, tried in March, 1950, and given a life sentence. He died or was
killed in prison.

[44] Later in the war Cheshmedzhiev took part in the Communist-sponsored Fatherland Front. He became a minister in the first postwar cabinet, but in the summer
of 1945, just before his death, he broke away from the coalition and joined the
anti-Communist opposition. After the war, Genovski collaborated with the Communists and later made an academic career for himself in the field of public law.

[45] The request by the defense lawyers to the Soviet government was communicated
to the Soviet legation in Sofia by the well-known Communist functionary Petur

of its technical apparatus, and other leading Communists, was held
during July, 1942. It ended with twelve death sentences (six of them
in absentia), several life sentences, and many long-term convictions.
On July 23 the six death sentences were carried out. Those executed
were Anton Ivanov, P. Bogdanov, G. Minchev, N. Vaptsarov (a poet
of some talent who served as the Central Military Commission's archi-
vist), A. Popov, and A. Romanov. Traicho Kostov, the Party secretary,
escaped execution, his sentence having been commuted to life imprisonment.[46]

In the spring of 1942, aided by the Gestapo, the Bulgarian police
uncovered and broke up a major pro-Soviet military spy center, in
which the Soviet legation in Sofia, the Communist Party, and the Communist underground in Czechoslovakia were all involved. The center
was headed by retired General Vladimir Zaimov, who was arrested on
March 22, 1942. Zaimov was a professional army officer. In the mid-
thirties he served as inspector of artillery in the Bulgarian army, and
he was a major figure in the Military League. In September, 1935,
following the overthrow of the Zveno regime which had taken power in

---

Vranchev. A similar request appears to have been made by Radoinov himself. A
written message by him was smuggled out of prison and also related to the Soviet
legation by Vranchev. (Vranchev, pp. 492–98.) The Communists and their
sympathizers, especially Ivan Kharizanov from Zveno, who had helped behind
the scenes in organizing the defense, were bitterly disappointed with the Russian
silence. Promoted a general after September, 1944, Vranchev pressed the question
of Moscow's silence on Soviet General Sereda, who had been the military attaché
in Sofia in 1942, but received no reply. Vranchev was himself purged in the late
forties but survived to write his memoirs. The purely legal question involved in
the defense lawyers' initiative and their hope of invoking the Geneva Convention
on prisoners of war remains unclear in view of the fact that Bulgaria was not
at war with the USSR.

[46] On the circumstances leading to the capture of the Central Committee members
and the various theories as to alleged responsibilities, see Vranchev, pp. 490–92.
The matter of guilt and responsibility has not been cleared up by Party historians
to this day. Nor is the problem of central importance. As Kostov himself said in
1945, "a great many of the defendants, including a few who were sentenced to
death, were unable to withstand police tortures and made confessions" (*Rabotnichesko delo*, July 23, 1945). In 1942 there was little that the police under the
capable hands of its political inspector, Geshev, did not know of matters pertaining to the Party.

Kostov's life appears to have been spared by none other than King Boris. The
man who intervened on his behalf with the monarch was A. Balan, a distinguished
philologist who was Boris's adviser and friend. Kostov was a friend of Balan's

the May *putsch* of the year before, Zaimov became the president of the Military League. He was implicated in Damian Velchev's abortive counter-*putsch* of 1935, tried, and released for lack of evidence. This experience marked the start of Zaimov's drift to the left. In 1938 he was nominated by the Communists in Sofia as candidate for the Subranie. His candidacy was withdrawn in the middle of the electoral campaign on the insistence of the Soviet legation in Sofia, which had other plans for Zaimov. The precise date of his recruitment by the Soviet military intelligence remains obscure. By the late thirties he was already involved in collecting military intelligence under the cover of a commercial enterprise set up for him by the Russians. He was provided with a radio transmitter for a direct link with Moscow. The Buro-in-Exile was fully aware of Zaimov's work, as were a number of Communist functionaries in Sofia who provided information and used the radio link for liaison with the Soviet Union. Zaimov's network was uncovered by the German Gestapo long before his actual arrest, which came about following the arrest in occupied Czechoslovakia of an underground Communist functionary who had traveled to Sofia and used Zaimov to reestablish contact with the Soviet Union. Zaimov was tried before a military court, sentenced to death, and shot on June 1, 1942.[47]

---

son, who in turn took Kostov's case to his father. There were no political considerations in Boris's commutation. The argument used by A. Balan was that Kostov was a brilliant young intellectual whose life should not be wasted. At first Boris refused to listen, but on the eve of the execution he met A. Balan and told him that "your hooligan has been saved." (In his trial in 1949, Kostov did not go into details, but explained his survival in 1942 as due "either to the intervention of his sister, or the fact that a school friend of his was secretary to King Boris." The above details were supplied to the author by Professor V. A. Nikolaev, a political exile since 1957, to whom the story was related by A. Balan in person. The two versions, Kostov's and Nikolaev's, are fully compatible.) In future years Kostov was accused of having capitulated to the police in 1942 and of having saved his life by agreeing to collaborate. Insinuations along the same lines were made by Tito's regime, which disliked Kostov because of his wartime support of Bulgaria's cause in Macedonia. Kostov was a tough man to break, as attested by his arrest in the twenties, related previously. In a way which had no precedent in all the trials of Communist leaders in Eastern Europe in the late forties, Kostov stood his ground and publicly denied the charges against him. For a comparative study on Soviet police techniques and Kostov's unique record, see Leites and Bernaut, pp. 456, 462–64.

[47] Zaimov's story is pieced together from his two biographies, namely, Danailov and Zaimov, *General Vladimir Zaimov,* and Poptsviatkov, *General Vladimir*

Contrary to established practice, the Soviet legation in Sofia, which was the center for all spy activities in the country, did not distinguish between its professional intelligence agents and local Communist functionaries. Its reliance on the latter was probably inevitable in view of the strict surveillance under which Soviet diplomatic personnel in Sofia were placed by the Bulgarian police and the German Gestapo. Had Zaimov not been introduced into matters involving the Communist underground, he could have proved more successful. In the spring of 1943, the Soviet military intelligence resident agent in Bulgaria, Dr. A. Peev, was uncovered, tried, and executed in November of the same year. His discovery was made possible by the arrest of a Communist functionary whom Peev used as a radio operator.[48]

With the collapse of the two leading Communist organs, the Central Committee and the Central Military Commission, the organizational life of the Party came to a virtual stop. At no time had Bulgarian Communists found themselves in a more hopeless situation. With their leaders dead or in jail, with half of European Russia occupied by the Germans, and with police blows falling one after another, there was little to sustain their spirits and morale, which in 1942 sank to their lowest level.

In the spring of 1942, only Yugov and Dragoicheva from the Politburo were out of jail. It was therefore on their shoulders that the

---

Zaimov: Biograficheski ocherk. On Zaimov's career in the middle thirties, see Swire, p. 314. His connections with the Czechoslovak underground are related by a Czech historian in *IIIBKP*, VI (1959), 401–2. His candidacy in the 1938 elections is related by Popzlatev, of Zveno in *Izgrev* (Sofia), December 26, 1944. Zaimov was not and never became a Communist. He was the son of a Bulgarian army officer and a Russian mother, spoke good Russian, and was close to the Soviet legation ever since its establishment in 1934. According to his indictment, he had worked for the Soviet Union since 1935. Having broken the underground cell in Czechoslovakia, the Gestapo continued to feed false information into the Zaimov network. The game would have continued longer if not for the intervention of King Boris, who insisted that the arrest be made on the very day on which he was meeting with Hitler. Boris's motives have been given various interpretations. By forcing the disclosure of Zaimov's intelligence work the Bulgarian monarch was probably hoping to impress the Führer with the prevalence of Russophile sentiments in the country and thus weaken any pressures on him to join the war against Russia. In 1964 the Soviet government awarded Zaimov the order of the "Red Banner" posthumously.

[48] Vranchev, pp. 545–47.

burden of Party affairs fell. Having to look after their own safety, and faced with an unbroken series of failures, they could do little. During 1942 the police broke up twenty-one local Party organizations and forty-six youth and students' groups involving a total of 1,771 persons, of whom 1,086 were brought to trial.[49] According to police estimates, during the same year there remained, all told, twenty-seven illegal groups with 381 functionaries living outside the law.[50] This figure included the entire active resistance force of the Party, its preoccupation being one of self-preservation rather than active opposition. Never having fully accepted the policy of armed resistance, Communists were convinced that the only sensible course for the Party was one of "watchful waiting." The concentration camps were crowded with Communist functionaries, and yet few if any attempted to escape despite the relative ease with which that could be undertaken.

In September, 1942, Anton Yugov brought the problem into the open:

Hiding under the cover of alleged preparations for the decisive blow, leading comrades are in effect interfering with the struggle of the masses. They say, "Let us wait until we are ready. Our turn has not yet come. Our conditions are different from those prevailing in Serbia and other places. Let us wait until we are able to strike simultaneously in all places, etc." Such is their talk, behind which one cannot but find evidence of most dangerous misunderstanding, and in many cases simple flight from the tasks of our day. It is such an attitude that condemns the Party to a state of paralysis.[51]

Also in the fall of 1942, on the occasion of the nineteenth anniversary of the September uprising, the passive attitude of the rank-and-file Communists was again attacked. This time Dragoicheva addressed herself to the subject:

Many expect our liberation . . . to come as a result of the favorable changes along the fighting fronts. We will take into account such changes, although we must remember that no foreign factor can substitute for our

[49] Gornenski, p. 124.

[50] *Ibid.*, p. 92.

[51] *Rabotnichesko delo*, September, 1942, reproduced in *Rabotnichesko delo, izbrani statii i materiali, 1927–1944*, pp. 627–29. The illegally published Party organ *Rabotnichesko delo*, discontinued after the outbreak of the Russo-German war, resumed publication on September 1, 1942.

own forces at home. It is on these home forces that in the final analysis the victory over Bulgarian Fascism will depend.[52]

In December the Party organ complained of the faintheartedness with which comrades behaved while in the hands of the police. It went on to give practical advice on the ways and means to be applied in order to withstand police torture.[53]

COMMUNISTS AND THE PROBLEM OF MACEDONIA

Macedonia was one of the principal issues around which Bulgarian political history had revolved ever since independence. More than being a mere political question, the destiny of Macedonia affected the Bulgarians' perception of themselves as a nation. Since Bulgaria's might did not suffice to impose a resolution of the Macedonian question to Bulgaria's liking, revolutionism—of the right and of the left—was substituted for military force and diplomatic influence. Of those actively engaged in the Macedonian struggles, the great majority joined the ranks of the Macedonian national revolutionary movement in its many subdivisions. A very sizable minority drifted to the left. For them, Socialism and Communism became the vehicles by which they hoped to travel the entire length of the tangled Macedonian problem, all the way to its ultimate solution. For the Communists, no less than for their enemies on the right, Macedonia was rightfully Bulgaria's, as were the Macedonian people essentially part of the "Bulgarian tribe." More than "the class struggle," the commitments and frustrations over Macedonia explained much of the special appeal of Communism in Bulgaria. This is not to suggest that Bulgarians of Macedonian origin who joined the ranks of Communism, and who populated much of the Bulgarian Party's elite, saw in the Party a mere temporary shelter. Inevitably, the Macedonian and Communist revolutionary impulses merged into what to them became a single meaningful whole. The meshing of complex sentiments defied logical definitions. In 1937, while addressing a congress of Soviet writers in Tiflis, Krustiu Belev, a well-known Bulgarian Communist of Macedonian origin, could at one and the same time speak "as a Bulgarian writer" of "Macedonian nationality" and claim both Blagoev

[52] *Ibid.*, pp. 630–32.
[53] *Ibid.*, pp. 300–3.

and Dimitrov as the great sons of the Macedonian people.[54] In the spring of 1944 while in Moscow, Djilas spoke to Kolarov and told him of the tremendous losses sustained by the Yugoslavs during the war, estimating the total at 1,200,000. "Yet," observed Djilas, all that Kolarov found "appropriate to ask me was the single question: 'In your opinion, is the language spoken in Macedonia closer to Bulgarian or to Serbian?' "[55]

Not unlike the case of Dobruja, the Communist line on Macedonia followed the Comintern's vicissitudes. The formula which Moscow fostered after World War I was expressed in the simplistic outcry of "the Balkans for the Balkan Peoples." When in 1924 the Communists endeavored to establish an alliance with IMRO, this slogan was modified to conform to a new formulation in favor of a Macedonian Republic "within a voluntary union of independent Balkan Republics." The Communist-IMRO united front, however, came to nothing. After 1925, the Comintern threw its support behind its own Macedonian revolutionary front, Dimitur Vlakhov's so-called United-IMRO, of which Vladimir Poptomov served as general secretary from 1924 to 1934. The United-IMRO also proved a failure.[56]

Vlakhov and his associates were placed in a dilemma following

[54] This unique speech is quoted in the Bulgarian-language *Narodna voliia*, March 4, 1938, published in Detroit. The majority of the paper's readership was made up of Bulgarian Americans of Macedonian origin for whom Belev's seemingly confused terminology represented no contradiction in terms. Belev was a major literary figure in Bulgarian Communist circles in the interwar period, and played an important role in cultural affairs immediately after 1944.

[55] Djilas, p. 35. Kolarov, unlike Blagoev, Dimitrov, and many other prominent leaders of the Party, was not of Macedonian origin.

[56] Vlakhov, a Bulgarian consular representative (Odessa, 1917; Vienna, 1924), was instrumental in the negotiation of the abortive Communist-IMRO pact of 1924. In the later twenties, Vlakhov served as publisher of a number of Macedonian pro-Communist publications, trying to keep his Comintern associations secret. In the early thirties, however, he appeared in Moscow, where, for a time, he served as *Inprecorr*'s commentator on Bulgarian and Macedonian affairs.

Poptomov's name has already appeared in these pages. He was a member of the Bulgarian Communist Party ever since the end of World War I. A Communist deputy during the Stamboliiski regime, he participated in the 1923 uprising, after which he fled the country. In addition to his position as general secretary of United-IMRO, Poptomov was editor of *Makedonsko delo*, and after 1934 a collaborator in the Comintern apparatus (*Novo vreme*, No. 5 [1952], pp. 14–18).

the May, 1934, coup in Bulgaria. Although the Georgiev-Velchev government was immediately attacked as a "military Fascist dictatorship," they felt some satisfaction with the measures taken against the "Macedonian Fascists" under Ivan Mikhailov. In 1935 Vlakhov continued to speak of the "revolutionary struggle" and "the right of self-determination of the Macedonian people" which would eventually lead to an "independent republic of the toiling masses of Macedonia." [57] Soon afterwards, in the summer of the same year that the Seventh Congress of the Comintern met, Communists were no longer concerned with the revolutionary possibilities of the nationalities question. The emphasis was now on peace and not on revolutionary action. In February, 1937, following the rapprochement between Yugoslavia and Bulgaria, the Central Committees of the Communist parties of both countries issued a joint declaration which approved the alliance.[58] As long as the period of the popular front lasted, the Communists continued to advocate Bulgaria's entry into the Balkan Pact.

The seemingly solid Communist front on Macedonia suffered its first break at the end of 1940. Within the Communist Party of Yugoslavia, to say nothing of the Greek Communists, there were always grave reservations toward the Macedonian line of the Comintern. They suspected the Bulgarian Communists of using their prestige and influence in the Comintern to swing its support to the side of Bulgaria. These suspicions were not wholly unjustified in view of Bolshevik sympathy for Bulgaria, particularly during the early postrevolutionary years.[59]

[57] D. Vlahov, "The Dictatorship in Bulgaria and the Revolutionary Movement in Macedonia," *Inprecorr*, June 15, 1935, pp. 663–64.

[58] For the text of the joint declaration, see *Sbornik ot lektsii po istoriiata na BKP*, pp. 420–21.

[59] The literature on Macedonia is legion. The only attempt in these pages is to give an outline of relations between the Bulgarian and Yugoslav Communists during the war. The best treatment of the Comintern's and the Bulgarian Communists' attitudes toward the problem of Macedonia is found in Rothschild. Bulgarian historiography has not been very helpful on the wartime period. Bulgaria having lost to Tito after 1943, Bulgarian sources have since concentrated on polemics. For the wartime years reliance is overwhelmingly on Yugoslav sources. The single most important collection of documents is the *Istorijski arhiv KPJ*, Vol. VII, published in Belgrade in 1951. The collection covers the period 1941–44 and contains texts of correspondence between the Yugoslav and Bulgarian CPs, on the one hand, and the Comintern on the other. The same docu-

At the end of 1940, with the launching of the Communist campaign for a Soviet-Bulgarian Pact, Yugoslav Communists became alarmed. The immediate cause was the distribution of leaflets by the Bulgarian Party in which it was claimed that the Soviet Union was ready to support Bulgaria's realization of some of her "national aspirations." Although Greek and Turkish territory alone was involved, the Soviets being careful not to antagonize their Yugoslav allies, the Yugoslav Communists felt uneasy.

When the Germans invaded Yugoslavia on April 6, Macedonia was cut off by German columns operating from Bulgaria and was occupied within a few days. Ten days later (April 15), the Bulgarian government broke diplomatic relations with Yugoslavia and ordered the Bulgarian army into Yugoslav Macedonia (except the upper Vardar and the northwestern district around Tetovo). On the conquest of Greece a few days later, the Bulgarians occupied Greek Macedonia (April 24) except for the Salonika area and a small part of western Macedonia. Bulgarian settlers were sent to Greek Macedonia to replace Greeks who were deported.[60] Even though the Germans did not permit the Bul-

---

ments were made available to Lazo Mojsov, who as early as 1948 published in Skoplje his *Bugarskata rabotnichka partija* (*kommunisti*) *i makedonskoto natsionalno prashanye*. More objectively, much the same grounds are covered by Elisabeth Barker in her *Macedonia: Its Place in Balkan Power Politics*, published in 1950. A good summary of the respective positions is given in U.S. Department of State, *Macedonian Nationalism and the Communist Party of Yugoslavia*, published in Washington in 1954. Some information, otherwise unavailable, appears in *KPJ i makedonskoto natsionalno prashanye*, which appeared in Skoplje in 1949. On wartime relations between the Bulgarian and Greek Communists one must rely on the controversial but informative monograph by P. Shterev, *Obshti borbi na bulgarskiia i grutskiia narod*, published in Sofia in 1966. Much of the information which follows is based on the above sources.

[60] In 1945, Greek sources estimated the number of those deported at 200,000 (*Bulgarian Atrocities in Greek Macedonia and Thrace, 1941–1944*, p. 14). Bulgarian officials, on the other hand, admitted 70,000, some of whom they claimed to have left voluntarily (Ministry of Foreign Affairs, "Bulgarian Occupation in Thrace and Eastern Macedonia," *Pamphlets*, p. 4). Eventually the Bulgarians handed over to the Germans all the Jews from the occupied territories (11,392 in number), who were in turn shipped to Poland and exterminated.

The Bulgarians behaved ruthlessly in Greek Macedonia, where there was only a very small Slav population (on this see the account of a British observer, C. M. Woodhouse, *Apple of Discord*, pp. 123, 129). At the end of September, 1941, the Bulgarian army was used to put down a small uprising in the Drama region.

garians to carry out a formal act of annexation, for all practical purposes Macedonia became part of Bulgaria.[61] Bulgarian administrators were sent to govern the "liberated lands," and were instructed to treat the Slav population as Bulgarians.

Once Macedonia was incorporated within the political boundaries of Bulgaria, the Communists had to take a stand. The official silence was first broken by Todor Pavlov, the Bulgarian Communist theoretician, who, in an open letter written in the spring of 1941, denied the existence of a Macedonian nation, saying that the Macedonians throughout their history had always felt themselves Bulgarians. The stand taken by Pavlov, himself of Macedonian origin, angered Yugoslav Communists. Kostov (writing under the name of "Grigorov") hastened to come out with an official qualification. He brushed aside the question of whether the Macedonians were or were not a nation as irrelevant for the present time, and therefore a meaningless waste of words. Kostov insisted that for the moment what was of primary importance for the Macedonians was to organize a struggle against the Filov regime, implying that such a struggle would have to be conducted under the leadership of the Bulgarian Communists.[62] Kostov's stand did not satisfy the Yugoslav Communists, who saw in it an attempt to avoid the main issue.

The implication that the anti-Filov effort would have to be carried out under the leadership of the Bulgarian Party, however, was of immediate importance. Right after the annexation of the "new territories" the Bulgarian Communist Party enunciated the principle of "one territory—one Party." This meant that, in the future, the Communist organi-

---

Bulgarian sources estimated the number of Greeks killed at 482 (*New York Times*, November 10, 1941), although the true figure was probably in the thousands. On the Drama uprising see the following sources: Dinev, pp. 388–89; Gornenski, pp. 105–7; *Bulgarian Atrocities in Greek Macedonia and Thrace, 1941–1944*, pp. 25–30; Gialistras, pp. 103–5. In the summer of 1943 the Germans ceded to the Bulgarians a new zone of occupation west of the river Struma. The Bulgarian occupation in Greece was further expanded in February, 1944, by the addition of three additional provinces in western Macedonia.

[61] The Bulgarians proceeded to establish schools, cultural centers, and libraries, as well as the first university in Macedonia established in Skoplje at the end of 1943. Bulgarian teachers and priests were obliged to spend some time in service in the "new lands."

[62] Mojsov, pp. 60–62.

zations in the annexed territories would have to obey the Central Committee of the Bulgarian Party rather than the Yugoslav or Greek Communist centers. This measure, the Bulgarian Communists insisted, was being taken purely on practical grounds of technical convenience. Since for the time being efforts would have to be concentrated against the Filov regime, they claimed it would be only natural for the Yugoslav and Greek Communists to join forces against the authority under which they were being ruled.[63]

In order to implement the principle, the Central Committee of the Bulgarian Party set up a committee of three empowered to proceed with the projected integration. Its members were Todor Pavlov, Mitko Zafirovski, and Khristo Kalaidzhiev. Pavlov was made responsible for the integration of the Communist organizations in Aegean Macedonia; Zafirovski, for the organizations in Vardar Macedonia; and Kalaidzhiev, for those operating in Thrace. Anton Yugov, in his capacity as Politburo member, was placed in over-all control. The Bulgarians tried but failed to bring about the integration by working through the various regional representatives. The matter soon passed into the hands of the Yugoslav Party in Belgrade, which rejected the Bulgarian plan. For Tito, integration with the Party in Sofia meant the secession of the Macedonian Communist organization from the Yugoslav Party. "Irrespective of the barbed-wire barriers set up by the occupiers between the various Communist organizations of Yugoslavia," read a CPY decision of May, 1941, "Tito was determined to maintain the unity of the working class of Yugoslavia." [64] Tito never abandoned this principle. However, its realization in Macedonia proved difficult and, at first, altogether impossible.

---

[63] *Ibid.*, pp.65–70. The claim that the principle of "one territory—one Party" was forwarded only because of practical considerations was made by the Bulgarians immediately following the break with Tito. In July, 1948, replying to Yugoslav charges made at the Fifth Congress of the CPY, the Bulgarian Party organ asked: "Why are the Yugoslav Communists charging the Bulgarian Communists with Great Bulgarian chauvinism? . . . Is it because during the occupation of Macedonia the Macedonian Communists for technical convenience obeyed the Central Committee of the Bulgarian Communist Party and not the Central Committee of the CPY, and because we called on them to fight together against the Filov regime?" Quoted from an article in *Rabotnichesko delo*, July 28, 1948.

[64] Mojsov, p. 47.

Active Communists in Macedonia were few and the regional organization weak. In the thirties, they received the attention of the Sofia Communists more than that of Belgrade. The more ambitious among the Macedonian Communists had long since gone to Sofia or to Moscow to pursue their revolutionism. When the dispute erupted, the secretary of the Macedonian regional organization was Metodi Shatarov (alias Sharlo), an old functionary of the Bulgarian Party. As early as 1927, Shatarov was a member of the Central Committee of the Bulgarian Party.[65] In the mid-thirties he headed the special center set up in Paris for the purpose of processing volunteers to the Spanish Civil War. It was natural for Shatarov to side with Sofia.

At the end of April, 1941, Shatarov appeared in Sofia, where he proclaimed his adherence to the Bulgarian Communist Party. He returned to Skoplje in May. To expose him the CPY sent Lazar Kolishevski to Macedonia at the end of May.

Thus the German attack on the USSR found the control over the Macedonian Party organization in dispute. On June 25, Tito addressed a letter to the regional organization of Macedonia denouncing Shatarov as a counterrevolutionary and stating that he had been expelled from the CPY.[66] Shatarov responded on July 2 by issuing an appeal of his own in which he called for a "free Soviet Macedonia." [67] Seeing that he was not going to be silenced as long as he continued to enjoy the support of the Bulgarian Communists, Tito wrote the Central Committee of the Bulgarian Party later in July, protesting the attempts at taking over the Macedonian organization and the protection being extended to Shatarov.[68] At this point the Comintern intervened.

The Comintern issued its decision in August, stating that since the cardinal problem of the moment was armed resistance against the occupation authorities, and that since the principal instrument in the struggle was the partisan movement now being organized in Yugoslavia, the Bulgarian Communists should join hands with the Yugoslavs in order to extend the resistance effort to Macedonia. Although the Comintern

[65] *BKP v rezoliutsii i resheniia*, p. 148.

[66] Mojsov, pp. 88–89.

[67] *Ibid.*, p. 65.

[68] *Ibid.*, p. 70.

ruling was by no means unequivocal on the long-term question of Macedonia, there was little doubt that it favored Tito primarily because he had adopted a policy of partisan war.[69] There was nothing for the Bulgarian Communists to do but to retreat. In a letter to the Central Committee of the CPY, the Central Committee of the Bulgarian Party stated that it accepted the Comintern decision "without reservation" and that, instead of trying to integrate the Macedonian organization, it would send to Macedonia a plenipotentiary who would help coordinate the common struggle. The Bulgarians condemned Shatarov for his "gross political and organizational errors" but objected to his being branded a class enemy. With this, Shatarov's role in Macedonia came to an end.[70] He went to Sofia and joined the leadership of the Bulgarian Party.

Following the Comintern ruling, the Yugoslavs began preparations for armed resistance. On August 25, 1941, a new Macedonian regional committee was established under Kolishevski. He set to work to fulfill Tito's directives for the establishment of partisan detachments. This proved a most difficult undertaking in view of the strict control imposed by the Bulgarian army of occupation. In the meantime, the Bulgarian Party sent Petur Bogdanov as its first representative to the regional Macedonian organization. He did not stay in Macedonia long. In October, 1941, he was succeeded by Boian Bulgaranov.[71]

[69] *Istorijski arhiv KPJ*, p. 50, reproduces the Comintern decision. The communication was sent to the Bulgarian CC in late August, 1941, and reached Tito via the Macedonian organization sometime in September.

[70] *Ibid.*, pp. 50–51, has the text of the Bulgarians' letter to the CPY; it also contains the letter by Shatarov to the CC of the CPY in which he asks permission to be allowed to join the partisans, confessing his mistake over the issue of "Soviet Macedonia." On his arrival in Sofia, Shatarov became the secretary of the Sofia district Party organization. His name will figure in connection with the executions of Bulgarian statesmen at the hands of the Communists. Later in the war, Shatarov became the commander of the Third Military Zone of the Bulgarian resistance. He was killed on September 4, 1944, near the town of Pazardzhik, only days before the entry of the Red Army into the country. In September, 1945, he was posthumously promoted to the rank of colonel (on his death announcement and the promotion decree, see, respectively, *Rabotnichesko delo*, September 20, 1944, and *Zemedelsko zname*, September 9, 1945). Considered a traitor by the Yugoslav Communists, Shatarov has remained a hero for the Bulgarians.

[71] Bogdanov, according to the Yugoslavs, continued the Shatarov line. On his return to Sofia, he fell victim to the great Central Committee collapse and was one of the six persons executed along with Anton Ivanov. Boian Bulgaranov had

"From the very beginning," reported Bulgaranov a few years later, "from our first meeting with them [the pro-Tito Macedonians], they accused our Party of opportunism" for failing to support the establishment of partisan units.[72] On this point, Kolishevski was determined not to follow the advice of the Bulgarians, who insisted that the resistance be carried out only by means of sabotage and subversion. In October, 1941, under the leadership of Kolishevski and his newly established regional organization, the first Macedonian partisan detachments at Kumanovo and Prilep were established. The results of their first encounter with the Bulgarian occupation authorities (October 11, 1941) were disastrous. The partisan units were destroyed and the Bulgarian army undertook additional reprisals and punitive measures. In November the regional organization decided to continue its partisan warfare efforts, although the main base of operations was shifted to western Macedonia, which was under Italian occupation. This decision could not be realized, since soon thereafter Kolishevski and a number of his regional organization members fell into the hands of the Bulgarian security authorities and were imprisoned.[73]

With the arrest of Kolishevski the Yugoslav Party in Macedonia suffered a severe setback from which it did not recover until 1943. The field was left wide open for the Bulgarians, who, under the leadership of Bulgaranov, held control. In December, 1941, the few remaining partisan units were dispersed and work on the creation of fresh detachments was suspended.

---

been sent to a Soviet military academy at the end of 1921. He returned to Bulgaria in time to participate in the 1923 uprising. After nine years in prison, he emigrated to the Soviet Union. In 1935 he was sent to Istanbul on Comintern work. Following his return to Bulgaria he participated in the Communist-Zveno secret talks. Bulgaranov's mission to Macedonia was only the beginning of a high-ranking career. After the entry of the Red Army into Bulgaria, he served successively as political commissar to the Second Bulgarian army, as director of the Communist militia, and as commander of the Political Administration of the Bulgarian army; on his life, see *Rabotnichesko delo*, November 25, 1956; *Kratka bulgarska entsiklopediia*, I, 320.

[72] Speech of Bulgaranov before the Fifth Congress of the Bulgarian Communist Party of December, 1948, reproduced in *Peti kongres na BKP*, I, 567–77.

[73] Barker, p. 90. Kolishevski spent the entire war years in Bulgarian jails, much of the time in the Pleven prison, together with Kostov and other leading Bulgarian Communists.

As in Bulgaria proper, the resistance in Macedonia throughout 1942 did not amount to much. The Bulgarians continued to press for subversive rather than armed activities, insisting that, under existing conditions, partisan warfare was unrealistic. When early in 1942 the Macedonian regional organization decided to oppose the Bulgarian government's attempt to recruit troops for the occupied territories and called for sabotage of the mobilization and for "flight to the woods," it was reproved by the Bulgarian Party. In a communication to the Macedonian regional organization, the Party insisted that for the moment efforts should be made to infiltrate rather than resist the army. "As far as winning over the army is concerned, this is a problem of the future," stated the communication. "Why then do you decide to 'run to the mountains'? Is it not better for us to subvert the army into a real revolutionary force which will eventually be of decisive importance in the realization of our goals? Is it not wiser for us to remain in the towns and villages with the army rather than oblige the enemy by running to the mountains?" The Party called for a middle course. "You can look either to the 'right' or to the 'left,' either running to the woods or opportunistic capitulation. There is, however, another way out." [74]

Throughout 1942 the Bulgarians continued to stress the "special conditions" under which Communists in Bulgaria proper, as well as in the occupied territories, were compelled to act. Fighting groups rather than full-fledged partisan units were the Bulgarian models. Again and again attempts were made to explain to the Yugoslav Communists the different situation existing in Bulgaria as compared to Yugoslavia. An all-out armed resistance in Bulgaria was difficult if not impossible, according to the Bulgarians,

because the old state apparatus in Bulgaria was not crushed as in Yugoslavia, because the Bulgarian army had not been defeated and its arms had not passed into the hands of the people, and, finally, because the Germans had entered Bulgaria not as an open force of occupation.[75]

It was not until the beginning of 1943 that Tito again tried to restore his position in Macedonia. In a letter to the Macedonian regional organization of January 16, he emphasized that "the freedom and inde-

[74] Mojsov, pp. 109–13.

[75] *Ibid.*, pp. 103–4.

pendence of all the peoples, and equally of the Macedonian people,"
would be decided by the "national liberation struggle" alone. He condemned the "outworn and liberal attitude toward autonomist tendencies
of a national character" (a clear reference to the traditional pro-
Bulgarian "autonomist" solution) and denied the existence of "specific
Macedonian conditions," stressing the leading role of the Yugoslav
Communist Party.[76] The message served as a prelude to the arrival of
Svetozar Vukmanovic (Tempo) in Macedonia at the end of February,
1943.

Tempo, an energetic Montenegrin, knew Macedonia, having
worked in Skoplje before the German invasion.[77] On his arrival, he
undertook several steps that marked a turning point in the development
of Macedonian affairs. First, he decided to transfer the main theater of
armed resistance from the Bulgarian-occupied territory to the area under
joint Albanian-Italian control.[78] Secondly, he managed to establish
contact with Enver Hoxha, the leader of the Albanian Communists, as
well as with the Greek resistance movement, ELAS.[79] Finally, Tempo
started organizing partisan detachments, which in time were substantially expanded. Gradually, the military initiative passed into Tito's
hands. In November, 1943, when the Anti-Fascist Council of National
Liberation of Yugoslavia met in Jajce, Macedonia obtained equal status
with the other five federal units of the new Yugoslav political framework
sponsored by Tito. To the pro-Yugoslav Macedonians this was a political achievement of the first magnitude. The Bulgarians, including the
Communist Party, did not like the new arrangement and said so,
although there was little they could do. In fact, it was not long before
the Bulgarians, under the anti-Fascist government of the Fatherland
Front, found themselves compelled to defend their claims to Bulgaria's
piece of Macedonia (the Pirin region), which Tito wanted to incorporate
into the newly established Macedonian federal republic within Yugoslavia.[80]

[76] Barker, p. 91.

[77] Clissold, p. 135.

[78] *Ibid.*, pp. 141–42.

[79] *Ibid.*, pp. 143–46.

[80] On the Jajce decisions as related to Macedonia, see Barker, pp. 93–98. Dimitur
Vlakhov became one of the five vice-presidents of the Presidium of the central

The coming of Tempo marked the end of the era of Bulgarian Communist influence in Macedonia. For a time, Bulgaranov, the representative of the Bulgarian Party, remained at Tempo's headquarters. He left early in 1944 to join the Bulgarian resistance forces operating in western Bulgaria. On the defensive immediately after the German invasion, the Yugoslav Communist Party

gradually moved over to the offensive. The Bulgarian Party started on the offensive and was gradually pushed back on to the defensive. Tito's minimum objective was to retain Yugoslav Macedonia within the frontiers of Yugoslavia. His maximum objective was to bring about the union of Bulgarian [Pirin] Macedonia . . . with Yugoslav Macedonia, under his own aegis. The Bulgarian Communist Party's maximum objective was to create an independent Greater Macedonia closely linked with Bulgaria or, perhaps, quite simply to annex Yugoslav Macedonia. Its minimum objective was to keep Bulgarian Macedonia out of Tito's hands, and inside Bulgarian frontiers.[81]

The above summation of the problems involved in "that eternal Balkan sore spot of rival nationalism," of which the period 1940–43 formed the opening scene, is accurate on the whole. With the Bulgarian Germanophile regime in physical control over the whole of Macedonia, and with the Axis still overwhelmingly victorious along the fighting fronts, both the Bulgarian and Yugoslav Communist parties proved only slightly less chauvinistic than the old-fashioned bourgeois parties had been in the past. In its Macedonian policy after 1940, the Bulgarian Communist Party aimed at least at an autonomous solution. This policy was not as sinister as it was described by the Yugoslavs after 1948, nor was it motivated purely by considerations of "technical convenience." The fact that on the Bulgarian side most of the leading Communists, namely, Kostov, Yugov, and Pavlov, were of Macedonian origin, must have affected the Party line.[82] Faced at the same time with the pro-

---

Anti-Fascist Council. Vladimir Poptomov, his long-time associate, on the other hand, was elected ordinary member of the same Council. After 1944, Poptomov returned to Bulgaria, becoming a Politburo member of the Bulgarian Communist Party, while Vlahov remained in Yugoslav Macedonia. The break of 1948 found the two on opposite sides of the fence, with Poptomov, as Bulgarian foreign minister after August, 1949, leading the anti-Tito attack.

[81] Barker, p. 83.

[82] After becoming a regent in 1944, Todor Pavlov led the campaign for the recognition of the Macedonians as a separate and distinct nation, thus reversing

Bulgarian enthusiasm of Macedonian Communists like Shatarov, the Communists could not but pursue a line contrary to that of Tito. At the end, of course, it was not the sentimental attachments of Bulgarian, Macedonian, or Yugoslav Communists which decided the issue, but the fact that in 1943, following the victory at Stalingrad, the success of Tito's resistance record cost the Bulgarian Communists their initiative as well as some of their confidence. From that point on, the Bulgarian Communists, who had hitherto thought themselves unequaled by their Balkan counterparts, found themselves in a secondary position.

---

his 1941 stand, according to which the Macedonians had always felt themselves to be Bulgarians. This change played directly into the hands of the opposition, which did not fail to capitalize on the inconsistencies of the Party line. "Imagine the gaps that would appear in the leadership of our country [wrote Trifon Kunev, a leading Agrarian oppositionist and an able satirist] if one of these days some of our leading personalities [meaning Kostov, Yugov, and Pavlov, among others] suddenly remember their Macedonian origin and decide to return to the land of Canaan." See Trifon Kunev, *Sitni-drebni kato kamilcheta* (Sofia, 1945), pp. 127–28; this volume is a collection of Kunev's satiric articles first printed in the Agrarian *Narodno zemedelsko zname.*

CHAPTER SEVEN

ARMED RESISTANCE

WITH THE RED ARMY'S VICTORIES at Stalingrad came new hope. For the first time since 1941 Bulgarian Communists regained some of their confidence. Those who had always believed in the invincibility of the Soviet army could now turn to their more skeptical comrades with "we told you so" arguments. The spring of 1943, therefore, saw an improvement of morale among Communists both in and out of jail.

Stalingrad was, however, far removed from the immediate Bulgarian reality. If anything, the Filov regime appeared stronger and more solidly entrenched. If Bulgarian statesmen were having second thoughts about the eventual outcome of the war, their doubts did not show on the surface. The organs of state security continued their anti-Communist campaign with increased vigor.

Compared with the estimated 10,600 Party members at the outbreak of the Russo-German war, the membership in 1943 stood at 8,500. The decline, however, was only relative, since a total of 6,700 Communists had been arrested during the two-year period.[1]

In the year following the 1942 collapse of the Central Committee,

---

[1] Vasilev, p. 210. There is, of course, no way in which to verify the figures. One's doubts are based not so much on the magnitude of the over-all Party membership as on the fact that, given the existing conditions of terror and jailings, the Party was able to make any estimate at all. It is possible that the figures are based on police estimates, although Vasilev gives no clues to their origin.

the composition of leading Party organs remained unstable. Yugov and Dragoicheva were joined later in 1942 by Dimitur Ganev,[2] the Party delegate to the Rumanian CP in Dobruja who was freed from a Rumanian jail in 1940. Also in 1942 the Central Military Commission was reestablished under the leadership of Yugov, with the following composition: Emil Markov, Spas Georgiev, Yosif Yosifov, Petur Vranchev, Svilen Rusev, and Lev Glavinchev.[3] The majority did not survive long. In February, 1943, Spas Georgiev and Yosif Yosifov fell into the hands of the police. Khristo Mikhailov, the leader of the Commission when first established in 1941, who had rejoined it in July, 1943, died at the hands of the police on February 8, 1944.[4]

During 1943 there were three important additions to the Party leadership, two of which were of long-range significance. In 1943, after almost two years in detention camps, Vlado Trichkov, a "Spaniard" and a Communist of long standing, regained his freedom and joined the Party resistance. He became one of the central leaders of the partisan movement just being organized.[5] In February, 1943, Georgi Chankov, a Central Committee member since 1936 and in prison since 1939, escaped from jail and rejoined the Central Committee.[6] Dobri Terpeshev, the third Communist functionary to join the Party leadership in the summer of 1943, was for the immediate future, at least, the most important of them all. With the application of Terpeshev's common touch and enthusiasm to the immediate problems, his reappearance marked a turning point in the Bulgarian Communist resistance. In September he took command of the general staff of the resistance. This was only a new name for the original Central Military Commission. In the spring of 1943 it was decided that all resistance units should enter what was then called the People's-Revolutionary Army of Liberation, or NOVA (*Narodnoosvoboditelna vustanicheska armiia*). During March–April, 1943, the country was subdivided into twelve clandestine military zones, each with

[2] *Rabotnichesko delo*, December 2, 1948.

[3] Vasilev, pp. 219–21.

[4] *Ibid.*, pp. 223–24.

[5] *Rabotnichesko delo*, October 6, 1944.

[6] *Ibid.*, December 12, 1947. Chankov entered the Party Politburo in 1944 and, following the September coup of that year, became one of three Party secretaries in charge of organizational matters.

its local military staff responsible to the underground general staff in Sofia.

For the immediate future, the establishment of a general staff and military zones was more a declaration of intent than a reality, its significance being more symbolic than actual. The decision to make the change was motivated by Tito's example and his successes in resisting the Germans. In view of the conditions in Bulgaria, however, imitation of the Yugoslavs could only be carried a certain distance. Of this, Bulgarian Communists were well aware. Even those who were emotionally and physically committed to armed resistance could not fail to realize that the resistance effort would not be promoted merely by insisting on armed struggle.

In their search for "new forms" of resistance, Bulgarian Communists in the spring of 1943 turned to political assassination. On February 13, 1943, retired General Khristo Lukov, the chief apologist for war with Russia and a leading figure in the crypto-Nazi Legion movement, was assassinated. The action was carried out by a Communist fighting group led by Violeta Yakova. The murder of Lukov was followed by more assassinations involving mostly politicians and suspected police agents. On April 6, 1943, Lukov's secretary was fired upon. A week later (April 15), Sotir Yanev, the chairman of the Committee on Foreign Relations of the Subranie and a former Socialist turned pro-German, was assassinated. A fortnight later (May 3), a Communist fighting group shot and killed Colonel Pantev, the chairman of the Military Court of the Sofia region. Pantev was credited with having introduced Gestapo methods to the Bulgarian police.

The moving spirit behind the political assassinations was Metodi Shatarov, the former secretary of the regional Communist organization in Macedonia. After being expelled from Skoplje, he became secretary of the district Party organization in Sofia. In September, 1942, Shatarov ordered a Communist functionary named Slavcho Radomirski to organize and train the special execution squads. The first act of assassination was carried out on November 18, 1942, against a police agent. The last act of political terrorism against individual persons was undertaken in May, 1943, after which political assassinations were suspended by orders of the Party high command. By that time the executioners were sustaining more casualties than their victims. Moreover, there was fear within the Party leadership that such unorthodox ventures might well get out of control and deteriorate into personal vendettas. There was no question that, while it lasted, the assassination campaign had the endorsement of the Party, even though official acknowledgement to this effect came years later. Of the killings, the removal of General Lukov was without doubt the most significant. In the thirties, Lukov was Boris's chief instrument in purging the army of its Military League elements. After 1941, Lukov favored Bulgaria's entry into the war against the Soviet Union and became an outspoken critic of the King. Because of his personal connections with leaders of the German Reich, Lukov was considered a potential Bulgarian dictator, if and when the Germans decided to replace the Boris regime. His murder caused no regrets within palace circles. On their part, the Communists spared no efforts to perpetuate the fiction that Lukov was the victim of Boris's stooges.[7]

The latter part of 1943 witnessed an increase in the level of armed resistance. Although the core of the resistance consisted of the so-called fighting groups, some partisan bands made their appearance. The difference between the two was basic. Fighting groups were formed around existing Party cells and were composed of Communists who, while living a legal existence, would occasionally take part in armed actions. Partisans, on the other hand, were those who, having been discovered by the police, chose to flee to the mountains.

On a very limited scale, partisan bands were in operation as early as 1941. The first such band (*cheta*) active in Pirin Macedonia was led by a veteran Communist named Nikola Parapunov. According to police estimates, at the end of 1942 there were 183 partisans organized in

---

[7] Full documentation exists on the entire spectrum of Communist assassinations in the winter and spring of 1943. The two most important sources on the subject are the memoirs of participants, namely, S. Radomirski, *Prez ogun i kurshumi*, and M. Grubcheva, *V imeto na naroda*, both published in 1962. Radomirski was in charge of the operational side of the executions. Grubcheva carried out the execution of Colonel Pantev. She later fought as a partisan and survived to participate in yet another purge. On September 13, 1944, several days after the entry of the Red Army into Bulgaria, she shot and killed General Stefanov, commander of the Pleven military district (Grubcheva, pp. 539–40). Violeta Yakova, General Lukov's assassin, perished as a partisan in June, 1944. A brief but authoritative account on the executions is given in Boris Stoinov, *Boinite grupi*, pp. 92–101. During the same period, similar actions, involving figures of less importance, were carried out in the provinces.

twenty-five bands in the country at large. Their number rose to 372 in March, 1943, and to 650 three months later. In June, 1943, the number of partisan bands was placed at forty-seven, with an average of ten to twelve partisans in each.[8] Occasionally a number of bands would come together under a single command to form a partisan detachment. One of the first formations of this kind was the partisan detachment "Anton Ivanov," operating in the Rodopi mountains. In May, 1943, "Anton Ivanov" included about 100 partisan members.[9] This unit was an exception, however. In most cases, bands remained small and largely isolated from each other as well as from the center.

One of the larger and more successful partisan formations which distinguished itself as early as the summer of 1943 was the detachment under the command of Slavcho Trunski. Operating in Trunsko, a region located on the Bulgarian-Yugoslav frontier, Trunski's detachment, in contrast to partisan units operating in the interior, proved a relative success. Their success was due largely to the assistance of Tito's partisans, with whom Trunski cooperated from the very beginning. Not only were Trunski's people supplied with arms by the Yugoslavs, but they could cross over into Tito's free zone and replenish their stocks in relative peace. Cooperation with the Yugoslavs involved occasional small-scale joint operations.

The Yugoslavs, who had always insisted that the Bulgarians abandon their fighting-group methods as ineffective, supported Trunski's methods, in which they saw the beginning of Bulgarian partisan warfare. Once armed, the Yugoslavs advised, the units should stay armed and in formation while retaining flexible tactics. Above all, and this conviction Tito never retracted, the Yugoslavs believed that the only way in which partisan units could operate effectively was for the Bulgarians to establish a territorial base, a free zone from which partisans could strike and to which they could retreat. For the Bulgarians this proved impossible.[10]

[8] Gornenski, p. 137.

[9] *Ibid.*, p. 142.

[10] Trunski became one of the few authentic heroes of the Bulgarian partisan movement. He played an important role in the early days of the Sovietization process after 1944. He was purged in the late forties, as were many other functionaries, but reemerged in the fifties, becoming the commander of the Rakovski Military Academy and a senior general in the Bulgarian army. He began his

THE ALLIES AND BULGARIAN RESISTANCE

All through 1942 and the first part of 1943, the Bulgarian resistance was overlooked by the major combatants. Following the discovery by the police of Dr. Dimitrov's resistance network in the early spring of 1941, the SOE lost interest in Bulgaria. In the Middle East, Dr. Dimitrov was provided with a small staff which prepared and edited a Bulgarian-language broadcast under the name of "Svobodna i nezavisima Bulgariia" (Free and Independent Bulgaria).[11] Moscow followed much the same course. In the aftermath of the abortive venture of the parachutists, the Buro-in-Exile satisfied itself with the broadcasts over the "Khristo Botev" station. This relative noninvolvement came to an end in the second part of 1943. The Bulgarians in Moscow and the British in the Middle East undertook separate efforts to reach the Bulgarian resistance. In both cases, the effort was pursued indirectly. The emissaries who were dispatched converged on free Yugoslav territory held by the Tito forces, from which they endeavored to establish physical contact with the Bulgarian resistance.

In September, 1943, the first group of Bulgarian émigrés from the Soviet Union was parachuted over Yugoslav territory. It was headed by Shteriu Atanasov, who was sent as Dimitrov's personal representative to Tito. Several more such groups were flown to Yugoslavia through the winter and spring of 1944. Having settled the dispute over the Macedonian question on Tito's terms, Dimitrov was determined to get Tito's assistance in bolstering the Bulgarian resistance movement. The newly arrived Bulgarians were few and did not constitute a fighting force. A

---

partisan career as a countryside brigand rather than a Communist of conviction. His success was due to his native intelligence and support from the Yugoslav partisans. He was in effect adopted by the Party after having made a reputation for himself as a successful leader. Trunski's experiences are recorded in great detail in his *Partizanski spomeni* (1955), *Neotdavna* (3d ed., 1965), and *Iz taktikata na partizanskata borba v Bulgariia* (1969). The idea of establishing a free partisan zone was considered but never materialized; on this, see *Iz taktikata*, pp. 161–64, and Vranchev, pp. 592–93 ff.

[11] The broadcasts originated from Jerusalem in British-held Palestine. The editorial staff was assembled from among Palestinian Jews of Bulgarian origin. Editorial policy was set by Dr. Dimitrov, under the nominal supervision of Major Hugh Seton-Watson, then in charge of Balkan affairs in the British Middle Eastern command.

few remained as liaison officers at Tito's headquarters. The remainder made their way eastward and joined Trunski's partisans along the Bulgarian-Yugoslav frontier.[12]

Unlike the initiative from Moscow, which remained essentially political in nature, the British effort, although modest in scope, centered on the military-operational sphere. The British high command in the Mediterranean, which by the middle of 1943 had already established close collaboration with Tito, knew little of the Bulgarian resistance effort. In August, 1943, the British decided to establish direct contact with the Bulgarian resistance in order to explore the possibilities for future actions. After undergoing special training, a small group of British military personnel headed by Major Mostyn Davies was parachuted over Albanian territory (September 15, 1943) with orders to proceed northward in order to establish liaison with the Bulgarians operating along the Yugoslav frontier.[13]

[12] Details on the Bulgarian groups flown from the Soviet Union to Yugoslavia are given in Atanasov, *Pod znameto na partiiata*, pp. 149–67, Vinarov, pp. 601–23, and in Gilin's *Komunisti*. The groups were made up of exiles whose dispatch to Bulgaria had been suspended following the failure of the parachutists in the summer of 1941. They were reinforced by those from the Comintern's Kushnarenkovo School, which was shut down after the dissolution of the Comintern. Tito's reaction to the arrival of the Bulgarians was mixed. His relations with Dimitrov were good. Following the extermination of the Yugoslav Communist leadership in the Great Purge, Dimitrov had helped Tito reorganize the Yugoslav Party, a fact which Tito appears never to have forgotten. Dimitrov was surprised with Tito's overwhelming success in developing the resistance movement in Yugoslavia, and disappointed with the performance of his own countrymen. In matters pertaining to the resistance and the partisan struggle, Dimitrov accepted the fact that Tito's role in the Balkans was primary. Yet, remembering the bitter experiences over Macedonia in the early years of the war, Tito remained suspicious of the Bulgarian emissaries. In a letter dated October 9, 1943, to Tempo, his representative in Macedonia, Tito urged that the Bulgarian resistance be aided, but that over-all initiative must remain in Yugoslav hands; see *Istorijski arhiv KPJ*, pp. 271–74.

[13] Unless otherwise indicated, the following accounts of the Davies and Thompson missions are based on three main sources. The first is a secret report prepared by the Bulgarian police following the failure of the two missions and is based on the testimony of some of those who fell prisoner. In 1946 the report was made public in Vasilev, pp. 564–73. The second is the memoir of Major Frank Thompson (*There Is a Spirit in Europe: A Memoir of Frank Thompson*), published in 1947 by his mother and brother. This is less valuable, since it is based on poorly prepared and poorly arranged materials supplied by the Fatherland Front government

Even though assisted by Yugoslav partisans on its way to the north, Davies's party faced great difficulties on its trek, which lasted more than two months. Finally on December 15, 1943, Davies and his men reached Tsurna-trava at Burko where they established contact with Slavcho Trunski, who in turn connected Davies with the general staff of the Bulgarian resistance in Sofia. Official contact between the general staff and the British party was established on January 3, 1944, with the arrival on the scene of Vlado Trichkov (the "Spaniard" freed from a concentration camp the year before) in his capacity as representative of the underground general staff.[14]

Talks between Davies and Trichkov produced two immediate decisions. First, it was agreed that arrangements should be made for the Bulgarian partisans in the interior to be supplied from the air by British planes. For that purpose, Trichkov asked the staff in Sofia to designate appropriate areas over which supplies could be dropped. Second, Davies requested Cairo for the dispatch of a second party so that contact with the Bulgarians could be broadened.

The first decision came to nothing. The staff in Sofia did not answer Trichkov's request, probably because of failure in communications, which were becoming more and more difficult in view of the large-scale Allied bombings of the capital. Davies's second demand, on the other hand, was fulfilled promptly. On January 25, 1944, a group under Major (then Captain) Frank Thompson, a radioman and a noncommissioned officer, was parachuted with supplies in the region of Dobro pole. Its members were ordered to remain in touch with Trichkov and the Bulgarians stationed in the free Yugoslav zone in order to inform themselves of conditions in Bulgaria.

In the meantime, the Bulgarian resistance underwent changes. On December 14, 1943, a detachment of seventy-five Bulgarian soldiers

---

sometime during 1946. Finally, there are the accounts of B. Sweet-Escott (who in the early spring of 1943 took over as chief of the Balkan desk of the SOE in the Mediterranean) in *Baker Street Irregular*, pp. 159, 193, 205–7, 211–13.

[14] Tito was unhappy with the arrival of the British mission for fear that his control over Bulgarian resistance affairs along the Bulgarian frontier would be lost to the British. Once arrived on Yugoslav-held territory, however, Davies was given the necessary assistance; on Tito's reactions to the matter, see *Istorijski arhiv KPJ*, pp. 271–74.

from the army of occupation led by Lieutenant Dicho Petrov deserted
to the Bulgarian partisans in the Yugoslav free zone and formed the first
soldiers' battalion of the Bulgarian resistance.[15] Early in 1944 the
Bulgarian partisans centered in the Yugoslav free zone were further
strengthened by the arrival of a number of prominent Party leaders,
among them Georgi Chankov, a member of the Party Central Committee, and his wife, Yordanka Chankova, who was the secretary of the
Party youth organization. They were sent to the village of Kalna following the decision of the general staff in Sofia to abandon the capital and
split the high command in two. At the same time, Terpeshev, Yugov, and
Dragoicheva established themselves in Plovdiv to direct the resistance
effort within the country.

Thus, in the spring of 1944, the Bulgarian partisans around the
area of Kalna in the Yugoslav free zone achieved a substantial concentration of forces. What they lacked most was weapons, which the British
had supplied to them in only limited quantities. Despite repeated efforts
on the part of Major Davies, from February 1 to March 15, 1944, only
three supply-drops (out of the requested fifteen) were made because of
bad weather conditions. The Bulgarians, always suspicious of the
British, became disappointed and angered. Relations between Davies
and Trichkov worsened until on March 1 the latter was recalled as
representative to the Davies mission and was replaced by a new man.

Throughout February and March, little or nothing was done to
carry out sabotage of railroad communications in western Bulgaria, an
endeavor in which the British high command in Cairo was particularly
interested. On March 18, having been tipped off, the Bulgarian army of
occupation attacked in force with orders to clear the Tsurna-trava
region. After some fighting, Davies and his people were killed. The survivors, Major Thompson and his two associates, escaped after a period
in hiding. With this calamity, the first stage of the British effort came to
an end.

British liaison with the Bulgarian partisans was now transferred
entirely to Thompson. Because of his knowledge of the Bulgarian
language, and partly because of his Communist inclinations dating back
to his student days in England, Thompson's relations with the Bulgarian
representatives were better than were those of Davies. Nevertheless,

---

[15] Gornenski, pp. 165–66. This became the "Khristo Botev" partisan detachment,
which later was fused into the Second Sofia Partisan Brigade.

because of the difficulties in supply, the Bulgarians remained dissatisfied.

On April 20, a conference between Thompson and a ranking Bulgarian resistance representative produced a plan calling for the establishment of a free zone in Macedonia to serve as a base of operations for both the Bulgarian and Macedonian partisans. According to this plan, the free zone was to cover an area stretching to the west of the town of Kiustendil (in Pirin Macedonia) and into occupied Macedonia, including the towns of Kratovo and Kumanovo. If the plan was realized, the territory controlled by the partisans would not only border on Tito's free zone but would also include part of Bulgaria proper.

The plan received the approval of both Cairo and Tito. Operations started on April 25, with the Bulgarians directing their effort on Kiustendil and the Yugoslavs concentrating on Kratovo and Kumanovo. The undertaking proved to be an immediate failure. Following some success by the Yugoslavs in the Kratovo region, the attacking forces were repulsed by the Bulgarian army of occupation. Only after much difficulty were the two Bulgarian partisan brigades able to extricate themselves and return to base.

Having failed in Macedonia, the Bulgarian partisans decided on a new plan more daring than the first. This time an attempt was to be made to establish a free zone in the Sredna-gora mountains in the very heart of Bulgaria proper. For the purpose a number of partisan detachments operating inside Bulgaria were directed to start on their way to Sredna-gora. The main effort was to be made by the Second Sofia Partisan Brigade under Vlado Trichkov, accompanied by the Thompson mission. Starting in the middle of May, they were expected to reach their destination sometime early in June.

The "long march" began on May 12. Under his command Trichkov had the Second Sofia Partisan Brigade (the First Sofia Brigade under Trunski remained in the Trun region) consisting of several partisan detachments equipped with British weapons, as well as the soldiers' battalion that had deserted from the Bulgarian army of occupation in December, 1943. From the first, the expedition faced misfortune. Thompson lost radio contact with Cairo early in the march. Partisan detachments operating in the Sofia region with which Trichkov was to establish contact on his way failed to show on time. These and other mishaps combined to make the effort a trying experience.

The surprising thing about the expedition was not that it failed but that it succeeded in making as much progress as it did. Toward the end of May, after a successful crossing of the Iskur River, the brigade was pushing forward in the direction of Botevgrad (to the northeast of Sofia) when it was intercepted by regular army units near the village of Lita-kovo. Most of the partisans were killed on the spot during the ensuing battle; some were captured and eventually executed. Others, who succeeded in breaking away, were rounded up in the following few days. Vlado Trichkov, Chankova, and all the other commanders were killed. Thompson was captured, brought to the village of Batuliia, court-martialed, and shot.[16] With his death the venture came to an end.

In all, the quantity of British arms and equipment handed over to the Bulgarian partisans was small. Had the Allies in the Mediterranean tried to establish contact earlier and had they been able to help the Bulgarian resistance more, there is little doubt that the partisans would have made a better showing. As it was, because of the other enormous commitments in the area, the effort remained very limited in scope. To the Bulgarian guerrillas, starved as they were for weapons of any kind, the assistance was not insignificant. "We have not forgotten and will never forget the valuable assistance in weapons, clothing, and munitions given our partisans along the western frontier by the Anglo-Americans," stated a letter of the Party Central Committee early in October, 1944.[17] Having thus acknowledged the Allied support, the Bulgarian Com-

---

[16] Thompson was shot on June 10, 1944; see Doinov and Draev, *Za svobodata*, pp. 268–80, on his life and death. Thompson's radio operator was captured and used by the Gestapo to feed Cairo with false information. The game failed, but the man survived and was repatriated after September, 1944; on this, see Sweet-Escott, pp. 211–13.

[17] Dimitrov, *Spasitelniiat put za Bulgariia*, p. 61. In the summer of 1944 some British arms were handed over to Bulgarian partisans operating in the Rodopi mountains in southern Bulgaria. Contact was made with a number of British officers from the SOE mission established in the Bulgarian-occupied Aegean area as early as October, 1943. Two of them, John Harington and Ian Macpherson, made their way into Bulgaria proper and found themselves in Sofia at the time of the September coup of 1944. A few days later they were ordered out of Bulgaria by the Red Army. The above events are related in some detail in Shterev, pp. 97–104, and Sweet-Escott, pp. 206, 220. The Shterev monograph treats in detail relations between the Bulgarian resistance and the various Greek resistance groups. No attempt is made to trace them here since their real importance emerged only after the September coup of 1944 when the Bulgarians were called upon to evacuate the Aegean area.

munists proceeded to forget as soon as they could that they had ever been recipients of material assistance from the British, probably because of their desire not to place the Soviet Union in an unfavorable light.

While direct contact with the British came to an end after the execution of Thompson, collaboration with the Yugoslavs continued until the very end of the war. Until September, 1944, the First Sofia Partisan Brigade under Trunski continued to enjoy Yugoslav hospitality, again and again returning to Tito's free zone in order to replenish its reserves.

RESISTANCE DURING 1944

In Bulgaria proper Dobri Terpeshev, the political commissar of the general staff, emerged as the commander in chief of the armed resistance as a whole. This high-sounding title bore little relation to reality because armed resistance remained largely decentralized with partisan bands isolated from each other and confined mostly to their respective geographic areas.

Early in 1944, the prime efforts of Terpeshev and Yugov centered on one major objective. Exploiting the great victories of the Red Army on the eastern front and the state of near panic in which the Bulgarian government found itself after the bombings of Sofia, the Communist leaders tried to broaden the resistance effort by bringing in those Communists who until that time had shown no enthusiasm for armed resistance.

Efforts were made to broaden the scope of the resistance by increasing Communist influence in the army. In February, 1944, a secret meeting between the underground general staff and representatives of the Military League took place. It was decided that close cooperation should be established between individual Communist and Military League officers on active service.[18]

Resistance grew despite government repressions, and in many cases because of it. Large-scale attempts aimed at dislodging the partisan bands from their two main areas of concentration—the region of the Sredna-gora mountains to the north of the Maritsa Valley and the area of the Rodopi mountains—were undertaken as early as the spring of

[18] Vasilev, pp. 394–96. A number of desertions took place in the occupied territories. Individual desertions continued throughout much of the war and were on the increase in 1944.

1943. During March and April of that year police, in collaboration with regular army units, imposed a twenty-day-long blockade in the region of Sredna-gora. A similar campaign was later undertaken in the Rodopi mountains. The results were mixed. In most cases partisans survived simply by standing still in their hiding places until the military withdrew. The government reacted by changing tactics. It pulled back the army but increased its police force, which was assigned to guard duties along the mountain roads as well as in villages, hoping to cut off supplies to the partisans. Early in 1944 the Subranie passed a special measure for the establishment of a gendarmery. Formed directly under the Ministry of the Interior, the gendarmery was an autonomous force with its own cavalry and mechanized units specializing in antipartisan activities.

Reprisals against the civilian population became the chief instrument on which the police and the gendarmery units relied in their partisan hunt. Tempted by money prizes of 50,000 *leva* for each partisan killed, policemen resorted to limitless brutality to extract information from relatives and friends of individual partisans. Villagers suspected of supplying partisan bands with food were tortured and their houses set on fire.[19]

Many fled and joined the partisans, if only to escape police repressions. The limiting factor as far as the partisans were concerned was no longer manpower but weapons and supplies. With the government forces increasing in numbers, the partisans used most of their energy to get food and to evade police patrols. Offensive actions were undertaken only out of desperation and hunger. Mountain lodges and isolated mountain villages were favorite objectives. Even so, the risks were enormous, since the government could generally rely on the village mayors and the forest guards (all of them civil servants) to serve as informers.

The winter of 1943–44 saw the partisans faced with their worst ordeals. Unable to leave their places of hiding for fear of the police, partisan bands could do little but freeze and starve. In desperation some tried to desert and return to their homes. To maintain discipline, partisan commanders were forced to resort to strict measures, including execu-

[19] During 1943–44, the government spent a total of 28,350,000 *leva* in the form of payments to those who could prove having killed a partisan; 2,139 houses were said to have been set on fire as a result of reprisals carried out by the government security forces throughout the war.

tions on charges of attempted desertion. In the case of the partisan detachment "Anton Ivanov," operating in the Rodopi mountains, partisans were executed for having stolen food from their own comrades.[20] In March, "Anton Ivanov" was annihilated. It lost 130 out of its 150 fighters in a matter of days.

As a rule partisans did not survive once in the hands of the police or the gendarmery. In many cases they were shot on the spot and their bodies mutilated. Suicide, and in some cases group suicide, was resorted to by partisans finding themselves in hopeless situations. In one case a group of seventeen partisans chose to take their lives instead of surrendering.

In April, 1944, the partisans created a new brigade, the first to be established in Bulgaria proper (the other two, the First and Second Sofia Brigades, having been organized in the Yugoslav free zone). The brigade was created out of the fast-growing "Chavdar" detachment. Two additional brigades were organized in May, "Vasil Levski" and "Khristo Botev." At that time "Chavdar," which was the largest partisan formation in Bulgaria, numbered 437 fighters.[21]

With growing strength came increased confidence. On March 24, partisan units temporarily occupied the mountain town of Koprivshtitsa. This was the first case in which partisans ever ventured into a town of any size. Usually there were no stand-up engagements, but at most small-scale running affrays. The partisans would raid a village, possibly shoot the mayor, its clerk, and the village policeman, destroy the village land register and other records, loot the village dairy, and make a few

---

[20] *Chetnishka borba*, No. 3, July, 1944, reproduced in Gorov, pp. 33–44. The Gorov volume is a collection of materials published illegally by the various partisan detachments operating in southern Bulgaria. Issued by the Fatherland Front committee of Plovdiv immediately after the September coup, with little or no time for editing and selection, the volume is one of the most illuminating on the subject of partisan activities and the prevailing conditions under which operations were carried out.

[21] The "Chavdar" brigade proved of significance beyond the context of the resistance. Its commander was Dobri Dzhurov and its political liaison officer in Sofia was Todor Zhivkov. In later years, the former became minister of defense and the latter first secretary of the Party and premier of Bulgaria. The history of "Chavdar" is told by its commander in Dzhurov and Dzhurova, *Murgash*, published in 1966.

propaganda speeches to the villagers. Then they would leave, having perhaps converted some of the peasants.

RESISTANCE: MYTH AND REALITY

The process of rewriting the Bulgarian resistance record began immediately after the coup of September 9, 1944. This was not an unusual procedure. Bulgaria had a new regime which wanted to dissociate itself from the past. Having emerged victorious, the government of the Fatherland Front undertook to do what new regimes have done repeatedly throughout history, namely, blacken the memory of its enemies and glorify its own march to power. Earlier, the Bulgarians had done the same with their struggle for liberation during the 1870s.

There were good reasons for the new regime to want to improve on the actual resistance record. Bulgaria was a defeated country. The one positive thing which the new regime could put forward in trying to better Bulgaria's position as a defeated power was to show the existence of a large and potent resistance movement within the country. In this aim, the Communists and their non-Communist partners in the government of the Fatherland Front were united: "tell a big story and serve the national interest."

This community of interests lasted even after the emergence of open opposition to the Communists in the fall of 1945. As long as the Bulgarian peace treaty was being negotiated, Petkov's Agrarians and their Social Democratic allies did nothing to deflate Communist resistance claims. By the time the foreign factor was no longer important, the peace treaties having been signed, the opposition had already been crushed.

During the decade following 1948, Communist writers did everything in their power to place the armed resistance movement in the most favorable light. Exaggeration followed exaggeration until a myth was created. The resistance effort came to be described as nothing less than a civil war. At the same time, compelled to take into account the consequences of intra-Party purges, the historians of the resistance resorted to open distortions. In most cases these distortions were falsifications based on omissions rather than overt inventions. One after another, the names of prominent Communists such as Kostov, Terpeshev, Chankov, and others disappeared from the history texts. In Gornenski's official history of the movement published in 1958, not a single mention is made of Terpeshev, the commander in chief of the resistance in the period 1943–44. Distortion and exaggeration in many cases had an effect opposite to that which was desired, in that they gave rise to total disbelief. The entire resistance effort was dismissed as nothing more than a "Communist skirmish" indefinitely inflated in order to foster the interests of the Party.

Fortunately, enough primary source material remained to reconstruct a truer picture. To a degree, Yugoslav accounts after 1948, as well as those of Bulgarian anti-Communists, subjective as they were, helped to balance the one-sidedness of the official history.

Of one thing there was little doubt. The resistance as a whole never became a popular movement. There were seldom more than a few thousand German troops in Bulgaria to fight against, and they kept out of the way. The partisans thus had to fight Bulgarians, which was a much less popular thing to do. Moreover, the partisan movement never became tightly organized. It consisted of a rather loosely linked series of groups with little central direction.

The leaders of the partisan bands were mostly Party members. Most rank-and-file partisans were young Communists or would-be Communists.[22] Some were Anarchists, others were supporters of the Agrarians, and still others had no fixed political ideas.[23] There were relatively large numbers of Jews among them.[24]

[22] Immediately after the September coup, the Party claimed 70 percent of all resistance fighters as members of the Communist youth organization; *Rabotnichesko delo*, September 18, 1944.

[23] After the war, Bulgarian Anarchists claimed to have collaborated with the Communists throughout the resistance period; on this see *Bulgaria, a New Spain*, p. 17. The Agrarians subsequently claimed to have helped the partisans rather than to have fought themselves. This did not mean that individual Agrarians did not join partisan bands.

[24] Unlike the Jews from the occupied territories, who were turned over to the Germans and shipped to the extermination camps in Poland, those in Bulgaria proper survived. Official Communist sources claimed that 400 Jews fought as partisans (*The Struggle of the Bulgarian People Against Fascism*, p. 56); of these, according to the Jewish Central Consistory, 123 lost their lives; Meyer *et al.*, p. 575. In 1958 the same Consistory assembled an illustrated and well-documented album dealing with the Jewish anti-Fascist effort in Bulgaria (*Evrei zaginali v antifashistkata borba*).

As in Yugoslavia, the Bulgarian partisan bands had their own political commissars, and when they were not fighting spent much time undergoing political indoctrination. Some of the larger partisan formations were able to produce propaganda material for their own use as well as for distribution among the villagers. The bulk of Communist illegal publications, however, originated in the towns and cities.[25]

Most of the time, it was neither indoctrination nor fighting that occupied the initiative and energy of the partisans, but the unending struggle against starvation. Years later, the Communists were to claim "an army" of 200,000 *yatatsi* (helpers and concealers) who assisted the partisans, providing them with food and clothing.[26] This claim was probably the most inflated of all. Had their actual number been only 20,000, the partisans would not have found themselves in so desperate a situation in terms of supply as they in fact did. "Hunger, the real terrible kind of hunger," wrote Vasilev in 1946, "was always present in absolutely every partisan band and detachment, bringing not only unbearable suffering but also terrible misfortune." [27]

How was it that an overwhelmingly agricultural population failed to support a few thousand partisans? In part, no doubt, it was prevented from doing so by the strict police controls and the brutal retaliations undertaken against all those suspected of assisting the partisans. "Not only were they [the partisans] killed and their bodies left lying naked in village and town squares—to intimidate the population," wrote a foreign observer in no way interested in helping the Communist cause, "but their relatives, including women and children, also were executed by firing squads, burned alive or hanged off the nearest telegraph pole." [28]

[25] On the nature of Party control over the resistance movement, see the monograph by Ivan Stoinov, *Politicheskata rabota v partizanskite otriadi, 1941–1944*. A comprehensive bibliography of Communist illegal publications is available in Direktsiia na pechata, *Bibliographiia na nelegalniia antifashistki pechat, 1923– 1944*, pp. 101–18.

[26] See the article by General Diko Dikov, deputy minister of defense, in *Rabotnichesko delo*, September 22, 1958. This was not the first time the 200,000 figure was mentioned. The main reason for the exaggeration was no doubt the desire to "prove" the wide popular support enjoyed by the partisans.

[27] Vasilev, p. 271.

[28] *New York Times*, January 14, 1945. The dispatch is by J. M. Levy, one of the first foreign correspondents to be allowed into Bulgaria. Writing from Istanbul

Directed against a rural population, this barbarity proved effective. Often the police and gendarmery did not have to resort to such extreme measures, for large segments of peasants had no intention of helping the partisans in any case.

In August, 1945, Vasil Kolarov said that at the time of the September coup there were "about 25,000 fighters" in the "revolutionary army." [29] In 1954 Dr. Kiril Dramaliev put the number of partisans operating in the fall of 1944 at 18,300.[30] Four years later, the Deputy Minister of Defense, himself a former resistance fighter, estimated at 30,000 the total number of both partisans and members of fighting groups.[31]

At the other extreme, the total number of partisans was estimated at no more than 2,000 to 3,000 people. This estimate was made by Ivan Docheff, the former leader of the pro-Fascist Legion, who succeeded in fleeing Bulgaria after the September coup.[32] It was in Docheff's interest to minimize Communist influence in Bulgaria. Foreign estimates of the over-all fighting strength of the resistance on the eve of the September coup vary anywhere from 12,000 to a maximum of 18,000.[33] These estimates, however, are not independent calculations but are based on modified Communist figures.

To some extent the variations in the official estimates were undoubtedly due to ambiguities in definition. There was confusion between partisans and members of fighting groups. Fifteen years after the coming to power of the Fatherland Front, a historian of the resistance confessed

---

after a six-week stay in Bulgaria, Levy was the first to report on the Communist repressions instituted after the September coup.

[29] Kolarov, *Bulgarskiiat narod v borbata za Nova Bulgariia* [The Bulgarian People in the Struggle for a New Bulgaria] (Sofia, 1945), p. 38.

[30] *Deset godini narodna vlast* [Ten Years of People's Rule] (Sofia, 1954), p. 69.

[31] See the article by General Diko Dikov in *Rabotnichesko delo*, September 22, 1958.

[32] Docheff, p. 38.

[33] An estimate of 12,000–15,000 is quoted by J. M. Levy (*New York Times*, January 14, 1945), who visited Bulgaria soon after the September coup and appears to have been well informed. A maximum estimate of 18,000 is quoted in R. R. Betts, ed., *Central and South East Europe, 1945–1948* (London, 1950), p. 27.

that the Party had never attempted to find out the number of partici-pants in fighting groups.[34]

Of the numerous official estimates supplied throughout the years, there is one that is both well defined and reasonable. In 1957, Voin Bozhinov, a political and diplomatic historian, stated that on the eve of the September coup "there were about 8,000 fighters in the partisan movement." The figure, according to the author, was based on unpub-lished sources and excluded members of fighting groups. Bozhinov also stated that "more than 1,700 partisans died in the uneven struggle." [35] This was the first time that official estimates were given for the partisans alone. Bozhinov's claim of 8,000 is reasonable. The figure represents the peak reached in September, 1944, the year in which the over-whelming majority of members joined the partisan movement. If an arbitrary but not unreasonable total of 2,000 members in the fighting groups is included, the grand total of the active Bulgarian resistance at its peak might well have been in the vicinity of 10,000.

Like resistance figures, official estimates of casualties were also in-flated. In 1954 the total of those allegedly killed during the war was put at 29,210, of whom 20,070 were classified as helpers and concealers of partisans (*yatatsi*) as well as relatives put to death in retaliation. This left at 9,140 the number of partisans and members of fighting groups killed during the entire resistance. While there is no way of checking the validity of the casualty figures involving the *yatatsi*, the actual figure of partisan casualties is not likely to be higher than a maximum of 5,000. In September, 1944, in the very first issue of the newly revived Party organ, official sources of the Communist youth organization stated that the young Communists (RMS members) "who formed 70 percent of the entire resistance force" lost a total of 3,000 killed.[36]

The partisans, irrespective of their numbers, could make no mili-tary contribution without equipment. Weapons remained a weak point throughout the resistance period. The following is an official estimate of the quantities of arms in the hands of the Bulgarian resistance during selected periods:

---

[34] *Istoricheski pregled*, No. 4 (1959), p. 133.

[35] Bozhinov, p. 117.

[36] *Rabotnichesko delo*, September 18, 1944.

Types of Weapons	End of 1943	Early Summer of 1944	Eve of the September Coup
Rifles	563	2,026	7,660
Machine guns	9	129	402
Submachine guns	13	190	850
Pistols	314	885	3,180
Hand grenades		1,800	5,700
Heavy machine guns		16	38
Mortars			9

Source: Gornenski, *Vuoryzhenata borba*, pp. 235–38.

The estimates do not include light automatic weapons dropped by Soviet aircraft toward the end of August, 1944. The drop, to be discussed in the next chapter, was made over Tito's free territory and the arms did not all go to the Bulgarians.

With this small quantity of arms, the military contribution of the Bulgarian resistance remained limited. If the Bulgarian partisans did not do much useful fighting—and certainly they did not hold down the German troops—they had, particularly during the last year, a big nuisance value. Bulgarian regular army troops, as well as the gendarmery, had to be used against them. "Toward the end of 1943 and the beginning of 1944, an army of 100,000 soldiers and gendarmes under Fascist command were involved in the struggle against the partisan movement," Georgi Dimitrov reported later. "Hitler's and King Boris' inability to send a single Bulgarian soldier to the Eastern front was due primarily to the fact that the main forces of the Bulgarian army were engaged in a struggle against the partisans in Bulgaria and Yugoslavia." [37] It was to this theme in particular that Bulgarian sources after September, 1944, returned repeatedly. "The Bulgarian army is comparatively small, but well trained," remarked an official postwar government memorandum prepared during the peace treaty negotiations for the benefit of the Allies:

There cannot be the slightest doubt that if this army had been used in World War II, as it had been used before, it would have cost the Allied

[37] Dimitrov, *Political Report Delivered to the V Congress of the Bulgarian Communist Party*, p. 36.

armies tens of thousands of lives and possibly more, not to mention other material losses.[38]

Boris opposed the sending of the Bulgarian army to the eastern front long before the partisans constituted a factor of any importance. This he did because of the pro-Russian sentiments of the Bulgarian population and because Bulgaria had nothing to gain from a conflict with Russia, with which it had no common frontier. By the time the partisans emerged as a fighting force, Boris was dead. By that time, too, it was the Red Army that had gained the upper hand on the eastern front.

Thus the military contribution of the armed resistance, both direct and indirect, would at best remain questionable. Of two things there was no doubt whatever. First, of the German satellites in Eastern Europe, Bulgaria was the only country that developed a significant anti-Fascist armed resistance. Second, of the many opposition elements in Bulgaria after June, 1941, it was only the Communists who organized partisan warfare. The Bulgarian Communists were thus in a position of strength at the end of the war in relation to the remaining political groups in Bulgaria. As far as the partisans were concerned, it would not be unfair to say that they were a good deal less important during the "German era" than they became when the moment arrived for the Fatherland Front to seize power. Then the partisans came down from the hills into the towns and villages and set up in a day or two what was at least nominally Fatherland Front rule.

[38] Bulgaria, *Memorandum: Bulgaria and Her Peace Problems* (1946), Annex 1, p. 7.

CHAPTER EIGHT

POLITICS OF THE FATHERLAND FRONT

BULGARIA CONTINUED TO HAVE the semblance of parliamentary government throughout the war years. With real power in the hands of the King, however, and with the Subranie packed with government supporters, parliamentarism was little more than a formality. The Subranie's main significance during those years was as a forum for a handful of oppositionists who, having won seats in the 1939–40 election, had retained them even after the expulsion of the Communist deputies in September, 1941. Thanks to them, the voice of opposition was never completely silenced.

THE "TOLERATED OPPOSITION"

Throughout the war, Aleksandur Tsankov counted himself as an oppositionist. He was dissatisfied primarily because the Germans had not turned to him but had chosen to work through the established authority of Boris. The Germans needed public order in Bulgaria and a smoothly functioning economy which could make available to the German army the greatest possible amounts of agricultural produce. As against this requirement, they were uninterested in Tsankov's theories for a "national social revival." Thus, not unlike the Rumanian Horia Sima, he was kept in reserve until such time when the Germans would no longer have confidence in the Bulgarian government. Tsankov continued to attack the regime for not allowing him to organize freely. All he wanted was for Germany to win the war and for himself to be allowed to reorganize Bulgarian society against Bolshevism, which according to him would continue to be a major threat even after the collapse of the Soviet Union.[1]

If the opposition of Tsankov was extremist, that of Nikola Mushanov was moderate and constitutionalist. "I understand the exceptional times in which we live," stated Mushanov in a speech in the Subranie on November 14, 1941, yet, he continued, "I plead before you for the preservation of minimum freedoms for our people." These words were typical of Mushanov. Having no sympathies for Communism, he was nevertheless one of the very few who protested the government's anti-Communist brutalities.[2] At the height of the government's anti-Semitic campaign, Mushanov protested the measures against the Jews.[3] Above all, Mushanov tried to warn the government against committing Bulgaria irrevocably on the side of Germany.

On December 13, 1941, when Filov proclaimed Bulgaria's formal declaration of war against the United States and Great Britain, Mushanov and Stainov protested.[4] Joined occasionally by Angel Derzhanski (of Pladne) and the independent Dr. Nikola Sakarov, they continued their criticism of the government throughout the war years.

Outside the Subranie, the leaders of the democratic groupings were all but immobilized. Gichev waited for events to develop. With the death of Yanko Sakuzov on February 2, 1941, the Social Democrats were dominated by Pastukhov. Legalistic by virtue of his training and temperament, and yet denied the parliamentary forum, Pastukhov did occasionally voice his opposition. For this he used the mildly oppositionist newspaper *Duga*, edited by Moskov, a fellow Social Democrat. Fundamentally, however, Pastukhov, Mushanov, and Gichev put their trust in Boris's political skill.

[1] See Tsankov's speech of November 18, 1941, in Narodno subranie, *Stenografski dnevnitsi*, pp. 179–86.

[2] *Ibid.*, pp. 162–71.

[3] See the session of June 25, 1942, *ibid.*, pp. 62–83.

[4] See the transcript of the session of December 13, 1941, in Narodno subranie, *Stenografski dnevnitsi na XXV obiknoveno narodno subranie: Treta i chetvurta redovni sesii*, I, 351–54. With the German and Italian ambassadors present in the Subranie chamber and being applauded wildly by the House, Filov and his government succeeded in turning the "debates" over the declaration of war into a noisy demonstration.

Of the "tolerated opposition," the Pladne group was the least tolerated, owing first to the greater militancy of Pladne than of the Gichev Agrarians, and secondly to the known pro-Western orientation of its leaders, who were suspected of connections with British Intelligence. As early as May, 1938, Kosta Todorov had been deported.[5] After a stay in Czechoslovakia he left for the United States, where he remained until April, 1941, when he joined Matsankiev, Dr. G. M. Dimitrov, and Ivan Kostov in Palestine. They formed the nucleus of a Bulgarian political exile group which, though never recognized by the Allies as an official committee, played a role throughout the war. Todorov returned to North America, from which he undertook whatever political work he could.[6] Matsankiev went to London and helped organize British broadcasts in the Bulgarian language. Dr. G. M. Dimitrov remained in the Middle East. He maintained clandestine contacts with his followers at home and advised the British Mediterranean command on developments in Bulgaria. His principal contribution to the opposition effort in Bulgaria consisted of radio broadcasts originating under his direction from Palestine that continued until the fall of 1943.

The leadership of Pladne within Bulgaria passed into the hands of Nikola Petkov. On the eve of the German entry into Bulgaria, Petkov was sent to the Gonda voda detention camp, where he remained imprisoned for a time, together with such other prominent Agrarians as Obbov and Boris Bumbarov (a future Pladne minister and a close associate of Dr. Dimitrov).

THE PROGRAM OF THE FATHERLAND FRONT

Bulgarian-Soviet relations remained in a state of crisis throughout 1942. In March of that year, Filov declared that the destruction of Bolshevism was the prime requisite for the establishment of the New Order. Efforts were made to clean out of the government apparatus all pro-Soviet elements and people suspected of Communist sympathies.[7]

---

[5] Todorov, *Balkan Firebrand*, p. 289.

[6] On this, see Kosta Todorov, "Can the Balkans Be United?" *American Mercury*, September, 1943, pp. 322–30.

[7] In a speech before the Military Club delivered on September 15, 1942, Filov announced that 400 state officials had been fired for their "Communist manifestations." Filov, *Ideite i delata na dneshniia bezpartien rezhim*, p. 38.

The government sponsored anti-Soviet propaganda, and an anti-Bol-shevik exhibition organized by the Germans was shown in the larger Bulgarian towns. The government joined in Goebbels's winter collection of warm clothing for the German troops on the eastern front.

Throughout these crucial months, the Party remained politically immobilized. The period was one of intensive police pressure leading to the collapse of the Central Committee. Except for a number of insignifi-cant sabotage actions, the Party did not rise to the challenge. Again, as in the summer of 1941, the initiative came from Moscow.

As early as December, 1941, Dimitrov spoke out in favor of re-viving the united front. "There is only one way out if our people are to be saved from ruin and our country from catastrophe," he wrote on December 15. "This is the way of the popular movement, of united action between the army and the people aimed at the country's rulers who have sold themselves to Hitler." [8] At that point no precise proposals were made.

In the summer of 1942 the Buro-in-Exile presented concrete pro-posals. On July 17 the broadcasting station "Khristo Botev" announced the text of what was later to become known as the program of the Fatherland Front.[9] The text was prepared by Vasil Kolarov.[10] The document represented a minimum Communist program.

Fundamentally the program of the Fatherland Front was no more than the revival of ideas propagated during the era of the popular front, tailored to suit the new Bulgarian conditions. It urged the creation of a "mighty Fatherland Front" for the realization of a number of major objectives. The Fatherland Front would bring down the present "Hitlerite government" and would create a "true Bulgarian national regime" which would insist on Bulgarian noninvolvement in war and the dissolu-tion of the alliance with Germany. The program called for the restora-tion of political freedom and an amnesty for all political prisoners. Once established, the Fatherland Front government would create the necessary

---

[8] *Govori radiostantiia "Khristo Botev,"* I, 347–48.

[9] For the complete text of the Fatherland Front program, see *BKP v rezoliutsii i resheniia*, pp. 451–53.

[10] Borov, p. 59. Kolarov, much more than Dimitrov, kept in touch with develop-ments in Bulgaria. This fact is not generally admitted in postwar Bulgaria, Dimitrov being given most of the credit.

conditions for the convocation of a Grand Subranie which would in turn decide on the future nature of the regime.

The program did not name the groups which were to enter the proposed Front. On the question of the occupied territories—the single most important issue of the day—the program merely urged the withdrawal of the Bulgarian army sent to fight "the brotherly Serbian people." This left the question of Macedonia's future open. It was a clever formulation, and a necessary one, since the Communists could not have advocated the abandonment of Macedonia and hope to attract any of the democratic groups or, for that matter, appeal to their own members.

For the Party in Bulgaria, the announcement of the program could not have come at a more desperate time. The collapse of the Central Committee in April (Anton Ivanov and the five Central Committee associates were executed only six days after the broadcast) had delivered a crippling blow to the leadership. Morale among the Communists was low and still sinking. With the Germans rapidly on their way toward Stalingrad, many were despondent.

On September 1, 1942, after a long pause, the Party organ *Rabotnichesko delo* resumed underground publication. Its first issue carried the text of the program as well as an appeal to the Agrarians, the Social Democrats, the Democrats, and the Radicals to give their support to the proposals and to join in establishing the proposed Front. The appeal went so far as to state that the program should be looked at not as a final draft but as a basis for negotiations. It invited those interested to come forward with amendments and additions.[11]

With the Politburo members in the underground, the Party required a negotiating machinery through which the various democratic leaders could be approached. For this purpose a special committee was created consisting of a number of known Communist intellectuals who were responsible directly to the Politburo through Dragoicheva. Not a formal body, the committee never had a stable composition. Those Communist negotiators who in one way or another became associated with the special committee formed an interesting group of individuals.

[11] For the text of the appeal as well as a photostatic reproduction of the original article, see *Rabotnichesko delo*, No. 1, September, 1942, cited in *Rabotnichesko delo, izbrani statii i materiali, 1927–1944*, pp. 607–10.

Dr. Kiril Dramaliev, an intellectual and a Party member since 1921, was from the very first the committee's principal figure. During the thirties he had served as secretary of the Communist-sponsored Teachers' Union, and as such participated in an international teachers' congress at Oxford in the mid-thirties. He later went to the Soviet Union, returning to Bulgaria in 1937.[12]

Dramaliev's chief aid during the early stage of negotiations was Dr. Racho Angelov. An old-time Socialist, Angelov had obtained his medical degree in Kiev in 1896 and had for many years been active in progressive medical circles in Sofia.[13] Sometime in 1943 Dramaliev and Angelov were joined by Dr. Mincho Neichev. A doctor of law, a Communist since 1923, Neichev was a member of the Bulgarian section of the Communist International Judicial Council.[14] Finally, early in 1944, Dr. Ivan Pashov joined the committee. In terms of service to the Party, Pashov was unequaled by the other three. A member of the Party since 1900, he had served in its Central Control Commission as early as 1919 and joined the Central Committee soon after the 1923 uprising, returning to Party work after eight years (1925–33) in jail.[15]

[12] On the life of Dramaliev, see *Rabotnichesko delo*, December 12, 1947. After the September coup, Dramaliev became a member of the Party Central Committee (*ibid.*, March 7, 1945) and served as political commissar to the Fifth Bulgarian Army, active in the fighting in Macedonia. Later he became minister of education and was instrumental in the reorganization of the educational system along Communist lines.

[13] Dr. Racho Angelov (1873–1956) became minister of public health in the first Fatherland Front government and was later a member of the Presidium of the Subranie. A mild Communist, Dr. Angelov was one of the very few Party functionaries whom the opposition admired throughout. On his career, see *Rabotnichesko delo*, December 10, 1956.

[14] Dr. Mincho Neichev (1887–1956) studied law and philosophy in Geneva, Bern, and Brussels. In 1944 he became minister of justice, in which capacity he was instrumental in setting up the People's Courts. He was later minister of education (1946–47), president of the Subranie (1947–50), and minister of foreign affairs from 1950 to his death. He was elected to the Central Committee in 1945; he became a candidate member of the Politburo in 1948 and a full member in the following year. On his life and career as a Party functionary, see *Rabotnichesko delo*, August 13, 1956.

[15] *Rabotnichesko delo*, August 18, 1945. In 1945 Pashov resumed his onetime position as member of the Party Central Control Commission (*ibid.*, March 7, 1945), while retaining his post as Party representative to the National Committee of the Fatherland Front.

NEGOTIATING WITH THE OPPOSITION

The first contacts with the opposition leaders were made by Dr. Racho Angelov in September, 1942.[16] One after another the various leaders were approached and invited to join in the proposed Fatherland Front. Although the Communist offer was not rejected offhand, the reception was cool.[17] Mushanov, the veteran Democrat, hesitated. Six months elapsed before he agreed to meet with Party representatives.[18] Gichev listened but was not persuaded. He expressed the conviction that Boris would steer the country on a different path at the first opportune moment. Atanas Burov, the leader of the conservative Narodniatsi, refused to have anything to do with the Communists. The same was true of the Social Democrat Pastukhov, who distrusted the Communists and resented their armed resistance, which, as he said later, "was in any case being directed not against the Germans, the real enemy, but against fellow Bulgarians." [19] Pastukhov did not speak for all Social Democrats. Several of their leaders—Grigor Cheshmedzhiev and Dimitur Neikov, both lifelong Socialists—listened to the Communist representatives and expressed readiness to join in the proposed Front.[20] Neither Cheshmedzhiev nor Neikov was a left-winger, as they were later described. At this point there was no question of splitting the Social Democrats, since, after years of illegality, the Social Democratic Party was for all practical purposes nonexistent. The different stands taken vis-à-vis the Communists were largely unknown outside a limited circle of Social Democrats living in the capital. Pastukhov and Cheshmedzhiev merely agreed to disagree.

The Communists succeeded in winning over Nikola Petkov of Pladne. Politically largely unknown, Petkov did not have the prestige of

[16] This information was related by Kimon Georgiev (then prime minister) in his speech at the First Congress of the Fatherland Front of March 9, 1945.

[17] Dr. Kiril Dramaliev, in *Deset godini narodna vlast* (Sofia, 1945), pp. 47–76.

[18] Kazasov, *Burni godini*, p. 725.

[19] Quoted from Pastukhov's last speech at his 1946 trial; *Svoboden narod*, June 23, 1946.

[20] At this stage, the position taken by Kosta Lulchev, another leading Social Democrat, was somewhat ambiguous. He appears to have assumed a middle position between Pastukhov and Cheshmedzhiev, although in 1944 he sided with the latter.

Gichev. Nevertheless, having Pladne as an ally was of significance since it promised a certain amount of mass support. On his part, Petkov was convinced that in order to beat down the Fascist regime of Filov, Bulgarian politicians would have to effect a combination of forces similar to the one realized on the international scene, namely, an alliance between the democratic and Communist elements. Petkov was sympathetic to the Soviet Union and admired the Communists for their energy, for their discipline, and for their daring and audacity.

The Communists also received the support of Kimon Georgiev of Zveno. Georgiev could not offer mass support because he and his group had none. As in the past, Georgiev's importance lay in his friendship with Velchev, who in turn continued to have some influence with the military, particularly the retired officers. Georgiev had nothing to lose in listening to the Communists. By agreeing to cooperate in the proposed Front, he was in effect breaking away from the political isolation imposed on him and his people by democratic leaders who remembered the 1934 coup.[21]

In the spring and early summer of 1943, therefore, after months of negotiations, the Party could count only on part of the Agrarians (Pladne), one part of the Social Democrats, and Zveno. The great prize, the winning over of Mushanov, Gichev, and Pastukhov, had not been obtained. Hoping that the coalition could eventually be broadened, the Party decided to leave things as they were, that is, to continue its connection with Petkov, Cheshmedzhiev, and Georgiev, but to avoid establishing a formal body of the Fatherland Front.

In March, 1943, the Subranie registered the first signs of sizable opposition within the government majority. The case in point involved a plan to deport 20,000 Jews, who were to be handed over to the Germans. An agreement to this effect had been reached in February, 1943, between A. Belev, the Bulgarian commissar for Jewish affairs, and SS-Obergruppenführer Dannecker. The deal was approved by the cabinet,

---

[21] Communist historians have produced a large body of literature devoted to the wartime interparty negotiations over the Fatherland Front. Most important are the following monographs: Dramaliev, *Istoriia na Otechestveniia front* (1947); Sharlanov's *Otechestveniiat front* (1964) and his *Suzdavane i deinost na Otechestveniia front* (1966); Petrova, *Borbata na BRP za ustanoviavane narodnodemokraticheskata vlast* (1964). None of the above sources are reliable in terms of their political interpretations, although they are important for the facts supplied.

but news of it leaked out and a storm of protest broke out within the government camp. Dimitur Peshev, the vice-president of the Subranie, a hitherto unqualified supporter of government policies, protested before the Minister of the Interior and insisted that the deportation order be countermanded. He organized forty-two additional deputies who affixed their signatures to a letter of protest which he took in person to the Prime Minister on March 17. Faced with a small-scale rebellion, the government compromised. The Jews from Bulgarian-occupied Macedonia and Thrace were indeed deported. The overwhelming majority of them ultimately perished in the German extermination camps. However, deportation action against the Jews within the pre-1941 frontiers was stopped. During April and May, the Germans through their representatives in Sofia continued to press for the deportation of all Bulgarian Jews. Following the parliamentary upheavals of March, however, the government vacillated. In the end, it decided to proceed with an alternative plan. The Jews of Sofia were to be sent to the provinces in the course of three days beginning May 25. Although nothing to this effect was definitely stated, the implication was that the resettlement would constitute a preliminary stage at the end of which all Jews would be deported to the East. On May 24—a national holyday—groups of Sofia Jews tried to organize a demonstration in the streets of the capital. They were prevented from doing so by the police. The Jews of Sofia were in fact resettled in the provinces. With this action, the high mark of actual persecution was reached. The gravest danger, that of deportation to the German-occupied eastern territories, had passed. Cognizant of the German defeats on the Russian front, and determined not to further commit themselves irrevocably and unnecessarily to the Reich, Bulgaria's rulers desisted from taking the ultimate step. Thus Bulgaria's Jews—unlike the Jews from Bulgarian-occupied Macedonia and Thrace—survived the war.

More than any other single cause, a particular combination of time factors and of Bulgaria's wartime circumstances brought about the exceptional escape of the Jewish community. The heroes of the Bulgarian Jewish drama, if there were any at all, were Peshev and his collaborators, whose intervention at a crucial moment slowed down and deflected the anti-Jewish course of events set in motion in February, 1943. On balance, their motives were political no less than humanitarian. Peshev and his supporters came from within the regime's majority rather than from the opposition. Personalities from the Church establishment and the democratic opposition added their voice on behalf of the Jews. The Communists took a hand in organizing the abortive demonstration of May 24. Throughout the war, the radio station "Khristo Botev" in the Soviet Union and the Communist underground publications at home protested against the government's anti-Jewish measures. The net contribution of all these acts, however, proved insignificant.[22]

In the summer of 1943, a German victory seemed very dubious. In August, after a visit to Berlin, Boris died suddenly under mysterious circumstances.[23] The unexpected death of the King gave rise to intensified political activity, in the course of which the Communists found themselves isolated.

The government of Bogdan Filov had no intention of surrendering its powers. To retain control, however, it had to overcome a constitutional obstacle involving the composition of the Regency Council, which had to be established in view of the minority of Boris's son. The Constitution of 1879 provided that a regency could be appointed by a special Grand Subranie elected by a popular vote. Filov and his col-

[22] Significant as the wartime Bulgarian Jewish problem is in itself, the subject falls outside the scope of this study. Some historians have claimed undue credit for the Communists on the question of the Jewish escape. It is only in order to restore a proper perspective that the above outline is made. For a more detailed analysis of the subject, see the author's "The Bulgarian Exception: A Reassessment of the Salvation of the Jewish Community," *Yad Vashem Studies*, VII (Jerusalem, 1968), 83–106. Comprehensive accounts of the entire spectrum of the wartime Jewish problem are found in the works of Meyer, Kishales, Arditi, Grinberg, Piti, Chary, and Oliver, all of which appear in the bibliography. For a pro-Communist view, see the article by Koen in *Istoricheski pregled*, No. 2–3, 1969.

[23] The enigma surrounding Boris's death has produced a large body of literature. None of the research provides conclusive evidence on the circumstances of his death. At the time of his departure to Berlin, the contention that the King had been murdered on Hitler's orders was widely held by leading Bulgarians from the democratic and Communist camps as well as by Allied spokesmen. The same view is held by the majority of Bulgarians to this day. Yet a convincing case to the contrary is made by Helmut Heiber in *Vierteljah,shefte fur Zeitgeschichte*, 9, Jahrgang 1961 (Stuttgart, Deutsche Verlags-Anstalt), pp. 384–416. There is no doubt that Boris was admired by Hitler. The Germans did not change their policies toward Bulgaria after August, 1943. Nor did they force on the Bulgarians any number of prospective Bulgarian Fascist dictators as they might have done had they been dissatisfied with Boris and his regime. At the time of Boris's death,

leagues were determined to avoid such an election by all possible means. The government maintained that under the unusual wartime conditions the holding of an election was a technical as well as a political impossibility. The government proposed instead that the Regency Council be elected by the existing ordinary Subranie, with the stipulation that once conditions became normalized, a Grand Subranie would be called upon to approve the election. Although outwardly not unreasonable, the government proposal meant in effect that Filov, thanks to his control over the deputies, would be in a position to select a Council of his liking.

Seeing the government's dilemma, the Communists tried to seize the initiative and create a united front of the entire opposition that would in turn insist on the application of the original constitutional provision for the election of a Grand Subranie. Mushanov and Gichev, as well as the would-be partners in the Fatherland Front, however, made their own plans. Instead of fighting the regime, they decided to exploit the government's difficulty in order to seek an accommodation with Filov. A delegation of ten opposition leaders visited the Prime Minister for the purpose of reaching an understanding on the vital political issues that would clear the atmosphere and allow the holding of elections for a Grand Subranie. The opposition offer was also put in writing and was signed by Mushanov, Pastukhov, Burov, Kimon Georgiev, Dimitur Gichev, Nikola Petkov, Professor Petko Stainov, Konstantin Muraviev, and Vergil Dimov.[24] In the case of a rejection, the opposition leaders worked out a compromise: insistence on an election for a Grand Subranie would not be pressed provided that Filov agreed to include one oppositionist in the Regency Council. In such a case, the opposition leaders

---

Hitler appears to have been convinced that he was murdered by agents of the Italian court, into which he had married (on this, see Rudolf Semmler, *Goebbels: The Man Next to Hitler* [London, 1947], p. 100; also, Franz von Papen, *Memoirs* [London, 1952], pp. 501–2; *Hitler's Table Talk* [London, 1953], pp. 379–80, 391, 396, 418). After years of silence on the subject, the Bulgarians reopened the case on the twenty-fifth anniversary of Boris's death. In a study prepared by one of the most reputable Bulgarian historians, Boris is described as having died of natural causes (see article by Ilcho Dimitrov in *Istoricheski pregled*, No. 2, 1968). This last contention conforms with the official statement made by the Bulgarian government at the time of the King's death. As in other controversial cases, the simplest explanations may well prove to be the closest to the truth.

[24] Kazasov, *Burni godini*, p. 728.

were ready to disregard the constitutional provision and have the three regents elected by the existing parliament.[25]

Filov felt strong enough to turn down all opposition deals. On September 9, the Subranie named him, Boris's brother Kiril, and the minister of war, General Mikhov, to the new Regency Council. On September 14, Dobri Bozhilov, who had served as minister of finance, became the new prime minister. Petur Gabrovski was dropped from the Ministry of the Interior and his place was assumed by Docho Khristov.

With these developments the crisis over the regency came to an end. Filov emerged as the single most powerful figure in Bulgarian politics. In their attempts, the opposition leaders had achieved nothing. The Communists were outmaneuvered both by Mushanov and by their would-be partners in the Fatherland Front.

Two days after the formation of the Bozhilov government, Georgi Dimitrov urged in the pages of *Pravda* that the people and the army unite in order to pry Bulgaria loose from the Axis. He expressed the belief that the Germans would not attempt to occupy Bulgaria because of their preoccupation on the Russian front.[26]

Prompted by Dimitrov's article, and in part, no doubt, determined to put an end to the freedom of action which both Petkov and Georgiev had exhibited during the crisis over the regency, the Party decided to take a step in the direction of solidifying its political position vis-à-vis the remaining opposition groups. In September, 1943, fourteen long months after the program of the Fatherland Front was originally broadcast, the first National Committee of the Fatherland Front came into being. It consisted of Dr. Kiril Dramaliev (Communist), Nikola Petkov (Pladne), Kimon Georgiev (Zveno), Grigor Cheshmedzhiev (Social Democrat), and Dimo Kazasov (Independent).[27]

[25] On the opposition compromise deal, see Professor Stainov's testimony in *The Trial of Nikola D. Petkov, August 5–15, 1947: Record of the Judicial Proceedings* (Sofia, 1947).

[26] *Pravda* (Moscow), September 16, 1943.

[27] On the establishment of the National Committee of the Fatherland Front, see Vasilev, p. 660, and Kazasov, *Burni godini*, p. 725. At this point, Kazasov's memoirs become of great importance. As a member of the National Committee, Kazasov remained in the center of Fatherland Front affairs until and after the September coup of 1944. Considering the date of publication (1949), his account retains a degree of objectivity absent in official Communist writings.

Communist expectations that the establishment of the National Committee would limit the freedom of action of those participating in it were not realized. The Pladne, Zveno, and Social Democratic leaders continued to maintain close contact with the other opposition leaders, much as before. The Communists, being the originators and prime movers of the Fatherland Front, took their own freedom of action for granted.

With the establishment of the National Committee, the attempts at broadening the coalition continued. As before, the main effort was directed at Mushanov and Gichev. On November 19, 1943, the two leaders were addressed by the Party Central Committee in two separate letters.

Today [read in part the letter to Mushanov], when the USSR, Great Britain, and the United States find it possible to work together and wage a common struggle despite all the differences that separate them, we Bulgarians who serve the same nation, speak the same language, and suffer the same oppressor have not been able to unite in our common struggle for the realization of Bulgaria's interests.

Stating that the Party was ready to follow anybody who was in a position to implement the program of the Fatherland Front, the letter continued:

While the stand you have taken in parliament has been good, and while on occasions your behavior has been applauded by the entire people, your position outside parliament, where the real fight between the people and the Fascist regime is going on, has been one of hesitation. More often than not, you have chosen to trust the Court and the Court cliques rather than listen to the voice of the people.

We understand your position, your advanced age, your social standing, and therefore we are not asking you to take the difficult road of illegality. . . . The only thing we do ask from you is to assume your place among the leaders of the Fatherland Front. Your active participation in the National Committee of the Fatherland Front would be a crucial factor in the national struggle.[28]

Despite its conciliatory tone, the letter bore no fruit. Mushanov was determined not to enter into any agreement with the Communists. He continued to object to their armed resistance and their partisans,

[28] For the complete text of the letter sent to Mushanov, see Vasilev, pp. 666–71.

hoping as he had always done for a change from above. By March, 1944, after the heavy Allied bombings of the capital, Mushanov and Professor Stainov were openly speaking from the floor of the Subranie in favor of a new government.

Gichev's reaction was fundamentally the same as Mushanov's. Not having received an answer to the letter of November 19, the Central Committee decided to send Dr. Ivan Pashov to confer with the Agrarian leaders. A meeting between Pashov and Gichev was held in late November. Like Mushanov, Gichev expressed objections to the Communist armed resistance. In any case, he maintained, the Fatherland Front itself was nothing more than a "Communist invention." Furthermore, Gichev objected to any kind of cooperation between himself and Zveno, whose coup of 1934 he could neither forget nor forgive.

In an endeavor to appease and deradicalize the country, in the fall of 1943 the Bozhilov government granted a broad political amnesty. The detention camps were closed down. All persons detained without trial since mid-1941 were thus released. The great majority were Communists or suspected Communists. They were asked to sign written statements to the effect that in the future they would undertake no political activities. The same procedure was applied to political prisoners serving short-term sentences in state prisons. In October, 1943, therefore, the Communist intellectual elite found itself free, even though in some cases prominent Communists were not allowed to reside in the capital. Only a few joined the resistance movement. The great majority, who had never accepted the idea of an armed rebellion, remained inactive and awaited developments.[29]

Anxious over the lack of visible results in the Communist campaign to recruit new allies from within the opposition, early in 1944 the Buro-in-Exile reappraised the strategy followed by the Party at home.

---

[29] At his trial in 1945, Bozhilov claimed to have freed a total of 6,000 people from detention camps and internment centers (Ministerstvo na propagandata, *Dnevnitsi*, January 12, 1945, p. 6). Communists not directly involved in armed resistance or conspiracies were treated harshly but not cruelly by the regime. Conditions in the detention camps were fair and relations with the commanding officers good and occasionally friendly. A revealing account of life in the largest of those camps is given by Milorad Zhivkovich in *Glas na bulgarite v Yugoslaviia*, January 16, 1950; also on the camps and the 1943 amnesty, see Zarkov, pp. 87–90; Kodzheikov, *Rozhdenie i suzizhdane*, the last four chapters; Natan, *Biakhme v "Enikioi."*

In a lengthy new directive prepared in March, the émigré leadership urged the Communists in Bulgaria to show greater flexibility and further reduce their demands for collaboration with the Mushanov-Gichev forces.[30]

The modification in the Communist position notwithstanding, the spring of 1944 witnessed no progress in the direction of widening the Fatherland Front. Here and there local Fatherland Front committees with a predominant Communist composition were established. They were few and isolated. Although armed resistance continued to be carried out under the label of the Fatherland Front, the effort remained exclusively in Communist hands. Petkov, the only other representative in the Fatherland Front who, because of the support which his group had in the villages, could have taken active part in the armed resistance by appealing to his followers to join the partisans, abstained from such a step. Nor did he later, despite the obvious political advantages involved, ever claim to have actively supported the partisans and the armed resistance in general. "Nikola Petkov did not agree with our basic policy to wrest power through an armed uprising and partisan detachments," said Dr. Kiril Dramaliev during the 1947 trial of Petkov. "He was in favor of a military *coup d'état*. That was the basic difference which he upheld from beginning to end." [31] The difference, as events were soon to show, was not so basic, since the Communists themselves in no way rejected the possibility of a *coup d'état*. However, in the spring of 1944 they went so far as to seek a separate deal with the ruling regime.

THE BAGRIANOV GOVERNMENT

In the spring of 1944, under the influence of fast-changing political and military conditions, the regime of Professor Filov found itself under ever increasing pressures. The most immediate changes took place on the military fronts. On April 8, 1944, the Red Army reached the Rumanian frontier along the Carpathians; two days later, Odessa was liberated. With this, the Black Sea naval and air facilities given to the Germans at the port towns of Varna and Burgas became of prime tacti-

---

[30] The March, 1944, directive is related and analyzed in Petrov, pp. 184–89.

[31] Quoted from the testimony of Dr. Kiril Dramaliev given at the trial of Petkov and reproduced in *The Trial of Nikola D. Petkov, August 5–15, 1947: Record of the Judicial Proceedings*, pp. 338–47.

cal importance to the Soviet armies. On April 17 the Soviet government protested the use of the Varna facilities by the Germans. The Bulgarians denied the charges, saying that the Black Sea bases were not being employed for offensive purposes. To this, the Soviets responded on April 26 by requesting the reopening of the Soviet consulate in Varna, which the Bulgarians had closed down in 1942, and the establishment of two new consulates in Burgas and Ruse in order to verify the Bulgarian contentions. Afraid to offend the Russians, but unwilling to agree, the government postponed its reply.[32]

On May 12, 1944, the three Allied governments warned Germany's Balkan satellites of the "inevitability of a crushing Nazi defeat." The longer they continued at war in collaboration with Germany, the more disastrous would be the consequences, the declaration said, and the more rigorous the terms imposed at the end of the war. This declaration was interpreted as an attempt to mitigate the unconditional surrender terms and thus hasten the breakup of the alliances with Germany.

The combination of Allied warnings and Soviet protests produced a crisis. On May 18, Bozhilov submitted his resignation.[33] Filov did not go to the "tolerated opposition" but turned to his own entourage for the selection of a new prime minister. He chose Ivan Bagrianov, an Agrarian from the right and a wealthy landowner. Bagrianov had resigned as minister of agriculture on the eve of the German entry into Bulgaria, but had remained in the government camp. Though his resignation in February, 1941, had not been over the pro-German policies of Boris and Filov, it was now hoped that his absence from the cabinet during the period in which Bulgaria was formally at war with the Western Allies would make him a more suitable candidate for an eventual rapproche-- ment with the West. At the same time, Bagrianov was not unacceptable to the Germans.

From the first, Bagrianov's government appeared less devoted to

[32] For the texts of notes exchanged between the Soviet and Bulgarian governments during the period April-September, 1944, see *Soviet Foreign Policy During the Patriotic War*, II, 111–19. The full range of inter-Allied diplomacy relating to Bulgaria, and the Anglo-Russian "percentage agreement" over the Balkans, are explored in *Foreign Relations of the United States: Diplomatic Papers, 1944*, III, 300–554; *The Memoirs of Cordell Hull*, II, 1451–61, 1570–82; Churchill, *The Second World War*, VI, 227–33.

[33] Bozhinov, pp. 69–72.

the Axis than its predecessor. Changes were made in the political police apparatus, while the anti-Jewish measures were appreciably relaxed.[34] Bagrianov now began to speak of "strict neutrality" and promised the introduction of sweeping social and agrarian reforms. The most important developments, however, took place behind the scenes.

The new cabinet formed in June had the following composition: Ivan Bagrianov, prime minister and minister of foreign affairs; Al. Stanishev, minister of the interior; Mikh. Arnaudov, minister of education; Dim. Savov, minister of finance; Khr. Vasilev, minister of trade, industry, and labor; Gen. Rusi Rusev, minister of war; Boris Kolchev, minister of railroads and posts; and Doncho Kostov, minister of agriculture. With the exception of the last-named, the cabinet was politically colorless. Doncho Kostov, however, was the person least expected to be given a seat in the government. A Soviet-educated agricultural-biologist and a close follower of Michurin's and Lysenko's theories on genetics, he returned from the Soviet Union sometime during 1943. His appointment to the Ministry of Agriculture created a small-scale sensation.[35]

From the first, the Party Central Committee endeavored to establish direct contact with the new prime minister. For that purpose, Dr. Ivan Pashov and Dr. Mincho Neichev met with Bagrianov.

The negotiations between the two sides were extensive and covered the entire spectrum of Communist activities. Bagrianov, with an eye toward improving relations with the Soviet Union, went a long way in assuring the Communist representatives of his good will and desire for an accommodation. He promised to institute personnel changes in the police *apparat* and to stop the persecution of the partisans if they in turn suspended their armed activities.[36]

In view of these developments, Dobri Terpeshev, acting in his

---

[34] The government's retreat on the "Jewish front" was most pronounced. Secret negotiations between Nikola Balabanov, the Bulgarian minister to Istanbul, and Ira Hirschmann, representative of the U.S. War Refugee Board, were opened already in July. In August, Balabanov addressed a letter to Hirschmann declaring that the Bulgarian government regretted all anti-Jewish measures. Finally, on August 17, Bagrianov announced in the Subranie the abrogation of all anti-Jewish laws; see Meyer *et al.*, pp. 573–74.

[35] Kazasov, *Burni godini*, pp. 748–49. After the Communist seizure of power, Doncho Kostov became the chief theoretician of Bulgarian agricultural sciences.

[36] *Ibid.*, p. 750.

capacity as commander in chief of the resistance movement, issued orders to the effect that partisan units stop fighting, while retaining their weapons. To this end a number of representatives from the center were sent to local partisan staffs.[37]

Throughout the interval of the Communist negotiations with Bagrianov, he continued to be attacked in the broadcasts of the Party Buro-in-Exile. In a "Khristo Botev" broadcast of June 5, the Bagrianov government was classified as basically pro-German, and its early downfall predicted. In a Moscow radio broadcast of June 12, Kolarov attacked the new government.[38] The overt inconsistencies between the activities of the Party at home and the statements made by the Buro-in-Exile remained unexplained; either Kolarov and Dimitrov were not informed of the actions taken by the Party at home, or they were better informed of Russia's ultimate plans for Bulgaria. In any case, it was Kolarov and Dimitrov who proved to be right and the Party at home wrong.

Before that, however, came the end of the Doncho Kostov episode. On June 12, less than a fortnight after its formation, the government of Bagrianov was reorganized. Doncho Kostov was dropped and Bagrianov took over the Ministry of Agriculture himself, while surrendering Foreign Affairs to Petur Draganov, Bulgaria's sometime minister to Berlin and Madrid respectively. Doncho Kostov disappeared from the scene and was not heard from until the September coup. His unexpected appointment and sudden dismissal remained something of a mystery. According to Kazasov, he was never consulted by Bagrianov when first appointed to the Ministry of Agriculture and in fact never assumed his post.[39] According to a second source, Kostov was retained in the government for several days against his will. Was his appointment in any way connected with the negotiations between the Communists and Bagrianov? If so, the Party never disclosed the nature of this connection. There was, of course, the possibility that the two events were not directly connected and that in both cases Bagrianov did what he did in order to mislead the public and buy time with the Soviet government. In a secret report pre-

---

[37] *Novo vreme*, No. 9 (1953), pp. 59–75.

[38] Kolarov, *Protiv khitlerizma i negovite bulgarski slugi*, pp. 639–43. See also pp. 633–38 for the text of the broadcast of May 31.

[39] Kazasov, *Burni godini*, p. 749.

pared for Prince Kiril (Boris's brother who was now one of the three regents), Bagrianov said that Bulgaria could be saved "from the approaching Red wave not by any strategic barriers but by the erection of a political barrier." [40]

In the meantime, the Party was discovering the futility of its "understanding" with Bagrianov. The antipartisan campaign continued. When the Communist representatives went to the Prime Minister to ask for an explanation, an apologetic Bagrianov begged their indulgence and asked for time to overcome the opposition of the regents and the army.[41] At the beginning of August the National Committee of the Fatherland Front decided to break off all connections with Bagrianov.[42]

The armed resistance in general and the partisan movement in particular were not greatly affected by the Communist-Bagrianov negotiations. After initial optimism over the talks, the struggle between the partisans and the gendarmery continued much as before. Following the September coup, the Communists maintained that the number of partisans killed during the three months of the Bagrianov government exceeded the total number killed during the entire preceding resistance period. In 1945, Kostov, speaking before the first postwar plenary session of the Party Central Committee, said:

There is no denying the fact that with his demagogy Bagrianov succeeded, at first in any case, in generating certain illusions, not only among the masses, but also within leading circles in the Party. He was soon unmasked, however, because his deeds stood in direct contradiction to his words. We must admit that it was the rank and file of the Party which reacted against the mistake of the Central Committee and that the Central Committee, in turn realizing its mistake, did everything to correct it.[43]

Having failed to effect a separate understanding with the Bagrianov government, the Communists reverted to their earlier stand. Essentially, this meant a return to the old-time effort of trying to secure the cooperation of the "tolerated opposition" within the framework of the Fatherland Front, and should this again prove impossible, outside it.

[40] *Rabotnichesko delo*, January 5, 1945.

[41] Kazasov, *Burni godini*, p. 750.

[42] *Ibid.*, p. 755.

[43] Kostov, *Politicheskoto polozhenie i zadachite na partiiata*, pp. 11–12.

With this aim in mind, the National Committee of the Fatherland Front, under Communist inspiration, drafted a "warning" to the Bagrianov regime by which it hoped to obtain the support of Mushanov and Gichev and thus seize the initiative.

The "warning" to Bagrianov, completed on August 10, proved to be a mild document. Opening with an analysis of the political situation as seen by the Fatherland Front, it pointed out a number of measures which should be taken immediately if Bulgaria was to be saved from disaster. First, the government was called upon to sever its alliance with Germany. Without this "first inevitable step," restoration of good relations with the Soviet Union and an end to the state of war with Great Britain and the United States were "unthinkable." The government was further asked to proclaim complete political amnesty and abolish all discriminatory laws. On the crucial issue of the occupied territories, the "warning" stated that the Bulgarian army should be withdrawn from the territories of "Serbia, Bosnia, Montenegro, and Greece." This implied the retention of Yugoslav and Greek Macedonia by the Bulgarians.[44]

The "warning" of August 10 was signed by thirty-three persons, all of them affiliated with the Fatherland Front. The leaders of the "tolerated opposition" refused to sign the document, stating that they themselves were in the process of drafting a note to the government. Thus, in the end, the Communists were again faced with the danger of being politically isolated unless they were ready to cooperate with Mushanov. This time the Party decided on full cooperation.

The note prepared by the leaders of the "tolerated opposition," later to become known, after the number of its signatories, as the "declaration of the thirteen," was a shorter document than the one drafted by the National Committee and, on the whole, more to the point. It read as follows:

We, the representatives of the political forces in Bulgaria, assembled in one of the most difficult moments for our fatherland, find that it is necessary: (1) to end the war with Britain and the United States; (2) to undertake a policy of open friendship and trust toward Russia, our liberator; (3) to withdraw the army from those territories for which Bulgaria has never pretended any interest; (4) to establish a state of strict compliance with the

[44] The full texts of this document and of the one immediately following are to be found in Kazasov, *Burni godini*, pp. 751–52.

Constitution and guarantee the rights and freedoms of all citizens; (5) to form a people's constitutional government enjoying the confidence of the entire nation in order to realize these policies.

The declaration was signed by Atanas Burov (Narodniatsi); Nikola Mushanov and Dr. Al. Girginov (Democrats); Dimitur Gichev, Konstantin Muraviev, and Vergil Dimov (Gichev Agrarians); Pastukhov and A. Moskov (Social Democrats); Kimon Georgiev and Professor Petko Stainov (Zveno); Nikola Petkov (Pladne); Dr. Ivan Pashov and Dr. Mincho Neichev (Communists). On August 12 Mushanov delivered the declaration to the Regency Council.[45]

The signing of the "declaration of the thirteen" was of far-reaching importance because it affected both the composition of the opposition in Bulgaria and the course the Bagrianov government was to take.

From the first the declaration went far beyond being a mere warning. In view of the international situation, which from the point of view of Bulgaria was deteriorating daily, and in view of the wide support which the declaration received, it constituted in effect an ultimatum to the government. It presented the regents with a united opposition to which they had to turn if Bagrianov failed to find a way out of the impasse. The thirteen political representatives who signed the declaration did not fail to appreciate this fact. Indeed, at the time of signing they saw themselves as a potential government. "It was then agreed," said Pastukhov later, "that the struggle would be continued until the *zavoi* [turnabout] was effected, after which a new government would be formed composed of all those who signed the declaration." [46]

Strictly speaking, therefore, with the signing of the declaration the Fatherland Front withered away because its four affiliates—Pashov, Neichev, Petkov, and Georgiev—acted not as a body but as the representatives of their respective groups.[47] This action was taken with the full agreement of the Communists, Neichev and Pashov having been

[45] Moshanov, pp. 52–53.

[46] Quoted from Pastukhov's statement to the court at his 1946 trial; *Svoboden narod*, June 23, 1946.

[47] Although an affiliate of Zveno, Professor Petko Stainov did not become involved in the Fatherland Front until it was about to assume power, at which time he was named foreign minister; on this, see Stainov's testimony at the trial of Pastukhov, in *Svoboden narod*, June 11, 1946.

authorized to do so by the Party Central Committee.[48] What is more, having once decided to cooperate with the "tolerated opposition," the two Communist representatives appeared anxious to have the declaration signed as soon as possible. "Mincho Neichev took a very moderate stand," Professor Stainov said later. "He insisted that an agreement be reached, and did all he could to facilitate the signing of the declaration." [49] Technically there were no difficulties. On the vital issue of the occupied territories, despite the difference in formulation, the two documents were in agreement in so far as both implied Bulgaria's retention of Macedonia.[50] Nevertheless, in agreeing to sign the declaration so short a time after the leaders of the "tolerated opposition" had refused to support the National Committee's own "warning," the Communists were in effect admitting a tactical as well as a moral defeat, for the initiative now passed into the hands of the opposition leaders outside the Fatherland Front.

The action of August 12 was taken because the Party was afraid of being left out of a future government, which the Communists knew would sooner or later take the place of Bagrianov's. Moreover, the Communists were afraid of the possibility that Bulgaria, not being at war with the Soviet Union, would find herself under the occupation of the Western Allies. What they did not know at the time was that Rumania was about to surrender and that within a matter of days the Soviet army would find itself on the Bulgarian frontier ready to cross the Danube into Bulgaria proper.

[48] On the Central Committee authorization, see Kazasov, *Burni godini*, p. 756.

[49] Quoted from Stainov's testimony at the trial of Pastukhov; *Svoboden narod*, June 11, 1946.

[50] Speaking of the discussions with the Communist representatives on the question of the occupied territories, Pastukhov later said: "I remember the words of Dr. Pashov, who said that on this question Russia had not yet spoken her last word. On every occasion during the period when the signing of the declaration was being negotiated, I continued to remind the Communist representatives: 'You have a strong Party in the country. You also have influential people in Russia. These things are usually done through pressure. Much as Soviet foreign policy appears predetermined, we can still get something for Bulgaria, assuming we continue to bring up the question. Let us not be too late and say that our chances have gone by.' To this, they used to answer: 'We are constantly reminding our people about this question, and we hope that they will succeed in finding a suitable solution.' " Quoted from Pastukhov's statement at his 1946 trial; *Svoboden narod*, June 23, 1946.

Reacting to the mounting foreign and domestic pressures, Bagrianov decided on two steps with which he hoped to save his government. First, early in August he opened negotiations with the Western Allies to find out whether Bulgaria could not somehow mitigate the severity of an unconditional surrender. A fortnight later, with the "declaration of the thirteen" already delivered, he called the Subranie to a special session. With this second move he hoped to demonstrate his and his government's popularity.

A separate approach to the Allies was not a new idea. In February, 1944, Bagrianov had told Moshanov that he personally was in favor of turning to the Soviet government with a request that it assist the Bulgarians in establishing contact with the United States and Britain.[51] After he became prime minister, Bagrianov again spoke of his ideas, although this time a request to the Soviet Union was vetoed by Draganov, the foreign minister, who maintained that before asking the Soviets for help, Bulgaria should try to establish direct contact with the West. Bagrianov hesitated until he perceived the urgency of the situation. The immediate cause was a speech by Churchill which, with its attacks on Bulgaria, greatly disturbed the government.

Thrice thrown into wars on the wrong side by a miserable set of criminal politicians, who seem to be available for their country's ruin generation after generation [said the British Prime Minister in his speech before the House of Commons], three times in my life has this wretched Bulgaria subjected a peasant population to all the pangs of war and chastisements of defeat. For them also, the moment for repentance has not passed, but it is passing swiftly. The whole of Europe is heading, irresistibly, into new and secure foundations. What would be the place of Bulgaria at the judgment seat, when the petty and cowardly part she has played in this war is revealed, and when the entire Yugoslav and Greek nations, through their representatives, will reveal at the Allies' armistice table the dismal tale of the work the Bulgarian Army has done in their countries as the cruel lackeys of the fallen Nazi power?[52]

On the day following Churchill's speech, Moshanov was summoned by the Prime Minister and authorized to go to Ankara to establish con-

---

[51] Unless otherwise stated, the account of Bulgaria's negotiations with the Western Allies is based on Moshanov, pp. 53–59. Moshanov, it should be remembered, was the Speaker of the 1938 Subranie.

[52] Quoted from Churchill's speech of August 2, 1944, as reproduced in Holborn, II, 509.

tact with the British minister there. This Moshanov did, reaching the Turkish capital on August 14, after being detained by the Germans on the Bulgarian-Turkish frontier for forty-eight hours.[53] Talks with the British minister were begun on August 16, at which time the Bulgarian delegate was told that the governments of the United States and the Soviet Union would be kept fully informed. Instructed by the Bulgarian government to remain in Ankara and await further developments, Moshanov accomplished little or nothing during the first stage of his mission. Following the Rumanian capitulation, he was recalled to Sofia for new instructions.

On August 17 the Subranie reconvened in a special session. In his opening speech, Bagrianov spoke of the Bulgarian people's desire for peace. He outlined a broad program with which he hoped to achieve a "democratic reconstruction." In order to show its good will, he said, the government had decided to put an end to anti-Jewish persecutions. A broad amnesty for political prisoners was promised, and the partisans were invited to discontinue their fight. The Prime Minister's declaration was wildly applauded. The very same deputies who in December, 1941, applauded Filov when he announced Bulgaria's entry into the war were now happy with Bagrianov for trying to bring an end to the conflict.

Then, on August 23, Rumania capitulated. The Fatherland Front, which only ten days earlier had been submerged so that its affiliates could collaborate with the "tolerated opposition," reappeared overnight. On the day the news of the Rumanian surrender broke, the National Committee decided to seek an interview with Bagrianov, which Dimo Kazasov proceeded to arrange in person.[54]

The meeting between the National Committee and Bagrianov took place on August 24 with Kazasov serving as spokesman. The National Committee came forward with the request that the Fatherland Front be brought to power. To this Bagrianov replied that he would be willing to step down from his post, but that the decision was up to the Regency Council. He invited the National Committee to meet with the three regents, but was refused on the grounds that it was up to him to raise the

[53] The Germans occupied a narrow strip of Bulgarian territory along the Bulgarian-Turkish frontier in 1941.

[54] The account of developments during August 23 and 24 is based on Kazasov, *Burni godini*, pp. 756–58.

problem. The Prime Minister then went to see the regents while the Fatherland Front representatives waited. Upon his return, Bagrianov told his visitors that "the regents could not receive the delegation because they were not faced with a cabinet crisis." With this the interview came to an end.

The following days saw intensified maneuvers on all sides. On August 25 the National Committee issued an appeal to the people which, like the "warning" of a fortnight earlier, spoke in generalities. "The time has arrived," concluded the appeal, "for the people and the army to stand together and be ready to assume in their own hands the destinies of the endangered fatherland." [55] On the following day the Communist Party Central Committee issued its "Circular No. 4," which was more strongly worded. It called for the establishment of a government of the Fatherland Front and asked all units of the armed resistance to begin concentrating on strategically important points. It also requested the withdrawal of the Bulgarian army from Yugoslavia (not just Serbia) and Greece.[56]

In the meantime the government did all it could to reassure both the Soviet and Turkish governments of Bulgaria's passivity. On August 25 the German troops on Bulgarian territory were ordered disarmed. The next day, Foreign Minister Draganov informed the Soviet Foreign Ministry of Bulgaria's determination to remain neutral in the Russo-German conflict and repeated the government's decision concerning the disarming of German troops.[57] On August 27 an official government statement made known Bulgaria's determination to leave the war and stated that for some time the government had been in touch with representatives of those countries with which Bulgaria was at war.[58] On the same day, the regents invited the leaders of all opposition groups to an audience. Nikola Petkov, Dr. Ivan Pashov, and Grigor Cheshmedzhiev, the spokesmen for the National Committee, insisted on being received as representatives of the Fatherland Front and not merely as leaders

[55] *Ibid.*, p. 758.

[56] For the complete text of the circular, see *BKP v rezoliutsii i resheniia*, pp. 462–65. The circular was a secret communication to the Party organizations and not an appeal to the people at large.

[57] Bozhinov, pp. 98–99.

[58] Kazasov, *Burni godini*, pp. 758–60.

of their respective groups. The request was rejected by the regents on the grounds that the meeting was exploratory and that the invitations were issued to individual political figures and not to opposition blocs. The three representatives of the Fatherland Front thereupon withdrew. The only one affiliated with the Front who attended the meeting along with the "tolerated opposition" and Tsankov was Kimon Georgiev, who on the same day had been brought by the government from his internment in Burgas. Georgiev had presumably been unable to confer first with his colleagues of the Fatherland Front.[59]

The audience brought no immediate results. The leaders of the "tolerated opposition" reiterated their position of August 12 and insisted on the creation of a new national government. The regents made no commitments. Filov clung to his position to the last. His hopes were based on two assumptions: (1) that the Russians would respect Bulgaria's neutrality and would not openly intervene in the internal affairs of the country so long as Bulgarian territory was not used by the Germans as a base of operations; and (2) that a separate understanding with the Western Allies allowing Bulgaria to get out of the war had not been totally ruled out. A new effort toward this end was made late in August.

On August 28 the Bulgarian government was notified by Balabanov, its minister to Ankara, of a communication from the British minister to Turkey to the effect that the Allies were ready to reveal their truce conditions but that these could be given only in Cairo. The British minister further indicated that a special plane would await the Bulgarian delegates in Istanbul to fly them to Allied headquarters if and when they were ready to undertake the mission.[60]

Bagrianov decided that the mission should be undertaken immediately. In order to strengthen his position, Moshanov asked that the government be reconstructed to include a number of people known for their pro-Western sympathies. Bagrianov, on his part, agreed and promised to bring Professor Petko Stainov to the Ministry of Foreign Affairs and Nikola Petkov to the Interior in the place of Stanishev, who, as a Macedonian, was an open Germanophile. The Prime Minister also promised that as soon as Professor Stainov was in the cabinet he would

---

[59] On the meeting of August 27, see *ibid.*, p. 760; see also the testimony of Professor Stainov as reported in *Svoboden narod*, June 11, 1946.

[60] Here again, the account of the Bulgarian contact with the Western Allies is based on Moshanov, pp. 53–59.

be asked to go to Cairo in person to assume the leadership of the Bulgarian negotiating delegation. With these reassurances, Moshanov left Sofia on August 29, arriving in Cairo on the following day.

Bagrianov's promises to Moshanov on the government reorganization remained unfulfilled. On August 30 the government's basic assumption that the Soviet Union would respect Bulgaria's neutrality suffered a blow. On that day, the Soviet news agency Tass categorically denied rumors to the effect that the Soviet government had officially recognized Bulgaria's neutrality. Bagrianov attempted to offset the Soviet statement by announcing that the Bulgarian occupation corps was being withdrawn from the occupied territories. This proved of no avail. The regents at last decided to drop Bagrianov, bringing his political career to a close.

THE MURAVIEV GOVERNMENT

On September 2 the Gichev Agrarians, the group with the largest popular support in the "tolerated opposition," were given a mandate to form a new government. As far as the regents were concerned, the choice was a logical one. In his centrist position Gichev enjoyed the confidence of Mushanov as well as of Pastukhov. It was hoped that he would be able to attract representatives of the Fatherland Front into a new government.

In the final event, however, the premiership did not go to Gichev, the real leader of his Agrarian faction, but to Konstantin Muraviev, his close associate.

Before announcing the composition of the new cabinet, the Gichev Agrarians and the Democrats did all they could to make the government as broad as possible. The Communists were approached but turned down an offer to participate. The Party stated that it would only enter a government composed purely of Fatherland Front elements.[61] Nikola Petkov took a similar stand. Great efforts were made to bring in Pastukhov, who, having no commitments to the Fatherland Front, was believed available. However, Pastukhov refused under pressure from the other Social Democratic leaders, with whom he conferred on the same day.[62]

---

[61] See Gichev's own account in *Svoboden narod*, June 11, 1946.

[62] Pastukhov, who together with A. Moskov appeared inclined to join the new government, called a meeting of the leadership in which the issue was debated. Cheshmedzhiev and those who had entered the Fatherland Front objected on the grounds that the Social Democrats had a commitment to the Front not to under-

The cabinet was formed during the night of September 2–3. Muraviev became prime minister as well as minister of foreign affairs. Gichev, Mushanov, and Atanas Burov, the three elder statesmen of the "tolerated opposition," became ministers without portfolios. Dr. Aleksandur Girginov from the Democrats was given the Ministry of Finance, and Vergil Dimov, the Ministry of the Interior. The ministries of Education, Trade, and Railroads remained unfilled. They were held in reserve for the members of the Fatherland Front if and when they decided to join.[63]

Fundamentally, the Muraviev cabinet was a re-creation of the People's Bloc government of the early 1930s. Its pro-Western sympathies were unquestionable. Yet its composition did not receive an enthusiastic reception in Western circles, particularly in Cairo where the Bulgarians were negotiating for a truce. "Premier Muraviev," wrote a Cairo observer on September 4, "is regarded here as a rather weak figure since his days as a Stamboliiski supporter twenty-one years ago, and M. Burov is regarded as fairly reactionary." [64] "The probability of a revolution," wrote the same observer on the following day, "resulting in a distinctly Left Wing government [appears] imminent." [65]

The Muraviev government undertook a number of moves. On September 3 it instructed Dr. K. M. Sarafov, the secretary-general of the Ministry of Foreign Affairs, to contact Yakovlev, under whose management the Soviet legation in Sofia had been left following the departure of the Soviet minister. The Bulgarian diplomat expressed "the government's firm determination to secure by all means at its disposal the absolute and complete application of the policy of neutrality made public by the preceding government." [66] On the following day, the Muraviev gov-

---

take independent action. Although the commitment in no way involved Pastukhov personally, he decided to comply with the desires of his colleagues in order not to create the impression of an open split in Social Democratic ranks.

[63] The other ministries were filled in the following manner: Boris Pavlov—Justice; General Ivan Marinov—War; Khr. G. Popov—Agriculture; St. Daskalov—Roads.

[64] *New York Times*, September 4, 1944.

[65] *Ibid.*, September 5, 1944.

[66] On Sarafov's mission, see Bozhinov, p. 122.

ernment in its first official statement repeated its determination not to allow the stationing of German troops on Bulgarian soil, and threatened to break off diplomatic relations with Germany in case of difficulties in this regard. The government declared the Tripartite Pact void and promised to continue the withdrawal of the Bulgarian occupation corps from territories held by it. Finally the government announced that it would continue its truce negotiations with the Western Allies.[67]

Tass at once published the opinion that the action of the Bulgarian government did not go far enough and that Bulgaria must join the Allies or suffer the consequences. It should follow Finland and Rumania and separate itself completely from Germany. Then suddenly, late in the next afternoon, Molotov asked the American and British ambassadors to call on him. "He gave them copies of a statement which the Soviet government was about to issue. This was a declaration of war against Bulgaria. Molotov evaded questions as to whether Soviet troops would enter Bulgaria. Asked also whether he expected to start armistice negotiations with Bulgaria, and how and when, he said that depended on what the Bulgarians did." [68]

Following the interview with ambassador Harriman and Clark Kerr, Molotov summoned the Bulgarian minister. The latter was presented with a lengthy note in which the Soviet government stated that, having tolerated Bulgaria's warlike attitude for more than three years, it had now decided to declare war on Bulgaria.

The news of the Soviet declaration of war reached Muraviev late on September 5 during a cabinet meeting. The surprise was complete. The government stayed in session until the early morning at which time a delegation was sent to Yakovlev, the Soviet representative in Sofia. It informed him (1) of the government's decision to break with Germany and (2) of its desire for an immediate truce.[69]

Later in the day on September 6, faced with the new situation, the Muraviev government took two decisions. First, it instructed the military

[67] The single most authoritative account of Muraviev's government is found in Ilcho Dimitrov's article in *Istoricheski pregled*, No. 5 (1964), pp. 3–33. The text of the government's official statement of September 4 is summarized in Kazasov, *Burni godini*, pp. 762–64.

[68] Herbert Feis, *Churchill, Roosevelt, Stalin* (Princeton, N. J., 1957), pp. 417–19.

[69] Bozhinov, p. 123.

that in case of Red Army penetrations into Bulgaria, "there was to be no resistance." Second, it declared war on Germany. However, on the advice of General Marinov, the minister of war, it was decided to hold up the official announcement and not to undertake immediate military action. Marinov argued that before the Bulgarian army could engage in any military campaign against the Germans it should be given time to improve its order of battle.[70] This the minister of war considered essential, particularly since on September 4 the Germans, afraid that the Bulgarians might capitulate suddenly, had undertaken to immobilize the Bulgarian army located in the occupied territories by taking captive the staffs of three of its divisions. The government agreed to delay publication of its declaration of war. It could no longer expect anything from the negotiations in Cairo, which had collapsed with the Soviet declaration of war.[71] Muraviev's one tangible achievement during these crucial hours was the resignation of Professor Filov from the Regency Council, obtained after prolonged insistence on the part of the government. Then, on September 8, with advanced Red Army units already in northeastern Bulgaria, the government at last announced its declaration of war on Germany. For a few short hours the Muraviev government found itself in the strange position of being at one and the same time at war with Russia and Germany.[72]

In a way, the fate of the Muraviev government was sealed on the very day of its formation. The only way in which Muraviev could have

[70] For Marinov's own account, see his article in *Istoricheski pregled*, No. 3, 1968.

[71] Following his arrival in Cairo on August 30, Moshanov was presented with an unofficial version of the armistice conditions. The talks, however, came to a standstill with the formation of the Muraviev government, since Moshanov needed his credentials renewed by that government. By the time Muraviev's authorization arrived, the negotiations had to be suspended since Bulgaria was already at war not only with the Western Allies but also with the USSR (Moshanov, p. 59). Later in September the Bulgarian delegates were flown to Turkey together with Dr. G. M. Dimitrov, with whom Moshanov had established contact in Cairo. At the end, under pressure from the Soviets, the Western Allies agreed that the Bulgarian armistice should be signed in Moscow. The actual signing took place in October, 1944, with the Bulgarians represented by a delegation of the Fatherland Front government.

[72] The fact that it was the Muraviev government and not that of the Fatherland Front which declared war on Germany is usually overlooked, and even denied by official Communist sources.

hoped to stabilize his position was immediately to declare war on Germany. This he did not do because he still hoped that Bulgaria could preserve her neutrality and because war with Germany might well have brought about the intervention of the Red Army. This was the last thing Muraviev wanted to happen. Until the last moment, he and his colleagues hoped that the Russians would not cross into Bulgaria.

The move undertaken by the Soviet government on September 5 was brutal and yet masterful. It brought about another change of government, placing in power groups that the Soviet government preferred to the ones on whom it was declaring war. It also put an end to the negotiations in Cairo, thus making the Soviet Union a party to the Bulgarian armistice negotiations.

THE COUP

August 23, 1944, the day of the Rumanian collapse, marked a turning point in Communist and Fatherland Front thinking. While before that date affiliates of the Front were still uncertain of their political future and did all they could not to be left out of political developments, such doubts all but disappeared after the entry of the Red Army into Rumania. At that point the Fatherland Front undertook an independent course which it pursued until the coup of September 9.

In late August, the Communist Party Buro-in-Exile executed two moves aimed at reassuring the Communists at home both militarily and politically. On the military side, arms were dropped to the Bulgarian partisans by Soviet aircraft over the region of Kalna in the Free Yugoslav zone. With this equipment, which was the first the Soviets had ever sent, the Bulgarian partisans organized their first partisan division, of which Trunski became the commander. Trunski's division, however, played no direct part in the subsequent coup itself. Being the largest armed formation on which the Party could rely, it played its major role after the coup.

On the political side, the Buro-in-Exile undertook to strengthen the Party leadership. As in 1935, when the purge of the so-called left sectarians was carried out, the choice of Kolarov and Dimitrov fell again on Stanke Dimitrov-Marek. In February, 1944, he had been withdrawn from his work with the broadcasting station "Naroden glas" and assigned to special parachute training.[73] Three days after the fall of Rumania, on August 26, Dimitrov-Marek with a group of associates left the Soviet Union. The mission, however, ended in tragedy. The aircraft crashed over Soviet soil killing Dimitrov-Marek and most of his companions.

Within Bulgaria, in the meantime, following the conference between the Regency Council and the opposition leaders on August 27 from which the representatives of the Fatherland Front withdrew, the main effort was directed against the Bagrianov government. On August 29 the National Committee issued a proclamation which called for the immediate resignation of the government, stating that only a government of the Fatherland Front could save Bulgaria.

The coming of power of Muraviev brought about several important developments. The Fatherland Front undertook to broaden the composition of its National Committee. With this move it was hoped to impress Muraviev and also to strengthen the Front's political position by bringing in some of the more prominent personalities who until that time had remained outside its formal framework. Closer collaboration was also established between the National Committee on the one hand and the general staff of the resistance movement on the other. This was particularly important because political and military activities could now be better coordinated. It also meant closer ties between the resistance and the army, in which Zveno was still influential.

The reorganized National Committee had a membership three times as large as the one originally constituted. It included the following: [74]

Communists	1.	Dr. Kiril Dramaliev
	2.	Dobri Terpeshev
	3.	Dr. Racho Angelov
	4.	Dr. Ivan Pashov
	5.	Dr. Mincho Neichev
Pladne	6.	Nikola Petkov
	7.	Angel Derzhanski
	8.	Khristo Stratev

---

[73] *Rabotnichesko delo*, August 27, 1946. After his departure from "Naroden glas," his place was taken by Svetoslav Kolev, who was eventually succeeded by Ferdinand Kozovski; see Kozovski's article in *Rabotnichesko delo*, September 8, 1958.

[74] The list of names is taken from Vasilev, p. 661.

Zveno	9.	Kimon Georgiev
	10.	Damian Velchev
	11.	Khristo Stoikov
Social	12.	Grigor Cheshmedzhiev
Democrats	13.	Dimitur Neikov
Independent	14.	Professor Venelin Ganev
	15.	Dimo Kazasov
	16.	Professor Petko Stoianov

In military terms, the significance of the reorganized National Committee was that it included Dobri Terpeshev, the Communist commander in chief, as well as Velchev, of Zveno. While Terpeshev constituted the connecting link between the National Committee and the general staff of the resistance movement, Velchev brought to bear his influence on the military inside and outside the army. This, as events were soon to show, proved decisive on the day of the coup.

Serious preparations for a coup were begun on September 2 when the Party Politburo outlined a general plan of action that called on partisan units to begin their movement toward urban centers.[75]

On September 4 a Fatherland Front delegation visited Muraviev. The Prime Minister was informed of the Front's determination to hold public demonstrations in the capital. Muraviev objected. Despite his opposition, and contrary to orders issued by Vergil Dimov, the minister of the interior, some demonstrations were held. On September 6 Sofia's transportation workers went on strike and demonstrations and public meetings against the government took place near the railroad station. On the same day, the "Shopski" partisan detachment entered the capital secretly and placed itself at the disposal of an operational staff headed by Todor Zhivkov, which was in turn made responsible for Communist activities within the city.[76] On September 7 the coal miners of Pernik went on strike. By that time, demonstrations had taken place in other

[75] Party accounts since 1950, as a direct result of Terpeshev's downfall, have tended to minimize the role of the general staff of the resistance and attribute important decisions to the Politburo as a body.

[76] *Rabotnichesko delo*, September 6, 1959. The name of Todor Zhivkov begins to be mentioned only after he became Party secretary in 1954. At the time of the coup, Zhivkov was a member of the Sofia Party district committee.

towns. On September 7 a mob stormed the Pleven prison house and freed all political prisoners, Kostov among them.[77]

While demonstrations were organized throughout the country, behind the scenes steps were taken to ensure the cooperation of key persons in the Muraviev administration. Such measures, after the Soviet declaration of war, became easier by the hour. Afraid that the government was about to fall, officials in high posts became more and more inclined to make a separate peace for themselves by coming to terms with those they believed would become the masters of tomorrow.

Inroads were made into the cabinet itself. Through the Zveno members in the National Committee, the minister of war, General Ivan Marinov, was kept informed of the intentions of the Fatherland Front. He was the only member of the government who knew of the impending coup. Approaches were also made to the police high command, whose cooperation was secured.

On September 8 [reported Petur Vranchev, a member of the resistance general staff, some years later], on the instruction of the Party, I met with the chief police inspector, Dimitur Chavdarov, and with Asen Boiadzhiev, the police commandant of Sofia. The police officials were prepared for the meeting in advance and were ready to cooperate. . . . Two conditions were agreed upon. First, it was agreed that all police patrols would be recalled to their quarters at 12 o'clock that night. Second, the entire police force was to remain passive throughout the night.[78]

The blow came in the early hours of September 9. The main effort was directed against the Ministry of War, where much of the government was concentrated. The building was taken at 2:15 A.M. without a shot. This action was made possible by a group of junior officers led by Captain Petur Iliev (later General) who, as employees of the ministry, were able to unlock the back doors from the inside. Vranchev, who concluded the agreement with the police chiefs, led a unit into the ministry. The Minister of War, placing himself openly at the disposal of the Fatherland Front, telephoned the Sofia garrison to secure its cooperation. The services of the "Shopski" partisan detachment, which, under

[77] *Rabotnichesko delo*, September 7, 1946.

[78] *Rabotnichesko delo*, September 5, 1957. Vranchev's close liaison with Zveno and with individual members of the Military League paid off. His memoirs (Vranchev, pp. 622–33) provide the most detailed account of the immediate preparations for the coup and the capture of the War Ministry building.

the command of Todor Zhivkov, had taken positions near the ministry, were not required.

During the night, army military units went over to the Fatherland Front one after another. Major communications centers and key buildings in the center of Sofia fell into the hands of Fatherland Front supporters. Early in the morning of September 9, Kimon Georgiev, as the new prime minister, read a proclamation over the Sofia radio in which he stated that the Fatherland Front had decided to seize power in order to save Bulgaria from further disaster.[79] Georgiev also made public the composition of the new government. It included the following:

Communists	Dobri Terpeshev (minister without portfolio)
	Anton Yugov (Interior)
	Dr. Mincho Neichev (Justice)
	Dr. Racho Angelov (Health)
Zveno	Kimon Georgiev (Prime Minister)
	Damian Velchev (War)
	Prof. Petko Stainov (Foreign Affairs)
	Prof. Stancho Cholakov (Education)
Agrarians	Nikola Petkov (minister without portfolio)
	Angel Derzhanski (Transportation)
	Asen Pavlov (Agriculture)
	Boris Bumbarov (Public Works)
Social Democrats	Grigor Cheshmedzhiev (Social Welfare)
	Dimitur Neikov (Trade and Industry)
Independent	Dimo Kazasov (Propaganda)
	Prof. Petko Stoianov (Finance)

The Regency Council was dismissed and its members arrested. Three new regents were appointed: Venelin Ganev, a distinguished law professor; Tsvetko Boboshevski, an affiliate of Zveno; and Todor Pavlov, the well-known Communist theoretician.[80] The monarchy was not

---

[79] For the full text of the proclamation, see Kazasov, *Burni godini*, pp. 771–72.

[80] Nominally independent, Professor Venelin Ganev, who entered the National Committee early in September, was a personal friend of Nikola Petkov. His appointment to the senior position in the Regency Council was made on Petkov's recommendation. Boboshevski was an old political figure. Pavlov was the Party's official theoretician.

abolished. General Ivan Marinov received his reward for cooperating with the Fatherland Front by being appointed chief of the army's General Staff.[81] Pro-German officers in senior positions were dismissed and many of them were arrested. Dobri Terpeshev, Slavcho Trunski, Petur Iliev, Petur Vranchev, and many others were promoted to the rank of general. Anton Yugov, the new minister of the interior, took personal control over the police, which became known as the People's Militia. The operational staff of the resistance under Todor Zhivkov was transformed into the general staff of the People's Militia with Zhivkov, now a colonel, as its commander.[82]

With the capital in the hands of the Fatherland Front, the provinces responded immediately. Fatherland Front committees assumed local control. In places where no local committees existed, Communist activists took over. Here and there, individual garrison commanders put up resistance. There was shooting in Turnovo, with a number of peasants being killed while trying to enter the town. In Plovdiv, the commander of the Second Army refused to collaborate. On September 10 his subordinates brought the garrison over to the side of the new regime.

On its march to the interior, the Red Army was not resisted. One of the first undertakings of the new government was to dispatch a special mission to Marshal Tolbukhin's headquarters with a request that hostilities be formally brought to an end. This time the Fatherland Front succeeded where Muraviev had failed on September 6. Tolbukhin agreed on an immediate cessation of hostilities to become effective as of 10 o'clock on the evening of September 9. On the whole, the Red Army received a favorable reception from the local population. Communists and old Russophiles made sure of the presence of a sufficient number of red flags as well as properly organized reception committees.

Emerging from the underground, from prisons and places of internment, the Communists began to assemble. Their ranks were strengthened by partisans, many of them newly converted members who came down from the mountains. Added to them were the first Communist exiles

[81] There was an added irony in Marinov's appointment to the General Staff, since it had been on his advice that Muraviev had not declared war on Germany on September 6. Marinov kept his post as commander in chief until July 11, 1945. Early in 1946 he was made Bulgaria's minister to France.

[82] *Rabotnichesko delo*, September 6, 1959. Zhivkov's role at this point should not be overemphasized. His entry into the People's Militia is pointed out primarily because of his future importance as first Party secretary.

returning from the Soviet Union. On September 9 there were, all told, about 15,000 Party members. These were surrounded by a great many ex-Communists and Communist sympathizers who, together with thousands of young Communists, created a substantial pool from which the leadership could draw. Four months later, in the middle of January, 1945, the Party already claimed a membership of a quarter of a million.

Leading Party organs were established one after another. Kostov reached Sofia on the day following the coup and assumed his position of general secretary of the Party. Soon a three-man Secretariat was established, composed of Kostov, Georgi Chankov, and Vulko Chervenkov, who arrived from the Soviet Union a short while after the coup. The Politburo, when first announced in March, 1945, had the following composition: [83]

Full Members		
	1.	Georgi Dimitrov
	2.	Vasil Kolarov
	3.	Traicho Kostov
	4.	Georgi Chankov
	5.	Vulko Chervenkov
	6.	Dobri Terpeshev
	7.	Anton Yugov
	8.	Tsola Dragoicheva
	9.	Dimitur Ganev
	10.	Raiko Damianov
	11.	Georgi Damianov
	12.	Petko Kunin
	13.	Vladimir Poptomov
Candidate	14.	Dimitur Dimov
Members	15.	Gocho Grozev
	16.	Titko Chernokolev

[83] *Rabotnichesko delo*, March 7, 1945. This issue contains a complete list of members of the Secretariat, the Politburo, the Central Committee, and the Central Control Commission elected at the first postwar plenary session of the Central Committee (February 27–March 1, 1945). At the time of the election, Vasil Kolarov was in Moscow. He returned to Bulgaria in the fall of 1945. Georgi Damianov was already back from Russia and heading the Military Department of the Central Committee. Titko Chernokolev, one of the youngest members of the Politburo, had become the secretary of the Party youth organization shortly before the coup.

The first postwar Politburo was a large body. In terms of age, experience, and personal background its diversity was marked. Kolarov, the oldest, had been a Socialist before Chernokolev was born. Some had left their mark on the Party before the September, 1923, insurrection. Others were little known until propelled to positions of leadership by the accidents of illegality. Kolarov, Kostov, Kunin, and Poptomov were revolutionary intellectuals. Dobri Terpeshev, Anton Yugov, and Georgi Damianov were men of action. Vulko Chervenkov was largely the product of Soviet education. Georgi Dimitrov, still in Moscow, was named president of the Central Committee.

CONCLUSION

THE MARCH OF THE RED ARMY into Bulgaria made the conquest of Communism inevitable. Yet the consolidation of Communist power did not come without struggle. Bulgarian peasants and townsmen resisted as few other East Europeans did. The anti-Communist opposition was not appeased. Rather, it was subdued and crushed by force. From the outset the contest was between two unequals. The Red Army did not intervene directly. It did not have to. Its mere presence provided the Communists with an overwhelming advantage which their opponents could not overcome.

After they assumed power, the Bulgarian Communists undertook to rewrite the earlier history of their Party. Past perspectives were made to fit present requirements. Historiography became an instrument of policy. As new functionaries emerged and old leaders were purged, the record of the past underwent corresponding adjustments. The compulsion to make the historic records comply with the interests of the victors at the end of any given intra-Party engagement added new distortions. For the objective historian, however, the process of permanent historical revision was not without value, because it necessitated the disclosure of hitherto unknown factual evidence.

Yet, unlike so many ruling Communist regimes in Eastern Europe, the Bulgarians did not have to invent, as it were, the history of Bulgarian

Communism for the years before 1944. The grip of Communism over the minds and deeds of a substantial segment of the Bulgarian people was there to be acknowledged by all.

A psychological predisposition for political radicalism was characteristic of the early Bulgarian Socialists. The late coming of modern nationalist consciousness was not unrelated to the upsurge of radical ideas in this backward peasant country. The urge to supplement the gift of political independence with a new social justice dominated the Bulgarian intelligentsia who sprang up in the eighties and nineties of the last century. The first awareness of the larger world of ideas was acquired in the universities of prerevolutionary Russia, Germany, Switzerland, and Austria to which the ambitious village sons traveled for their education. For most of them, Marxism became a passion. Their very eagerness for learning and understanding led to a state of infatuation with a doctrine which promised a systematic and comprehensive ordering of all knowledge. Yet realities in Bulgaria stood far removed from the fixations of scientific socialism. Doctrinal affinities alone would not have sufficed to make Bulgarian Communism what it in fact became.

Important inflows from the political sphere, relevant to Bulgaria's national stature, reinforced Bulgarian Communism and gave it buoyancy and vitality that persisted despite great odds. A small people, occupying a central position in the Balkans, the Bulgarians were one of the last in Europe to attain state sovereignty. From the outset the underlying impulse of their political behavior was—and remains—to bring about the unification of the entire "Bulgarian tribe" within the boundaries of the Bulgarian state. The fact that their perception of who was a Bulgarian differed profoundly from the views of their neighbors gave rise to complexities which made Balkan politics what they became.

Since national goals always exceeded national capabilities, the Bulgarians were cast in a revisionist role from the beginning. The permanent need for at least one big European power as protector remained predetermined throughout. So long as the German Empire lasted and Russia was Tsarist, the margins of political maneuvering remained wide. Orientations toward Russia or toward Germany and Austria characterized the alignments of political forces in Bulgaria before World War I. Small but vigorous political groupings came forward with comprehensive party programs aimed at resolving Bulgaria's national problems by fostering a link with Germany or with Russia. In the twenties, however, this was no longer true. Weimar Germany was young and weak, while Italy in the Balkans represented only a temporary choice of the second best. As for Russia, the coming of Bolshevism undercut the traditional Russophiles in Bulgaria. The Communists alone could step into the position of claiming Russia as a protector. Although traditional Russophilism did not correlate with political radicalism, the Communists mastered and exploited the endemic pro-Russian sentiments to reinforce themselves. The Communists were further reinforced by a revolutionist temperament which had come about in the Bulgarian peasant during the period of national revival. The catastrophe of the Balkan wars was as much the logical consequence of Bulgaria's desire to master the entirety of Macedonia as the outcome of World War I was the result of the earlier defeats. The impact of compounded catastrophe on the domestic political scene was shattering. Many a Bulgarian of Macedonian origin saw in Communist revolutionism the one hope for the realization of Bulgarian national aspirations. The displacement of large numbers of people at the end of the war created a new refugee class in the country which in itself constituted a reservoir on which the Communists could draw.

The abortive uprising in the early twenties gave rise to two distinct and separate Communist bureaucracies—the one in Bulgaria proper and the other in the Soviet Union. Neither was safe or immune. The Party at home was continuously persecuted by the monarchic regime. The emigration in the Soviet Union was not spared the brunt of the Stalin terror machine. Yet the physical schism within the ranks of the Party gave Communism in Bulgaria a certain resiliency throughout the interwar period. While it is true that personal cleavages gave rise to endless rivalries and crosscurrents which consumed a great deal of energy and wasted much talent, the desire of the émigrés to return to their homeland and make right the earlier defeat constituted an important impetus.

In the course of its development, Bulgarian Communism produced a few revolutionary intellectuals as well as a large number of capable and devoted cadres. At no time were they able to turn up a revolutionary strategist of the first rank. Schooled as professional revolutionaries, they remained inept as revolutionary diagnosticians. The blame was not all theirs. Their dependence on Stalin's Russia was too overwhelming. Only seldom did Russia's interests in the Balkans conform with the interests of revolution in Bulgaria. The result was an almost perpetual disharmony on the plane of tactical maneuvers. The switch in the Soviet Comintern line came too late to salvage political pluralism in Bulgaria. Any real prospects for a popular front which alone might have constituted a countervailing force against an autocratic monarch had disappeared with the military coup of May, 1934. Even though in the thirties and early forties the Party line was tilted in the direction of making it conform more closely to Bulgaria's revisionism on the national question, the Communist bid could not match that of Bulgaria's pro-Axis regime. While Soviet Russia could promise, the Germans could deliver. The contribution of Soviet diplomacy and that of the Bulgarian Communists in Dobruja remained unacknowledged when the region finally reverted back to Bulgaria. The Yugoslav Communists, whom their Bulgarian comrades had treated patronizingly throughout the interwar period, won the quiet battle in the contest for dominion over wartime Macedonia. The Communist-fostered armed resistance against Bulgaria's wartime regime, organized and maintained against all odds, was impressive only when compared with the resistance movements in the countries which were Germany's clients. Unlike the resistance in the lands under German occupation, particularly Yugoslavia and Greece, the Communists of Bulgaria could not and did not succeed in harmonizing their efforts with the national sentiments of the people at large. The result was that when the time came and the Communists were called upon to take power, the Party élan had been blunted. The Sovietization campaign in Bulgaria was thus carried out by a Party whose prestige and self-esteem had been impaired. This caused the Russians to take their Bulgarian comrades for granted even more so than before. The full price was paid by all the Bulgarians. The accusations which in earlier years the Bulgarian Anarchists had made against their Communist comrades for having in effect adopted the thesis of the "three-fourths from abroad" had proved prophetic: three-fourths of the force behind a triumphant revolution in Bulgaria had indeed come from the outside.

BIBLIOGRAPHY

This is a working bibliography rather than a comprehensive listing of materials published on the subject of Bulgarian Communism. Only items consulted and found directly relevant to the subject and the period have been included. The bibliography is further limited by the exclusion of articles, the most important of which appear in the footnotes. A section on the newspapers and periodicals used is provided at the end of the bibliography.

Angelov, V. *Stopanskata razrukha na Bulgariia* [The Economic Devastation of Bulgaria]. Sofia, 1945.
—— *Zemedelskiiat vupros v Bulgariia* [The Agricultural Problem in Bulgaria]. Sofia, 1947.
Antonov, A., and S. Vladimirov. *Belezhnikut "Sampa"* [The Notebook "Sampa"]. Sofia, 1963.
Arditi, B. *Roliata na tsar Boris III pri izselvaneto na evreite ot Bulgariia* [The Role of King Boris III in the Deportation of the Jews from Bulgaria]. Tel-Aviv, 1952.
—— *Yehudei bulgariya beshnot hamishtar hanatsi* [The Bulgarian Jews During the Years of the Nazi Regime]. Holon, Israel, 1962, |In Hebrew.)
Atanasov, Shteriu. *Pod znameto na partiiata* [Under the Party Banner]. Sofia, 1962.
—— *Pokhodut na zapad* [The Westward March]. Sofia, 1966.
—— *Zapiski na revoliutsionera* [Notes of the Revolutionary]. Sofia, 1969.
Atanasov, Shteriu, *et al. Bulgarskoto voenno izkustvo prez kapitalizma* [The Military Art in Bulgaria under Capitalism]. Sofia, 1959.
Avramov, Mois. *Po stupkite na suprotivata* [In the Footsteps of the Resistance]. Sofia, 1969.
Barker, Elisabeth. *Macedonia: Its Place in Balkan Power Politics*. London, 1950.
Barouh, Victor. *Beyond the Law*. Sofia, 1965.
Barov, Nikola St. *BKP v noviia podem na antifashistkoto dvizhenie, 1929–1935*

[The Bulgarian Communist Party in the New Advance of the Anti-Fascist Movement]. Sofia, 1968.

Barzilai [Berger], Joseph. *Zohar behatsot* [Glow at Midnight]. Tel-Aviv, 1963. (In Hebrew.)

Batakliev, Ivan. *Stopanskoto znachenie na belomorieto* [The Economic Significance of the Lands Along the Aegean Sea]. Sofia, [1943].

Beamish, Tufton. *Must Night Fall?* London, 1950.

Bekhar, Alfred. *Germanskiiat imperializm i otrazhenieto mu v Bulgariia* [The German Imperialism and Its Reflection in Bulgaria]. Sofia, 1949.

Belev, Krustiu. *Ispaniia zove* [The Call of Spain]. Paris, 1937.

—— *Katorgata na fashizma* [The Fascist Inquisition]. Sofia, 1945.

—— *V moiata rodina Makedoniia* [In My Macedonian Homeland]. Sofia, 1945.

Berger, Joseph. *See* Barzilai, Joseph.

Berov, L. *Polozhenieto na rabotnicheskata klasa v Bulgariia* [The State of the Working Class in Bulgaria]. Sofia, 1968.

Bitsin, Georgi, and Mircho Yurukov. *Vladimir Poptomov.* Sofia, 1957.

Black, C. E. *The Establishment of Constitutional Government in Bulgaria.* Princeton, N.J., 1943.

Blagoev, D. *Izbrani proizvedeniia* [Selected Works]. 2 vols. Sofia, 1950–51.

—— *Iz istoriiata na ruskata revoliutsiia* [From the History of the Russian Revolution]. Sofia, 1919.

—— *Prinos kum istoriiata na sotsializma v Bulgariia* [Contribution to the History of Socialism in Bulgaria]. Sofia, 1954.

Blagoeva, Stela. *Georgi Dimitrov: Biografichen ocherk* [Georgi Dimitrov: A Biographic Outline]. 6th ed. Sofia, 1953.

Bogdanov, Boris. *Vlado Georgiev.* Sofia, 1957.

Boiadzhiev, Asen. *Istoriia na sindikalnoto dvizhenie v Bulgariia* [History of the Syndicalist Movement in Bulgaria]. Sofia, 1948.

——*Spomeni* [Memoirs]. Sofia, 1969.

Boiadzhiev, Asen, ed. *50 godini revoliutsionno profsuiuzno dvizhenie v Bulgariia, 1904–1954* [Fifty Years of the Revolutionary Trade-Union Movement in Bulgaria]. Sofia, 1955.

Borkenau, F. *World Communism.* New York, 1939.

Borov, T., ed. *Vasil Kolarov: Bio-bibliografiia* [Vasil Kolarov: Bio-Bibliography]. Sofia, 1947.

Bozhinov, Voin. *Politicheskata kriza v Bulgariia prez 1943–1944* [The Political Crisis in Bulgaria During 1943–44]. Sofia, 1957.

Bulgaria. *Memorandum: Bulgaria and Her Peace Problems.* Sofia, 1946.

Bulgaria, a New Spain: The Communist Terror in Bulgaria. Chicago, 1948.

Bulgarian Atrocities in Greek Macedonia and Thrace, 1941–1944: A Report of Professors of the Universities of Athens and Salonica. Athens, 1945.

Bulgarska akademiia na naukite. *Izvestiia na instituta za bulgarska istoriia* [Bulgarian Academy of Sciences. Announcements of the Institute for Bulgarian History]. 7 vols. Sofia, 1951–57.

—— *Kratka istoriia na Bulgariia* [A Brief History of Bulgaria]. Sofia, 1958.

Bulgarskata komunisticheska partiia v rezoliutsii i resheniia [The Bulgarian Communist Party in Resolutions and Decisions]. Vol. III. Sofia, 1954.

Burks, R. V. *The Dynamics of Communism in Eastern Europe.* Princeton, N.J., 1961.

Burmeister, Alfred. *Dissolution and Aftermath of the Comintern: Experiences and Observations, 1937–1947.* New York, 1955.

Castro Delgado, Enrique. *Mi fe se perdio en Moscu.* Mexico, 1951.

Chakalov, A. *Formi, razmer i deinost na chuzhdiia kapital v Bulgariia* [Forms, Size, and Activity of the Foreign Capital in Bulgaria]. Sofia, 1962.

—— *Natsionalniiat dokhod i razkhod na Bulgariia, 1924–1945* [The National Income and Expenditure in Bulgaria]. Sofia, 1946.

Chary, F. B. "Bulgaria and the Jews: 'The Final Solution,' 1940 to 1944." Unpublished doctoral dissertation, University of Pittsburgh, 1968.

Cherniavski, G. I. *Borbata na BKP za suzdavane i ukrepvane na RMS, 1926–1929* [The Struggle of the Bulgarian Communist Party for the Creation and Strengthening of the Workers' Youth League]. Sofia, 1958.

Chervenkov, Vulko. *Bio-bibliografiia, 1900–1950* [Bio-Bibliography]. Sofia, 1950.

[——] Vladimirov, A., and G. Tsonev [Gavril Genov]. *Sentyabr'skoe vosstanie v Bulgarii 1923 goda* [The September Insurrection in Bulgaria of 1923]. Moscow, 1934.

Christopoulos, George. *Bulgaria's Record.* Chicago, 1944.

Ciliga, Anton. *The Russian Enigma.* London, [1940].

Clissold, Stephen. *Whirlwind.* New York, 1949.

Communist International. *Seventh Congress of the Communist International: Abridged Stenographic Report of the Proceedings.* Moscow, 1939.

Confino, Dr. Baruch. *Aliya "B" mehupei bulgariya, 1938–1940* [Illegal Emigration from the Shores of Bulgaria]. Jerusalem–Tel-Aviv, 1965. (In Hebrew.)

Conquest, Robert. *The Great Terror: Stalin's Purge of the Thirties.* New York, 1968.

Damianov, Georgi. *Izbrani proizvedeniia, 1892–1958* [Selected Works]. Sofia, 1966.

Danailov, L., and S. Zaimov. *General Vladimir Zaimov.* Sofia, 1957.

Dedijer, Vladimir. *Tito Speaks.* London, 1953.

Degras, Jane. *Soviet Documents on Foreign Policy.* Vol. III. London, 1953.

Dellin, L. A. D., ed. *Bulgaria.* New York, 1957.

Deset godini Otechestven front, 1942–1952 [Ten Years of the Fatherland Front]. Sofia, 1953.

Deveti septemvri: Spomeni [The Ninth of September (1944): Memoirs]. Sofia, 1957.

Dimitrov, Georgi. *Political Report Delivered to the V Congress of the Bulgarian Communist Party.* Sofia, 1949.

—— *Rechi, dokladi, statii, 1942–1947* [Speeches, Reports, Articles]. Vol. III. Sofia, 1947.

—— *Spasitelniiat put za Bulgariia* [Bulgaria's Road to Salvation]. Sofia, 1945.

—— *Suchineniia* [Works]. 14 vols. Sofia, 1951–55.

Dimitrov, Mikhail. *Poiava, razvitie i ideologiia na fashizma v Bulgariia* [Emergence, Development, and Ideology of Fascism in Bulgaria]. Sofia, 1947.

Dimitrova, Stela. *Moskovskoto suveshtanie na BKP, 1925* [The Moscow Consultation of the Bulgarian Communist Party]. Sofia, 1959.

Dimitrov-Marek, Stanke. *Izbrani proizvedeniia* [Selected Works]. Sofia, 1952.

Dinev, Angel. *Politichkite ubistva vo Bulgarija* [The Political Assassinations in Bulgaria]. Skoplje, 1951.

Direktsiia na pechata. *Bibliografiia na nelegalniia antifashistki pechat, 1923–1944* [Department of the Press. Bibliography of the Illegal Anti-Fascist Press]. Sofia, 1948.

Djilas, Milovan. *Conversations with Stalin*. New York, 1962.

Docheff, Ivan. *A New Danger for World's Peace: Red Bulgaria*. N.p., 1950.

Documents on German Foreign Policy, 1918–1945. Series D. Vols. V–XII. Washington, 1953–62.

Doinov, D., and I. Draev, eds. *Bulgari bortsi za svobodata na drugi narodi* [Bulgarian Fighters for the Freedom of Other Nations]. Sofia, 1963.

—— *Za svobodata na bulgarskiia narod* [For the Freedom of the Bulgarian Nation]. Sofia, 1967.

Drachkovich, M., and B. Lazitch, eds. *The Comintern: Historical Highlights. Essays, Recollections, Documents*. New York, 1966.

Dragoliubov, P. *General-maior Tsviatko Radoinov* [Major-General Ts. Radoinov]. Sofia, 1960.

Dramaliev, Kiril. *Istoriia na Otechestveniia front* [History of the Fatherland Front]. Sofia, 1947.

Dumanov, P., ed. *Galeriia ubiti durzhavni muzhe* [A Gallery of Assassinated Men of State]. Sofia, 1928.

Dzhurov, D., and E. Dzhurova. *Murgash*. Sofia, 1966.

Evrei zaginali v antifashistkata borba [Jews Killed in the Anti-Fascist Struggle]. Sofia, 1958.

Filov, Bogdan. *Ideite i delata na dneshniia bezpartien rezhim* [The Ideas and Deeds of the Present Non-Party Regime]. Sofia, 1942.

—— *Putut na Bulgariia* [Bulgaria's Road]. Sofia, 1941.

Fischer, Louis. *Men and Politics*. New York, 1941.

Fischer, Ruth. *Stalin and German Communism*. Cambridge, Mass., 1948.

Genov, K. *Nashata memoarna literatura za partizanskoto dvizhenie* [Our Memoir Literature on the Partisan Movement]. Sofia, 1958.

Genovski, Mikhail. *Filosofskata osnova na zemedelskata ideologiia* [The Philosophic Foundation of the Agrarian Ideology]. Sofia, 1945.

—— *I v smurta sa zhivi* [They Live in Their Death]. Sofia, 1945.

—— *Zemedelskoto dvizhenie i leninizma* [The Agrarian Movement and Leninism]. Sofia, 1948.

Georgi Dimitrov pred fashistkiia sud [Georgi Dimitrov at the Fascist Trial]. Sofia, 1945.

Georgiev, Ivan. *Dobrudzha v borbata za svoboda, 1913–1940* [Dobruja in the Struggle for Freedom]. Sofia, 1962.

Geroichno minalo: Spomeni na partiini deitsi [Heroic Past: Recollections of Party Functionaries]. Sofia, 1965.

Geshkoff, T. I. *Balkan Union: A Road to Peace in Southeastern Europe*. New York, 1940.

Gialistras, Serge A. *Hellenism and Its Balkan Neighbours*. Athens, 1945.

Gilin, D. *Komunisti* [Communists]. Sofia, 1960.

Gindev, Panaiot. *Kum vuprosa za kharaktera na narodnodemokraticheskata revoliutsiia v Bulgariia* [Concerning the Character of the People's Democratic Revolution in Bulgaria]. Sofia, 1956.

Giovanna di Bulgaria [Queen of Bulgaria]. *Memorie.* Milan, 1964.

Gonzalez, Valentin, and Julian Gorkin. *El Campesino: Life and Death in Soviet Russia.* New York, 1952.

Gornenski, Nikifor. *Vuoruzhenata borba na bulgarskiia narod za osvobozhdenie ot khitleristkata okupatsiia i monarkho-fashistkata diktatura, 1941–1944* [The Armed Struggle of the Bulgarian People for Liberation from Hitlerite Occupation and the Monarchic-Fascist Dictatorship]. Sofia, 1958.

Gorov, Khr., ed. *Vuzstanicheska borba* [Insurrectionary Struggle]. Plovdiv, 1944.

Govori radiostantsiia "Khristo Botev" [The Voice of the Radio Station "Khristo Botev"]. 7 vols. Sofia, 1950–52.

Grigorov, Boian. *BKP prez perioda na vremennata i chastichna stabilizatsiia na kapitalizma, 1925–1929* [The Bulgarian Communist Party During the Period of the Temporary and Partial Stabilization of Capitalism]. Sofia, 1961.

Grigorov, K. I. *Razvitie na burzhoaznata ikonomicheska misul v Bulgariia mezhdu dvete svetovni voini* [Development of Bourgeois Economic Thought in Bulgaria in the Interwar Period]. Sofia, 1960.

Grinberg, Natan. *Khitleristkiiat natisk za unishtozhavane na evreite ot Bulgariia* [The Hitlerite Pressure for the Extermination of the Jews in Bulgaria]. Tel-Aviv, 1961.

Grinberg, Natan, ed. *Dokumenti* [Documents]. Sofia, 1945.

Gross, F., ed. *European Ideologies.* New York, 1948.

Grubcheva, Mitka. *V imeto na naroda* [In the Name of the People]. Sofia, 1962.

Hernandez, Jesus. *Yo, Ministro de Stalin en España.* Madrid, 1954.

Holborn, Louise, W., ed. *War and Peace Aims of the United Nations.* 2 vols. Boston, 1943–48.

Hugessen, Sir Hughe M. K. *Diplomat in Peace and War.* London, 1949.

Hull, C. *The Memoirs of Cordell Hull.* 2 vols. New York, 1948.

Ionescu. G. *Communism in Rumania.* London, 1964.

Istoriia na BKP [History of the Bulgarian Communist Party]. Sofia, 1969.

Istoriia na Bulgariia [History of Bulgaria]. Vol. II. Sofia, 1955.

Istorijski arhiv KPJ. [Historic Archive of the Communist Party of Yugoslavia]. Vol. VII. Belgrade, 1951.

Ivanov, V. *Ispaniia v plamutsi* [Spain in Flames]. Sofia, 1959.

Izvestiia na Instituta po Istoriia na BKP [Announcements of the Institute for the History of the Bulgarian Communist Party]. 21 vols. Sofia, 1957–69.

Kabakchiev, Khristo. *Bio-bibliografiia* [Bio-Bibliography]. Sofia, 1958.

—— *Spomeni* [Memoirs]. Sofia, 1955.

Karaivanov, Ivan. *Ljudi i pigmeji* [People and Dwarfs]. Belgrade, 1953.

—— *Narodna republika Makedonija* [People's Republic of Macedonia]. Skoplje, 1949.

Karakostov, Stefan. *Kultura i fashizum* [Culture and Fascism]. Sofia, 1945.

Kasher-Dimitrova, Regina. *Stanke Dimitrov-Marek: Biografichen ocherk* [Stanke Dimitrov-Marek: A Biographic Outline]. Sofia, 1966.

Kazasov, Dimo. *Bez put i bez idei* [Without Direction and Ideas]. Sofia, 1926.

—— *Burni godini, 1918–1944* [Stormy Years]. Sofia, 1949.

—— *Dneshna Yugoslaviia* [Contemporary Yugoslavia]. Sofia, 1938.
—— *Political Bulgaria Between 1913–1944*. Sofia, 1945.
—— *Vidiano i prezhiviano* [Seen and Outlived]. Sofia, 1969.
—— *Zveno bez grim* [Zveno Unmasked]. Sofia, 1936.
Khadzhiliev, D., ed. *Partizanite razkazvat* [Partisan Tales]. Sofia, 1961.
Khadzhinikolov, V. *Internatsionalisticheskite traditsii na BKP* [The Internationalist Traditions of the Bulgarian Communist Party]. Sofia, 1962.
—— *Stopanski otnosheniia i vruzki mezhdu Bulgariia i suvetskiia suiuz do deveti septemvri, 1917–1944* [Economic Relations and Ties Between Bulgaria and the Soviet Union up to September Ninth]. Sofia, 1956.
Khadzhinikolov, V., *et al. Stachnite borbi na rabotnicheskata klasa v Bulgariia* [Labor Strikes of the Working Class in Bulgaria]. Sofia, 1960.
Khristov, F. *Voenno-revoliutsionnata deinost na BKP, 1912–1944* [The Military-Revolutionary Activity of the Bulgarian Communist Party]. Sofia, 1959.
Khristov, K. *Revoliutsionnata kriza v Bulgariia prez 1918–1919* [The Revolutionary Crisis in Bulgaria During 1918–19]. Sofia, 1957.
Khristov, K., and K. Vasilev. *Dimitur Blagoev*. Sofia, 1956.
Kiosev, D. G. *Istoriia na makedonskoto natsionalno revoliutsionno dvizhenie* [History of the Macedonian National Revolutionary Movement]. Sofia, 1954.
Kishales, Haim. *Korot yehudei bulgariya* [History of the Bulgarian Jews]. Vol. III. Tel-Aviv, 1969. (In Hebrew.)
Kodzheikov, Dragoi. *Materiali po sindicalnoto dvizhenie v Bulgariia* [Materials on the Syndicalist Movement in Bulgaria]. Sofia, 1948.
—— *Rozhdenie i suzizhdane* [Birth and Life]. Sofia, 1966.
Kodzheikov, Dragoi, *et al. Revoliutsionnoto profsuiuzno dvizhenie v Bulgariia* [The Revolutionary Trade-Union Movement in Bulgaria]. Sofia, 1957.
Koen, David B. *Ograbvaneto i razoriavaneto na bulgarskoto stopnastvo ot germanskite imperialisti prez vtorata svetovna voina* [The Devastation of the Bulgarian Economy by the German Imperialists During World War II]. Sofia, 1966.
Kolarov, Vasil. *Izbrani proizvedeniia* [Selected Works]. 3 vols. Sofia, 1954–55.
—— *Protiv Khitlerizma i negovite bulgarski slugi* [Against Hitlerism and Its Bulgarian Stooges]. Sofia, 1947.
—— *Protiv liiavoto sektantstvo i trotskizma v Bulgariia* [Against the Left Sectarianism and Trotskyism in Bulgaria]. Sofia, 1949.
—— *Spomeni* [Memoirs]. Sofia, 1968.
Kolev, S. *Borbata na BKP za naroden front, 1935–1939* [The Struggle of the Bulgarian Communist Party for a Popular Front]. Sofia, 1959.
Kolinkoev, I. K. *Shest mesetsa na zatochenie v kontslagera pri selo Krusto pole* [Six Months' Imprisonment in the Concentration Camp near the Village of Krusto Pole]. Svishtov, 1945.
Kostov, Traicho. *Izbrani statii, dokladi, rechi* [Selected Articles, Reports, Speeches]. Sofia, 1964.
—— *Politicheskoto polozhenie i zadachite na partiiata* [The Political Situation and the Tasks of the Party]. Sofia, 1945.
Kosturkov, Stoian.*Vurkhu psikhologiiata na bulgarina* [On the Psychology of the Bulgarian]. Sofia, 1949.

Kousoulas, D. G. *Revolution and Defeat: The Story of the Greek Communist Party*. London, 1965.

KPJ i makedonskoto natsionalno prashanye [The Communist Party of Yugoslavia and the Macedonian National Problem]. Skoplje, 1949.

Krapchev, Danail. *Izminut put, 1906–1936* [The Road Behind]. Sofia, 1936.

Leites, N., and E. Bernaut. *Ritual of Liquidation: The Case of the Moscow Trials*. Glencoe, Ill., 1954.

Leonhard, Wolfgang. *Child of the Revolution*. London, 1957.

Lipper, E. *Eleven Years in Soviet Prison Camps*. Chicago, 1951.

Logio, G. *Bulgaria: Past and Present*. Manchester, 1936.

Lukacs, John A. *The Great Powers and Eastern Europe*. New York, 1953.

Macartney, C. A., and A. W. Palmer. *Independent Eastern Europe*. London, 1962.

Malinov, A. *Pod znaka na ostrasteni i opasni politicheski borbi* [Under the Sign of Passionate and Dangerous Political Struggles]. Sofia, 1934.

—— *Stranichki ot nashata nova politicheska istoriia: Spomeni* [Pages from Our New Political History: Memoirs]. Sofia, 1938.

Materiali po istoriia na BKP [Materials on the History of the Bulgarian Communist Party]. Sofia, 1960.

Meyer, Peter, *et al. The Jews in the Soviet Satellites*. Syracuse, 1953.

Michev, D., and S. Kolev. *Borbite na narodnoto studentstvo nachelo s Bulgarskiia obsht naroden studentski suiuz, 1930–1944* [The Struggles of the People's Students under the Guidance of the Bulgarian General People's Student Union]. Sofia, 1960.

Mikhailov, Vasil. *Anton Ivanov*. Sofia, 1964.

Milev, Georgi V. *Subi Dimitrov*. Sofia, 1956.

Mitev, I. *Fashistkiiat prevrat na deveti iuni 1923 godina i iunskoto antifashistko vustanie* [The Fascist Putsch of June 9, 1923, and the June Anti-Fascist Insurrection]. Sofia, 1956.

—— *Kratka istoriia na bulgarskiia narod* [A Short History of the Bulgarian People]. Sofia, 1951.

Mitrev, Dimitar. *Pirinska Makedonija vo borba za natsionalno osvoboduvanje* [Pirin Macedonia in the Struggle for National Liberation]. Skoplje, 1950.

Mojsov, Lazo. *Bulgarskata rabotnichka partija (komunisti) i makedonskoto natsionalno prashanye* [The Bulgarian Workers' Party (Communists) and the Macedonian National Question]. Skoplje, 1948.

Molho, M., and J. Nehama. *Shoat yehudei yavan* [The Holocaust of the Greek Jews]. Jerusalem, 1965. (In Hebrew.)

Moshanov, Stoicho. *Vunshnata politika na demokraticheskata partiia* [The Foreign Policy of the Democratic Party]. Sofia, 1946.

Narodno subranie. *Stenografski dnevnitsi na Narodnoto subranie* [National Subranie. Stenographic Minutes of the National Assembly]. Selected volumes. Sofia, 1931–44.

Natan, Zhak. *Biakhme v "Enikioi"* [We Were in "Enikioi" (Detention Camp)]. Sofia, 1967.

—— *Ikonomicheska istoriia na Bulgariia* [Economic History of Bulgaria]. Sofia, 1957.

Natan, Zhak, and L. Berov. *Monopolisticheskiiat kapitalizum v Bulgariia* [Monopoly Capitalism in Bulgaria]. Sofia, 1958.

Nedev, Nediu T. *Otrazhenie na laiptsigskiia protses v Bulgariia* [Reflections of the Leipzig Trial in Bulgaria]. Sofia, 1962.

Nelegalni pozivi na BKP [Illegal Leaflets of the Bulgarian Communist Party]. Sofia, 1954.

Nestorov, Khristo. *Vlado Trichkov*. Sofia, 1956.

Nollau, G. *International Communism and World Revolution*. New York, 1961.

Oliver, Kh. D. *Nie, spasenite* [We, the Saved]. Sofia, 1967.

Padev, M. *Escape from the Balkans*. New York, 1943.

Panaiotov, Panaiot. *Prinosut na bulgari za pobedata na Oktomvriiskata revoliutsiia* [The Contribution of Bulgarians to the Victory of the October Revolution]. Sofia, 1967.

Pavlov, Todor. *Izbrani proizvedeniia* [Selected Works]. Sofia, 1957.

—— *Protiv oburkvaneto na poniatiata* [Against the Confusion of the Terms]. Sofia, 1939.

—— *Teoriia na otrazhenieto* [The Theory of Reflection]. 3d ed. Sofia, 1947.

—— *Za marksicheska estetika, literaturna nauka i kritika* [On Marxist Aesthetics, Literary Science, and Criticism]. Sofia, 1954.

Pavlova, Gana. *Ruka za ruka* [Hand in Hand]. Sofia, 1962.

Penchev, Gencho. *Nelegalnite pechatnitsi na partiiata* [The Illegal Party Presses]. Sofia, 1965.

Peti kongres na Bulgarskata komunisticheska partiia [Fifth Congress of the Bulgarian Communist Party]. Vol. I. Sofia, 1949.

Petrov, Stoian. *Strategiiata i taktikata na BKP v borbata protiv monarchofashizma 1941–1944* [The Strategy and Tactics of the Bulgarian Communist Party in the Struggle Against Monarcho-Fascism]. Sofia, 1969.

Petrova, Dimitrina V. *BZNS i narodniiat front, 1934–1939* [The Bulgarian Agrarian Union and the Popular Front]. Sofia, 1967.

—— *BZNS v kraia na burzhoaznoto gospodstvo v Bulgariia, 1939–1944* [The Bulgarian Agrarian Union at the End of the Bourgeois Domination in Bulgaria]. Sofia, 1970.

Petrova, Slavka. *Borbata na BRP za ustanoviavane narodnodemokraticheskata vlast* [The Struggle of the Bulgarian Workers' Party for the Establishment of the People's Democratic Rule]. Sofia, 1964.

—— *Devetoseptemvriiska khronika* [Ninth of September (1944) Chronicle]. Sofia, 1969.

Pipinelis, M. P. *Caitiff Bulgaria*. New York, [1943].

Piti, B. *Bulgarskata obshtestvenost za rasizma i antisemitizma* [The Bulgarian Public on Racism and Anti-Semitism]. Sofia, 1937.

—— *Te, spasitelite* [They, the Saviors]. Tel-Aviv, 1969.

Popov, N., and Z. Petrov. *Todor Pavlov*. Sofia, 1958.

Popovski, B. D. *Shpiuni* [Spies]. Skoplje, 1949.

Poptsviatkov, G. *General Vladimir Zaimov: Biograficheski ocherk* [General Vladimir Zaimov: A Biographic Outline]. Sofia, 1958.

Pundeff, Marin V. "Bulgaria's Place in Axis Policy, 1936–1944." Unpublished doctoral dissertation, University of Southern California, 1958.

Purvanov, P. *Khristo Mikhailov*. Sofia, 1955.
Rabotata na BKP v armiiata, 1941–1944 [The Work of the Bulgarian Communist Party in the Army]. Sofia, 1959.
Rabotnicheskata partiia v Bulgariia, 1927–1938 [The Workers' Party in Bulgaria]. Sofia, 1966.
Rabotnicheski vestnik. Izbrani statii i materiali, 1923–1939 [Worker's Newspaper. Selected Articles and Materials]. Vol. III. Sofia, 1954.
Rabotnichesko delo, izbrani statii i materiali, 1927–1944 [Worker's Deed, Selected Articles and Materials]. Sofia, 1954.
Radomirski, Slavcho. *Prez ogun i kurshumi* [Through Fire and Bullets]. Sofia, 1962.
Rendel, Sir George. *The Sword and the Olive*. London, 1957.
Rothschild, Joseph. *The Communist Party of Bulgaria: Origins and Development, 1883–1936*. New York, 1959.
Samuilov, I. *Leon Tadzher*. Sofia, 1956.
Sarafis, Stefanos. *Greek Resistance Army: The Story of ELAS*. London, 1951.
Sbornik ot lektsii po istoriiata na BKP [A Collection of Lectures on the History of the Bulgarian Communist Party]. 2d ed. Sofia, 1948.
Septemvriiski dni: Spomeni za deveti septemvri 1944 g. [September Days: Recollections on September 9, 1944]. Sofia, 1970.
Serge, Victor. *Memoirs of a Revolutionary*. London, 1963.
Sharlanov, D. *Otechestveniiat front, 1942–1944* [The Fatherland Front]. Sofia, 1964.
—— *Suzdavane i deinost na Otechestveniia front* [Creation and Function of the Fatherland Front]. Sofia, 1966.
Sharlanov, D., and P. Damianova. *Miastoto i roliata na Otechestveniia front v sistemata na narodnata demokratsiia* [The Place and the Role of the Fatherland Front in the System of the People's Democracy]. Sofia, 1968.
Shterev, P. *Obshti borbi na bulgarskiia i grutskiia narod sreshtu khitlerofashistkata okupatsiia* [Common Struggles of the Bulgarian and Greek People Against the Hitlerite-Fascist Occupation]. Sofia, 1966.
Sirkov, D. *V zashtita na ispanskata republika* [In Defense of the Spanish Republic]. Sofia, 1967.
Soviet Foreign Policy During the Patriotic War: Documents and Materials. 2 vols. London, 1946.
Stavrianos, L. S. *Balkan Federation: A History of the Movement Toward Balkan Unity in Modern Times*. Northhampton, Mass., 1944.
Stefanov, Tsvetan. *Komunisticheskiiat i antifashistkiiat pechat prez vremeto na fashistkata diktatura v Bulgariia* [The Communist and Anti-Fascist Press During the Fascist Dictatorship in Bulgaria]. Sofia, 1960.
Stoev-Shvarts, Dr. G. *Voina: Spomeni na interbrigadista* [War: Recollections of a Member of the International Brigades]. Sofia, 1965.
Stoikov, A., ed. *Nie biakhme partizani* [We Were Partisans]. Sofia, 1949.
—— *Poslednata im duma* [Their Last Word]. Sofia, 1948.
Stoinov, Boris. *Boinite grupi, 1941–1944* [The Fighting Groups]. Sofia, 1969.
Stoinov, Ivan. *Politicheskata rabota v partizanskite otriadi, 1941–1944* [The Political Work in the Partisan Groups]. Sofia, 1969.

The Struggle of the Bulgarian People Against Fascism. Sofia, 1946.
Sweet-Escott, Bickham. *Baker Street Irregular.* London, 1965.
Swire, Joseph. *Bulgarian Conspiracy.* London, 1939.
Telge, Dr. Oskar [Tsvetan Kristanov], *et al. Ispaniia! Ispaniia!* [Spain! Spain!] Sofia, 1966.
Terpeshev, Dobri. *Spomeni ot zatvora* [Recollections from Prison]. Sofia, 1955.
There Is a Spirit in Europe: A Memoir of Frank Thompson. London, 1947.
Thomas, Hugh. *The Spanish Civil War.* New York, 1961.
Tobias, Fritz, *The Reichstag Fire: Legend and Truth.* London, 1963.
Todorov, Kosta. *Balkan Firebrand.* New York, 1943.
—— *Iz mojih uspomena* [From My Recollections]. Belgrade, 1934.
—— *Politichka istorija savremene Bugarske* [Political History of Contemporary Bulgaria]. Belgrade, 1938.
The Trial of Traicho Kostov and His Group. Sofia, 1949.
Trunski, Slavcho. *Iz taktikata na partizanskata borba v Bulgariia* [On the Tactics of the Partisan Struggle in Bulgaria]. Sofia, 1969.
—— *Neotdavna* [Recently]. 3d ed. Sofia, 1965.
—— *Partizanski spomeni* [Partisan Recollections]. Sofia, 1955.
Tsanev, Petur. *Marksistko-leniniskata kniga prez perioda na fashistkata diktatura, 1923–1944* [The Marxist-Leninist Literature During the Period of the Fascist Dictatorship]. Sofia, 1965.
Tsankov, Professor A. *Trite stopanski sistemi* [The Three Economic Systems]. Sofia, 1942.
Tsion, [Rabbi] Daniel. *Pet godini pod fashistki gnet* [Five Years under Fascist Oppression]. Sofia, 1945.
United States Department of State. *Macedonian Nationalism and the Communist Party of Yugoslavia.* Washington, 1954.
Vasilev, Orlin. *Vuoruzhenata suprotiva sreshtu fashizma v Bulgariia, 1923–1944* [The Armed Resistance Against Fascism in Bulgaria]. Sofia, 1946.
V boi s fashizma [In Battle Against Fascism]. Sofia, 1960.
Velichkov, Kiril. *Dobrovoltsi na svobodata* [Volunteers for Freedom]. Sofia, 1965.
Vidinski, Kiril. *Podvodnicharite* [The Submariners]. Sofia, 1963.
Vinarov, Ivan. *Boitsi na tikhiia front: Spomeni na razuznavacha* [Warriors of the Silent Front: Memoirs of an Intelligence Agent]. Sofia, 1969.
Vladimirov, A. *See* Chervenkov, Vulko.
V pomosht na izuchavashtite istoriiata na mladezhkoto revoliutsionno dvizhenie v Bulgariia [An Aid to the Students of the History of the Youth Revolutionary Movement in Bulgaria]. Sofia, 1959.
Vranchev, Petur. *Spomeni* [Memoirs]. Sofia, 1968.
Vulkov, Georgi Iv. *Selski voini* [Peasant Wars]. 2d ed. Sofia, 1945.
Vuoruzhenata borba na bulgarskiia narod protiv fashizma, 1941–1944: Dokumenti [The Armed Struggle of the Bulgarian People Against Fascism: Documents]. Sofia, 1962.
Woodhouse, C. M. *Apple of Discord: A Survey of Recent Greek Politics in their International Setting.* London, [1948].
Yarki imena v nashata istoriia [Vivid Names from Our History]. Sofia, 1955.
Zagoroff, S. D. *The Economy of Bulgaria.* Council for Economic and Industrial Research, Inc. Report No. A–19. Washington, 1955.

Zagoroff, S. D., et al. *The Agricultural Economy of the Danubian Countries, 1935–45.* Stanford, 1955.

Zarkov, V. *Zapiski na politzatvornika* [Notes of a Political Prisoner]. Sofia, 1959.

NEWSPAPERS AND PERIODICALS

Rabotnichesko delo [Worker's Deed], the daily organ of the Central Committee of the Bulgarian Communist Party, is the single most important newspaper source on the history of the Party. The complete collection of the original issues for the period September, 1944, to date has been used extensively. In 1954, two comprehensive volumes of selections from *Rabotnichesko delo* and *Rabotnicheski vestnik* [Worker's Newspaper] were published, covering the periods 1927–44 and 1923–39, respectively. Both volumes appear in the general bibliography. A selection of illegally published Party leaflets in the thirties and the wartime period is available in a published volume entitled *Nelegalni pozivi na BKP* [Illegal Leaflets of the Bulgarian Communist Party] (Sofia, 1954). The Comintern's *Inprecorr* [*International Press Correspondence*], published during 1930–38, is indispensable.

The pro-Communist *Narodna voliia* [People's Will], published in Detroit after 1938, is both important and useful. From among the various anti-Communist exile publications, the most important are *Svobodna i nezavisima Bulgariia* [Free and Independent Bulgaria], the organ of the Bulgarian National Committee in Washington, *Bulgarian Review*, published in Rio de Janeiro since 1961, and *Osvobozhdenie* [Liberation], which appeared briefly in the United States during the mid-fifties. *Glas na bulgarite v Yugoslaviia* [Voice of the Bulgarians in Yugoslavia], published in Yugoslavia during the late forties and early fifties, is of particular value for the history of the Bulgarian Communist emigration in the Soviet Union and its fate during the Great Purge.

Four nominally nonpartisan dailies published in Sofia, namely, *Mir* [Peace], *Utro* [Morning], *Den* [Day], and *Zora* [Dawn], have been used to check and document particular events in the thirties and the war years.

Novo vreme [New Time], the theoretical official monthly of the Communist Party, and *Istoricheski pregled* [Historic Review], the official bi-monthly of the Bulgarian Academy of Sciences, which have appeared ever since the end of World War II, are indispensable.

Narod [People], the daily organ of the Social Democrats published in Sofia after September, 1944, and *Svoboden narod* [Free People], the organ of the Social Democrats in opposition after the summer of 1945, contain important information on the pre-1944 period. Of particular importance is the daily organ of the Agrarian Union, *Zemedelsko zname* [Agrarian Banner], principally the issues published during the first year following the coup of September 9, 1944. The anti-Communist daily *Politika*, which appeared briefly in the winter of 1944–45, contains valuable information. Finally, *Otechestven front* [Fatherland Front], the official daily of the Fatherland Front and later of the Bulgarian Communist government, which has appeared ever since September, 1944, represents an important source on all aspects of Communist policy.

INDEX

Agrarian Union: reemerges as governing party, 5; in 1920s, 7–8, 16–20; in Malinov government, 8–9, 25; leaders of, in exile, 20–24; splits within, 21, 25; denounced by Communists, 115, 155; after coup of *1934*, 117; in Subranie of *1938*, 130; leaders of, arrested, 163; in resistance, 215*n*; and Fatherland Front, 255
—— Agrarians of Gichev (Vrabcha 1): in People's Bloc, 8; as dominant faction, 19; after coup of *1934*, 119; almost eliminated, 149; denounced by Communists, 160; in Muraviev government, 247
—— Pladne group (Agrarian Union—Al. Stamboliiski): formation of, 21, 23–24; membership of, 26; in local elections of *1934*, 26; negotiations for entry of, into government, 31; and Dimitrov, 70; after coup of *1934*, 119; and popular front, 121–22; in Subranie of *1938*, 131; and Spanish Civil War, 133; in elections of *1939–40*, 148; suppressed, 223; and Fatherland Front, 227–28, 252
—— Agrarians of Kosta Tomov, 8, 11
Aleksandrov, Ivan Nikolaevich, *see* Ganchev-Koprinkov, V.

Alexander, king of Yugoslavia, 20
Alexander Stamboliiski Peasant Union, 23–24
Alexandrov, G. F., 99
Amnesty bill, 21–22, 24–25
Anarchists, Bulgarian: in interwar period, 137; in Spanish Civil War, 137; in resistance, 215
Andreichin, Georgi, 39, 89
Angelov, D., 131*n*
Angelov, Racho, 226, 227, 252, 255
Ankara, Anglo-Bulgarian talks in, 243–44
Anti-Bolshevism, in Bulgarian government, 6, 101–2, 223–24
Anti-Communist repressions, 102–3
Anti-Fascist Council of National Liberation of Yugoslavia, 197
Anti-Semitism, 156, 237, 244; *see also* Jews
"Anton Ivanov" partisan detachment, 204, 213
Apriltsi, 40–41
Army, Bulgarian, 175, 219, 250
Arnaudov, M., 237
Asher, Zhak, 134*n*
Assassination, as political weapon, 202
Atanasov, Georgi, 88
Atanasov, Metodi, *see* Shatarov, Metodi

EAST CENTRAL EUROPEAN STUDIES OF COLUMBIA UNIVERSITY

The East Central European Studies comprise scholarly books prepared at Columbia University and published under the auspices of the Institute on East Central Europe of Columbia University. The faculty of the Institute on East Central Europe, while not assuming responsibility for the material presented or the conclusions reached by the authors, believe that these studies contribute substantially to knowledge of the area and should serve to stimulate further inquiry and research.

DIVERSITY IN INTERNATIONAL COMMUNISM. Alexander Dallin, ed., in collaboration with the Russian Institute. Columbia University Press, 1963.
A documentary record of the issues agitating the international Communist movement in the years 1961–63.

POLITICAL SUCCESSION IN THE USSR. Myron Rush. Published jointly with the RAND Corporation. Columbia University Press, 1965.
A theoretical and historical account of the problem of political succession in the Soviet regime.

MARXISM IN MODERN FRANCE. George Lichtheim. Columbia University Press, 1966.
A historical study of French Socialist and Communist theory and practice since World War I.

POWER IN THE KREMLIN. Michel Tatu. Viking Press, 1969. First published in 1967, by Bernard Grasset, under the title Le Pouvoir en URSS, and also in England by William Collins Sons and Co., Ltd., in 1968.
An analysis of the shifting balance of power within the Soviet leadership in the 1960s.

THE SOVIET BLOC: UNITY AND CONFLICT. Zbigniew Brzezinski. Revised and enlarged edition. Harvard University Press, 1967.
Focuses on the role of ideology and power in the relations among the Communist states.

VIETNAM TRIANGLE. Donald Zagoria. Pegasus Press, 1968.
A clarification of the factors governing the relations among the Communist parties and states involved in Vietnam.

COMMUNISM IN MALAYSIA AND SINGAPORE. Justus van der Kroef. Nijhoff Publications, The Hague, 1967.
The first book-length study of the Communist movement in the Malaysian-Singapore region today.

RADICALISMO CATTOLICO BRASILIANO. Ulisse A. Floridi. Istituto Editoriale Del Mediterraneo, 1968.
A discussion of the problems faced by the Catholic Church when it becomes actively involved in the struggle for social justice.

STALIN AND HIS GENERALS. Seweryn Bialer, ed. Pegasus Press, 1969.

An anthology of war memoirs from Soviet books, journals, and other writings which gives a picture of the Soviet military elite and of Stalin's role during World War II.

MARXISM AND ETHICS. Eugene Kamenka. Macmillan and St. Martin's Press, 1969.

The author examines both Marx's positive ethics of the truly human man freed from alienation and Marx's materialist critique of moralities as class-bound ideologies.

DILEMMAS OF CHANGE IN SOVIET POLITICS. Zbigniew Brzezinski, ed. and contributor. Columbia University Press, 1969.

A collection of essays which appeared in *Problems of Communism* in 1966–68 discussing prospects for the Soviet political system.

THE USSR ARMS THE THIRD WORLD: CASE STUDIES IN SOVIET FOREIGN POLICY. Uri Ra'anan. The M.I.T. Press, 1969.

Using Egypt and Indonesia as case studies, the author analyzes Soviet involvement in the Third World.

COMMUNISTS AND THEIR LAW. John N. Hazard. The University of Chicago Press, 1969.

The author analyzes the Marxian socialist legal system and examines the implementation of policy by law in the Communist world.

FULCRUM OF ASIA. Bhabani Sen Gupta. Published jointly with the East Asian Institute. Pegasus Press, 1970.

The author analyzes and documents the relations among China, India, Pakistan, and the Soviet Union during 1947–68.

LE CONFLIT SINO-SOVIÉTIQUE ET L'EUROPE DE L'EST. Jacques Lévesque. Les Presses de l'Université de Montreal, 1970.

The author examines the impact of the Sino-Soviet conflict on the relations between the USSR and Poland (1956–59) and between the USSR and Rumania (1960–68).

BETWEEN TWO AGES. Zbigniew Brzezinski. Viking Press, 1970.

The author projects the impact of technology and electronics on the political and social values of the United States, the Soviet Union, and the Third World, and analyzes the implications of the above for the United States.

THE CZECHOSLOVAK EXPERIMENT, 1968–1969. Ivan Svitak. Columbia University Press, 1971.

This book presents an extensive selection of Professor Svitak's own writings from occasions during the Dubcek era. They document in a unique way the manner in which Czechoslovak New Left touched the raw nerve of Soviet Communism by questioning the vanguard, omniscient role of the Communist Party. This anthology of personal political documents, written by a Marxist philosopher in the midst of national crisis, not only testifies to the possibilities of political action undertaken by the new coalition of intellectuals and workers in a potentially revolutionary period, but also reveals something of the universality of man's quest for freedom as it was reflected in the brief hour of Czechoslovakia's trial in 1968.

COMMUNIST CHINA AND LATIN AMERICA, 1959–1967. Cecil Johnson. Columbia University Press, 1970.

The author describes the Chinese efforts to become a major force in Latin America. He compares the Chinese theory of revolution with those developed by the Latin Americans; and he analyzes the efforts to establish pro-Chinese parties and movements as well as the strategy of these pro-Chinese groups.

LES REGIMES POLITIQUES DE L'U.R.S.S. ET DE L'EUROPE DE L'EST. Michel Lesage. Presses Universitaires de France, 1971.

The author describes and analyzes the principles which govern the relations between the political regimes of Eastern Europe.

COMMUNISM AND NATIONALISM IN INDIA: M. N. ROY AND COMINTERN POLICY, 1920–1939. John P. Haithcox. Princeton University Press, 1971.

Focusing on the career of M. N. Roy, the founder of the Communist Party of India, Professor Haithcox traces the development of Communism and nationalism in India from the Second Comintern Congress in 1920 to the defeat of the left wing of the Indian National Congress in 1939. In the process he provides new interpretations of the Roy-Lenin debate on colonial policy at the Second Comintern Congress, Roy's role in the development of the Indian Communist movement, Roy's activities in China, and the circumstances surrounding his expulsion from the international Communist movement.